Instructor's Manual

ARCHITECTURE
Residential Drafting and Design

by

Clois E. Kicklighter, CSIT
Dean Emeritus, School of Technology
and Professor Emeritus of Construction Technology
Indiana State University
Terre Haute, Indiana

Joan C. Kicklighter, CFCS
Coauthor of *Residential Housing*
Naples, Florida

Publisher
The Goodheart-Willcox Company, Inc.
Tinley Park, Illinois

Copyright © 2008

by

The Goodheart-Willcox Company, Inc.

Previous Editions Copyright 2004, 2000, 1995, 1990

All rights reserved. No part of this work may be reproduced for resale.
Manufactured in the United States of America.

Instructor's Manual
ISBN-13: 978-1-59070-701-2
ISBN-10: 1-59070-701-X

Instructor's Resource Binder
ISBN-13: 978-1-59070-702-9
ISBN-10: 1-59070-702-8

Instructor's Resource CD-ROM
ISBN-13: 978-1-59070-703-6
ISBN-10: 1-59070-703-6

3 4 5 6 7 8 9 – 08 – 12 11 10 09

Contents

Introduction

Chapter Resources

Introduction

Overview

Architecture: residential drafting and design provides a complete teaching package for use in residential architectural drafting and design courses. The package includes the textbook, workbook, and instructor's manual, in addition to the Instructor's Resource Binder, the Instructor's Resource CD, and the Instructor's PowerPoint Presentations CD. The Instructor's Resource Binder contains answer keys, color transparencies, and test masters. Included on the Instructor's Resource CD are the Architecture Software, the G-W Test Creation Software, handouts and visual masters, and the color transparency materials in electronic form. The Instructor's PowerPoint Presentations CD contains electronic slide presentations corresponding to key concepts in the text. The textbook and supplements provide comprehensive coverage of design fundamentals and procedures used to represent design ideas in traditional, as well as state-of-the-art, technology. The teaching package helps students solve problems related to the design of structures, helps to reinforce the topics discussed, and assists the student in becoming proficient in illustrating residential designs in proper form using both manual and CADD methods.

The **Architecture: residential drafting and design** textbook supplies key knowledge required for designing most types of residential structures. It provides instruction for making drawings employing traditional manual methods as well as CADD systems. Clear and concise drawings illustrate current drafting standards that are consistent with the skills required by modern design and construction firms. The textbook also serves as a resource for design and building principles and techniques. Additionally, it can be used to assist in developing the skills required to convey design ideas in an intelligent and precise manner as required in the field.

The subject matter of the textbook is presented in a systematic arrangement. It includes step-by-step instructions written in understandable language. The textbook is extensively illustrated with quality photographs and drawings. The functional use of color is used throughout to create interest and add clarity. For each chapter, Internet resources are identified to provide a wealth of new information on topics related to the chapter content.

Each textbook chapter is enhanced with corresponding chapter materials in the workbook and instructor's manual. Various types of questions, problems, and activities are included to reinforce the material presented in the textbook. They are intended to be applied before starting and upon completion of each chapter. In addition, teaching strategies, display suggestions, and pretests and posttests are provided in this instructor's resource for each chapter to assist the instructor with the topics presented. The student will gain a thorough understanding of architectural drafting and design applications and residential construction practices after utilizing all of the materials in the package.

The Textbook

The textbook contains 39 chapters dealing with all phases of architectural drafting and design. The chapters are divided into 11 sections. Two chapters discuss house styles and basic house designs, while another deals with factors to be considered when evaluating homesites. Traditional and computer-aided design and drafting equipment and procedures are presented and illustrated. Two chapters are devoted to computer-aided drafting and design and CADD commands and functions. Three chapters are devoted to planning activity areas for efficient use of space. Materials and construction methods are discussed, in addition to detailed instructions for drawing each of the different types of architectural plans—plot plans, foundation plans, floor plans, elevations, electrical plans, plumbing plans, climate control plans, and presentations. The various systems and elements of the residential structure are presented in detail and fully illustrated. These include floor, wall, and roof systems, in addition to doors and windows, stairs, fireplaces, and chimneys. Several chapters are devoted to systems planning for electrical, plumbing, HVAC, and security and home automation systems. Innovations in architecture, such as earth-sheltered dwellings, solar heating systems, and dome structures, are covered. Methods of presenting architectural designs through pictorial drawings and CADD models are covered in depth. Modular applications, the influence of building costs, building codes, and zoning regulations with respect to the site and design are also presented. The textbook also covers remodeling, preservation, and designing for health and safety.

In addition to providing information on architectural drafting, design, and construction, the text includes excellent coverage of industrialized housing, tradework specifications, career opportunities, and an extensive reference section. This edition includes three new chapters—*Information, Communication, and Security Wiring*; *Architectural Remodeling, Renovation, and Preservation*; and *Designing for Health and Safety*. Included in these chapters are topics on the latest approaches to home security and automation systems and information and communication systems. Also covered are the major types of remodeling, adding on to a structure, historic preservation,

and preparing remodeling plans. Topics on fire prevention and detection, carbon monoxide and radon detection, moisture and mold problems, weather and nature-related safety issues, and general home safety practices are also included. CADD coverage has been completely revised, updated, and integrated throughout the text.

Numerous new topics have been added throughout the text to keep it on the cutting edge. Sample topics include: Weather-resistant decking and roofing, new code requirements, outdoor low voltage lighting, budgeting for housing, shallow foundations, three-coat stucco, autoclaved aerated concrete, programmable digital thermostats, applying shading and shadows to drawings, computer-generated rendering methods, freehand sketching, and new electrical symbols.

The textbook has been designed to develop an awareness of the types and styles of housing and factors to be considered when selecting a style. It is intended to help the student make wise choices when selecting materials and methods of construction, and to develop the skills necessary to communicate these decisions through architectural drawings. A comprehensive reference section and glossary are provided in the text to serve as a resource and to identify and define relevant terms.

Each chapter of the text is divided into various parts, including learning objectives, key terms, the text body, Internet resources, review questions, and suggested activities. These components are discussed in the following sections.

Learning Objectives

Learning objectives are listed at the beginning of each chapter. Students should use the objectives to become familiar with the content of each chapter. They can also be used as a review tool after completing the chapter to determine if the major concepts of the chapter have been learned.

Key Terms

Key terms are listed at the beginning of each chapter. They appear in bold type in the text when initially discussed. An explanation of each term is provided when it is first referenced. The student is immediately made aware that the term is important and that he or she should become familiar with the definition. Each key term is also defined in the textbook glossary.

Text Body

The text body is separated into main headings and subheadings. The main headings define the major concepts explained in the chapter content. The subheadings further define the organization of material within each main concept. The content areas are presented in a logical sequence that aids in learning the material. Each content area builds a foundation for further learning.

Identifying Disabled-Accessible Features

Throughout the text, a special icon is used to identify portions where disabled-accessible features and design requirements are discussed. A standard disabled-accessible graphic is used for this icon. The icon appears in the text body margin next to each reference as shown here.

Internet Resources

Several Web sites are listed at the end of each chapter for additional sources of information related to the chapter content. They include sites for manufacturers, associations, and government agencies.

Review Questions

Review questions appear at the end of each chapter. They may be used by students to evaluate their understanding of the subject matter. A variety of multiple choice, completion, and short answer questions are used to help assess the student's knowledge. The review questions may also be used as assigned homework, or selected questions may be used for quizzes to test students on the material presented.

Suggested Activities

The suggested activities at the end of each chapter enable the student to learn more about different aspects of construction and architectural drafting and design. They are designed to provide hands-on experiences or allow students to research further designs, construction materials, elements, and methods.

Some of the activities are designed to be completed with a CADD system. These are identified with a special icon in the margin as shown here. These activities do not necessarily correlate to the problems included in the Architecture Software package.

More specifically, the suggested activities provide opportunities to:

- Study local building codes and regulations.
- Seek information on the Internet.
- Assemble a collection of various styles and designs of residential architecture.
- Interview practitioners in the field.
- Assemble literature from manufacturers. Secure speakers for the class.
- Write letters to obtain information.
- Design a variety of architectural plans. Build scale models.
- Prepare bulletin board illustrations. Lead class discussions.
- Participate in a CADD demonstration. Evaluate software.
- Participate in field trips.
- Evaluate home styles in the community. Perform a survey.
- Write a report.
- Plan and execute a fund-raising event.
- Evaluate existing plans to meet specific requirements. Develop a materials list.
- Measure actual construction. Test building elements.
- Plan for a restoration.
- Prepare schematics.
- Secure estimates.
- Compare systems.
- Determine labor rates.

- Make detail drawings.
- Evaluate use of materials.
- Visit and evaluate a building site.
- Photograph construction features.
- Examine cutaway models.
- Redesign a house plan.
- Prepare specifications.
- Study magazines in the field.
- Use the library to locate manufacturers.
- Participate in a group project.
- Perform calculations.
- Evaluate construction techniques.
- Plan furniture arrangements.
- Prepare charts and reports.
- Perform historical research.
- Make a rendering.

Reference Section

The comprehensive reference section in the rear portion of the text includes a wide variety of resources commonly used in the field of architecture. The reference section includes the following, plus much more: A complete list of symbols used in the field of architecture, standard sizes and designs of cabinetry and windows, grades of lumber, engineered lumber specifications, design data for roof and floor trusses, floor and ceiling joist and beam span data, resistivity to heat loss of common building materials, steel beam data, weights and measures conversions, weights of building materials, brick and block courses, plywood grades, asphalt roofing products, welded wire reinforcement styles, gypsum wallboard applications, reinforcing bar sizes, recommended foot-candle levels, and abbreviations. One of the great strengths of this textbook is the material covered in this section. It is not only an excellent source of information for the student, but also for the professional.

Glossary

The glossary comprises a complete alphabetical listing of terms commonly used in architecture. Terms new to the field are also included. Each entry consists of the term printed in bold type followed by its definition. All key terms identified in the text are included in the glossary.

Index

The index contains a thorough listing of the topics presented in the text. Each topic is followed by page number references indicating where the topic is discussed.

The Workbook

The workbook is designed to assist the student in mastering the subject matter presented in the text. It is also intended to aid in developing skill in representing ideas in acceptable form. The workbook contains questions and problems/activities. These enable the instructor to determine how the student is progressing. The workbook is also designed for the student to use as a study guide. Students can measure their own progress by completing the questions and problems/activities and then verifying the answers. The workbook includes many examples of construction drawings that serve as models of professional quality work.

The workbook is arranged to correspond to the chapters of the textbook. An instructor can use each workbook chapter to review the information or test comprehension of the major concepts in the textbook. The questions are comprehensive and include multiple choice, short answer/listing, completion, matching, and calculation questions.

The problems/activities enable the student to perform many of the same problem-solving tasks that would be performed by a professional. They are designed to create student interest. Some answers will be individual responses requiring evaluation based on a set of principles rather than specific responses.

Questions

The student is expected to complete the questions in the workbook after careful study of the material presented in the textbook. Several types of questions are given to determine the student's understanding of the material. The student should read each question carefully and then proceed to answer it. Spaces are provided to record the appropriate answers.

Problems/Activities

The problems enable students to gain experience and practice in further refining the techniques presented in the textbook. They are designed to give the student experience in using traditional and computer-aided drafting and design equipment. A variety of problems is included to meet the needs of students with varying abilities.

The activities encourage student exploration of community resources such as local building departments, building materials centers, architectural firms, and construction companies. The students are also exposed to the many mechanical and electrical systems and building practices currently used in residential construction. In addition, the activities require the student to develop design ideas and collect building material samples for use in the classroom.

The Instructor's Manual

The Instructor's Manual is invaluable for use with the **Architecture: residential drafting and design** textbook and workbook. It provides plans and methods for teaching architectural drafting and design courses, recommendations for working with students of various abilities, including those with special needs, activities to expand the student's experience outside the classroom, tools for evaluating student progress, and resources for further study.

Each chapter section in the chapter resources portion of this instructor's resource contains specific suggestions for teaching the contents of the textbook. Also included in each chapter section are learning objectives, display suggestions, references to textbook and workbook pages, teaching strategies, and a chapter pretest and chapter posttest. In addition, each chapter section contains the answers and solutions to the review questions in the textbook, the answers to the questions and problems/activities in the workbook, and the answers to each chapter pretest and chapter posttest.

Instructor's Resource Binder

The Instructor's Resource Binder provides teaching materials similar to those found in the Instructor's Manual. It contains chapter resources, teaching suggestions, and chapter pretests and posttests. In addition, color transparencies are provided. These summarize key concepts in the text and can be used as a resource for classroom discussion. They are designed to add variety to the classroom presentation of the text material.

Instructor's Resource CD

As previously discussed, the Instructor's Resource CD contains a number of teaching components in electronic form. These include the contents of the Instructor's Resource Binder, the Architecture Software, and the G-W Test Creation Software. In addition, handout and visual masters are provided. The software packages are discussed in the following sections.

The Architecture Software Package

The Architecture Software package contains 93 problems. Many of these problems are taken from the workbook. The problems selected for the software package are designed to be completed with a CADD system. The Architecture Software package is not intended to replace the workbook, but rather to facilitate the use of a CADD system in solving many of the workbook problems. There are two versions of the Architecture Software package. The Student Version contains the problems designed to be completed by students. The Instructor's Version is designed for the instructor and contains the problem solutions. A custom architectural lettering font is also included in the software, which enables the students to prepare professional-looking drawings.

The following Progress Chart lists specific problems included in the Architecture Software package. The problems are arranged by chapter.

Software Progress Chart

Chapter 2		Chapter 8		Chapter 11		Chapter 18		Chapter 23		Chapter 29	
2-1		8-1		11-1		18-1		23-1		29-1	
Chapter 4		8-2		11-2		18-2		23-2		29-2	
4-1		8-3		11-3		18-3		23-3		29-3	
4-2		8-4		11-4		Chapter 19		Chapter 24		Chapter 30	
4-3		8-5		Chapter 12		19-1		24-1		30-1	
4-4		Chapter 9		12-1		19-2		24-2		Chapter 31	
4-5		9-1		12-2		19-3		24-3		31-1	
Chapter 5		9-2		Chapter 13		19-4		Chapter 25		Chapter 32	
5-1		9-3		13-1		Chapter 20		25-1		32-1	
5-2		9-4		13-2		20-1		25-2		32-2	
Chapter 6		9-5		13-3		20-2		25-3		32-3	
6-1		9-6		Chapter 14		20-3		Chapter 26		32-5	
6-2		Chapter 10		14-1		20-4		26-1		32-6	
6-3		10-1		14-2		Chapter 21		26-2		32-7	
6-4		10-2		Chapter 15		21-1		Chapter 27		Chapter 33	
Chapter 7		10-3		15-1		21-2		27-1		33-4	
7-1		10-4		15-2		Chapter 22		27-2		Chapter 37	
7-2		10-5		Chapter 16		22-1		Chapter 28		37-1	
7-3		10-6		16-1		22-2		28-1		Chapter 38	
7-4				16-2				28-2		38-1	
				Chapter 17							
				17-3							

When installing the software, electronic DWG files for the problems are installed to the hard drive. Installing the Student Version of the software installs the problem files. Installing the Instructor's Version of the software installs the problem solution files. The files are then opened in a CADD system that reads DWG files. The files are accessed from the path specified during the installation. When a student opens a problem and works on the activity, the file can then be saved as a separate file under a different name. This allows the user to make use of the problem file without changing the original problem. Students will then have their own copy of the problem with their own solution when they have completed the problem. In the instructor's case, he or she can view the completed problem, compare it against the problem solution file, make changes, and plot the student file for grading purposes.

The Architecture Software can be used by a single student, a group of students, or an entire class, depending on the workstations available. A mixed class can proceed along together with some students using the workbook worksheets and others using the Architecture Software for the problems where CADD is appropriate. All students should use the workbook worksheets for lettering, sketching, and all non-CADD related activities.

ExamView® Test Generator Software

The ExamView® Test Generator Software provides a convenient way to create your own tests or quizzes in a professional format from a question bank of over 2000 questions. The questions range from very basic to difficult. Several styles of questions—true or false, multiple choice, matching, short answer, listing, calculation, and completion—are included. If you desire, you can add your own questions to the question bank.

Instructor's PowerPoint Presentations CD

The Instructor's PowerPoint Presentations CD provides slide presentations designed for display in the classroom. The presentations are tied to material in the text and highlight key concepts and visual materials. They can be used with the PowerPoint Viewer utility, which is included with the CD. Presentations are provided for each chapter in the text. They are intended as special lecture supplements to generate student interest and classroom discussion.

Planning Course Content

The **Architecture: residential drafting and design** teaching package provides material sufficient for two years of study in architectural drafting and design. For example, the first-year course could teach the production of a set of standard residential construction drawings and would include the following related chapters:

1. The World of Architecture
2. Basic House Designs
3. Primary Considerations
4. Drawing Instruments and Techniques
5. Introduction to Computer-Aided Drafting and Design
6. CADD Commands and Functions
7. Room Planning—Sleeping Area and Bath Facilities
8. Room Planning—Living Area
9. Room Planning—Service Area
10. Plot Plans
11. Footings, Foundations, and Concrete
12. The Foundation Plan
13. Sill and Floor Construction
14. Wall and Ceiling Construction
15. Doors and Windows
16. Stairs
17. Fireplaces, Chimneys, and Stoves
18. The Floor Plan
19. Roof Designs
20. Elevations
21. Residential Electrical
22. Information, Communication, and Security Wiring
23. The Electrical Plan
24. Residential Plumbing
25. The Plumbing Plan
26. Residential Climate Control
27. Climate Control Plan

The second-year course would cover the following chapters:

28. Solar Space Heating
29. Nontraditional Structures
30. New Products and Methods of Construction
31. Modular Applications
32. Perspective Drawings
33. Presentation Drawings
34. Architectural Models
35. Material and Tradework Specifications
36. Estimating Building Cost
37. Architectural Remodeling, Renovation, and Preservation
38. Designing for Health and Safety
39. Career Opportunities

Applying Teaching Methods

A variety of teaching methods and techniques should be used to create and maintain student interest in the classroom. Common techniques include the use of lectures, problem-solving activities, overhead transparencies, group discussions, demonstrations, and movies or videos. Several different types of techniques should be utilized to ensure student understanding since students learn from a variety of methods. The appropriate method for each specific situation is based on experience and standard practice.

The primary tool used in teaching, in most instances, will be the textbook. It not only provides material for use in the classroom, but it also has reference material for use outside the classroom. The workbook is also an important aid in teaching, serving to reinforce textbook understanding. The lectures, group discussions, and demonstrations, supplemented with overhead transparencies, slides or photos, and movies or videos, help to provide variety in learning. Using different methods and techniques will help maintain interest in the topics being presented.

This instructor's resource details suggestions for integrating these methods to obtain optimum results. It will help you to maintain a balance by combining lectures with activities and problems. This resource describes suggested teaching displays that may be used to create interest in the materials being presented.

The teaching strategy presented in each chapter section of this instructor's resource follows the content and organization presented in the textbook. As previously discussed, the textbook is arranged to provide an appropriate learning sequence. For example, concepts that must be understood to construct a floor plan are presented prior to the chapter on floor plans. The teaching strategy also provides an organized, step-by-step procedure for teaching the content of each chapter. It integrates pretests, displays, handout materials, suggested activities from the textbook, and the workbook problems/activities into a cohesive lesson plan. For example, the chapter pretest is given prior to the student's review of chapter content. The review questions in the textbook will be assigned after the material has been presented. The students are to first answer the review questions without the textbook. They may then refer to the text for any question they do not know. The instructor will then discuss the answers with the students. The answers to the review questions in the textbook, therefore, allow interaction and discussion to occur. Next, the students will be expected to answer the chapter questions in the workbook and check their own answers. This is then followed up by a chapter posttest.

An important element of this teaching strategy is that the instructor returns assignments promptly and with comments. Another inherent part of the teaching strategy is that the instructor is expected to spend an appropriate amount of time collecting materials for the chapter, preparing bulletin board materials, making drawings to illustrate proper procedures, and being familiar with the **Architecture** package in preparation for teaching the material.

At the beginning of the course, the students should be encouraged to do a cursive study of the book to become familiar with it. Have them review the units to be covered during the course as well as the reference section, glossary, and index. This procedure results in less time needed to become familiar with the contents and greater ease in finding information. This leaves valuable class time for instruction and other learning activities. During the course, the students will find it necessary to review sections and materials previously studied to assure understanding of concepts. The students will need to perform a number of the activities and problems outside the classroom due to the limited amount of instruction time and the vast amount of subject matter provided in the textbook.

Understanding the Importance of Planning

Have a plan for teaching the course. It is important to determine the goals and objectives of the course from the start. Goals and objectives provide structure as well as direction for the course. Planning is also critical when developing chapter lessons, as well as when carrying out the lesson plans. Conscientious planning is necessary in order for the class to run smoothly and allow students to accomplish as much as possible. Your job as an instructor will be simpler if you plan your work. You will make more efficient use of your time, enabling you to accomplish more and allowing your teaching to be more effective.

Generating Motivation

Motivation is any factor that starts an individual toward a goal and then sustains the individual until that goal is realized. The instructor should constantly motivate students until they realize their goals. Research indicates that motivated students are never bored and that they want to learn.

All instructors should be conscious of student motivation even though laboratory courses, such as architectural drawing, are generally of interest to most students. Instructional strategies in your presentation of topics can be used to create interest in learning. Use a variety of teaching techniques to stimulate interest. Stand while lecturing and use the chalkboard or overhead projector instead of sitting at your desk. Move about the classroom to communicate with the students at their workstations to offer advice and encouragement. Keep the students informed of their progress. Encourage them to research topics in which they have an interest. Be interested in your students and get to know them as individuals. They will be more comfortable and receptive to learning if the instructor is friendly. Students need attention and recognition. They also need approval from their peers and people of authority. The instructor should use praise and encouragement freely to help provide motivation for his or her students.

Objectives provide a basis for motivation. When students determine what their goals and objectives are, they become motivated to attain them. The instructor can be instrumental in helping students realize their objectives by continuously providing motivation.

Promoting Student Participation

Encourage student participation. Students who are actively involved in class activities generally learn better and are more successful. Try to predict where failure might occur in the learning process. Put forth extra effort to help your students avoid failure and feel successful. They will have a more positive attitude toward learning if they feel successful. Let your students know that you are there to help and that you have confidence in them. The extra amount of attention that you give them will inspire them to work harder to achieve success. Plan techniques that permit your students to achieve as much as possible. Encourage them to strive for higher levels of accomplishment.

Share the latest research and developments in the field with the class and encourage your students to read publications related to architecture. Suggest that students choose an area in which they have an interest, learn more about it, and share it with the class. For example, if a student is interested in the restoration of older homes, assign the task of library research for articles and photographs of restoration projects. Have the student seek out companies that manufacture products used in restoration and obtain their product literature. Determine whether there are builders in the local area who specialize in restoration. Also, determine whether there are older homes currently under restoration. Sharing the information with the class, and possibly arranging a field trip to see the restoration in progress, would complete the task.

Creating Enthusiasm and Excitement

Enthusiasm is contagious. When an instructor is enthusiastic about the subject, the students will also be enthusiastic. It sets the stage for learning and helps to maintain the student's interest in the subject throughout the time in class. Showing enthusiasm is a positive way of keeping student morale at a high level and results in better recall of the material studied.

Create excitement in the classroom. This can be accomplished by incorporating a wide range of learning techniques and hands-on activities. Attractive bulletin board displays with drawings or designs from the chapter being studied can stimulate excitement. Meet the needs of your students, for example, by showing them that the drawing techniques currently being practiced can be applied to drawing plot plans, floor plans, elevations, etc. When the students view the activities and problems as meaningful (rather than busy work), the learning experience will be more exciting.

Applying Problem-Solving Methods

Problem solving is fundamental to student learning. In all probability, it is the key element responsible for student success. Problem solving is a technique that the student can use to carry out research, develop a project, or write a paper. The instructor can help students develop problem-solving abilities by utilizing methods that are conducive to teaching problem solving. The instructor should develop exercises in problem solving to serve two purposes: (1) To enable the student to develop the art of reasoning, and (2) To provide the student practical knowledge or skill valuable in life. The steps required in the problem-solving process are:

1. Identifying and explaining the problem.
2. Gathering information.
3. Developing a plan for examining the facts.
4. Analyzing the facts to determine solutions.
5. Evaluating the results.

It is the instructor's responsibility to determine if the students understand the procedure and can apply it to different problem-solving situations. The laboratory and resources in the community provide excellent opportunities for students to practice their knowledge of problem solving. The instructor can help students move from abstract to actual situations of problem solving by using realistic problems. Students should be given the opportunity to discuss and formulate ideas, construct models for testing theories, and simulate actual situations. Problem-solving ability is not only important for the students in their current class, it will be invaluable to them for the remainder of their lives. Students can expect to encounter endless situations requiring experience in problem solving and decision making, regardless of their ultimate walks in life.

Keeping Current

The instructor should maintain a current status with the field of architecture and construction in order to challenge and lead students. Read the latest journals and other publications to learn about new building codes and construction techniques. Periodically visit the local building materials center and collect brochures on the latest building materials on the market. Visit construction sites to determine the building materials and construction techniques currently used in your locality. Keep abreast of new designs and identify examples of these new designs in your area. Be aware of the latest computer equipment and software on the market with architectural applications. Make as many of these sources as possible available to the students in your classroom.

Addressing Varying Student Abilities

The students in your classroom possess a wide range of skills. Some have a great deal of drawing skill, while others have limited skill. Some have decided to make architectural drafting and design a career choice, while others are merely interested in exploring it.

It is important to recognize that the students in your classroom possess a variety of abilities. There may be students with special needs who have mental or physical impairments. There may also be students who are gifted and possess the potential to exceed the limits of the course. You must challenge students along the entire range of abilities.

Identifying Students with Special Needs

Generally, students with special needs will be identified before enrolling in architectural drafting and design classes. This identification is usually performed by school personnel specifically trained to evaluate learning problems. However, there may be instances in which these students have been enrolled in classes without identification. The responsibility then rests with the instructor to identify any students who require special help.

A number of symptoms often occur in students with special needs and may include disturbances in intellectual, conceptual, motor skill, and social behavior. Many of these students are diagnosed early on in their educational years, while some remain undetected. Therefore, it is necessary that the instructor be aware of the behaviors commonly exhibited by special needs students. (Keep in mind that an occasional incident probably does not indicate that a student should be labeled as having special needs.) Behaviors typically found in students having special needs include:

- Short attention span.
- Attendance problems.
- Below-grade level ability in reading, writing, and mathematics.
- Low self-concept.
- Tendency toward incorrect social behavior.
- Lack of eye-hand coordination.
- Tendency toward disruptive behavior.
- Poor relationships with peers.
- Lack of class participation.
- Poor motivation.
- Hearing, sight, or speech impairments.
- Repeated failure to do homework.

This is only a partial listing of behaviors found in special needs students. If you have a student who exhibits several of these behaviors, discuss your observations with the student's counselor. If the student is displaying these behaviors in other classes, then further diagnostic testing should be requested. After the student's specific learning disabilities are determined, then the instructor can proceed to modify the teaching techniques to meet the student's needs.

Mainstreaming the Special Needs Student

Mainstreaming is, in essence, placing special needs students in a regular classroom. The passing of the Federal Education of All Handicapped Children Act in 1975 mandated that all handicapped children have available a free education in a relatively unrestricted environment suitable to their needs. Many schools have taken the necessary steps to better educate special needs students.

Prior to the passing of the act, special needs students were taught entirely by instructors trained to work with handicapped students in resource classrooms set aside for these students. These instructors often lacked the specialized training to teach in areas such as architecture. In most cases, the rooms were not equipped with the facilities required for the instruction of the particular subject. Mainstreaming special needs students into the regular classroom enables these students to experience and investigate a greater variety of subjects. Whenever possible, special needs students are placed in regular classrooms and receive assistance from special education instructors or aides. Some special needs students are mainstreamed into a number of regular classes and spend the remaining time in resource classrooms, while others are fully mainstreamed into regular classes.

Architecture instructors will have more opportunities to work with special needs students as more schools participate in mainstreaming. As an instructor, it may be necessary to adapt your teaching practices to enable these students to develop the required skills. Special needs students have the same desire to be successful as the majority of students in architectural classes. It is imperative that the instructor inform these students that high standards and expectations are just as applicable to them as to the remainder of the class. Setting high expectations and providing a great deal of encouragement result in the students putting forth extra effort to meet goals and achieve success. Special needs students can be successful in architecture classes. In architecture, the students study and learn the subject matter in the textbook and then apply this knowledge to generate drawings. Hands-on experiences, such as drawing, usually provide a high rate of success for special needs students.

Teaching Students with Special Needs

The instructor will generally have a wide range of special needs students in his or her classes. The range includes students with learning disabilities, mild retardation, emotional disturbances, speech impairments, hearing impairments, visual impairments, and physical disabilities. The success of the students depends, to a large extent, on how the instructor approaches their needs and modifies his or her teaching to meet their needs. The following suggestions can be incorporated into the teaching process to help special needs students be successful:

1. Furnish reading material appropriate for the reading level.
2. Provide outlines of subject matter to help the student follow the lecture. Also, provide outlines that the special education instructor may use when working with the student.
3. Simplify handouts as much as possible by using diagrams, drawings, etc.
4. Provide work that is simple and short in length.
5. Give encouragement frequently.
6. Emphasize the student's successes rather than failures.
7. Integrate special needs students with the remainder of the class whenever possible, through group projects, class discussions, and other activities. Encourage participation.
8. Use several different teaching techniques. Assign individual research projects when necessary.
9. Simplify processes into smaller segments.

10. Return assignments and evaluations quickly with helpful comments and discussion.
11. Design repetitive activities appropriate to the student's ability to help build skill.
12. Administrate oral and written tests using a variety of test questions.
13. Be consistent, reasonable in expectations, and flexible.
14. Pair special needs students with students who can help with the assignment.
15. Permit extra time for special needs students to complete activities and assignments.
16. Work in cooperation with your special needs students and the special education instructor to develop a suitable grading and evaluating system.

When working with hearing-impaired students, face the student when speaking, maintain eye contact, and speak clearly, distinctly, and in a normal voice. Be sure that you have the student's attention when making assignments. Allow vision-impaired students to examine the classroom at the beginning of the course to become familiar with the layout. Use materials with large type when possible. Be specific when referring to parts of a drawing, for instance. Vision-impaired and hearing-impaired students should sit near the front of the classroom.

Students with physical disabilities may require ramps instead of stairs and special access to drawing or computer tables. Tables should be at least 31" from the floor to accommodate a wheelchair. Special drawing or computer tables may be necessary for students with physical disabilities. A clearance space of 36" is needed for a wheelchair to pass between objects. Eliminate as many physical barriers as possible from the classroom.

Instructors can use their influence, creativity, and imagination to ensure the success of special needs students. You may have to experiment with a variety of instructional techniques before finding which ones are successful. The ultimate goal is to challenge these students to work up to their potential and realize their specific goals.

Identifying Gifted Students

It is likely that the majority of gifted students entering the classroom will have been identified. Generally, school counselors work with gifted students to guide them into interesting and challenging classes. Counselors identify the gifted students to the classroom instructor and work with the instructor to lend any assistance needed to create a positive learning atmosphere.

There may be gifted students who have not been identified prior to entering the classroom. Identifying gifted students may be a little more difficult than identifying special needs students. However, as with special needs students, unless gifted students are identified and modifications are made to challenge their learning potential, behavior problems may result.

In some cases, gifted students may intentionally conceal their identity and become difficult to distinguish from other students in the classroom. However, several behavior characteristics normally exhibited by gifted students help make their identification possible. The instructor should be aware of these characteristics in order to help identify any gifted students in the classroom. Some behaviors may include finishing work well before the remaining students in the class, boredom or restlessness, and uniformly high test scores.

Physically, gifted students are often stronger, taller, healthier, and more energetic than their classmates. Mentally, they learn quickly and are skillful thinkers. They tend to be imaginative, creative, persevering, and curious. Socially, they display leadership, self-confidence, and friendliness. They are usually charitable and critical of themselves as well as others. In addition, there are other characteristics often exhibited by gifted students. The following list is not comprehensive, but it should help the instructor determine whether gifted students are in the classroom. Gifted students tend to:

- Show ability to deal with abstraction to a great degree.
- Show ability to generalize at a high level.
- Display self-directed behavior.

- Practice considerable independent study.
- Possess an abundant amount of background knowledge and tend to apply it to new objects quickly and easily.
- Have long attention spans.
- Have vocabularies that are well above average. Have many and varied interests.
- Show the tendency to ask relevant questions.
- Desire challenges.
- Love learning for its intrinsic rewards.
- Have unusual abilities to build meanings and concepts and establish relationships.
- Express interest in experimenting with ideas and objects.
- Have tremendous ability to solve problems, invent new objects, and construct technical devices.
- Show sensitivity.
- Have high ideals.
- Have a worthy set of values and objectives.
- Have a great ability to work independently.
- Exhibit high levels of attention, concentration, and interest in intellectual subjects.
- Show interest in knowing how and why things work. Become completely preoccupied in their work. Possess great organizational ability.
- Notice clutter and try to organize the clutter.
- Have an abundance of general and specific information.
- Have high expectations of themselves and those around them.
- Express criticism of the system when it prevents them from expanding their learning experiences.
- Think deeply.
- Become completely absorbed in the problem at hand.

Gifted students perform best in an unrestricted learning environment that provides an atmosphere for their abilities and diverse interests to grow. They achieve easily when they are given the opportunity to learn in surroundings compatible to their interests and abilities.

Teaching Gifted Students

Programs for teaching gifted students differ from those used for special needs students or students with average abilities. The instructor needs to understand gifted students and should be willing to establish the appropriate atmosphere for creative learning activities to take place. The instructor must determine the program modifications that will result in the greatest achievements. The students' capabilities to think critically, establish relationships, and construct meanings and concepts should be refined. Their self-direction, independence, and desire to experiment with ideas and objects should be encouraged. Gifted students need to understand the amount and kind of education required to develop their abilities. The thrill of uncovering ideas, meanings, and relationships, as well as the opportunity to draw from a broad base of knowledge, provides the challenge of learning for gifted students.

There are a number of features that can be incorporated into a program to address the needs of gifted students. The following list includes a number of features to be considered:

- Employment of resources outside the classroom.
- Encouragement of individual research and problem solving.
- Provision for a research-oriented classroom.
- Development of a self-motivating and challenging learning atmosphere.
- Establishment of surroundings that do not set boundaries to learning.
- Application of situations that involve problem-solving and creative thought.
- Incorporation of activities requiring self-directed exploration, development, and communication.
- Development of a program that is inherently inter- and intradisciplinary.
- Establishment of a fast-track program involving in-depth technical subjects and individualization.
- Awareness that student outcomes should result in delayed success—not failure.

- Incorporation of an appropriate instructor-student ratio (1:10 is considered ideal).
- Involvement of the instructor as a resource person as well as a stimulator.
- Use of small groups to conduct research or investigations.
- Development of abstract concepts and models.
- Awareness and understanding of recent technical and research developments in science, math, and technology.
- Employment of research tools and equipment and related classroom communication.
- Involvement of community agencies and businesses to enhance classroom experiences.

Additionally, the instructor can provide activities to challenge any gifted students in the classroom. Gifted students may be asked to serve as an aid or assistant to the instructor to help other students having difficulty. They may be encouraged to work ahead on their own or be given more advanced work to challenge their potential. They may be assigned to work on a project for a local organization or a business in industry under the instructor's guidance. This would not only give them a chance to tap their potential, it would provide real-world experience outside the classroom.

The relationship of the instructor to gifted students will be somewhat different than that to average-ability students. The instructor is no longer the total authority, but rather the focal point for interaction. The new role as the resource person requires that the instructor be aware of where answers are to be found. These conditions require that an instructor be willing to experiment and not feel threatened by any perceived loss of authority.

Incorporating Additional Student Experiences

Student interest and learning can be generated by providing a variety of activities in addition to those listed in the chapter resources of this instructor's resource. Students learn inside as well as outside the classroom. There are a number of student experiences and resources the instructor can utilize to help expand the students' knowledge. They include the use of architecture and construction resources, field trips, participation in student organizations, and summer work experience. Architecture and construction resources can be used in several ways. Reading materials can be obtained to give students a broader understanding of the field. When used, they allow students to research a particular topic or learn of new innovations. Field trips enable students to see current building practices or techniques first-hand. Participation in student organizations helps students develop professionally. Summer work experience in the field of architecture and construction provides invaluable practice. The instructor can create an atmosphere that imparts an abundance of knowledge by providing as many activities and experiences as time allows.

Architecture and Construction Resources

In the Suggested Activities sections in the textbook and the Problems/Activities sections in the workbook, many experiences are presented for students to expand their knowledge inside or outside the classroom. In addition to having students participate in these activities, a number of associations and institutes can be used as resources to give students more information about their course of study. The intention of these organizations is to enlighten the public, provide information, and generally publicize the field, products, or purpose of their association or group. The following list of architectural and construction resource providers is not meant to be comprehensive, but it should help the instructor in gathering ideas and materials to enhance the educational process.

Associations and Institutes
Acoustical Society of America
2 Huntington Quadrangle
Melville, NY 11747-4502
http://asa.aip.org

Adhesive and Sealant Council, Inc.
7979 Old Georgetown Road, Suite 500
Bethesda, MD 20814
www.ascouncil.org

Air-Conditioning and Refrigeration Institute
4100 N. Fairfax Drive, Suite 200
Arlington, VA 22203
www.ari.org

Air Conditioning Contractors of America
2800 Shirlington Road, Suite 300
Arlington, VA 22206
www.acca.org

Aluminum Association, Inc.
900 19th Street NW
Washington, DC 20006
www.aluminum.org

American Architectural Mfgrs. Assn.
1827 Walden Office Square, Suite 550
Schaumburg, IL 60173-4268
www.aamanet.org

American Assn. of State Highway and
    Transportation Officials
444 N. Capitol St. NW, Suite 249
Washington, DC 20001
www.aashto.org

American Concrete Institute
38800 Country Club Drive
Farmington Hills, MI 48331
www.aci-int.org

American Fiberboard Association
1210 West Northwest Highway
Palatine, IL 60067
www.fiberboard.org

American Gas Association
400 North Capitol Street NW
Washington, DC 20001
www.aga.org

American Hardboard Association
1210 West Northwest Highway
Palatine, IL 60067
www.hardboard.org

American Hardware Mfgrs. Assn.
801 North Plaza Drive
Schaumburg, IL 60173-4977
www.ahma.org

American Institute of Building Design
2505 Main Street, Suite 209B
Stratford, CT 06615
www.aibd.org

American Institute of Architects
1735 New York Ave. NW
Washington, DC 20006
www.aia.org

American Institute of Constructors
466 94th Avenue North
St Petersburg, FL 33702
www.aicnet.org

American Institute of Steel Construction, Inc.
One East Wacker Drive, Suite 3100
Chicago, IL 60601-2001
www.aisc.org

American Institute of Timber Construction
7012 South Revere Parkway, Suite 140
Englewood, CO 80112
www.aitc-glulam.org

American Insurance Association
1130 Connecticut Avenue NW, Suite 1000
Washington, DC 20036
www.aiadc.org

American Iron and Steel Institute
1101 17th Street NW, Suite 1300
Washington, DC 20036
www.steel.org

American Lumber Standards Committee, Inc.
PO Box 210
Germantown, MD 20875-0210
www.alsc.org

American National Standards Institute
1819 L Street NW, 6th Floor
Washington, CD 20036
www.ansi.org

American Pipe Fittings Assn., Inc.
111 Park Place
Falls Church, VA 20046-4513
www.apfa.com

American Society of Civil Engineers
1801 Alexander Bell Drive
Reston, VA 20191-4400
www.asce.org

American Society of Plumbing Engineers
8614 West Catalpa Avenue, Suite 1007
Chicago, IL 60656-1116
www.aspe.org

American Society of Concrete Contractors
1801 Royal Lane, Suite 704
Dallas, TX 75229-3168
www.ascconline.org

American Society of Heating, Refrigeration,
and Air-Conditioning Engineers, Inc.
1791 Tullie Circle NE
Atlanta, GA 30329
www.ashrae.org

American Society of Interior Designers
608 Massachusetts Avenue NE
Washington, DC 20002-6006
www.interiors.org

American Society of Mechanical Engineers,
International
22 Law Drive
Fairfield, NJ 07007-2900
www.asme.org

American Society of Landscape Architects
636 Eye Street NW
Washington, DC 20001-3736
www.asla.org

American Society of Professional Estimators
11141 Georgia Avenue, Suite 412
Wheaton, MD 20902
www.aspenational.com

American Society of Sanitary Engineering
901 Centerbury, Suite A
West Lake, OH 44145
www.asse-plumbing.org

American Society for Testing and Materials
International
100 Barr Harbor Drive
West Conshohocken, PA 19428-2959
www.astm.org

American Subcontractors Assn., Inc.
1004 Duke St.
Alexandria, VA 22314-3588
www.asaonline.com

American Walnut Manufacturers Assn.
PO Box 5046
Zionsville, IN 46077
www.walnutassociation.org

American Welding Society, Inc.
550 NW LeJeune Rd.
Miami, FL 33126
www.aws.org

American Wood Council
1111 Nineteenth Street NW, Suite 800
Washington, DC 20036
www.awc.org

American Wood Preservers Institute
2750 Prosperity Avenue, Suite 550
Fairfax, VA 22031
www.preservedwood.com

Architectural Precast Assn.
6710 Winkler Road, Suite 8
Ft. Myers, FL 33919
www.arch.precast.org

Architectural Woodwork Institute
1952 Isaac Newton Square West
Reston, VA 20190
www.awinet.org

Asphalt Institute
Research Park Drive
PO Box 14052
Lexington, KY 40512-4052
www.asphaltinstitute.org

Associated Builders and Contractors, Inc.
1300 North 17th Street, Suite 800
Rosslyn, VA 22209
www.abc.org

Associated General Contractors of America
333 John Carlyle Street, Suite 200
Alexandria, VA 22314
www.agc.org

Association of the Wall & Ceiling Industries
   Intl.
803 West Broad Street, Suite 600
Falls Church, VA 22046
www.awci.org

The Brick Industry Association
11490 Commerce Park Dr.
Reston, VA 20191-1525
www.brickinfo.org

Builders Hardware Mfgrs. Assn., Inc.
355 Lexington Avenue, 17th Floor
New York, NY 10017
www. buildershardware.com

Building Officials and Code Administrators
   International
4051 W. Flossmoor Rd.
Country Club Hills, IL 60478
www.bocai.org

Building Systems Council of NAHB
1201 15th Street NW
Washington, DC 20005
www.buildingsystems.org

California Redwood Association
405 Enfrente Drive, Suite 200
Novato, CA 94949
www.calredwood.org

Carpet and Rug Institute
PO Box 2048
Dalton, GA 30722
www.carpet-rug.com

Cast Stone Institute
10 West Kimball Street
Winder, GA 30680
www.caststone.org

Cedar Shake & Shingle Bureau
PO Box 1178
Sumas, WA 98295-1178
www.cedarbureau.org

Center for Resourceful Building Technology
PO Box 100
Missoula, MT 59806
www.crbt.org

Ceramic Tile Institute of America
12061 Jefferson Blvd.
Culver City, CA 90230-6219
www.ctioa.org

Chain Link Fence Manufacturers Institute
10015 Old Columbia Road, Suite B-215
Columbia, MD 21046
www.chainlinkinfo.org

Composite Panel Association
18922 Premier Court
Gaithersburg, MD 20879-1574
www.pbmdf.com

Concrete Reinforcing Steel Institute
933 N. Plum Grove Rd.
Schaumburg, IL 60173
www.crsi.org

Construction Employers Associations
(Refer to The Blue Book of Building and
   Construction for individual listings)
www.thebluebook.com

Construction Specifications Institute
99 Canal Center Plaza, Suite 300
Alexandria, VA 22314
ww.csinet.org

Copper Development Assn., Inc.
260 Madison Avenue, 16th Floor
New York, NY 10016
http://marine.copper.org

Design Build Institute of America
1010 Massachusetts Avenue NW, 3rd Floor
Washington, DC 20001-5402
www.dbia.org

Door and Hardware Institute
14150 Newbrook Drive, Suite 200
Chantilly, VA 20151-2223
www.dhi.org

Ductile Iron Pipe Research Assn.
245 Riverchase Parkway East, Suite O
Birmingham, AL 35244
www.dipra.com

Engineered Wood Association (APA)
PO Box 11700
Tacoma, WA 98411-0700
www.apawood.org

Environmental Protection Agency
Ariel Rios Building
1200 Pennsylvania Avenue NW
Washington, DC 20460
www.epa.gov

Expanded Shale, Clay and Slate Institute
2225 E. Murray Holladay Road
Suite 102
Salt Lake City, UT 84117
www.escsi.org

Forest Products Laboratory
One Gifford Pinchot Dr.
Madison, WI 53705-2398
www.fpl.fs.fed.us

Forest Products Society
2801 Marshall Ct.
Madison, WI 53705-2295
www.forestprod.org

ForestryUSA.com
www.forestryusa.com

Gypsum Association
810 First Street NE, Suite 510
Washington, DC 20002
www.gypsum.org

Hardwood Manufacturers Association
Hardwood Information Center
400 Penn Center Blvd, Suite 530
Pittsburgh, PA 15235
www.hardwood.org

Hardwood Plywood and Veneer Assn.
PO Box 2789
Reston, VA 20195-0789
www.hpva.org

Home Improvement Research Institute
3922 Coconut Palm Drive, 3rd Floor
Tampa, FL 33619
www.hiri.org

House of Glass
www.glasschange.com

Illuminating Engineering Society of North
America
120 Wall Street, 17th Floor
New York, NY 10005
www.iesna.org

Indiana Limestone Institute of America
400 Stone City Bank Building
Bedford, IN 47421
www.iliai.com

Indoor Air Quality Information Clearing
House
PO Box 37133
Washington, DC 20013-7133
www.epa.gov/iaq

Industrial Heating Equipment Association
1111 North 19th Street, Suite 425
Arlington, VA 22209
www.ihea.org

Institute for Business and Home Safety
1408 N. Westshore Blvd., Suite 208
Tampa, FL 33607
www.ibhs.org

Institute of Electrical and Electronics
Engineers
3 Park Avenue, 17th Floor
New York, NY 10016-5997
www.ieee.org

Insurance Information Institute
110 William Street
New York, NY 10038
www.iii.org

International Association of Lighting
Designers
Merchandise Mart, Suite 9-104
200 World Trade Center
Chicago, IL 60654
www.iald.org

International Assn. of Plumbing and
  Mechanical Officials
20001 Walnut Drive South
Walnut, CA 91789-2825
www.iapmo.com

International Brotherhood of Electrical
  Workers
1125 15th Street NW
Washington, DC 20005
www.ibew.org

International Brotherhood of Painters and
  Allied Trades
1750 New York Avenue NW
Washington, DC 20006
www.ibpat.org

International Code Council
5203 Leesburg Pike, Suite 600
Falls Church, VA 22041
www.intlcode.org

International Council of Building Officials
5360 W. Workman Mill Rd.
Whittier, CA 90601-2298
www.icbo.org

International Institute for Lath & Plaster
PO Box 1663
Lafayette, CA 94549
www.iilp.org

International Masonry Institute
The James Brice House
42 East Street
Annapolis, MD 21401
www.imiweb.org

International Solid Surface Fabricators Assn.
975 American Pacific Drive, Suite 102
Hendersen, NV 89014-7823
www.issfa.com

International Union of Bricklayers & Allied
  Craftworkers
1776 Eye Street, NW
Washington, DC 20006
www.bacweb.org

International Union of Operating Engineers
1125 17th Street NW
Washington, DC 20036
www.iuoe.org

International Wood Products Association
4214 King Street West
Alexandria, VA 22302
www.ihpa.org

Laborers' International Union of North
  America
905 16th Street NW
Washington, DC 20006
www.liuna.org

Kitchen Cabinet Manufacturers Association
1899 Preston White Drive
Reston, VA 20191-5435
www.kcma.org

Manufactured Housing Institute
2101 Wilson Blvd., Suite 610
Arlington, VA 22201-3062
www.manufacturedhousing.org

Maple Flooring Manufacturers Assn.
60 Revere Dr., Suite 500
Northbrook, IL 60062
www.maplefloor.org

Marble Institute of America
28901 Clemens Road, Suite 100
West Lake, OH 44145
www.marble-institute.com

Masonry Advisory Council
1480 Renaissance Drive, Suite 401
Park Ridge, IL 60068
www.maconline.org

The Masonry Society
3970 Broadway, Suite 201-D
Boulder, CO 80304-1135
www.masonrysociety.org

Mason Contractors Association of America
33 Roselle Road
Schaumburg, IL 60193
www.masonryshowcase.com

Mechanical Contractors Assn. of America
1385 Piccard Drive
Rockville, MD 20850
www.mcaa.org

National Assn. of Demolition Contractors
16 North Franklin Street, Suite 203
Doylestown, PA 18901-3536
www.demolitionassociation.com

National Association of Home Builders
1201 15th Street NW
Washington, DC 20005
www.nahb.org

National Assn. of Housing Redevelopment
Officials
630 Eye Street NW
Washington, DC 20001
www.nahro.org

National Assn. of Plumbing, Heating, &
Cooling Contractors
180 South Washington Street
P.O. Box 6808
Falls Church, VA 22040
www.phccweb.org

National Association of Women in
Construction
327 S. Adams St.
Fort Worth, TX 76104
www.nawic.org

National Concrete Masonry Association
13750 Sunrise Valley Drive
Herndon, VA 20171-3499
www.ncma.org

National Council on Radiation Protection
and Measurement
7910 Woodmont Ave., Suite 800
Bethesda, MD 20814-3095
www.ncrp.com

National Electrical Contractors Association
3 Bethesda Metro Center, Suite 1100
Bethesda, MD 20814
www.necanet.org

National Electrical Manufacturers
Association
1300 North 17th Street, Suite 1847
Rosslyn, VA 22209
www.nema.org

National Fenestration Rating Council
8484 Georgia Avenue, Suite 320
Silver Spring, MD 20910
www.nfrc.org

National Fire Protection Association
1 Batterymarch Park
P.O. Box 9101
Quincy, MA 02269-9101
www.nfpa.org

National Glass Association
8200 Greensboro Dr., Suite 302
McLean, VA 22102-3881
www.glass.org

National Housing Rehabilitation Assn.
1625 Massachusetts Ave. NW, Suite 601
Washington, DC 20036-4435
www.housingonline.com

National Institute of Building Sciences
1090 Vermont Avenue NW, Suite 700
Washington, DC 20005-4905
www.nibs.org

National Institute of Standards and
Technology
100 Bureau Drive, Stop 2200
Gaithersburg, MD 20899-2200
www.nist.gov

National Kitchen and Bath Association
687 Willow Grove Street
Hackettstown, NJ 07840
www.nkba.org

National Lime Association
200 North Glebe Road, Suite 800
Arlington, VA 22203
www.lime.org

National Lumber and Building Material
    Dealers Assn.
40 Ivy Street SE
Washington, DC 20003
www.dealer.org

National Oak Flooring Manufacturers Assn.
PO Box 3009
Memphis, TN 38173-0009
www.nofma.org

National Paint & Coatings Assn.
1500 Rhode Island Ave. NW
Washington, DC 20005
www.paint.org

National Particleboard Association
18928 Premier Court
Gaithersburg, MD 20879-1569

National Precast Concrete Association
10333 N. Meridian Street, Suite 272
Indianapolis, IN 46290
www.precast.org

National Ready Mixed Concrete Assn.
900 Spring St.
Silver Spring, MD 20910
www.nrmca.org

National Roofing Contractors Assn.
10255 West Higgins Road, Suite 600
Rosemont, IL 60018
www.nrca.net

National Society of Professional Engineers
1420 King St.
Alexandria, VA 22314
www.nspe.org

National Stone, Sand, and Gravel Assn.
2101 Wilson Blvd., Suite 100
Arlington, VA 22201
www.aggregates.org

National Terrazzo & Mosaic Assn.
110 E. Market Street, Suite 200A
Leesburg, VA 20176
www.ntma.com

National Tile Contractors Association
PO Box 13629
Jackson, MS 39236
www.tile-assn.com

National Wood Window & Door Assn.
164 N. Lake Street
Neenah, WI 54957-1050
www.nwwda.org

North American Insulation Mfgrs. Assn.
44 Canal Center Plaza, Suite 310
Alexandria, VA 22314
www.naima.org

Occupational Safety and Health
    Administration
200 Constitution Avenue NW
Washington, DC 20210
www.osha.gov

Painting & Decorating Contractors of
    America
3913 Old Lee Highway, 2nd Floor
Fairfax, VA 22030
www.pdca.org

Perlite Institute, Inc.
1924 North Second Street
Harrisbug, PA 17102
www.perlite.org

Plastics Pipe Institute
1825 Connecticut Avenue NW, Suite 680
Washington, DC 20009
www.plasticpipe.org

Plumbing and Drainage Institute
45 Bristol Drive
South Easton, MA 02375
www.pdionline.org

Plumbing Manufacturers Institute
1340 Remington Road, Suite A
Schaumburg, IL 60173
www.pmihome.org

Portland Cement Association
5420 Old Orchard Rd.
Skokie, IL 60077
www.portcement.org

Precast/Prestressed Concrete Institute
209 W. Jackson Blvd., Suite 500
Chicago, IL 60606
www.pci.org

Resilient Floor Covering Institute
401 E. Jefferson Street, Suite 102
Rockville, MD 20850
www.rfci.com

Screen Manufacturers Association
2850 South Ocean Blvd., Suite 114
Palm Beach, FL 33480-5535
www.screenmfgassociation.org

Sheet Metal & Air Conditioning Contractors
    National Assn., Inc.
4201 Lafayette Center Drive
Chantilly, VA 20151-1209
www.smacna.org

Small Homes Council
Building Research Council
University of Illinois
One East Saint Mary's Road
Champaign, IL 61820
http://brc.arch.uiuc.edu/council.htm

Society for Protective Coatings
40 - 24th Street, 6th Floor
Pittsburgh, PA 15222-4656
www.sspc.org

Southern Bldg. Code Congress International,
    Inc.
900 Montclair Rd.
Birmingham, AL 35213-1206
www.sbcci.org

Southern Forest Products Assn.
P.O. Box 641700
Kenner, LA 70064
www.sfpa.org

Steel Door Institute
30200 Detroit Road
Cleveland, OH 44145-1967
www.steeldoor.org

Steel Joist Institute
3127 10th Avenue North Ext.
Myrtle Beach, SC 29577-6760
www.steeljoist.com

Steel Window Institute
1300 Sumner Avenue
Cleveland, OH 44115-2851
www.steelwindows.com

Stucco Manufacturers Association
2402 Vista Nobleza
Newport Beach, CA 92660
www.stuccomfgassoc.com

Sustainable Building Industry Council
1331 H Street, NW, Suite 1000
Washington, DC 20005
www.sbicouncil.org

Systems Builders Assn.
28 Lowry Drive
P.O. Box 117
West Milton, OH 45383-0117
www.systemsbuilders.org

Tile Contractors Assn. of America, Inc.
4 East 113th Terrace
Kansas City, MO 64114
www.tcaainc.org

Tile Council of America
100 Clemson Research Blvd.
Anderson, SC 29625
www.tileusa.com

Tilt-up Concrete Association
107 First Street W
PO Box 204
Mt. Vernon, IA 52314
www.tilt-up.org

Truss Plate Institute
583 D'Onofrio Drive, Suite 200
Madison, WI 53719
www.tpinst.org

Underwriters' Laboratories, Inc.
333 Pfingsten Rd.
Northbrook, IL 60062-2096
www.ul.com

United Brotherhood of Carpenters and
   Joiners of America
101 Constitution Ave. NW
Washington, DC 20001
www.carpenters.org

U.S. Army Corps of Engineers
441 G Street NW
Washington, DC 20314
www.usace.army.mil

U.S. Department of Housing and Urban
   Development
451 7th Street SW
Washington, DC 20410
www.hud.gov

Valve Manufacturers Association of America
1050 17th St. NW, Suite 280
Washington, DC 20036
www.vma.org

The Vermiculite Association
Whitegate Acre
Metheringham Fen
Lincoln
LN4 3AL
UK
www. vermiculite.org

Vinyl Siding Institute
1801 K Street NY, Suite 600K
Washington, DC 20006-7005
www.vinylsiding.org

Wallcovering Association
401 North Michigan Avenue
Chicago, IL 60611
www.wallcoverings.org

Western Red Cedar Lumber Association
1200 - 555 Burrard Street
Vancouver, BC. Canada V7X1S7
www.wrcla.org

Western Wood Products Assn.
522 SW Fifth Avenue, Suite 500
Portland, OR 97204-2122
www.wwpa.org

Wire Reinforcement Institute
942 Main Street, Suite 300
Hartford, CT 06103
www.wirereinforcementinstitute.org

Wood Flooring Manufacturers Assn.
PO Box 3009
Memphis, TN 38173-0009
www.nofma.com

Wood Truss Council of America
6300 Enterprise Lane
Madison, WI 53719
www.woodtruss.com

In addition to these resource providers,
there are a number of publications that can be
used to supply reference materials in relation
to architecture and construction. These publications should be made available in the classroom or school library. Useful published
materials include ANSI manuals, Architectural Graphic Standards texts, Time-Saver
Standards texts, Sweet's Catalog Files, and
texts on architecture, design and drafting,
construction, manufacturing, materials, and
processes. The list of publications that follows
indicates the variety of information available
to enhance learning.

Publications

Architecture
Bill Communications, Inc.
770 Broadway
New York, NY 10003
www.architecturemag.com

Architectural Digest
Conde Nast Publications, Inc.
4 Times Square
New York, NY 10036
www.archdigest.com

Architectural Record
McGraw-Hill, Inc.
1221 Avenue of the Americas
New York, NY 10120-1095
www.architecturalrecord.com

Builder
A Hanley-Wood, Inc. Publication
One Thomas Circle NW, Suite 600
Washington, DC 20005-5811
www.hanley-wood.com/inprint/builder

Building Design & Construction
Reed Business Information
360 Park Avenue South
New York, NY 10010
www.bdcmag.com

Building Products
Hanley-Wood, LLC
One Thomas Circle, Suite 600
Washington, DC 20005
www.hanley-wood.com/inprint/products

Computer-Aided Engineering
Penton Media, Inc.
1300 East Ninth Street
Cleveland, OH 44114
www.caenet.com

Computer Graphics World
PennWell Publishing Co.
98 Spitbrook Road
Nashua, NH 03062-2800
http://cgw.pennnet.com

Concrete Construction
Hanley-Wood, LLC
426 South Westgate
Addison, IL 60101-4546
www.hanley-wood.com/inprint/
   concreteconst

Construction Digest
Associated Construction Publications
30 Technology Parkway South
Suite 100
Norcross, VA 30092
www.acppubs.com/pub_cod.html

Construction Equipment
Reed Business Information
360 Park Avenue South
New York, NY 10010
www.coneq.com

Design News
Cahners Publishing Co.
275 Washington St.
Newton, MA 02458
www.manufacturing.net/dn

Environmental Resource Guide
American Institute of Architects
1735 New York Avenue, N.W.
Washington, DC 20006
http://es.epa.gov/new/business/aia/
   aia.html

Environmental Building News
BuildingGreen, Inc.
122 Birge Street, Suite 30
Brattleboro, VT 05301
www.buildnggreen.com

Fine Homebuilding
The Taunton Press
63 South Main Street
P.O. Box 5506
Newtown, CT 06470-5506
www.taunton.com/finehomebuilding

Fine Woodworking
The Taunton Press
63 South Main Street
P.O. Box 5506
Newtown, CT 06470-5506
www.taunton.com/finewoodworking

Heating/Piping/Air Conditioning
   Engineering
Penton Media, Inc.
1300 East Ninth Street
Cleveland, OH 44114
www.hpac.com

House & Garden
Conde Nast Publications
4 Times Square
New York, NY 10036
http://condenet.com/mags/hg

Interior Design
Reed Business Information
360 Park Avenue South
New York, NY 10010
www.interiordesign.net

The Journal of Light Construction
Hanley-Wood, LLC
186 Allen Brook Lane
Williston, VT 05495
www.hanley-wood.com/inprint/journallc
www.jlconline.com

Landscape Architecture
American Society of Landscape Architects
636 Eye Street, NW
Washington, DC 20001-3736
www.asla.org/nonmembers/lam.cfm

Masonry Construction
Hanley-Wood, LLC
426 South Westgate
Addison, IL 60101-4546
www.hanley-wood.com/inprint/masonry

Metal Construction News
Modern Trade Communications, Inc.
7450 N. Skokie Blvd.
Skokie, IL 60077-3374
www.metalarchitecture.com/mtcinc/
    mcn.htm

Modern Steel Construction
American Institute of Steel Construction, Inc.
One E. Wacker Drive, Suite 3100
Chicago, IL 60601-2001
www.aisc.org/msctemplate.cfm

Multi-Housing News
VNU Publications, Inc.
770 Broadway
New York, NY 10003-9595
www.multi-housingnews.com

Nation's Building News
National Association of Home Builders
1201 Fifteenth Street NW
Washington, DC 20005-2842
www.nahb.com/newsroom/nbnpage.htm

The Old House Journal
Restore Media, LLC
129 Park Street
North Reading, MA 01864
www.oldhousejournal.com

Preservation
National Trust for Historic Preservation
1785 Massachusetts Avenue, NW
Washington, DC 20036
www.nationaltrust.org/magazine

Professional Builder
Reed Business Information
360 Park Avenue South
New York, NY 10010
www.housingzone.com/pb

Qualified Remodeler
Cygnus Business Media
1233 Janesville Avenue
Ft. Atkinson, WI 53538
www.qrmagazine.com

Remodeling
Hanley-Wood, LLC
One Thomas Circle, NW, Suite 600
Washington, DC 20005-5811
www.hanley-wood.com/inprint/remodel

Woodshop News
Sounding Publications, Inc.
35 Pratt Street
Essex, CT 06426-1185
www.woodshopnews.com

Woodsmith
August Home Publishing Co.
2200 Grand Avenue
Des Moines, IA 50312-5306
www.woodsmith.com

Planning Field Trips

Field trips are a valuable educational experience for students. They provide a useful source of information and instruction. There are generally a number of sites in the local community that can provide first-hand knowledge of applications in the field of architecture and construction. A field trip can be planned to show your students how their classroom activities relate to industry.

Most companies are willing to cooperate with instructors and will welcome student groups if arrangements are made ahead of time. An instructor should make contact with a representative of the company well in advance of the trip. The instructor should maintain a working relationship with the representative so that all parties involved have a complete understanding of the areas to be covered, the scheduled activities, and other related information. Some companies may provide materials for use in the classroom to help prepare the students for the trip.

Prior to the trip, the students should be informed of the day's activities. Any background information that will help the students understand what they will see on the trip should be presented. After completing the field trip, the instructor should discuss it with the students and evaluate it with them.

In an architecture course, field trips provide students with information that they cannot typically learn in the classroom. They are given an opportunity to learn about careers in the architecture and construction field. They can actually see the duties that must be performed by employees of firms. Materials and construction practices can also be viewed.

Some ideas for field trips include trips to home construction sites, architectural firms, building materials centers, and companies manufacturing industrialized homes. Field trips can also be planned to visit sites incorporating recent architectural innovations, such as residential sites utilizing solar applications, dome structures, and earth-sheltered dwellings. Sites involving restorations of older homes are yet another source for field trips.

Participation in Professional and Student Organizations

Participating in recognized professional or student organizations provides many rewards. Participation in these types of organizations helps students grow as individuals. There are opportunities for developing leadership skills and interacting with professionals in the field. The variety of activities offered by these organizations expand student interest and help to develop technical skills. Organizations that offer activities for students studying architecture and construction include the following:

ACM SIGGRAPH
Professional and Student Chapters
www.siggraph.org

American Design Drafting Association
PO Box 11937
Columbia, SC 29211
www.adda.org

American Institute of Building Design
2505 Main Street, Suite 209 B
Stratford, CT 06615
www.aibd.org

American Institute of Architects
1735 New York Avenue NW
Washington, DC 20006
www.aia.org

American Society of Landscape Architects
636 Eye Street NW
Washington, DC 20001-3736
www.asla.org

Association for Career and Technical
  Education (ACTE)
1410 King St.
Alexandria, VA 22314
www.acteonline.org

Association of Collegiate Schools of
  Architecture
1735 New York Avenue NW
Washington, DC 20006
www.acsa-arch.org

International Technology Education
  Association
(ITEA)
1914 Association Dr., Suite 201
Reston, VA 20191-1539
www.iteawww.org

National Association of Industrial
  Technology
3300 Washtenaw Avenue, Suite 220
Ann Arbor, MI 48104-4200
www.nait.org

Society of American Registered Architects
305 East 46th Street
New York, NY 10591
www.sara-national.org

SkillsUSA (formerly VICA)
Box 3000
Leesburg, VA 20177-0300
www.skillsusa.org

Student competitions are often sponsored by businesses in industry, organizations, training centers, or state education associations. Contact these organizations in your community and state for information.

Summer Work Experience

Summer work experience provides short-term opportunities for responsible students who have completed advanced courses. This allows certain students to work in the fields they have chosen. The instructor may help the students find employment, or the students may find it on their own. To be most beneficial, the type of experience gained should coincide with the student's career goals.

There are several advantages to summer work experience. On one hand, it is an excellent way for students to gain actual work experience. It gives them an opportunity to use and refine the skills they have learned in the classroom. They also have the opportunity to learn new skills. Students gain a better understanding of all the aspects involved in the career of their choice by actually performing the day-to-day activities. They also have an opportunity to learn about other careers. Students who work jobs in the summer can earn money, and the employer can also benefit by getting a good worker at little cost.

Evaluation Methods

Purposeful evaluation is an important part of the teaching/learning process. Appropriate evaluation should play a key role in the instructor's method of teaching. There should be a conscious effort on the part of the instructor to evaluate each and every learning activity. Evaluation measures the influence of the class on the students in addition to their performance in the class. It includes deciding how students are performing as well as their feelings about the class. The conscientious instructor will constantly be aware of the students' thoughts and how they are growing intellectually. The instructor should care about the students' comprehension as well as their outlook. He or she should also be concerned about the students' capabilities in addition to what they accomplish.

Instructor evaluation should take into consideration not only the quality of teaching, but also how well students learn. Evaluation reveals to the instructor whether his or her teaching methods and strategies are effective. The evaluation methods that the instructor uses should make it easier for the students to comprehend and utilize the theory to be mastered in the class.

The overall goal of teaching a course is to assist the students in meeting the required objectives. A combination of efforts by the instructor and student learning can accomplish this goal. The students' ability to learn, plus the effectiveness of the teaching, is made evident by an evaluation of the technical skills gained, the concepts learned, and the mental processes of identifying and solving problems.

Evaluation should be an ongoing process—a process that the instructor as well as the student can use. Some typical evaluation methods include observations, self-evaluations, tests and examinations, the use of progress charts, and individual as well as group project evaluations. By using a wide variety of methods to measure student progress, an ongoing evaluation process by the instructor and the students should result.

The **Architecture: residential drafting and design** teaching package provides a variety of ways to evaluate progress. A chapter pretest is provided for each chapter of the text in this instructor's resource. This enables the instructor to measure more precisely the degree of understanding of the subject matter before students are introduced to the material. The same questions are presented in the chapter posttest in a different sequence. This ensures an accurate measure of student progress. The results of the chapter pretest compared to those of the chapter posttest will provide a real assessment of the learning that took place.

The evaluation process begins with the instructor administering the pretest for the chapter. Then the instructor presents the overall objectives to the students and lets them know exactly what is expected from them. The instructor should relate to them what they are expected to know, how they should perform, what areas they need to work on, and what class behavior is acceptable. The various class procedures should also be explained. The students should have a clear understanding of what will be taught, what they are expected to learn, and how they will be evaluated.

A vital part of the evaluation process is immediate feedback. The observation technique does just that. The student knows immediately if he or she is correctly applying the knowledge learned. The instructor should always emphasize what the student is doing correctly and show the student areas that require improvement. The instructor should always return drawings, tests, and other assignments as quickly as possible and make suggestions for improvement while also commending good work.

As previously discussed, a variety of techniques should be used to evaluate student progress. These techniques should be integrated into the teaching/learning process wherever possible. For instance, the instructor can use several evaluation techniques during a single class period. As material is presented, the instructor should observe the expressions on the students' faces. Do they understand the presentation or are there puzzled looks on their faces? If the instructor notices that the students do not understand the material being presented, it should be reviewed again or presented to them in a different way to ensure understanding. An instructor should encourage students to enter into the discussion so that he or she is sure that the students understand the concepts being presented. As the students begin to draw, observe them at their workstations. Is their work correct or should suggestions be made for improvement? Let the students know immediately if their performance is correct or if they need to make changes.

Using a variety of evaluation methods permits students to express themselves in different ways. Students with good eye/hand coordination frequently can perform successfully using drawing equipment. Those who can visualize a completed project before even starting the drawing process can be successful using computer or traditional techniques. Other students can perform well on written work. The instructor should provide opportunities for each student to find success.

The evaluation method used should be appropriate to achieve the desired results. Some methods are more suitable for one type of evaluation than others. If necessary, the instructor should make note of the various methods used for each situation and make reference to what is noted periodically.

The evaluation should always be based on guidelines and models. For example, several guidelines are given in the textbook for good window design. When evaluating designs for windows, base the evaluation on whether the design follows these guidelines. The drawings in the textbook should be used as models for the student to follow. In other words, they should serve as models for the students to pattern their work. When evaluating the students' drawings, use the models for comparison. How does the students' work compare to the work shown in the models?

The instructor should use evaluation methods that differentiate between the desired results and the actual results. The methods used should indicate how the students behave, how they comprehend, or how they carry out their work. The methods used should not only measure small differences, but meaningful differences as well. The instructor can determine which methods differentiate to the fullest extent for any given situation by experimenting with various methods.

The weight (emphasis) given to evaluations should vary among the different projects. All of the projects should not be worth the same amount. Values should be assigned to the projects so that the students will know the worth of each one. For example, a set of plans for a structure should have greater value than a quiz. The students should be told at the beginning of the course the values placed on the various projects.

The instructor should use evaluation methods that are dependable, effective, and complete. Dependable evaluation methods produce similar results time after time. Effective evaluation methods produce results that they are expected to produce. In other words, a test item designed to measure a certain concept should measure that concept. If it does not, then the test item is not effective. Evaluation methods that are complete should cover the concepts presented. The methods should be inclusive to the point that they cover the objectives to be learned. The instructor should keep these points in mind when selecting evaluation methods.

The instructor can use demonstration as an evaluation technique. He or she can set up a drawing table and actually draw a project along with the students. The students can see a professional at work. They gain confidence in their instructor's ability and this, in turn, helps to build confidence in themselves. The students can observe habits, drawing procedures, and techniques, as well as the sequence of methods demonstrated. They can see what the drawing actually looks like. The students will then set higher expectations for themselves when they see the instructor's performance.

Meaningful evaluation includes commending students when they succeed. It also includes constant feedback. It entails providing constant motivation and encouragement for students to reach their goals. Meaningful evaluation also involves teaching students to be responsible for their own development.

Flexibility in teaching methods may be required to use evaluation effectively. An instructor may need to modify his or her teaching methods to meet the various needs of the students. Extra attention and time may be required for some students to complete their projects. For example, the laboratory should be available for student use in addition to regular class time. This addresses students who need extra time to complete their projects and provides time for advanced students who wish to work on extra projects.

A number of specific evaluation tools and teaching strategies are provided in this instructor's resource. The contents are arranged by chapter and appear in the chapter resources section. The components of the chapter resources are discussed next.

Chapter Resources

This instructor's resource includes chapter resources for each chapter in the textbook and workbook. Each chapter resource section contains objectives for the chapter, display suggestions for bulletin boards, and teaching strategies. Also included are answers to the review questions in the textbook and answers to the questions and problems/activities in the workbook. There is also a chapter pretest and a chapter posttest in each chapter resource section. The answers are provided following the answers to the textbook and workbook questions.

Objectives

The objectives are the same as those found at the beginning of each chapter in the textbook. They are included in each chapter resource section to aid the instructor in developing the lesson plan.

Displays

Display suggestions for bulletin boards and other visual materials are provided for each chapter. Displays are designed to create interest, provide information, or display student work. They are an excellent medium for visual resources such as informational leaflets showing the latest building components available or current building techniques. Encourage student participation in collecting the items to be displayed and in arranging the display itself.

Instructional Materials

The resources necessary to teach the contents of each chapter are listed in the instructional materials section. Instructors should first examine the chapter pretest, answer the questions, and compare their answers to those given in this instructor's resource. They should then answer the review questions in the textbook and workbook, complete the problems/activities in the workbook, and answer the chapter posttest questions before the assignments are made to the students. This enables the instructor to thoroughly understand the material and be prepared to explain every detail. In addition, it gives the instructor an idea of the length of time required by students to complete a given project. It also allows the instructor to identify areas where students may encounter difficulties in comprehending concepts or mastering techniques.

Teaching Strategy

Suggestions and strategies for teaching the contents of each chapter are presented in this section. Instructors are given information about using the textbook, including guidelines on assigning the review questions and suggested activities in the text and the questions and problems/activities in the workbook. The instructor can utilize as many of the suggestions and activities as he or she desires in the time allotted. Some modifications will most likely be necessary to meet the needs of the students and curriculum. The instructor should keep a record of the teaching strategies he or she finds effective and continue to add ideas to keep his or her teaching current and relevant.

Transparency/Duplicating Masters

Transparency and duplicating masters may be utilized to reinforce concepts presented in the teaching strategies. They may be created from the solutions to the problems/activities presented in the workbook or from illustrations presented in the textbook. Transparency masters can reduce the time required to construct drawing examples on the chalkboard. They can be used as precise models for the students to work with when completing assignments. Duplicating masters are designed to be used in class or for out-of-class assignments. In some instances, concepts may be presented best by using a combination of transparency and duplicating masters.

Color Transparencies

A set of full-color transparencies has been produced to help the instructor reinforce concepts presented in the teaching strategies. These transparencies are available with the Instructor's Resource Binder and the Instructor's Resource CD. The Instructor's Resource CD contains 112 transparencies in electronic form. The Instructor's Resource Binder contains 96 printed transparencies.

Pretests and Posttests

A chapter pretest is provided for each chapter in this instructor's resource. This test may be used to determine a student's knowledge about the content before studying the chapter.

A chapter posttest is also provided and should be administered after students complete the review questions, problems, and activities for a given chapter. As previously discussed, the chapter posttest questions are the same as those given in the pretest with a different sequence. In this way, the chapter posttest serves as an accurate measure of student comprehension of the chapter content.

Portfolio Activity

A student portfolio activity is also provided in this instructor's resource. This appears before the chapter resources and can be reproduced for student use. After students have completed each chapter, they are instructed to collect architecture-related materials that pertain to the content just studied. The materials are to be gathered, entered into the portfolio, and checked by the instructor. After completing this activity, each student will have a comprehensive portfolio of architectural design.

Architecture and Construction Internet Resources

In each chapter of the textbook, a section listing various manufacturers, associations, and government agencies related to the chapter content is provided. The Internet Resources section is intended to be used as a reference for additional information pertaining to the chapter material. A Web address is provided with each listing. Where necessary, a description of the company or organization is also included. For reference purposes, the following is a comprehensive list of the organizations and Web sites included in each chapter.

AbbiSoft
www.abbisoft.com

Abracadata
www.abracadata.com

Acorn Stairlifts
www.acornstairlifts.com

Air Conditioning and Refrigeration Institute
www.ari.org

Alside, Inc.
www.alside.com

Alumax
www.alumag.com

Aluminum Company of America (ALCOA)
  Building Products, Inc.
www.alcoahomes.com

American ConForm Industries
www.smartblock.com

The American Contractor
www.amercon.com

American Forest and Paper Association
www.afandpa.org

American Institute of Architects
www.aia.org

American Institute of Building Design
www.aibd.org

American Iron and Steel Institute
www.steel.org

American National Standards Institute
www.ansi.org

American Rockwool Association
www.amerrock.com

American Society of Landscape Architects
www.asla.org

American Solar Energy Society
www.ases.org

American Standard
www.americanstandard.com

Anchor Retaining Wall Systems
www.anchorwall.com

Aqua Glass
www.aquaglass.com

Architectural Details, Inc.
www.details-details.com

Architectural Digest
www.archdigest.com

Architectural Ornament, Inc.
www.architectural-ornament.com

Archtek Telecom Corp.
www.archtek.com

Arcways, Inc.
www.arcways.com

Armstrong World Industries, Inc.
www.armstrong.com

ART Incorporated
www.chiefarch.com

ASTM International
www.astm.org

A-Systems Corporation
www.a-systems.net

ATAS International, Inc.
www.atas.com

Autodesk, Inc.
www.autodesk.com

Auton Motorized Systems
www.auton.com

Avis America
www.avisamerica.com

Babb International Inc.
www.hebel.com

Jim Barna Log Systems
www.logcabins.com

Better Homes and Gardens Magazine
www.bhg.com

Boise Cascade Engineered Wood Products
www.bcewp.com

Boral Bricks
www.boralbricks.com

Brass Light Gallery
www.brasslight.com

Eric Brown Design Group
www.designgroupstudio.com

The Buckminster Fuller Institute
www.bfi.org

Builder Magazine Online
www.builderonline.com

Builder Software Tools, Inc.
www.buildertools.com

Builders Software Enterprises
www.builders-software.com

Building Systems Councils, National
    Association of Home Builders
www.buildingsystems.org

Buildsoft Construction Scheduling and
    Estimating Software
www.buildsoft.com

Cadalyst magazine
www.cadalyst.com

CADENCE magazine
www.cadence.com

CADSOFT Corporation
www.cadsoft.com

California Closets
www.calclosets.com

California Redwood Association
www.calredwood.org

Caradco
www.caradco.com

Cardinal Homes, Inc.
www.cardinalhomes.com

Carrier Corporation
www.carrier.com

Cemplank
www.cemplank.com

Centers for Disease Control and Prevention
www.cdc.gov

CertainTeed Corporation
www.certainteed.com

Compaq computers
www.compaq.com

Composite Technologies Corporation
www.thermomass.com

Computer Presentation Systems, Inc.
www.cpsenet.com

Congoleum Corporation
www.congoleum.com

Construction Data Control, Inc.
www.cdci.com

Consumer Electronics Association,
    TechHome Division
www.hanaonline.org

Cooper Lighting
www.cooperlighting.com

Cooper Wiring Devices
www.eagle-electric.com

Cor-A-Vent, Inc.
www.cor-a-vent.com

CPI Plastics Group Ltd.
www.eonoutdoor.com

Cultured Stone
www.culturedstone.com

Customized Structures, Inc.
www.custruct.com

DATACAD, LLC
www.datacad.com

DealBuilder
www.dealbuilder.com

Deere and Company
www.deere.com

Dell Computers
www.dell.com

Deltec Homes
www.deltechomes.com

Department of Energy, Office of Energy
    Efficiency and Renewable Energy
www.eren.doe.gov

Department of Veterans Affairs
www.va.gov

Design Basics, Inc.
www.designbasics.com

Discreet Logic Inc.
www.discreet.com

Dryvit Systems, Inc.
www.dryvit.com

Earthship Global Website
www.earthship.org

Echelon Corporation
www.echelon.com

ELAN Home Systems
www.elanhomesystems.com

Eldorado Stone
www.eldoradostone.com

Eljer Plumbingware, Inc.
www.eljer.com

Elk Corporation of America
ww.elkcorp.com

ELK Products, Inc.
www.elkproducts.com

The Engineered Wood Association (APA)
www.apawood.org

Enterprise Computer Systems, Inc.
www.ecs-inc.com

EPS Molders Association
www.epsmolders.org

Federal Emergency Management Agency
www.fema.gov

FlowGuard Gold®
www.flowguardgold.com

Forest Products Laboratory
www.fpl.fs.fed.us

GAF Materials Corporation
www.gaf.com

Geist Manufacturing, Inc.
www.flexiduct.com

General Electric
www.ge.com/product/home/lighting.htm

Georgia Pacific Corporation
www.gp.com/build/index.html

GlowCore A.C., Inc.
www.glowcoreac.com

James Hardie Building Products, Inc.
www.jameshardie.com

Hartco Flooring
www.hartcoflooring.com

Harter Industries
www.harterindustries.com

HB&G Building Products
www.hbgcolumns.com

Heliodyne, Inc.
www.heliodyne.com

Hewlett-Packard
www.hp.com

Home Controls, Inc.
www.homecontrols.com

HomeCrest Cabinetry
www.homecrestcab.com

Homes of Elegance
www.homesofelegance.com

Honeywell Home and Building Controls
www.honeywell.com/yourhome

Hoover
www.hoovercompany.com

Hunter Fan Company
www.hunterfan.com

Hurd Windows and Patio Doors
www.hurd.com

Increte Systems
www.increte.com

Institute for Business and Home Safety
www.ibhs.org

Insulating Concrete Form Association
www.forms.org

Insulspan, Inc.
www.insulspan.com

Insurance Information Institute
www.iii.org

International Organization for
  Standardization
www.iso.ch

International Zinc Association
www.iza.com

Invensys Climate Controls
www.invensysclimate.com

ITT Industries
www.ittnss.com

Jacuzzi, Inc.
www.jacuzzi.com

Keeva International, Inc.
www.oikos.com/keeva

Kern Electrics and Lasers, Inc.
www.kernlasers.com

Keystone Retaining Wall Systems
www.keystonewalls.com

KitchenAid
www.kitchenaid.com

Knauf Fiber Glass
www.knauffiberglass.com

Kohler Company
www.kohler.com

Lennox Indoor Comfort Systems
www.lennox.com

Leviton
www.leviton.com

Lightolier® Controls
www.lolcontrols.com

Lindal Cedar Homes
www.lindal.com

Lite-Form Incorporated
www.liteform.com

Log Cabin Homes
www.logcabinhomes.com

Louisiana-Pacific Corporation
www.lpcorp.com

Lutron
www.lutron.com

M & S Systems
www.mssystems.com

Martin Industries, Inc.
www.martinindustries.com

Marvin Windows and Doors
www.marvin.com

Masonite International Corporation
www.masonite.com

McFeely's Square Drive Screws
www.mcfeelys.com

Media Lab
www.homesalespro.com

Melroe Co./Bobcat
www.bobcat.com

Melton Classics, Inc.
www.meltonclassics.com

Met-Tile
www.met-tile.com

MI Home Products
www.mihomeproducts.com

MicroStation publisher
www.bentley.com/products

Modern Plastics Co.
www.modernplastics.com

Modern Plastics magazine
www.modplas.com

Modular Radiant Technologies, Inc.
www.pfgindustries.com

Moen, Inc.
www.moen.com

NAHB Research Center
www.nahbrc.org

Napoleon Fireplaces
www.napoleon.on.ca

National Concrete Masonry Association
www.ncma.org

National Gypsum Company
www.nationalgypsum.com

National Hardwood Lumber Association
www.natlhardwood.org

National Institute for Standards and
    Technology—Material Science and
    Engineering Laboratory
www.msel.nist.gov

National Institute of Building Sciences
www.nibs.org

National Oceanic and Atmospheric
    Administration
www.noaa.gov

National Precast Concrete Association
www.precast.org

National Renewable Energy Laboratory
www.nrel.gov

Nemetschek North America
www.nemetschek.net

Norcraft Companies L.L.C.
www.norcraftcompanies.com

North American Housing Corporation
www.northamericanhousing.com

Owens Corning
www.owenscorning.com

Parametric Technology Corporation
www.ptc.com

Pease Entry Systems
www.peasedoors.com

Pella Corporation
www.pella.com

Pinecrest, Inc.
www.pinecrestinc.com

Plasti-Fab
www.plastifab.com

Portland Cement Association
www.concretehomes.com

Pozzi Wood Windows
www.pozzi.com

Price Pfister
www.pricepfister.com

Progress Lighting
www.progresslighting.com

Progressive Programming Corporation
www.bidrite.net

Raynor Garage Doors
www.raynor.com

Reddi-Form, Inc.
www.reddi-form.com

Reemay, Inc.
www.reemay.com

The Reinforced Earth Company
www.recousa.com

Renew Plastics
www.renewplastics.com

Renewable Energy Policy Project
www.crest.org

Reward Wall Systems
www.rewardwallsystems.com

Reynolds Building Products
www.reynoldsbp.com

Rockler Woodworking and Hardware
www.rockler.com

The Sater Design Collection, Inc.
www.saterdesign.com

Schulte Corporation
www.schultestorage.com

Sea Gull Lighting Products, Inc.
www.seagulllighting.com

The Siemon Company
www.homecabling.com

Slate/Select, Inc.
www.stone-slate.com

Smarthome®, Inc.
www.smarthome.com

A. O. Smith Water Products Company
www.hotwater.com

SoftPlan Architectural Design Software
www.softplan.com

Solar Energy Industries Association
www.seia.org

Southern Pine Council
www.southernpine.com

Staedtler Mars GmbH & Co.
www.staedtler-usa.com

Sterling Plumbing
www.sterlingplumbing.com

Studer Residential Designs
www.studerdesigns.com

Sweet's Catalog File
www.sweets.com

Synthetic Industries Concrete Systems
www.fibermesh.com

Thermal Industries, Inc.
www.thermalindustries.com

Thomas Register
www.thomasregister.com

TimberTech Limited
www.timbertech.com

The Trane Company
www.trane.com/residential

Trex Company
www.trex.com

US Department of Energy
www.energy.gov

US Department of Labor's Occupational
   Outlook Handbook
www.bls.gov/oco/

US Environmental Protection Agency
www.epa.gov

US Naval Observatory
aa.usno.navy.mil/data

Vanguard Piping Systems, Inc.
www.vanguardpipe.com

VELUX Group
www.velux.com

Vemco Corporation
www.vemcocorp.com

Ventamatic, Ltd.
www.bvc.com

Wausau Homes
www.wausauhomes.com

The Weather Channel
www.weather.com

West Penn Wire/CDT
www.westpenn-cdt.com

Western Wood Products Association
www.wwpa.org

Whirlpool Corporation
www.whirlpool.com

Windsor Door
www.windsordoor.com

Windsor Windows and Doors
www.windsorwindows.com

Woodcraft Supply Corp.
www.woodcraft.com

Woodshop News Magazine
www.woodshopnews.com

Woodworker's Supply, Inc.
www.woodworker.com

X10 Home Solutions
www.x10.com

Basic Skills Chart

The Basic Skills Chart identifies activities in the **Architecture: residential drafting and design** teaching package that encourage the development of basic skills. Included are activities in the text, *Workbook,* and *Instructor's Resource Binder* (listed in the chart as IRB).

Activities are broken down by chapter. In addition, hands-on activities are identified with the symbol ✍ preceding the activity listing.

<table>
<tr>
<th colspan="2"></th>
<th>Chapter 1</th>
<th>Chapter 2</th>
</tr>
<tr>
<td rowspan="3">Verbal/Communication Skills</td>
<td>Reading</td>
<td>Text: People and their Structures; Contemporary Structures; Trends in Architecture; Multifamily Housing; Americans with Disabilities Act (ADA).

IRCD: Early Traditional Home Styles, Handout 1-1; Americans with Disabilities Act, Handout 1-2.</td>
<td>Text: One-Story Ranch Designs; One-and-One-Half-Story Designs; Two-Story Designs; Split-Level Designs; Traffic Circulation; ✍Activity 7.</td>
</tr>
<tr>
<td>Writing</td>
<td>Text: ✍Activity 1; ✍Activity 2; ✍Activity 4.</td>
<td>Text: ✍Activity 2.</td>
</tr>
<tr>
<td>Verbal</td>
<td>Text: ✍Activity 3; ✍Activity 5.</td>
<td>Text: ✍Activity 4; ✍Activity 5.</td>
</tr>
<tr>
<td rowspan="2">Quantitative</td>
<td>Math</td>
<td></td>
<td>Text: ✍Activity 3.</td>
</tr>
<tr>
<td>Science</td>
<td></td>
<td></td>
</tr>
<tr>
<td>Analytical</td>
<td>Analytical</td>
<td></td>
<td>Text: ✍Activity 1; ✍Activity 6; ✍Activity 8; ✍Activity 9.

Workbook: Traffic Circulation, Activity 2-1.</td>
</tr>
</table>

		Chapter 3	**Chapter 4**
Verbal/Communication Skills	**Reading**	Text: Site Considerations; The Community; Zoning and Codes; Topographical Features; Family Needs; Other Considerations; Drawings Included in a Set of Plans. IRCD : Drawings Included in a Set of Plans, Handout 3-1.	Text: Orthographic Projection; Three Principal Views; Architectural Drafting Equipment; Freehand Sketching; Computer-Aided Drafting and Design; Lines Used in Architectural Drawing; CADD Symbols Library. IRCD : Typical Architectural Drafting Equipment, Handout 4-1; Architectural Style Lettering, Visual Master 4-1.
	Writing		Text: Architectural L ettering; ✍Activity 1; ✍Activity 2; ✍Activity 3; ✍Activity 5. Workbook: Architectural Lettering, Activity 4-5.
	Verbal		
Quantitative	**Math**	Text: Cost and Restrictions; Budgeting for Housing; ✍Activity 3.	Text: ✍Activity 4. Workbook: Measuring to Scale, Activity 4-3.
	Science		
Analytical	**Analytical**	Text: ✍Activity 1; ✍Activity 2; ✍Activity 4;✍Activity 5; ✍Activity 6.	Text: ✍Activity 6. Workbook: Orthographic Projection, Activity 4-1; Orthographic Projection, Activity 4-2; Alphabet of Lines, Activity 4-4.

		Chapter 5	Chapter 6
Verbal/Communication Skills	Reading	Text: What is CADD?; Why Use CADD?; Architectural CADD Applications; CADD Workstation; Selecting a CADD Package. IRCD : Benefits of CADD in Architecture, Handout 5-1.	Text: Drawing Commands; Editing and Inquiry Commands; Display Control Commands; Dimensioning Commands; Drawing Aids; Layers; Colors and Linetypes; Blocks and Attributes; 3D Drawing and Viewing Commands; 3D Animation and Rendering Commands. IRCD : Drawing Commands, Visual Master 6-1; Editing and Inquiry Commands 1, Visual Master 6-2; Editing and Inquiry Commands 2, Visual Master 6-3; Display Control Commands, Visual Master 6-4; Dimensioning Commands, Visual Master 6-5; Drawing Aids, Visual Master 6-6; Utility Commands and Functions, Visual Master 6-7.
	Writing		
	Verbal	Text: ✍Activity 1.	
Quantitative	Math		
	Science		
Analytical	Analytical	Text: ✍Activity 2; ✍Activity 3; ✍Activity 4. Workbook: General Purpose CADD, Activity 5-1; AEC CADD Characteristics, Activity 5-2. IRCD : 3D CADD Drawing, Visual Master 5-1.	Text: ✍Activity 1; ✍Activity 2; ✍Activity 3; ✍Activity 4. Workbook: Drawing Commands, Activity 6-2; Editing and Inquiry Commands, Activity 6-3; Dimensioning Commands, Activity 6-4. IRCD : CADD-Generated Section, Handout 6-1.

		Chapter 7	Chapter 8
Verbal/Communication Skills	Reading	Text: Areas of a Residence; Designing with CADD; Sleeping Area. IRCD : Small Bathroom with Adaptable Features, Handout 7-1; Large Bathroom with Adaptable Features, Handout 7-2.	Text: Designing with CADD; Living Rooms; Dining Rooms; Entryway and Foyer; Family Recreation Room; Special-Purpose Rooms; Patios, Porches, Courts, and Gazebos. IRCD : Handicapped Accessibility, Handout 8-1.
	Writing	Text: ✍Activity 1.	
	Verbal		
Quantitative	Math	IRCD : Minimum Clear Width for Wheelchairs, Visual Master 7-1; Wheelchair Turning Space, Visual Master 7-2; Minimum Clear Floor Space for Wheelchairs, Visual Master 7-3; Forward Reach, Visual Master 7-4; Side Reach, Visual Master 7-5; Clear Floor Space at Water Closets, Visual Master 7-6; Water Closets and Urinals, Visual Master 7-7; Clear Floor Space at Bathtub, Visual Master 7-8.	IRCD : Accessible Routes, Visual Master 8-1; Protruding Objects, Visual Master 8-2; Two Hinged Doors in Series, Visual Master 8-3.
	Science		
Analytical	Analytical	Text: ✍Activity 2; ✍Activity 3; ✍Activity 4; ✍Activity 5; ✍Activity 6; ✍Activity 7. Workbook: Basic Areas, Activity 7-1; Furniture Cutouts, Activity 7-2a; Bedroom Planning, Activity 7-2b; Bathroom Planning, Activity 7-3; Bathroom Planning, Activity 7-4.	Text: ✍Activity 1; ✍Activity 2; ✍Activity 3; ✍Activity 4; ✍Activity 5; ✍Activity 6; ✍Activity 7. Workbook: Living Room Planning, Activity 8-1; Dining Room Planning, Activity 8-2; Entry/Foyer Planning, Activity 8-3; Recreation Room Planning, Activity 8-4; Patio and Porch Planning, Activity 8-5.

		Chapter 9	Chapter 10
Verbal/Communication Skills	Reading	Text: Designing with CADD; Kitchen; Clothes Care Center; Garage or Carport. IRCD : Wheelchair Accessibility, Handout 9-1.	Text: Topographical Features; Location of the Structure on the Site; Landscape Plans; Procedure for Drawing a Plot Plan—CADD. IRCD : Plot Plans, Handout 10-1.
	Writing		Text: ✍Activity 3; ✍Activity 4. Workbook: Topographical Symbols, Activity 10-1.
	Verbal	Text: ✍Activity 1.	
Quantitative	Math	Text: ✍Activity 2; ✍Activity 5. Workbook: Kitchen Planning, Activity 9-1; Kitchen Planning, Activity 9-2; Clothes Care Center Planning, Activity 9-4; Garage Planning, Activity 9-5; Driveway Turnaround Planning, Activity 9-6. IRCD : Handrail and Guardrail Requirements, Visual Master 9-1; Stair Handrails, Visual Master 9-2; Storage Shelves and Closets, Visual Master 9-3.	Text: Property Lines; Contour Lines; Procedure for Drawing a Plot Plan—Manual Drafting; ✍Activity 1. Workbook: Bearings, Activity 10-2; Property Lines, Activity 10-3; Contour Lines, Activity 10-4; Site Plans, Activity 10-5, Plot Plans, Activity 10-6.
	Science		
Analytical	Analytical	Text: ✍Activity 3; ✍Activity 4; ✍Activity 6. Workbook: Kitchen Planning, Activity 9-1; Kitchen Planning, Activity 9-2; Kitchen Design, Activity 9-3; Clothes Care Center Planning, Activity 9-4; Garage Planning, Activity 9-5; Driveway Turnaround Planning, Activity 9-6.	Text: ✍Activity 2; ✍Activity 5; Activity 6. Workbook: Site Plans, Activity 10-5; Plot Plans, Activity 10-6.

		Chapter 11	Chapter 12
Verbal/Communication Skills	**Reading**	Text: Excavation; Footing Shapes and Specifications; Foundation Walls; Concrete and Masonry Basement Walls; Concrete and Masonry; Concrete Blocks; Paving. IRCD: Paving Pattern Bonds, Handout 11-1; High Planter or Retaining Wall, Visual Master 11-1; Low Planter or Retaining Wall, Visual Master 11-2; Porch Foundation Wall, Visual Master 11-3.	Text: Preliminary Steps to Drawing a Foundation Plan; Drawing a Foundation Plan; The Basement/Foundation Plan; Procedure for Drawing a Basement Plan; Using CADD to Draw a Foundation and Basement plan. IRCD : Foundation Plans, Handout 12-1.
	Writing		
	Verbal		
Quantitative	**Math**	Text: Staking out House Location, Beams and Girders; ✎Activity 1; ✎Activity 2; ✎Activity 3; ✎Activity 4; ✎Activity 5. IRCD : Concrete Masonry Units 1, Visual Master 11-4; Concrete Masonry Units 2, Visual Master 11-5; Concrete Masonry Units 3, Visual Master 11-6; Concrete Masonry Units 4, Visual Master 11-7.	Text: ✎Activity 4. IRCD : Typical Foundation Wall, Visual Master 12-1.
	Science		
Analytical	**Analytical**	Text: ✎Activity 6; ✎Activity 7. Workbook: Slab Foundation Section, Activity 11-1; Foundation with Crawl Space, Activity 11-2; Cast Concrete Basement, Activity 11-3; Wood Foundation/Basement, Activity 11-4.	Text: ✎Activity 1; Activity 2, ✎Activity 3. Workbook: Foundation Plan, Activity 12-1; Activity 12-2.

		Chapter 13	Chapter 14
Verbal/Communication Skills	**Reading**	Text: Platform Framing; Balloon Framing; Joists and Beams; Floor Trusses; Subfloor; Cantilevered Joists; Framing under Slate or Tile; Engineered Wood Products; Post and Beam Construction. IRCD : Redwood Deck Construction, Handout 13-1; Deck Stair Construction, Handout 13-2; Average Moisture Content, Handout 13-3; Lateral Support, Handout 13-6; Residential Steel Framing, Handout 13-7; Residential Steel Framing, Handout 13-8; Brick Veneer on Wood Frame 1, Visual Master 13-1; Brick Veneer on Wood Frame 2, Visual Master 13-2; Brick Veneer on Metal Studs, Visual Master 13-3.	Text: Frame Wall Construction; Steel Framing, Ceiling Construction, General Framing Considerations, Masonry Wall Construction, Brick Names and Sizes, Traditional Three-Coat Stucco. IRCD : Using Redwood Siding over Rigid Foam, Handout 14-3.
	Writing	Text: ✍Activity 2; Activity 3.	
	Verbal		
Quantitative	**Math**	IRCD : Floor Joist Spans for Western Woods, Handout 13-4; Floor Joist Spans for Southern Pine, Handout 13-5; Brick Veneer on Wood Frame 1, Visual Master 13-1; Brick Veneer on Wood Frame 2, Visual Master 13-2; Brick Veneer on Metal Studs, Visual Master 13-3. Workbook: Wall Section Parts, Activity 13-1; Floor Framing Problems, Activity 13-2.	Workbook: Wall Framing Details, Activity 14-1. IRCD : Ceiling Joist Spans for Western Woods, Handout 14-1; Ceiling Joist Spans for Southern Pine, Handout 14-2; Using Redwood Siding over Rigid Foam, Handout 14-3; Residential Steel Framing 1, Visual Master 14-1; Residential Steel Framing 2, Visual Master 14-2; Residential Steel Framing 3, Visual Master 14-3; Residential Steel Framing 4, Visual Master 14-4; Residential Steel Framing 5, Visual Master 14-5; Residential Steel Framing 6, Visual Master 14-6; Residential Steel Framing 7, Visual Master 14-7.
	Science	IRCD : Average Moisture Content, Handout 13-3.	
Analytical	**Analytical**	Text: ✍Activity 1; ✍Activity 4; ✍Activity 5. Workbook: Wall Section Parts, 13-1; Floor Framing Problems, Activity 13-2. IRCD : Residential Steel Framing, Handout 13-7; Residential Steel Framing, Handout 13-8.	Text: ✍Activity 1; ✍Activity 2; ✍Activity 3; ✍Activity 4; ✍Activity 5; ✍Activity 6; ✍Activity 7; ✍Activity 8. Workbook: Wall Framing Details, Activity 14-1; Masonry Wall Symbols, Activity 14-2.

		Chapter 15	Chapter 16
Verbal/Communication Skills	**Reading**	Text: Designing with CADD; Interior and Exterior Doors; Specifying Doors; Door Details; Windows. IRCD : Custom Fixed Straight-Sided Windows, Handout 15-1; Custom Fixed Curved Windows, Handout 15-2.	Text: Types of Stairs; Stair Terminology; Designing with CADD; Stair Design; Structural Details; Code Requirements for Handrails and Guardrails; Adaptations for Special Needs. IRCD : Interior Stairway Framing, Visual Master 16-1; Framing for Stairway with a Landing, Visual Master 16-2.
	Writing	Text: ✐Activity 1. Workbook: Exterior Door Detail, Activity 15-3.	
	Verbal		
Quantitative	**Math**	Text: ✐Activity 4.	Text: Stair Calculations and Drawing Procedure; ✐Activity 1; ✐Activity 2. IRCD : Calculating Stair Dimensions, Handout 16-1.
	Science		
Analytical	**Analytical**	Text: ✐Activity 2; ✐Activity 3; ✐Activity 5. Workbook: Plan View Door Symbols, Activity 15-1; Plan View Window Symbols, Activity 15-2; Exterior Door Detail, Activity 15-3.	Text: ✐Activity 3; ✐Activity 4; ✐Activity 5. Workbook: Stairs, Activity 16-1.

		Chapter 17	**Chapter 18**
Verbal/Communication Skills	**Reading**	Text: Fireplace Design Considerations; Fireplace/Chimney Terms; Designing with CADD; Hearth and Fire Chamber; Damper and Smoke Shelf; Flue; Framing around Fireplace and Chimney; Fireplace Specifications; Stoves. IRCD : Floor Framing around Fireplace, Visual Master 17-1.	Text: Required Information; Drawing a Floor Plan. IRCD : Floor Plans, Handout 18-1; Drawing Floor Plans, Handout 18-2; CADD-Generated Floor Plan, Visual Master 18-4.
	Writing	Text: ✎Activity 1. Workbook: Fireplace Parts, Activity 17-1.	Text: ✎Activity 1.
	Verbal	Text: ✎Activity 2; ✎Activity 3; ✎Activity 5.	
Quantitative	**Math**	Text: ✎Activity 4. Workbook: Fireplace Dimensions, Activity 17-2; Fireplace Details, Activity 17-3. IRCD : Single Face Fireplace Dimensions, Handout 17-1; 42″ Built-in Wood Burning Fireplace, Handout 17-2; Single Story Installation with Attic, Handout 17-3.	Text: ✎Activity 3. IRCD : Typical Floor Plan, Visual Master 18-1; Zero Lot Line Residence, Visual Master 18-2; Garden House Floor Plan, Visual Master 18-3.
	Science		
Analytical	**Analytical**	Text: ✎Activity 1; ✎Activity 6. Workbook: Fireplace Parts, Activity 17-1; Fireplace Dimensions, Activity 17-2; Fireplace Details, Activity 17-3.	Text: ✎Activity 2; ✎Activity 4; ✎Activity 5. Workbook: Floor Plan Symbols, Activity 18-1; Dimensioning Floor Plans, Activity 18-2.

		Chapter 19	Chapter 20
Verbal/Communication Skills	Reading	Text: Types of Roofs; Traditional Frame Roof Construction; New Roofing Materials; ✐Activity 1. Workbook: Roof Framing Plan, Activity 19-4. IRCD : Rafter Framing Details, Handout 19-1; Steel Framing at Roof Eave, Visual Master 19-1; Steel Framing Truss Details, Visual Master 19-2.	Text: Required Information; Drawing a Typical Wall Section; Procedure for Drawing an Elevation—Manual Drafting; Procedure for Drawing an Elevation—CADD. IRCD : Elevations, Handout 20-1.
	Writing	Text: ✐Activity 2. Workbook: Roof Framing Parts, Activity 19-1.	
	Verbal		
Quantitative	Math	Text: ✐Activity 5. Workbook: Roof Framing Parts, Activity 19-1; Cornice Section, Activity 19-3; Roof Framing Plan, Activity 19-4. IRCD : Rafter Spans for Western Woods, Handout 19-2; Rafter Spans for Southern Pine, Handout 19-3.	Workbook: Exterior Elevation Symbols, Activity 20-1; Colonial House Elevation, Activity 20-2; Garden House Elevation, Activity 20-3. IRCD : Exterior Elevations—Windows, Visual Master 20-1; Front Elevation—15′ Classic Gazebo, Visual Master 20-2; Garden House Front Elevation, Visual Master 20-3.
	Science		
Analytical	Analytical	Text: ✐Activity 3; ✐Activity 4; ✐Activity 6. Workbook: Roof Slope, Activity 19-2; Roof Framing Plan, Activity 19-4.	Text: ✐Activity 1; ✐Activity 2; ✐Activity 3; Activity 4; Activity 5. Workbook: Floor Plan Symbols, Activity 18-1; Dimensioning Floor Plans, Activity 18-2. IRCD : CADD-Generated Elevation, Visual Master 20-4.

		Chapter 21	**Chapter 22**
Verbal/Communication Skills	**Reading**	Text: Electrical Terms; Service Entrance and Distribution Panel; Branch Circuits; Outlets and Switches; Ground-Fault Circuit Interrupter (GFCI); Low Voltage Exterior Lighting; ✍Activity 4. IRCD : Typical Appliance Requirements, Handout 21-1.	Text: Information and Communication Wiring; Signaling Circuits; Data and Video Conductors; Security Wiring; Home Automation; Low-Voltage Switching. IRCD : Modern Technology Features, Visual Master 22-1; UTP Cable, Visual Master 22-2; Low-Voltage Switching, Visual Master 22-3.
	Writing	Text: ✍Activity 3. Workbook: Residential Electrical Outlets, Activity 21-1.	Text: ✍Activity 1; ✍Activity 2.
	Verbal		
Quantitative	**Math**	Text: Circuit Requirement Calculations; ✍Activity 1; ✍Activity 2. IRCD : Typical Appliance Requirements, Handout 21-1.	
	Science	Workbook: Residential Electrical Outlets, Activity 21-1.	
Analytical	**Analytical**	Text: ✍Activity 5; ✍Activity 6. Workbook: Switches and Outlets, Activity 21-2.	Text: ✍Activity 3; ✍Activity 4. Workbook: Activity 22-1; Activity 22-2.

		Chapter 23	Chapter 24
Verbal/Communication Skills	Reading	Text: Required Information; Procedure for Drawing an Electrical Plan—Manual Drafting; Procedure for Drawing an Electrical Plan—CADD. IRCD : The Electrical Plan, Handout 23-1.	Text: Water Supply System; In-House Water Treatment Devices; Water and Waste Removal; Plumbing Fixtures; Water Conservation; Private Sewage Disposal System. IRCD : Bathroom Clearances, Handout 24-1.
	Writing	Text: ✐Activity 4.	Text: ✐Activity 3.
	Verbal	Text: ✐Activity 3.	Text: ✐Activity 2.
Quantitative	Math		Text: ✐Activity 4; ✐Activity 5. Workbook: Well/Septic Placement, Activity 24-3. IRCD : Bathroom Clearances, Handout 24-1; Typical Bathtub Roughing-in, Handout 24-2; Typical Pedestal Lavatory Roughing-in, Handout 24-3; Typical Siphon-Action Toilet Roughing-in, Handout 24-4.
	Science	IRCD : Electrical Circuit Data Chart, Visual Master 23-1.	Workbook: Waste Removal System, Activity 24-2.
Analytical	Analytical	Text: ✐Activity 1; ✐Activity 2; ✐Activity 5; ✐Activity 6. Workbook: Electrical Symbols, Activity 23-1; Garage Electrical Plan, Activity 23-2.	Text: ✐Activity 1; ✐Activity 6. Workbook: Water Supply System, Activity 24-1; Waste Removal System, Activity 24-2; Well/Septic Placement, Activity 24-3. IRCD : Typical Bathtub Roughing-in, Handout 24-2; Typical Pedestal Lavatory Roughing-in, Handout 24-3; Typical Siphon-Action Toilet Roughing-in, Handout 24-4.

		Chapter 25	**Chapter 26**
Verbal/Communication Skills	**Reading**	Text: Required Information; Procedure for Drawing Plumbing Plan—Manual Drafting; Procedure for Drawing Plumbing Plan—CADD. IRCD : The Plumbing Plan, Handout 25-1.	Text: Temperature Control; Humidity Control; Air Circulation and Cleaning; Programmable Thermostats; Cooling Systems; Types of Heating Systems; Ground-Source Heat Pumps; True Window R-Value; CADD Heat Loss Calculations. IRCD : Heating Systems, Visual Master 26-1.
	Writing	Text: ✎Activity 1.	Text: ✎Activity 5.
	Verbal	Text: ✎Activity 5.	Text: ✎Activity 1; ✎Activity 3; ✎Activity 4.
Quantitative	**Math**		Text: Heat Loss Calculations; ✎Activity 2. Workbook: Heat Loss Calculations, Activity 26-2. IRCD : R-Value Recommendations, Handout 26-1; Roof Ventilation—Clay Tile, Visual Master 26-2; Roof Ventilation—Concrete Low Profile Tile, Visual Master 26-3; Roof Ventilation—Concrete Shake, Visual Master 26-4; Roof Ventilation—Standing Seam Metal, Visual Master 26-5.
	Science		Text: Carbon Monoxide Detectors. Workbook: Heat Loss Reduction, Activity 26-1; Heat Loss Calculations, Activity 26-2. IRCD : R-Value Recommendations, Handout 26-1.
Analytical	**Analytical**	Text: ✎Activity 2; ✎Activity 3; ✎Activity 4; ✎Activity 6. Workbook: Plumbing Symbols, Activity 25-1; Piping Arrangements, Activity 25-2; Plumbing Plan, Activity 25-3.	Text: ✎Activity 6. Workbook: Heat Loss Reduction, Activity 26-1.

		Chapter 27	Chapter 28
Verbal/Communication Skills	**Reading**	Text: Required Information; Distribution System; Thermostats and Climate Control Equipment; Schedules, Calculations, and Notes; Procedure for Drawing Climate Control Plan—Manual Drafting; Drawing Climate Control Plans Using CADD. IRCD : Climate Control Plan, Handout 27-1.	Text: Insulation.
	Writing		Text: ✍Activity 3; ✍Activity 4.
	Verbal	Text: ✍Activity 1.	
Quantitative	**Math**	Workbook: Heating Duct System, Activity 27-2.	Text: Calculation of BTUs Possible for Any Given Location; ✍Activity 1; ✍Activity 2. Workbook: Active Solar System, Activity 28-2.
	Science	IRCD : Climate Control Plan, Handout 27-1.	Text: Passive Solar Systems; Active Solar Systems. Workbook: Passive Solar Heating, Activity 28-1; Active Solar System, Activity 28-2. IRCD : Annual Heating Degree Hours for 65°, Handout 28-1; Annual Cooling Degree Hours for 85°, Handout 28-2; Daily Mean Solar Radiation for January, Handout 28-3; Daily Mean Solar Radiation for June, Handout 28-4.
Analytical	**Analytical**	Text: ✍Activity 2; ✍Activity 3; ✍Activity 4. Workbook: Climate Control Symbols, Activity 27-1; Heating Duct System, Activity 27-2.	Text: Advantages of Solar Heating; Disadvantages of Solar Heating; ✍Activity 5.

		Chapter 29	**Chapter 30**
Verbal/Communication Skills	**Reading**	Text: Earth-Sheltered Dwellings; Dome Structures; ✐Activity 4. Workbook: Earth-Sheltered Site, Activity 29-2. IRCD : Soil Classification Chart, Handout 29-1; 30′ Dome Home Floor Plan, Visual Master 29-1.	Text: Introduction to Products and Methods; Exterior Insulation Finish Systems (EIFS); Structural Foam Sandwich Panels; Concrete Wall Systems; Insulated Concrete Block Systems; Frost-Protected Shallow Foundation; Weather-Resistant Deck Materials; The Hebel Wall System; ✐Activity 3. IRCD : Panel-to-Metal Framing, Visual Master 30-1.
	Writing		
	Verbal	Text: ✐Activity 2; ✐Activity 3.	Text: ✐Activity 1; ✐Activity 2; ✐Activity 4.
Quantitative	**Math**	Text: ✐Activity 6. Workbook: Earth-Sheltered Home, Activity 29-1; Earth-Sheltered Site, Activity 29-2; Dome Home, Activity 29-3; Dome Model, Activity 29-4. IRCD : 30′ Dome Home Floor Plan, Visual Master 29-1.	
	Science	Workbook: Earth-Sheltered Home, Activity 29-1; Earth-Sheltered Site, Activity 29-2. IRCD : Soil Classification Chart, Handout 29-1.	
Analytical	**Analytical**	Text: ✐Activity 1; ✐Activity 5. Workbook: Earth-Sheltered Home, Activity 29-1; Earth-Sheltered Site, Activity 29-2; Dome Home, Activity 29-3; Dome Model, Activity 29-4.	Workbook: New Deck Materials, Activity 30-1.

		Chapter 31	**Chapter 32**
Verbal/Communication Skills	**Reading**	Text: Standardization; Modular Components; Industrialized Housing.	Text: Perspectives; Perspective Grids; Complex Features in Perspective; ✎Activity 3; ✎Activity 4. IRCD : Types of Pictorials, Handout 32-1, Computer-Generated One-Point Perspective, Visual Master 32-2; One-Point Perspective, Visual Master 32-4.
	Writing	Workbook: Modular Construction, Activity 31-1.	Text: ✎Activity 1. Workbook: Two-Point Perspective, Activity 32-1. IRCD : Types of Pictorials, Handout 32-1.
	Verbal	Text: ✎Activity 2.	
Quantitative	**Math**	Text: Standardization. Workbook: Modular Construction, Activity 31-1. IRCD : Modular Grid, Handout 31-1.	IRCD : Two-Point Perspective Method, Visual Master 32-1; One-Point Perspective Method, Visual Master 32-3; One-Point Perspective, Visual Master 32-4.
	Science		
Analytical	**Analytical**	Text: ✎Activity 1; ✎Activity 3; ✎Activity 4; ✎Activity 5.	Text: ✎Activity 2; ✎Activity 5. Workbook: Two-Point Perspective, Activity 32-1; Two-Point Perspective, Activity 32-2; Two-Point Perspective, Activity 32-3; Two-Point Perspective, Activity 32-4; One-Point Perspective, Activity 32-5; One-Point Perspective, Activity 32-6; One-Point Perspective, Activity 32-7. IRCD : Computer-Generated One-Point Perspective, Visual Master 32-2.

		Chapter 33	**Chapter 34**
Verbal/Communication Skills	**Reading**	Text: Rendering; Shading and Shadows; Entourage; Types of Presentation Plans; ✐Activity 2.	Text: Types of Models; Materials Used in Model Construction; ✐Constructing a Balsa Model; Laser-Cut Model Parts.
	Writing		Text: ✐Activity 1.
	Verbal		
Quantitative	**Math**	Text: ✐Activity 2; ✐Activity 4.	
	Science		
Analytical	**Analytical**	Text: ✐Activity 1; ✐Activity 3; ✐Activity 4; ✐Activity 5; ✐Activity 6; ✐Activity 7. Workbook: Pencil Rendering, Activity 33-1; Ink Rendering, Activity 33-2; Rendering, Activity 33-3. IRCD : Pen and Ink Rendering, Visual Master 33-1; Computer-Generated Presentation, Visual Master 33-2.	Text: ✐ Activity 3; ✐Activity 5; ✐Activity 6. Workbook: Architectural Model, Activity 34-1; Structural Model, Activity 34-2; Ranch House Model, Activity 34-3.

		Chapter 35	Chapter 36
Verbal/Communication Skills	Reading	Text: Purpose of Specifications; Specification Formats; Examples of Specifications. IRCD : CSI MasterFormat Sections, Handout 35-1; CSI MasterFormat Divisions, Visual Master 35-1.	Text: Preliminary Estimates; More Accurate Estimates. IRCD : CSI MasterFormat, Visual Master 36-1.
	Writing	Text: ✍Activity 1; ✍Activity 2; ✍Activity 3; ✍Activity 4. Workbook: Contract Specifications, Activity 36-1.	Workbook: Materials List, Activity 36-1.
	Verbal		
Quantitative	Math		Text: Preliminary Estimates; More Accurate Estimates. ✍Activity 1; ✍Activity 2; ✍Activity 3.
	Science		
Analytical	Analytical	Text: ✍Activity 5.	

		Chapter 37	**Chapter 38**
Verbal/Communication Skills	**Reading**	Text: Choosing to Remodel; Types of Remodeling; Renovation; Historic Preservation; Preparing Remodeling, Renovation, and Preservation Plans. IRCD : Types of Remodeling, Visual Master 37-1; Resources for Remodeling Assistance, Visual Master 37-2.	Text: Smoke and Fire Detection; Moisture and Mold Problems; Weather- and Nature-Related Safety; General Home Safety. IRCD : Designing for Health and Safety, Visual Master 38-1; Weather- and Nature-Related Safety, Visual Master 38-2.
	Writing	Text: ✎Activity 1.	Text: ✎Activity 1; ✎Activity 2; ✎Activity 3; ✎Activity 4.
	Verbal		
Quantitative	**Math**		
	Science		Text: Carbon Monoxide (CO) Detection; Radon Detection.
Analytical	**Analytical**	Text: ✎Activity 2; ✎Activity 3. Workbook: Remodel plan, Activity 37-1.	Workbook: Health and Safety, Activity 38-1.

		Chapter 39
Verbal/Communication Skills	**Reading**	Text: Careers in Architecture and Construction; Keeping a Job and Advancing a Career; Entrepreneurship. IRCD : Careers in Architecture and Construction, Visual Master 39-1.
	Writing	Text: ✍Activity 1; ✍Activity 3. Workbook: Careers, Activity 39-1.
	Verbal	Text: ✍Activity 4; ✍Activity 5; ✍Activity 6.
Quantitative	**Math**	
	Science	
Analytical	**Analytical**	Text: ✍Activity 2.

Scope and Sequence Chart

The Scope and Sequence Chart identifies the major concepts presented in each chapter of the **Architecture: residential drafting and design** text. The chart is divided into three sections labeled Chapters 1 through 13, 14 through 26, and 27 through 39. Within these sections, entries are identified by a bold chapter number. Topics follow the chapter number for easy reference to the text.

Chapters 1–13

Care and Use of Tools and Equipment

4: Architectural drafting equipment; pencils; erasers; erasing shields; paper; drawing boards; T-square; triangles; protractors; scales; how to use a scale; dividers; the compass; lettering guides; irregular curves; case instruments; lettering devices; technical pens; templates; grids; freehand sketching; sketching technique; sketching horizontal lines; sketching vertical lines; sketching inclined lines and angles; sketching circles and arcs; sketching ellipses; sketching irregular curves; proportion in sketching.

Safe and Efficient Work Practices and Techniques

3: Drawings included in a set of plans; brief plan descriptions; other plans.
4: Orthographic projection; three principal views; lines used in architectural drawing; border lines; object lines; hidden lines; centerlines; extension lines; dimension lines; long and short break lines; cutting-plane lines; section lines; guidelines; construction lines; line type application; architectural lettering; notes on developing a style of lettering; letter spacing; word spacing; letter size; CADD symbols library.
5: Why use CADD?; productivity; flexibility; uniformity; scale; selecting a CADD package.
10: Procedure for drawing a plot plan—manual drafting; procedure for drawing a plot plan—CADD.
11: Excavation; footing shapes and specifications; foundation walls; T-foundations; slab foundations; pier and post foundations; wood foundations; concrete and masonry basement walls; concrete and masonry; paving.
12: Preliminary steps to drawing a foundation plan; drawing a foundation plan; procedure for drawing a foundation plan.
13: Platform framing; balloon framing; joists and beams; subfloor; cantilevered joists; framing under slate or tile; post and beam construction.

Basic Skills in Communication, Math, and Science

3: Budgeting for housing.
4: How to use a scale.
10: Property lines; contour lines; topographical features; location of structure on the site; landscape plans.

11: Staking out house location; footing shapes and specifications; beams and girders; weight calculations; beam calculations; post calculations; concrete blocks.
13: Platform framing; balloon framing; joists and beams; framing under slate or tile.

Design/Problem-Solving Processes

1: The Cape Colonial; the New England Gambrel; the Garrison; the Salt Box; the Southern Colonial; the contemporary style; the ranch design; cooperatives; condominiums; rental apartments.
2: One-story ranch designs; one-and-one-half story designs; two-story designs; split-level designs; variations of split-level designs; traffic circulation.
5: Selecting a CADD package.
7: Areas of a residence; designing with CADD; sleeping area; bedrooms; bathrooms.
8: Designing with CADD; living rooms: size, location, windows and doors, and décor; dining rooms: plan, size, location, and décor; entryway and foyer; family recreation room: size, décor, and applications; special-purpose rooms: patios, porches, courts and gazebos, and applications.

9: Designing with CADD; kitchen; kitchen planning; straight-line kitchen; L-shaped kitchen; corridor kitchen; U-shaped kitchen; peninsula kitchen; island kitchen; cabinets and appliances; location and ventilation; décor; applications; kitchen eating areas; clothes care center; garage or carport; size and location; design; doors; driveway; applications.
10: Procedure for drawing a plot plan—manual drafting; procedure for drawing a plot plan—CADD.
11: Staking out house location; concrete and masonry basement walls; beams and girders.
12: Preliminary steps to drawing a foundation plan; drawing a foundation plan; procedure for drawing a foundation plan; the basement/foundation plan; using CADD to draw a foundation and basement plan.
13: Joists and beams; floor trusses; subfloor; post and beam construction.

Material Properties and Specifications

3: Site considerations; cost and restrictions; zoning and codes.
11: Footing shapes and specifications.
13: Floor trusses; engineered wood products;

oriented strand board (OSB); parallel strand lumber (PSL); laminated veneer lumber (LVL); glue-laminated lumber; wood I-beams or joists.

Computer Applications and Literacy

4: Computer-aided drafting and design; CADD hardware; CADD software; output devices; CADD symbols library.

5: What is CADD?; Why use CADD?; productivity; flexibility; uniformity; scale; architectural CADD applications; schedule automation; renderings; animations; CADD workstation; computer components; storage devices; display types and sizes; input devices; output devices; selecting a CADD package; general purpose CADD packages; AEC CADD packages.

6: Drawing commands; line; double line; circle; arc; rectangle; polygon; text; hatch; editing and inquiry commands; erase; undo; move; copy; mirror; rotate; scale; fillet; chamfer; extend; array; list/properties; distance; area; display control commands; zoom; pan; view; redraw/regenerate; dimensioning commands; drawing aids; grid; snap; ortho; layers; color and linetypes; blocks and attributes; 3D drawing and viewing commands; isometric drawing; 3D modeling; 3D views; 3D animation and rendering commands.

7: Designing with CADD.

8: Designing with CADD.

10: Procedure for drawing a plot plan—CADD.

12: Using CADD to draw a foundation and basement plan.

Social/Cultural Impacts of Technology

1: People and their structures; contemporary structures; trends in architecture; multifamily housing; Americans with Disabilities Act (ADA).

3: The community; family needs; quality of living.

7: Areas of a residence.

Future of Technology

13: Engineered wood products.

Career Information and Employable Skills

4: Notes on developing a style of lettering.

11: Weight calculations.

Chapters 14–26

Care and Use of Tools and Equipment

19: Roof trusses; ventilation; flashing.

21: Lighting circuits; outlets; switches.

Safe and Efficient Work Practices and Techniques

14: Frame wall construction; plates; headers; exterior corners and bracing; interior walls; steel framing; advantages of steel framing; disadvantages of steel framing; steel framing components; wall and roof systems; ceiling construction; masonry wall construction; stonework; masonry veneer; traditional three-coat stucco; preparing for stucco; moisture barrier and flashing; lath (reinforcement); scratch or foundation coat; brown coat; finish coat.

16: Stair calculations and drawing procedure; structural details; code requirements for handrails and guardrails.

18: Required information (floor plan); location and size of walls; location and size of windows and doors; cabinets, appliances, and permanent fixtures; stairs and fireplaces; walks, patios, and decks; room names and material symbols; dimensioning; scale and sheet identification; metric system of dimensioning; drawing a floor plan; procedure—manual drafting; procedure—CADD.

19: Traditional frame roof construction; rafters; cornice; rake or gable end; roof trusses; ventilation; flashing; gutters and downspouts; roof sheathing and roofing.

20: Drawing a typical wall section; procedure for drawing an elevation—manual drafting; procedure for drawing an elevation—CADD.

21: Electrical terms; service entrance and distribution panel; branch circuits; lighting circuits; special appliance circuits; individual appliance circuits; outlets; switches; ground-fault circuit interrupter (GFCI); low voltage exterior lighting; planning low voltage exterior lighting; low voltage wiring considerations.

23: Required information (electrical plan); service entrance; switches; convenience outlets; lighting; other devices; branch circuits; procedure for drawing an electrical plan—manual drafting; procedure for drawing an electrical plan—CADD.

24: Water supply system; in-house water treatment devices; water and waste removal; plumbing fixtures; private sewage disposal system; septic tank; disposal field; disposal field soil tests; calculation of disposal field size.

25: Required information (plumbing plan); waste lines and vent stacks; water supply lines; drain locations; size and type of pipe; plumbing fixture schedule; symbols and legend; notes.

26. Carbon monoxide detectors; true window R-value.

Basic Skills in Communication, Math, and Science

15: Window schedules.

16: Stair terminology; treads and risers; stair calculations and drawing procedure.

17: Dimensioning; scale and sheet identification; metric system of dimensioning.

19: Rafters.

21: Lighting circuits; circuit requirement calculations.

24: Calculation of disposal field size.

26: Heat loss calculations; calculation procedure; example of heat loss calculation.

Design/Problem-Solving Processes

14: General framing considerations.

15: Interior and exterior doors; interior doors; exterior doors; door details; windows; window types.

16: Types of stairs; stair design; stringers; treads and risers; structural details; adaptations for special needs; stairlifts/elevators; ramps.

17: Fireplace design considerations; hearth and fire chamber; damper and smoke shelf; flue; framing around fireplace and chimney.

18: Required information (floor plan); location and size of walls; location and size of windows and doors; cabinets, appliances, and permanent fixtures; stairs and fireplaces; walks, patios, and decks; room names and material symbols; dimensioning; scale and sheet identification; metric system of dimensioning.

19: Types of roofs; gable roof; winged gable; hip roof; dutch hip; flat roof; shed roof; mansard roof; gambrel roof; butterfly roof; A-frame roof; folded plate roof; curved panel roof; contemporary roof types.

20: Required information (elevation); elevation identification; grade line, floors, and ceilings; walls, windows, and doors; roof features; dimensions, notes, and symbols.

21: Low voltage exterior lighting; planning low voltage exterior lighting; low voltage wiring considerations.

22: Monitoring functions; switching (activating) functions; programming functions; communication/recording functions; alarm functions; information and communication wiring; signaling circuits; data and video conductors; structured wiring; radio grade 6 cable; home automation summary questions; low voltage switching.

23: Procedure for drawing an electrical plan—manual drafting; procedure for drawing an electrical plan—CADD.

25: Procedure for drawing plumbing plan—manual drafting; procedure for drawing plumbing plan—CADD.

26: Temperature control; humidity control; air circulation and cleaning; programmable thermostats; cooling systems; types of heating systems; forced-air systems; hydronic systems; electric radiant systems; heat pumps; ground-source heat pumps.

Material Properties and Specifications

14: Brick names and sizes.

15: Specifying doors.

17: Fireplace specifications; single-face fireplace; two-face opposite fireplace; two-face adjacent fireplace; three-face fireplace; prefabricated metal fireplaces and stoves; stoves.

Computer Applications and Literacy

15: Designing with CADD.

16: Designing with CADD.

17: Designing with CADD.

18: Procedure—CADD.

20: Procedure for drawing an elevation—CADD.

23: Procedure for drawing an electrical plan—CADD.

25: Procedure for drawing plumbing plan—CADD.

26: CADD heat loss calculations.

Social/Cultural Impacts of Technology

14: Adaptations for special needs.

22: Communication/recording functions; alarm functions; security wiring; systems to protect occupants and property; home automation; types of home automation systems.

24: Water conservation; private sewage disposal system.

26: Carbon monoxide detectors; hydronic systems.

Future of Technology

19: New roofing materials; asphalt laminate shingles; metal roofing.

22: Home automation.

Career Information and Employable Skills

18: Procedure for drawing a floor plan—manual drafting; procedure for drawing a floor plan—CADD.

Chapters 27–39

Care and Use of Tools and Equipment

32: Two-point perspective drawing sequence; one-point perspective drawing sequence.

Safe and Efficient Work Practices and Techniques

27: Required information (climate control plan); schedules, calculations, and notes.
28: Insulation.
29: Typical dome construction.
30: Exterior insulation finish systems (EIFS); advantages of EIFS; disadvantages of EIFS; installation/application; structural foam sandwich panels; advantages of structural foam sandwich panels; disadvantages of structural foam sandwich panels; installation/application; concrete wall systems; insulated concrete wall forms; insulated concrete wall systems; welded-wire sandwich panels; insulated concrete block systems; Integra™; Therma-Lock™; frost-protected shallow foundation; weather-resistant deck materials; weather-resistant tropical hardwoods; synthetic decking; the Hebel wall system.
31: Modular components.
32: Perspectives; terminology; two-point perspectives; two-point perspective drawing sequence; one-point perspectives; one-point perspective drawing sequence; computer-generated perspectives; perspective grids; complex features in perspective.

33: Rendering; pencil rendering; ink rendering; watercolor rendering; tempera rendering; colored pencil rendering; felt-tipped pen rendering; scratchboard rendering; appliqué rendering; airbrush rendering; shading and shadows; entourage.
34: Types of models; materials used in model construction; constructing a balsa model; laser-cut model parts.
36: Preliminary estimates; more accurate estimates.
38: Smoke and fire detection; fire prevention; smoke detectors; fire safety code requirements; fire extinguishers; carbon monoxide (CO) detection; CO detectors; radon detection; radon in the home; radon testing; radon mitigation; moisture and mold problems; migration of water vapor; sources of water vapor, preventative measures; ventilation; mold prevention and removal; weather- and nature-related safety; earthquakes; floods; tornadoes; hurricanes; general home safety.
39: Model ethics code; work ethic; job site safety; leadership on the job.

Basic Skills in Communication, Math, and Science

28: Calculation of BTUs possible for any given location; calculation procedure for hours of sunshine; calculation procedure for total solar radiation available in BTUs.
29: Site considerations.
31: Standardization.
32: Perspectives; terminology; two-point perspectives; one-point perspectives.
33: Types of presentation plans.

36: Preliminary estimates; square foot method; cubic foot method; more accurate estimates.
38: Carbon monoxide poisoning; radon in the home; migration of water vapor; sources of water vapor; health hazards associated with mold; earthquakes; floods; tornadoes; hurricanes.

Design/Problem-Solving Processes

27: Distribution system; planning outlet and inlet locations; planning ductwork; planning piping for a hydronic system; thermostats and climate control equipment; procedure for drawing climate control plan—manual drafting; drawing climate control plans using CADD.

28: Insulation; passive solar systems; direct gain systems; indirect gain systems; isolated gain systems; summary of principles; active solar systems; warm air solar systems; warm water solar systems.

29: Earth-sheltered dwellings; site considerations; design variations on earth-sheltered dwellings; advantages of earth-sheltered housing; disadvantages of earth-sheltered housing; dome structures; dome variations; advantages of domes; disadvantages of domes.

30: Exterior insulation finish systems (EIFS); advantages of EIFS; disadvantages of EIFS; installation/application; structural foam sandwich panels; advantages of structural foam sandwich panels; disadvantages of structural foam sandwich panels; installation/application; concrete wall systems; insulated concrete wall forms; insulated concrete wall systems; welded-wire sandwich panels; insulated concrete block systems; Integra™; Therma-Lock™; frost-protected shallow foundation; weather-resistant deck materials; weather-resistant tropical hardwoods; synthetic decking; the Hebel wall system.

31: Standardization; modular components.

32: Perspectives; complex features in perspective.

33: Types of presentation plans; exterior perspectives; rendered elevations; presentation plot plans; presentation floor plans; rendered sections; walkthrough animation.

37: Preparing remodeling, renovation, and preservation plans; interior designer; architect; contractor.

Material Properties and Specifications

31: Standardization.

35: Purpose of specifications; specification format; examples of specifications.

39: Specifications writer.

Computer Applications and Literacy

27: Drawing climate control plans using CADD.

31: Industrialized housing.

32: Computer-generated perspectives.

33: Computer-generated renderings; entourage; walkthrough animation.

Social/Cultural Impacts of Technology

28: Advantages of solar heating; disadvantages of solar heating.

31: Industrialized housing.

37: Choosing to remodel; types of remodeling; changing lived-in areas; making unused space livable; adding on; buying to remodel; renovation; historic preservation; restoration; preservation through remodeling; adaptive reuse.

Future of Technology

30: Introduction to products and methods; exterior insulation finish systems (EIFS); structural foam sandwich panels; concrete wall systems; insulated concrete block systems; frost-protected shallow foundation; weather-resistant deck materials; the Hebel wall system.

31: Industrialized housing.

Career Information and Employable Skills

39: Careers in architecture and construction; architect; architectural drafter; architectural illustrator; specifications writer; estimator; surveyor; teaching architectural drafting; construction technologist; residential designer; keeping a job and advancing a career; model ethics code; work ethic; job site safety; leadership on the job; entrepreneurship.

37: Interior designer; architect; contractor.

Portfolio Activity

Name _____

Period_____Date _____Score_____

After completely studying a chapter in **Architecture: residential drafting and design**, read the portfolio instructions related to that chapter. When the instructions are completely understood, perform the task. Materials collected, constructed, and/or reproduced are to be gathered and entered into the portfolio. The instructor will check the portfolio after each entry. After completing this portfolio activity, you will have a comprehensive portfolio of architectural design.

Chapter 1

Start a collection of architectural designs. Collect pictures from magazines, newspapers, and advertising pamphlets, or use your own photographs to illustrate the various traditional and contemporary house styles. Include pictures of the current trends in architecture as well. Label the house style illustrated by each picture and list the identifying features of each design. Add this material to your portfolio.

Instructor_____Date _____

Chapter 2

Clip pictures or take photographs of the four basic house designs studied in this chapter—ranch, one-and-one-half-story, two-story, and split-level. Write a brief description of each style. Add this material to your portfolio.

Instructor_____Date _____

Chapter 3

Collect several real estate advertisements describing homes for sale. Identify the information included that relates to the primary considerations covered in the text—site considerations, the community, cost and restrictions, zoning and codes, topographical features, family needs, and other considerations such as modular aspects and quality of living. Add this material to your portfolio.

Instructor_____Date _____

Chapter 4

Collect descriptive literature describing traditional drafting equipment (instruments, tools, and guides). Add this material to your portfolio for future reference.

Instructor_____Date _____

Chapter 5

Visit or call several architectural firms in your area to determine the following:
1. How many are using CADD systems to generate drawings?
2. What CADD packages are they using?
3. What are their feelings toward using CADD in architecture?

Compile a report that includes a summary of the information collected. Include the report in your portfolio.

Instructor_____Date _____

Chapter 6

Prepare a list of commands that are used to draw and manipulate objects using your CADD system. Briefly describe what each command does. Add this material to your portfolio for future reference.

Instructor_____Date _____

Chapter 7

Collect pictures of bedrooms and baths that appeal to you. Identify elements such as arrangement, color scheme, fixtures, and furniture that you would like to use in some of your designs. Add these designs to your portfolio.

Instructor_____Date _____

Chapter 8

Collect pictures of living rooms, dining rooms, family recreation rooms, special-purpose rooms, foyers, and outside patios to add to your portfolio. Indicate what features you especially like about each selection. Add this material to your portfolio.

Instructor_____Date _____

Chapter 9

Collect pictures of kitchens, clothes care centers, utility rooms, storage facilities, and garage or carport designs that have elements of good design. Highlight the design features that you like. Include the pictures in your portfolio.

Instructor_____Date _____

Chapter 10

Obtain a site plan, plot plan, or landscape plan for a specific piece of property. Sources might include a local builder, real estate firm, home loan agency, or local building department. Study the plan and list the information included on it. Compare your list with the features identified in the text.

Instructor_____Date _____

Chapter 11

Perform a load calculation to determine the size of American Standard S-beam needed for the following residential structure:

- Type of structure: Two-story with basement, 24′ × 48′
- First-floor live load: 50 lbs./square foot
- Second-floor live load: 50 lbs./square foot
- Interior wall height: 9′ first floor, 8′ second floor
- Roof trusses will transfer roof weight to exterior walls

Assume the beam runs the length of the house with two supporting posts equally spaced along the length of the beam. Make a sketch of the layout and show your calculations for future reference. Follow the example in the text. Add this material to your portfolio.

Instructor_____Date _____

Chapter 12

Obtain the following design data for your area of the country for a one-story residential frame structure with an insulated slab foundation: Average maximum frost penetration depth, minimum foundation depth below grade, recommended minimum foundation wall thickness, and any reinforcing and/or anchor bolts required (spacing, number, and size). Record this data and add it to your portfolio for reference.

Instructor_____Date _____

Chapter 13

Collect product literature for each of the following popular structural wood panel products: plywood, oriented strand board, composite plywood, structural particleboard, and waferboard. Identify the typical construction applications for each material. Add this information to your portfolio.

Instructor_____Date _____

Chapter 14

Clip pictures or take your own photographs of as many different types of stonework (wall applications) as you can. Identify each type as one of the following: Ashlar, coursed rubble, random rubble, coursed cobweb, polygonal rubble, or other. Add this material to your portfolio.

Instructor_____Date _____

Chapter 15

Collect pictures or take photographs of as many of the following types of windows and doors as you can.

Window types:
1. Sliding windows: Double-hung, horizontal sliding
2. Swinging windows: Casement, awning, hopper, jalousie
3. Fixed windows: Picture, circle top, random shapes
4. Combination windows: Bay, bow
5. Skylights and clerestory windows

Door types:
1. Interior doors: Flush, panel, bi-fold, sliding, pocket, double-action, accordion, Dutch, French
2. Exterior doors: Flush, panel, swinging, sliding, garage

Identify each picture and photograph. Add this material to your portfolio.

Instructor_____**Date** _____

Chapter 16

Collect pictures and manufacturer's literature of various stair designs. Try to include at least one example from each of the following categories: Straight run stairs, L stairs, double-L stairs, U stairs, winder stairs, spiral stairs, and circular stairs. Add this material to your portfolio.

Instructor_____**Date** _____

Chapter 17

Collect pictures and/or photographs and manufacturer's literature (where appropriate) of the various types of fireplaces and stoves. Try to include at least one example of each of the following types:
- Fireplaces: Single-face, two-face opposite, two-face adjacent, three-face, and prefabricated steel heat-circulating
- Stoves: Radiant, circulating

Add this material to your portfolio.

Instructor_____**Date** _____

Chapter 18

Collect sample floor plans from magazines, catalogs, newspapers, and builder's literature. Make notes of features you particularly like about each plan. Add this material to your portfolio.

Instructor_____**Date** _____

Chapter 19

Collect pictures and/or photographs of houses with interesting and well-designed roof styles. Note the style and materials used. Try to represent as many of the following roof styles as possible: Gable, hip, flat, shed, mansard, gambrel, butterfly, A-frame, folded plate, curved panel, parasol, warped, and free-form. Add this material to your portfolio.

Instructor_____**Date** _____

Chapter 20

Collect several high-quality elevation drawings of well-designed houses from magazines, catalogs, or newspapers. Be sure to select drawings that include the proper information as described in your text. Add this material to your portfolio.

Instructor_____Date _____

Chapter 21

Prepare a list of standard electrical hardware items used in a residence. Examples are switches, outlets, Number 12 conductor, conduit, electrical boxes, and circuit breakers. Visit your local building supply store and list the price of each item. Add this data to your portfolio.

Instructor_____Date _____

Chapter 22

Collect product literature related to information, communication, and security residential systems. This effort is aimed at understanding what is available. Add this material to your portfolio.

Instructor_____Date _____

Chapter 23

Collect literature specifying regulations regarding residential electrical systems in your area of the country. Sources for this information might be electricians, a local electrician's union, a building department, or a real estate appraisal service. Add this information to your portfolio.

Instructor_____Date _____

Chapter 24

Compile a list of handicapped accessible considerations for the plumbing fixtures generally used in a residential structure. The considerations might relate to style or type, height, placement, or clearance. Include this information in your portfolio for future reference.

Instructor_____Date _____

Chapter 25

Collect drawings or pictures of bathrooms and kitchens that are designed to accommodate handicapped individuals. Identify the specific features that make these areas accessible. Add this material to your portfolio.

Instructor_____Date _____

Chapter 26

Perform a heat loss calculation for the following exterior wall section:
- Wall size: 8' × 20'
- Windows: 3' × 5' (2) with metal edge insulating glass
- Wall materials: APA 303 plywood siding (11/32"), R4 rigid foam insulation (sheathing), 2" × 4" studs, R13 batt insulation, vapor barrier (inside), and 1/2" gypsum drywall
- Outside design temperature: 0°F.
- Inside design temperature: 70°F.

Follow the procedure outlined in the text and record all of your calculations. Add this material to your portfolio.

Instructor_____**Date**_____

Chapter 27

Collect manufacturer's literature that describes the various types of heating systems used in residential structures. Study the literature and highlight key information. Literature can be obtained from local suppliers or distributors, lumber companies, or manufacturers of furnaces. Add this material to your portfolio.

Instructor_____**Date**_____

Chapter 28

Prepare a record of your local weather for each day of the year. Concentrate on the time of sunrise and sunset (number of hours of sunlight), the high and low temperature, and degree days during the heating season. This information is generally available on CD-ROM at your library, from a weather forecast office, or in the daily newspaper. Add this information to your portfolio.

Instructor_____**Date**_____

Chapter 29

Collect articles related to earth-sheltered dwellings and dome structures. The articles should cover such topics as the quality of life in these types of housing structures, the cost to build them, special code considerations, energy efficiency advantages, and availability in your area. Add these articles to your portfolio.

Instructor_____**Date**_____

Chapter 30

Collect manufacturer's literature about the new products and methods of construction discussed in the text. Consider the following: Steel framing, exterior insulation finish systems, oriented strand board, parallel strand lumber, laminated veneer lumber, glue-laminated lumber, wood beams or joists, structural foam sandwich panels, insulated concrete wall forms, insulated concrete wall systems, welded-wire sandwich panels, and insulated concrete block systems. Add this material to your portfolio.

Instructor_____**Date**_____

Chapter 31

Collect articles about modular applications, modular components, and industrialized housing. Highlight information about advantages and disadvantages, cost, availability, and future expectations. Add these articles to your portfolio.

Instructor_____Date _____

Chapter 32

Collect several perspective illustrations of homes from magazines, catalogs, or newspapers. Select illustrations that exhibit good form, style, and technique. Identify what you like about each one. Use the examples as models for your own work. Add them to your portfolio.

Instructor_____Date _____

Chapter 33

Start a collection of presentation drawings. Collect at least one of each of the following types: Pencil rendering, ink, tempera, colored pencil, felt-tipped pen, watercolor, scratchboard, appliqué, airbrush, and computer-generated. Add this material to your portfolio.

Instructor_____Date _____

Chapter 34

Visit a local hobby shop and make a list of materials available for model home construction. Include the price of each material and the address of the hobby shop. Add this material to your portfolio.

Instructor_____Date _____

Chapter 35

Obtain a typical material specification form or description of materials form that is used for residential construction. Possible sources include: Office supply stores, local builders, governmental agencies, and architects. Add this to your portfolio for future projects.

Instructor_____Date _____

Chapter 36

Prepare a chart showing the current wage rate per hour earned in your area by carpenters, plumbers, electricians, masons, drywallers, and roofers who work in the housing industry. Sources include your local association of homebuilders, an Associated General Contractors trade association, and local unions. Add this material to your portfolio.

Instructor_____Date _____

Chapter 37

Collect photos or pictures of historic homes in your community that have been remodeled or need remodeling. Attach information about each one. Add this material to your portfolio.

Instructor_____Date _____

Chapter 38

Make a list of the major weather events to happen in your local community or county in the last dozen years. List the damage done by each event. Add this information to your portfolio.

Instructor_____**Date** _____

Chapter 39

Select one of the positions described in the text and collect as much information as you can about it. Be sure to include the responsibilities and skill required, type of work done, and opportunities for advancement. Add the report to your portfolio.

Instructor_____**Date** _____

The World of Architecture

Objectives

After studying this chapter, the student will be able to:
- Identify the historical influences that helped shape today's home designs.
- Recognize and describe the elements of contemporary dwellings.
- Discuss current trends and influences in architecture.
- Identify types of multifamily housing.

Displays

1. **House Styles**. Select several photos of homes, each representing a different basic style. Identify the styles represented. Form an attractive arrangement on your bulletin board.
2. **Famous House**. Make a large "blueprint" from a slide of a famous house like the Falling Water House at Bear Run, Pennsylvania, designed by Frank Lloyd Wright. Display the print on your bulletin board. Use the following procedure to make the "blueprint." Set up a slide projector in a dark room. Select the slide you wish to make a print from and focus the image on a wall so that it is about the size of a sheet of blueprint (blue line or black line) paper. Tape a sheet of print paper to the wall and make a test copy by covering most of the unexposed sheet with cardboard. Expose the uncovered portion for 5 minutes. Move the cardboard over to expose another portion and expose that section for another 5 minutes. Continue the process until the first portion exposed has had an exposure time of about 30 minutes. Develop the sheet and select the exposure time best suited for your slide. Expose a new sheet for the appropriate amount of time to produce a blueprint of the slide. The exposure time will depend on the speed of the print paper and density of the slide.

Instructional Materials

Text: Pages 17–36
    Review Questions, Suggested Activities
Workbook: Pages 7–8
    Questions, Problems/Activities
Teacher's Resources:
    Chapter 1 Pretest
    Chapter 1 Teaching Strategy
    Chapter 1 Posttest

Teaching Strategy

- **Knowledge Assessment:** Administer the Chapter 1 Pretest. Correct the test and return. Highlight the topics in which the individual student is deficient.
- Prepare Display #1 to set the stage for this chapter.
- Review the chapter objectives.
- Introduce the world of architecture by showing photos or slides of a variety of architectural styles. Point out similarities and differences.
- Discuss several historical influences that helped shape home designs. Study characteristics of the Cape Colonials (Cape Cod and Cape Ann), Garrison, Salt Box, and Southern Colonial.
- Prepare Display #2 to coincide with the discussion on influences of home styles.
- Discuss and illustrate a variety of contemporary home designs. Emphasize the structure as related to the local environment—South, West, North, etc.
- Share information concerning trends in residential architecture. For example, cover postmodern architecture, the revival of previous styles, and experimentation with unique materials and building techniques.
- Assign one or more of the Suggested Activities in the text.
- **Chapter Review:** Assign the Review Questions in the text. Discuss the correct answers. Assign the questions in the

workbook. Have students check their own answers.

- **Evaluation:** Administer the Chapter 1 Posttest. Correct the test and return.

Answers to Review Questions, Text

Page 35

1. climate
2. Sensitivity to design, skill in drawing techniques, and a knowledge of the latest construction materials.
3. b. Containers in village stores.
4. 1) The separate corner posts on each floor make it possible to use shorter, stronger posts. 2) The short, straight lines provide an economy in framing materials. 3) Extra space is added to the second level by the overhang at very little extra cost.
5. The front colonnade and the giant portico.
6. The roof pitch is abruptly changed between the ridge and eaves.
7. The terms contemporary and modern do not denote any one particular architectural style because most modern homes borrow some distinctive features from more traditional structures while others appear almost independent of past designs.
8. low-pitched
9. ranch
10. 1) Dramatic, yet comfortable, living styles. 2) Homes designed to fit particular sites. 3) Providing a feeling of openness. 4) Retain necessary privacy.
11. postmodern architecture
12. Unlike the owner of a cooperative who buys stock, the owner of a condominium buys the apartment and a share of the common ground.
13. They offer a variety of lifestyles and are readily available. Rental apartments usually require less expense and effort in upkeep than other types of housing. In addition, rental apartments provide housing for those who do not have the money for a down payment on a purchase or have less than perfect credit and cannot qualify for a mortgage.
14. The ADA is enforced in the courts.
15. The ADA makes it illegal to discriminate against disabled persons in the areas of employment, public and private transportation, and access to public and commercial buildings.

Answers to Workbook Questions

Page 7

Part I: Matching

1. G. Salt Box
2. A. Cape Ann
3. D. Garrison
4. H. Southern Colonial
5. B. Cape Cod
6. F. Ranch
7. C. Contemporary
8. E. New England Gambrel

Part II: Completion

1. hillside
2. provide a feeling of openness
3. Postmodern
4. energy-efficient
5. restored
6. corporation
7. condominiums
8. 1990

Part III: Short Answer/Listing

1. 1) The separate corner posts on each floor make it possible to use shorter, stronger posts. 2) The short, straight lines provide an economy in framing materials. 3) Extra space is added to the second level by the overhang at very little extra cost.
2. Postmodern architecture, renovation of older homes, and experimentation with new materials and designs such as earth-protected homes and dome homes.
3. Cooperatives, condominiums, and rental apartments.

Answers to Chapter 1 Pretest

Completion

1. extra headroom
2. Cape Cod
3. climate
4. Colonials
5. shape
6. condominiums

Multiple Choice

1. A. postmodern
2. A. gambrel
3. B. Colonial
4. D. Salt Box
5. D. 200
6. C. central chimney
7. C. ranch
8. D. All of the above.

Short Answer

1. The ADA makes it illegal to discriminate against disabled persons in the areas of employment, public and private transportation, and access to public and commercial buildings.

Answers to Chapter 1 Posttest

Completion

1. climate
2. shape
3. Cape Cod
4. extra headroom
5. Colonials
6. condominiums

Multiple Choice

1. D. 200
2. B. Colonial
3. C. central chimney
4. A. gambrel
5. D. Salt Box
6. C. ranch
7. A. postmodern
8. D. All of the above.

Short Answer

1. The ADA makes it illegal to discriminate against disabled persons in the areas of employment, public and private transportation, and access to public and commercial buildings.

Chapter 1 Pretest
The World of Architecture

Name _____

Period _____ **Date** _____ **Score** _____

Completion

Complete each sentence with the proper response. Place your answer on the space provided.

1. An advantage of the gambrel roof is the _____ and usable space.

2. The _____ originated as a fairly small house with a steep roof and no overhang.

3. Many architectural styles developed over the years so that structures would be suited for the _____ and needs of families in various parts of the country.

4. One of the most gracious of all the _____ is the traditional Southern Colonial.

5. Some house styles that gained popularity over time took on names related to their _____, the period of time when they were developed, or the area of the country in which they were built.

6. Home ownership and convenience of apartment living are just two advantages of cooperatives and _____.

1. _____

2. _____

3. _____

4. _____

5. _____

6. _____

Multiple Choice

Choose the answer that correctly completes the statement. Write the corresponding letter in the space provided.

_____ 1. A current trend in architectural design that combines traditional and contemporary influences into designs for truly modern structures is called _____ architecture.

    A. postmodern
    B. revival
    C. modern
    D. art deco

_____ 2. The basic roof style of the Cape Ann style is a _____ roof.

    A. gambrel
    B. gable
    C. mansard
    D. hip

_____ 3. The Cape Cod is one of the earliest and best known of the traditional _____ styles.

    A. Southern
    B. Colonial
    C. Eastern
    D. European

_____ 4. The_____ style house gets its name from the shape of coffee, tea, cracker, and salt boxes found in colonial stores.

    A. Cape Ann
    B. Gambrel
    C. Garrison
    D. Salt Box

_____ 5. Two popular home styles developed over _____ years ago are the Cape Cod and Cape Ann.

    A. 1000
    B. 600
    C. 400
    D. 200

_____ 6. A primary feature of the Cape Ann home style was its _____.

    A. large windows
    B. double entry doors
    C. central chimney
    D. metal roofing

_____ 7. The _____ home style is basically a long, low, one-story house that originated in the southwestern part of the United States.

    A. contemporary
    B. split-level
    C. ranch
    D. Cape Cod

_____ 8. _____ are not considered under the term "public accommodation" by the ADA.

    A. Multifamily housing structures
    B. Private clubs
    C. Religious organizations
    D. All of the above.

Short Answer

Provide a brief answer to the following question.

1. The ADA makes it illegal to engage in what action? _____

_____

_____

_____

Chapter 1 Posttest
The World of Architecture

Name _____

Period _____**Date** _____**Score** _____

Completion

Complete each sentence with the proper response. Place your answer on the space provided.

1. Many architectural styles developed over the years so that structures would be suited for the _____ and needs of families in various parts of the country.

1. _____

2. Some house styles that gained popularity over time took on names related to their _____, the period of time when they were developed, or the area of the country in which they were built.

2. _____

3. The _____ originated as a fairly small house with a steep roof and no overhang.

3. _____

4. An advantage of the gambrel roof is the _____ and usable space.

4. _____

5. One of the most gracious of all the _____ is the traditional Southern Colonial.

5. _____

6. Home ownership and convenience of apartment living are just two advantages of cooperatives and _____.

6. _____

Multiple Choice

Choose the answer that correctly completes the statement. Write the corresponding letter in the space provided.

_____ 1. Two popular home styles developed over _____ years ago are the Cape Cod and Cape Ann.

    A. 1000
    B. 600
    C. 400
    D. 200

_____ 2. The Cape Cod is one of the earliest and best known of the traditional _____ styles.

    A. Southern
    B. Colonial
    C. Eastern
    D. European

_____ 3. A primary feature of the Cape Ann home style was its _____.

    A. large windows
    B. double entry doors
    C. central chimney
    D. metal roofing

_____ 4. The basic roof style of the Cape Ann style is a _____ roof.

    A. gambrel
    B. gable
    C. mansard
    D. hip

_____ 5. The_____ style house gets its name from the shape of coffee, tea, cracker, and salt boxes found in colonial stores.

    A. Cape Ann
    B. Gambrel
    C. Garrison
    D. Salt Box

_____ 6. The _____ home style is basically a long, low, one-story house that originated in the southwestern part of the United States.

    A. contemporary
    B. split-level
    C. ranch
    D. Cape Cod

_____ 7. A current trend in architectural design that combines traditional and contemporary influences into designs for truly modern structures is called _____ architecture.

    A. postmodern
    B. revival
    C. modern
    D. art deco

_____ 8. _____ are not considered under the term "public accommodation" by the ADA.

    A. Multifamily housing structures
    B. Private clubs
    C. Religious organizations
    D. All of the above.

Short Answer

Provide a brief answer to the following question.

1. The ADA makes it illegal to engage in what action? _____

_____

_____

_____

Basic House Designs

Objectives

After studying this chapter, the student will be able to:
- List the four basic house designs.
- Explain the chief advantages of each house design.
- List disadvantages of each house design.
- Explain traffic circulation in a floor plan.

Displays

1. **Basic House Designs**. Form a bulletin board display from the best basic house designs submitted by your students for Activity #1 in the Suggested Activities in the text.
2. **House Styles**. Contact real estate firms to obtain photos of ranch, two-story, and split-level homes they are marketing. Group the photos according to house style to form a bulletin board display.

Instructional Materials

Text: Pages 37–50
    Review Questions, Suggested Activities
Workbook: Pages 9–14
    Questions, Problems/Activities
Teacher's Resources:
    Chapter 2 Pretest
    Chapter 2 Teaching Strategy
    Chapter 2 Posttest

Teaching Strategy

- **Knowledge Assessment:** Administer the Chapter 2 Pretest. Correct the test and return. Highlight the topics in which the individual student is deficient.
- Prepare Display #1 to show basic house designs.
- Review the chapter objectives.
- Introduce the four basic designs—one-story ranch, one-and-one-half-story, two-story, and split-level.
- Assign one or more of the Suggested Activities in the text.
- Discuss one-story ranch designs with respect to advantages, disadvantages, characteristics, and variations within the design.
- Discuss one-and-one-half-story designs. Again, cover the advantages, disadvantages, characteristics, and variations within the design.
- Discuss two-story designs. Cover the advantages, disadvantages, characteristics, and variations within the design.
- Prepare Display #2.
- Discuss split-level designs in the same way as previous designs.
- Discuss traffic circulation in terms of functional analysis.
- Assign Problem 2-1 in the workbook.
- Assign one or more of the Suggested Activities in the text.
- **Chapter Review:** Assign Review Questions in the text. Discuss the correct answers. Assign the questions in the workbook. Have students check their own answers.
- **Evaluation:** Administer the Chapter 2 Posttest. Correct the test and return. Return Problem 2-1 with grade and comments.

Answers to Review Questions, Text

Page 49

1. One-story ranch, one-and-one-half-story, two-story, and split-level.
2. It lends itself to indoor-outdoor living, there are no stairs when on a crawl or slab, outside maintenance is easy, the low height simplifies construction, and it easily lends itself to expansion and modification.
3. It usually costs more to build than other designs of the same square footage, it requires a larger lot, there may be heating problems for certain areas of the house because of the distance from the furnace, maintenance costs may be higher because

of the large roof and exterior wall surfaces, and considerable hall space may be required.
4. steep roof, dormers
5. low cost per unit of habitable living space, built-in expandability
6. two-story
7. General exterior maintenance is usually more difficult and costly because of the height, there is a need for stairs from level to level, and it does not lend itself to variations in style.
8. split-level
9. Basement, intermediate, living, and sleeping.
10. Side-by-side, front-to-back, and back-to-front.
11. To provide additional light and ventilation in the attic area.
12. c. 40 to 60 percent.
13. The back-to-front variation of the split-level design.
14. movement

Answers to Workbook Questions
Page 9
Part I: Multiple Choice
1. C. Easily adapted to indoor-outdoor living.
2. A. One-story ranch.
3. B. It has a low-pitched roof.
4. B. One-and-one-half-story.
5. D. All of the above.
6. C. It is economical to build, it requires a smaller lot, and it has a small roof and foundation area compared to the interior space of most other designs.
7. A. Heating is relatively simple and economical because heat naturally rises from the first to the second floor.
8. C. Two-story.
9. D. Split-level.
10. B. Intermediate level.
11. D. All of the above.

Part II: Short Answer/Listing
1. Zoned heating (separate thermostats for various areas of the house) can be used to solve the problem.
2. Side-by-side, front-to-back, and back-to-front.

3. The front-to-back split-level.
4. It is a split entry (the foyer is halfway between levels).
5. The foyer should be centrally located and convenient to all areas of the house, since some family members and all guests will be using this entrance. The distance from the garage to the kitchen should be direct for transporting food and household items.
6. One-story ranch, one-and-one-half-story, two-story, and split-level.

Part III: Problems/Activities
1. Solution on page 94 of this manual.

Answers to Chapter 2 Pretest
Completion
1. economical
2. indoor-outdoor
3. Ranch
4. split-level
5. crawl space

Multiple Choice
1. B. front-to-back
2. D. dormers
3. D. traffic circulation
4. A. it requires more roof area and more foundation length
5. C. general exterior maintenance is usually more difficult and costly

Short Answer
1. side-by-side, front-to-back, back-to-front
2. One-story ranch, one-and-one-half-story, two-story, and split-level.
3. Answer may include any five of the following: Space available for the house, site contour, climate, convenience, cost, surroundings, personal preference, and personal needs.

Answers to Chapter 2 Posttest
Completion
1. indoor-outdoor
2. crawl space
3. Ranch
4. economical
5. split-level

Multiple Choice

1. A
2. D
3. C
4. B
5. D

Short Answer

1. One-story ranch, one-and-one-half-story, two-story, and split-level.
2. Answer may include any five of the following: Space available for the house, site contour, climate, convenience, cost, surroundings, personal preference, and personal needs.
3. side-by-side, front-to-back, back-to-front

Workbook Solution

1.

Directions:
Show the traffic circulation through the major living areas of the home below. Study the example in the text to see how traffic circulation is represented on a plan.

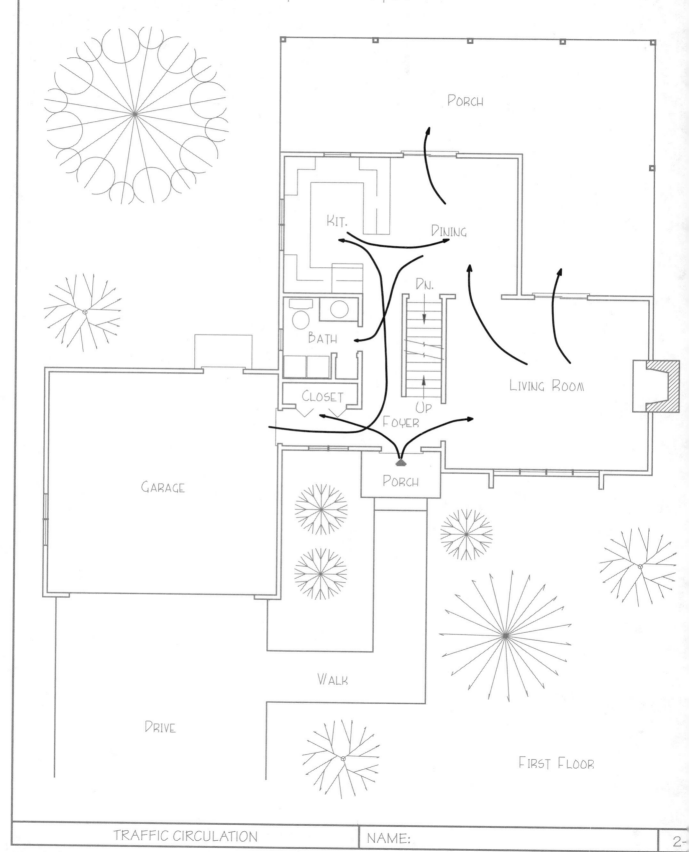

Architecture: Residential Drafting and Design

TRAFFIC CIRCULATION

NAME:

Copyright by Goodheart-Willcox Co.,

Chapter 2 Pretest
Basic House Designs

Name _____

Period _____**Date** _____**Score** _____

Completion
Complete each sentence with the proper response. Place your answer on the space provided.

1. Compared to ranch and one-and-one-half-story houses, the two-story house is more _____ to build.

1. _____

2. One chief advantage of the ranch design is that it lends itself to _____ living.

2. _____

3. _____ homes generally require a considerable amount of hall space.

3. _____

4. The _____ house was conceived for the hilly or sloping site.

4. _____

5. A ranch home may be built with a basement, a _____, or on a slab.

5. _____

Multiple Choice
Choose the answer that correctly completes the statement. Write the corresponding letter in the space provided.

_____ 1. In the _____ split-level home design, the house looks like a ranch from the front and a two-story from the back.

    A. back-to-front
    B. front-to-back
    C. side-by-side
    D. reversed

_____ 2. One-and-one-half-story homes generally have _____ to provide additional light and ventilation.

    A. skylights
    B. glass sliding doors
    C. picture windows
    D. dormers

_____ 3. An analysis should be made of _____ to determine if a house plan is as functional as it could be.

    A. walking paths
    B. air circulation
    C. traffic movement
    D. traffic circulation

_____ 4. The reason that a ranch design is generally more expensive to build than a two-story home of the same size is that _____.

    A. it requires more roof area and more foundation length
    B. it requires more windows and doors
    C. permits cost more to build a ranch home
    D. All of the above.

_____ 5. One disadvantage of a two-story house is that _____.

    A. it is more costly to heat because of the height
    B. it has little resale value
    C. general exterior maintenance is usually more difficult and costly
    D. None of the above.

Short Answer

Provide brief answers to the following questions.

1. List the three basic variations of the split-level home design. _____

_____

_____

2. List the four basic designs that a residential home designer has to choose from. _____

_____

_____

3. List five factors that should play a role in the final decision as to house design chosen. _____

_____

_____

_____

_____

Chapter 2 Posttest
Basic House Designs

Name _____

Period _____**Date** _____**Score** _____

Completion
Complete each sentence with the proper response. Place your answer on the space provided.

1. One chief advantage of the ranch design is that it lends itself to _____ living.

1. _____

2. A ranch home may be built with a basement, a _____, or on a slab.

2. _____

3. _____ homes generally require a considerable amount of hall space.

3. _____

4. Compared to ranch and one-and-one-half-story houses, the two-story house is more _____ to build.

4. _____

5. The _____ house was conceived for the hilly or sloping site.

5. _____

Multiple Choice
Choose the answer that correctly completes the statement. Write the corresponding letter in the space provided.

_____ 1. The reason that a ranch design is generally more expensive to build than a two-story home of the same size is that _____.

  A. it requires more roof area and more foundation length
  B. it requires more windows and doors
  C. permits cost more to build a ranch home
  D. All of the above.

_____ 2. One-and-one-half-story homes generally have _____ to provide additional light and ventilation.

  A. skylights
  B. glass sliding doors
  C. picture windows
  D. dormers

_____ 3. One disadvantage of a two-story house is that _____.

  A. it is more costly to heat because of the height
  B. it has little resale value
  C. general exterior maintenance is usually more difficult and costly
  D. None of the above.

_____ 4. In the _____ split-level home design, the house looks like a ranch from the front and a two-story from the back.

    A. back-to-front
    B. front-to-back
    C. side-by-side
    D. reversed

_____ 5. An analysis should be made of _____ to determine if a house plan is as functional as it could be.

    A. walking paths
    B. air circulation
    C. traffic movement
    D. traffic circulation

Short Answer

Provide brief answers to the following questions.

1. List the four basic designs that a residential home designer has to choose from. _____

_____

_____

2. List five factors that should play a role in the final decision as to house design chosen. _____

_____

_____

_____

_____

3. List the three basic variations of the split-level home design. _____

_____

_____

Primary Considerations

Objectives

After studying this chapter, the student will be able to:

- Discuss key site considerations, restrictions, zoning, and codes.
- Evaluate a site with respect to important considerations.
- Record topographical features of a site.
- List family needs that should be considered when planning or purchasing a dwelling.
- Develop a budget for purchasing or constructing a house.
- Describe the basic construction drawings used to build a structure.

Displays

1. **Our Community**. Obtain a large map of your school district and mount it on the bulletin board. Have each student locate his or her residence on the map by placing a map tack at the location. Shade in shopping areas, churches, recreation areas, and other services offered by the community. Locate the school with a distinct symbol.
2. **Permits Required to Build a Home.** Display sample permits required in your area to build a new residence. Attach an estimation of cost for each permit for an "average" new home in your community.
3. **Site Considerations.** Use materials generated by Activity #6 in the Suggested Activities to develop a bulletin board that illustrates the advantages of proper site considerations when planning a house.

Instructional Materials

Text: Pages 51–65
   Review Questions, Suggested Activities
Workbook: Pages 15–20
   Questions, Problems/Activities
Teacher's Resources:
   Chapter 3 Pretest
   Chapter 3 Teaching Strategy
   Chapter 3 Posttest

Teaching Strategy

- **Knowledge Assessment:** Administer the Chapter 3 Pretest. Correct the test and return. Highlight the topics in which the individual student is deficient.
- Prepare Display #1 to show student residences and other locations in the local community.
- Review the chapter objectives.
- Discuss site considerations as a part of the total planning process.
- Discuss the community influence in terms of planning a particular residence.
- Prepare Display #2. Discuss cost and restrictions. Discuss zoning and codes that affect building practices in your area.
- Introduce topographical features. Prepare Display #3.
- Emphasize family needs as a primary consideration. Review the list of activities in the text. Discuss modular aspects and quality of living as two additional factors to be considered.
- Describe in detail the various drawings included in a set of construction plans. Refer to drawings in the text.
- Assign one or more of the Suggested Activities in the text.
- **Chapter Review:** Assign the Review Questions in the text. Discuss the correct answers. Assign the questions in the workbook. Have students check their own answers.
- **Evaluation:** Administer the Chapter 3 Posttest. Correct the test and return. Return graded problems with comments.

Answers to Review Questions, Text

Page 64

1. Site considerations, community, cost, zoning restrictions, location, style, schools, neighbors, climate, shopping, transportation, and room for expansion.
2. title

3. deed
4. Slope, contour, size, shape, elevation, trees, rocks, and soil conditions.
5. one acre
6. A house is functional if the house fits the lifestyle of those who occupy it.
7. Answer may include any 10 of the following: Accommodating guests, bathing, dining, relaxing, dressing, entertaining, family recreation, hobbies, housekeeping, laundering, planning, preparing food, sleeping, storage, studying, and working.
8. To minimize waste and custom work, thereby reducing construction costs.
9. 4′, or at least 2′
10. Plot plan, foundation plan, floor plan, elevations, electrical plan, construction details, and pictorial presentations.
11. To verify that there are no legal claims to the property.
12. Income, other expenses and obligations, housing needs, and expected future income.
13. deed
14. Take-home pay is your earnings after taxes and other deductions have been subtracted. In other words, it is the amount of the check or direct deposit. Gross annual income is the amount of money you earn before taxes and other deductions.
15. 2-1/2

Answers to Workbook Questions

Page 15

Part I: Completion

1. site
2. split-level
3. site
4. title
5. Zoning
6. building
7. building
8. shape
9. size
10. materials
11. modules
12. 4′ × 8′
13. 4′
14. 15′
15. quality

Part II: Matching

1. F. Title search.
2. B. Deed.
3. D. Restrictions.
4. C. Easements.
5. A. Building codes.
6. G. Topographical drawings.
7. E. Specifications.

Part III: Multiple Choice

1. D. Electrical plan.
2. A. Construction details.
3. C. The location of the house on the site, utilities, and topographical features.
4. B. Shows the size and material of the support structure. Gives information pertaining to excavation, waterproofing, and supporting structures.
5. B. Plumbing plan.
6. C. Floor plan.

Part IV: Short Answer/Listing

1. Evaluate responses individually.
2. The site price should be examined carefully to determine if it takes into consideration needed improvements, such as grading, fill, tree removal, and drainage. The cost of the lot should also take into account the amount of frontage it has and whether or not it is a corner lot.
3. If the site is rural and you must provide water and septic systems, extra care must be taken to consider whether very hard water, iron water, or a lack of water are problems to be aware of. Also, some soil types can prevent the installation of a septic system, and a site smaller than one acre may not meet zoning and code requirements for a rural site.
4. Evaluate responses individually.
5. The plot plan, foundation plan, floor plan, elevations, electrical plan, construction details, and pictorial presentations.

Part V: Problems/Activities

1. Evaluate responses individually.
2. Evaluate responses individually.
3. Evaluate responses individually.

Answers to Chapter 3 Pretest

Completion
1. lifestyle
2. central
3. surroundings
4. Topography
5. Building codes

Multiple Choice
1. D. 4 or 2
2. C. elevations
3. A. title
4. A. $4' \times 8'$
5. D. $40' \times 60'$
6. C. assessments

Short Answer
1. Answer may include any 12 of the following: Accommodating guests, bathing, dining, relaxing, dressing, entertaining, family recreation, hobbies, housekeeping, laundering, planning, preparing food, sleeping, storage, studying, and working.
2. Answer may include any five of the following: Slope, contour, size, shape, elevation, trees, rocks, and soil conditions.
3. The plot plan, foundation plan, floor plan, elevations, electrical plan, construction details, and pictorial presentations.

Answers to Chapter 3 Posttest

Completion
1. Topography
2. surroundings
3. central
4. Building codes
5. lifestyle

Multiple Choice
1. C. assessments
2. A. title
3. D. $40' \times 60'$
4. D. 4 or 2
5. A. $4' \times 8'$
6. C. elevations

Short Answer
1. Answer may include any five of the following: Slope, contour, size, shape, elevation, trees, rocks, and soil conditions.
2. Answer may include any 12 of the following: Accommodating guests, bathing, dining, relaxing, dressing, entertaining, family recreation, hobbies, housekeeping, laundering, planning, preparing food, sleeping, storage, studying, and working.
3. The plot plan, foundation plan, floor plan, elevations, electrical plan, construction details, and pictorial presentations.

Chapter 3 Pretest
Primary Considerations

Name _____

Period _____ **Date** _____ **Score** _____

Completion
Complete each sentence with the proper response. Place your answer on the space provided.

1. A truly functional house will represent the _____ of those who occupy it.

2. A well-planned community is preferred over one that has no _____ theme or forethought.

3. The house should appear to blend in with the _____.

4. _____ is the characteristics of the land on the site.

5. _____ specify requirements for construction methods and materials for plumbing, electrical, and general building construction.

1. _____

2. _____

3. _____

4. _____

5. _____

Multiple Choice
Choose the answer that correctly completes the statement. Write the corresponding letter in the space provided.

_____ 1. Exterior walls of residential structures should be modular lengths in multiples of _____ feet.

    A. 16
    B. 10
    C. 8
    D. 4 or 2

_____ 2. Plan drawings that are drawn for each side of the structure to show exterior features are called _____.

    A. floor plans
    B. pictorial presentations
    C. elevations
    D. foundation plans

_____ 3. A _____ search should be instituted before purchasing a lot to determine if there are any legal claims against the property.

    A. title
    B. library
    C. quit claim deed
    D. property

_____ 4. Plywood and paneling are produced in sheets that are generally _____ in size.

    A. $4' \times 8'$
    B. $3' \times 6'$
    C. $4' \times 12'$
    D. $6' \times 12'$

_____ 5. A house with the overall dimensions _____ would be more economical to build than one that did not apply modular principles.

    A. $28' \times 59'$
    B. $50' \times 51'$
    C. $39' \times 59'$
    D. $40' \times 60'$

_____ 6. Corner lots generally have higher _____ because the length of frontage is longer than that for a typical lot.

    A. resale potential
    B. risk factors
    C. assessments
    D. insurance costs

Short Answer

Provide brief answers to the following questions.

1. Identify 12 individual and family activities that should be provided for in a functional house.

_____

_____

_____

_____

_____

2. List five topographical features that may limit the type of structure that may be built on a site.

_____

_____

_____

3. List the seven types of drawings that are frequently included in a set of typical residential construction drawings. _____

_____

_____

_____

Chapter 3 Posttest
Primary Considerations

Name _____

Period _____ **Date** _____ **Score** _____

Completion

Complete each sentence with the proper response. Place your answer on the space provided.

1. _____ is the characteristics of the land on the site.

1. _____

2. The house should appear to blend in with the _____.

2. _____

3. A well-planned community is preferred over one that has no _____ theme or forethought.

3. _____

4. _____ specify requirements for construction methods and materials for plumbing, electrical, and general building construction.

4. _____

5. A truly functional house will represent the _____ of those who occupy it.

5. _____

Multiple Choice

Choose the answer that correctly completes the statement. Write the corresponding letter in the space provided.

_____ 1. Corner lots generally have higher _____ because the length of frontage is longer than that for a typical lot.

    A. resale potential
    B. risk factors
    C. assessments
    D. insurance costs

_____ 2. A _____ search should be instituted before purchasing a lot to determine if there are any legal claims against the property.

    A. title
    B. library
    C. quit claim deed
    D. property

_____ 3. A house with the overall dimensions _____ would be more economical to build than one that did not apply modular principles.

    A. $28' \times 59'$
    B. $50' \times 51'$
    C. $39' \times 59'$
    D. $40' \times 60'$

_____ 4. Exterior walls of residential structures should be modular lengths in multiples of _____ feet.

    A. 16
    B. 10
    C. 8
    D. 4 or 2

_____ 5. Plywood and paneling are produced in sheets that are generally _____ in size.

    A. $4' \times 8'$
    B. $3' \times 6'$
    C. $4' \times 12'$
    D. $6' \times 12'$

_____ 6. Plan drawings that are drawn for each side of the structure to show exterior features are called _____.

    A. floor plans
    B. pictorial presentations
    C. elevations
    D. foundation plans

Short Answer

Provide brief answers to the following questions.

1. List five topographical features that may limit the type of structure that may be built on a site.

_____

_____

_____

2. Identify 12 individual and family activities that should be provided for in a functional house.

_____

_____

_____

_____

_____

3. List the seven types of drawings that are frequently included in a set of typical residential construction drawings. _____

_____

_____

_____

Drawing Instruments and Techniques

Objectives

After studying this chapter, the student will be able to:
- Define the three principal views in orthographic projection.
- List and explain the use of architectural drafting equipment.
- Explain the difference between size and scale.
- Reproduce the standard alphabet of lines.
- Demonstrate an acceptable architectural lettering style.
- Freehand sketch.
- Identify the basic components of a CADD workstation.

Displays

1. **Typical Manual Drafting Equipment**. Using photos from drafting equipment supply company catalogs, prepare a bulletin board display that shows the type of drafting equipment commonly used by manual drafters.
2. **Typical CADD System**. Obtain photos of the components of a typical CADD system. Attach the photos to the bulletin board using a residential CADD drawing as a background. Identify each of the CADD system components.
3. **Architectural Lettering Styles**. Display several samples of architectural lettering styles produced by your students. Encourage the class members to examine these examples in an effort to improve their individual lettering styles.

Instructional Materials

Text: Pages 67–90
  Review Questions, Suggested Activities
Workbook: Pages 21–34
  Questions, Problems/Activities
Teacher's Resources:
  Chapter 4 Pretest
  Chapter 4 Teaching Strategy
  Chapter 4 Posttest

Teaching Strategy

- **Knowledge Assessment:** Administer the Chapter 4 Pretest. Correct the test and return. Highlight the topics in which the individual student is deficient.
- Prepare Display #1.
- Review the chapter objectives.
- Review basic orthographic projection.
- Assign Problems 4-1 and 4-2 in the workbook.
- Discuss the principal views in architecture.
- Cover traditional architectural drafting equipment.
- Discuss freehand sketching. Assign Activity #4 in the Suggested Activities in the text.
- Discuss CADD drafting. Prepare Display #2 for reference.
- Explain how to use the scale and describe how to draw to scale.
- Assign Problem 4-3 in the workbook.
- Discuss the alphabet of lines. Draw the various lines on the chalkboard.
- Assign Problem 4-4 in the workbook.
- Discuss architectural lettering. Show the class how to make each letter on the chalkboard.
- Assign Problem 4-5 in the workbook.
- Prepare Display #3.
- Assign one or more of the Suggested Activities in the text.
- **Chapter Review:** Assign the Review Questions in the text. Discuss the correct answers. Assign the questions in the workbook. Have students check their own answers. Use the answers to Problems 4-4 and 4-5 in the workbook to make transparencies for review with the class.
- **Evaluation:** Administer the Chapter 4 Posttest. Correct the test and return. Return graded problems with comments.

Answers to Review Questions, Text

Page 89

1. top, front, right side
2. floor plan
3. erasing shield
4. 11″ × 17″, 12″ × 18″
5. 30°-60°, 45°
6. one half of a degree
7. engineer's
8. half size
9. 1/4″ = 1′-0″
10. dividers
11. compass
12. help letter a manual drawing
13. communicate
14. border
15. object
16. hidden
17. dimension
18. artistic
19. variable; *also acceptable:* not consistent
20. 1/8″, 3/32″
21. 1-1/2″
22. inclined
23. CPU, input devices, storage devices, and output devices.
24. Computer software is the programming that tells the computer hardware which tasks to perform.
25. A symbols library is a collection of drafting symbols saved to a file that can be quickly inserted into a CADD drawing.

Answers to Workbook Questions

Page 21

Part I: Matching

1. D. Dimension lines
2. E. Freehand sketching
3. F. Grids
4. B. Floor plan
5. A. Construction lines
6. H. Orthographic projection
7. G. Hand pivot method
8. C. Plan view

Part II: Multiple Choice

1. A. A
2. B. 18″ × 24″
3. C. The drawing is only half as large as the object in real life.
4. D. All of the above.
5. C. Hidden lines.
6. A. Centerlines.

Part III: Completion

1. top
2. front
3. side, lead
4. vellum
5. plastic
6. drafting
7. vernier
8. 12
9. 1/2″
10. F
11. Lettering
12. engineering
13. hard drive
14. pen
15. long
16. Section
17. construction

Part IV: Short Answer/Listing

1. Front, right, left, and rear.
2. Some pink erasers leave a pinkish color that detracts from the appearance of the finished drawing.
3. 45° and 30°-60°.
4. Semicircular and circular.
5. Dividers are used to divide a line into proportional parts and provide a quick method of measuring a length that must be used a number of times.
6. Hold the compass between the thumb and forefinger and rotate it in a clockwise manner while leaning it slightly forward.
7. Line up at least four points and draw the line through three of the points. Continue this process until the curve is completed.
8. Plotters and printers.
9. To communicate ideas accurately and clearly.
10. Cutting-plane lines.
11. Allow approximately a letter-height distance between words.

Part V: Problems/Activities

1. Solution on page 110 of this manual.
2. Solution on page 111 of this manual.
3. Solution on page 112 of this manual.
4. Solution on page 113 of this manual.
5. Solution on page 114 of this manual.

Answers to Chapter 4 Pretest

Completion

1. 10
2. plan
3. larger
4. parallel
5. B

Multiple Choice

1. D. monitor
2. C. front
3. C. compass
4. B. 17″ × 22″
5. B. adjustable triangle
6. A. Computer-Aided Drafting and Design

Short Answer

1. Architect's scale, engineer's scale, and combination scale.
2. Locate the end points of the line. Position your arm for a trial movement. Sketch a series of short, light lines. Darken the line in one continuous motion.
3. Pen plotters, laser printers, ink jet printers, and ink jet plotters.
4. top, front, and right side
5. The central processing unit (CPU), input devices, storage devices, and output devices.

Matching

1. A. Very light lines used in the drawing process.
2. G. Heavy lines used to show where the object is to be sectioned.
3. D. Used to indicate the center of symmetrical objects.
4. I. Used to show size and location.
5. B. Used to form a boundary.
6. F. Used for objects that are not visible.
7. H. Used in lettering.
8. C. Freehand lines used to reveal an underlying feature or part of the object removed.
9. E. Used for interior walls, steps, and doors.

Answers to Chapter 4 Posttest

Completion

1. parallel
2. plan
3. B
4. 10
5. larger

Multiple Choice

1. C. front
2. B. 17″ × 22″
3. B. adjustable triangle
4. C. compass
5. A. Computer-Aided Drafting and Design
6. D. monitor

Short Answer

1. top, front, and right side
2. Locate the end points of the line. Position your arm for a trial movement. Sketch a series of short, light lines. Darken the line in one continuous motion.
3. The central processing unit (CPU), input devices, storage devices, and output devices.
4. Pen plotters, laser printers, ink jet printers, and ink jet plotters.
5. Architect's scale, engineer's scale, and combination scale.

Matching

1. D. Used to form a boundary.
2. F. Used for interior walls, steps, and doors.
3. H. Heavy lines used to show where the object is to be sectioned.
4. C. Freehand lines used to reveal an underlying feature or part of the object removed.
5. A. Used for objects that are not visible.
6. E. Used to indicate the center of symmetrical objects.
7. I. Used in lettering.
8. G. Very light lines used in the drawing process.
9. B. Used to show size and location.

1.

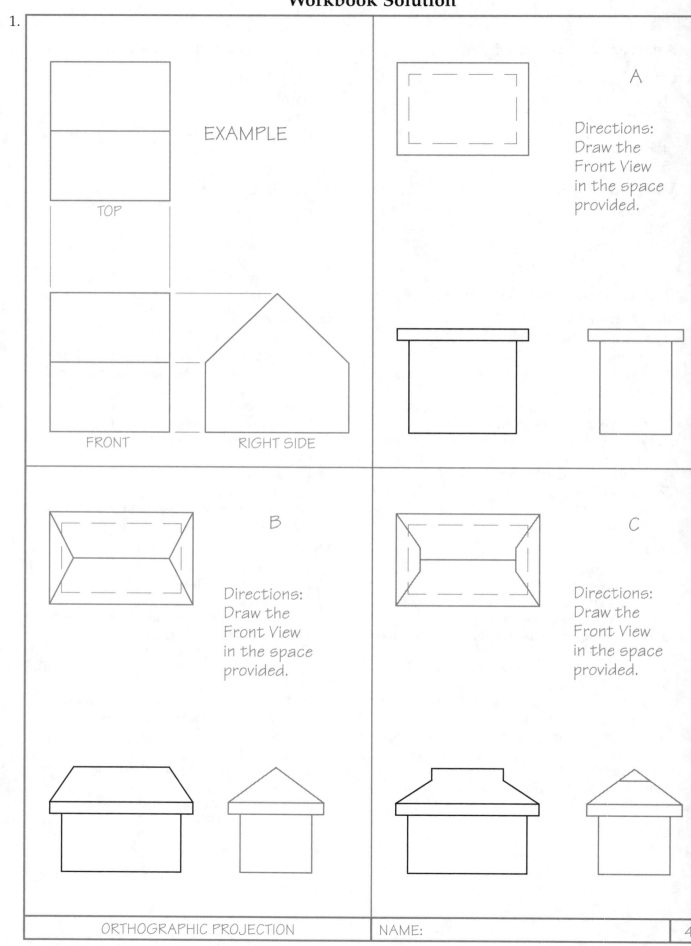

EXAMPLE

TOP

FRONT   RIGHT SIDE

A

Directions:
Draw the
Front View
in the space
provided.

B

Directions:
Draw the
Front View
in the space
provided.

C

Directions:
Draw the
Front View
in the space
provided.

ORTHOGRAPHIC PROJECTION

NAME:

4

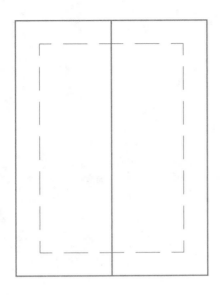

Directions:
Construct the Right Side view of
the object in the space provided.
Be sure to project the heights
from the Front View and transfer
depth dimensions.

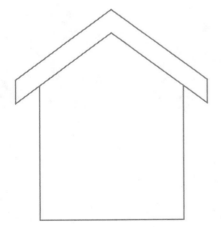

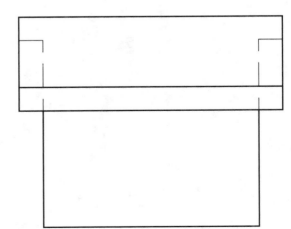

Chapter 4 Drawing Instruments and Techniques   **111**

Workbook Solution

3.

Directions:
Measure each of the lines below using the scale indicated and letter the length of the line 1/8" high just above the dimension line. Use guidelines.

3-5/8"
Full Size

7-1/4"
Half Size

14-1/2"
1/4 Size

29'-0"
1/8" = 1'-0"

16'-3"
1/4" = 1'-0"

8'-6"
1/2" = 1'-0"

6'-1"
3/4" = 1'-0"

5'-0"
1" = 1'-0"

MEASURING TO SCALE   NAME: 4-

Workbook Solution

Directions:

Draw each of the lines illustrated below in the space provided to the right of each line. Be sure to pay close attention to the thickness of each line and the size of each element.

Border line

Object line

Cutting-plane line

Short break line

Hidden line

Centerline

Long break line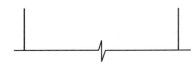

Leader

Workbook Solution

5.

4-

Directions:
Practice lettering the alphabet and numbers using a style similar to one illustrated in the text.
Practice "your" style until it becomes comfortable to use.

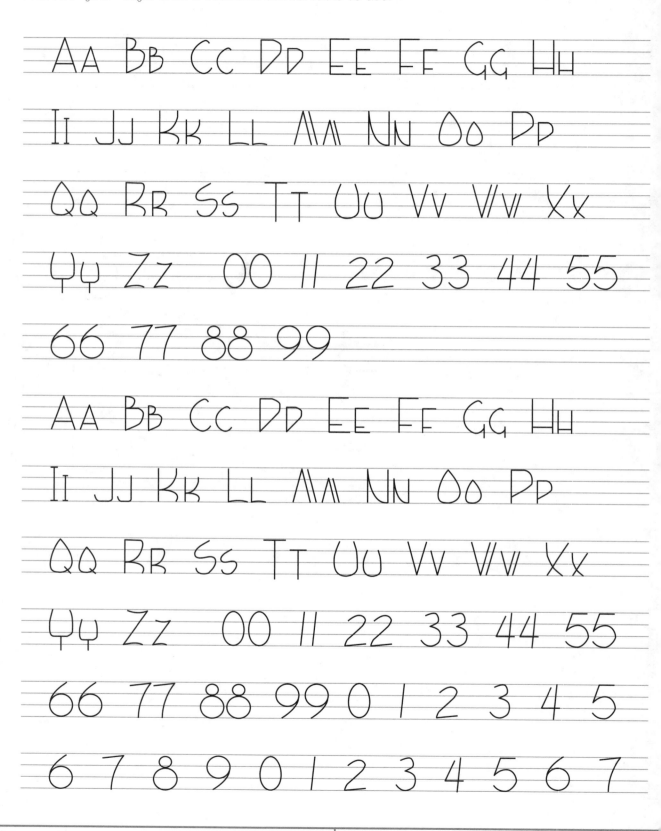

Chapter 4 Pretest
Drawing Instruments
and Techniques

Name _____

Period _____**Date** _____**Score** _____

Completion
Complete each sentence with the proper response. Place your answer on the space provided.

1. The divisions on an engineer's scale are based on _____ units to the inch.

   1. _____

2. The _____ view is used as the basis for most of the other views in a set of drawings for a house.

   2. _____

3. A drawing of an object made at 1/2 size will be _____ than a drawing made at 1/8 scale.

   3. _____

4. In orthographic projection, projection lines are _____ to each other.

   4. _____

5. Architectural drawing sheets measuring 11″ × 17″ are designated with the letter _____.

   5. _____

Multiple Choice
Choose the answer that correctly completes the statement. Write the corresponding letter in the space provided.

_____ 1. A _____ is an example of an output device used by a CADD system.

   A. mouse
   B. keyboard
   C. digitizing tablet
   D. monitor

_____ 2. The front view of an object in mechanical drawing is the same as the _____ elevation in architectural drawing.

   A. right side
   B. left side
   C. front
   D. rear

_____ 3. The _____ is used to draw circles and arcs.

   A. T-square
   B. protractor
   C. compass
   D. triangle

_____ 4. The size of a standard architectural drawing C-size sheet is _____.

   A. 11″ × 17″
   B. 17″ × 22″
   C. 22″ × 34″
   D. 24″ × 36″

_____ 5. A traditional drafting device that allows the drafter to draw a line at any angle is a(n) _____.

   A. straightedge
   B. adjustable triangle
   C. scale
   D. protractor

_____ 6. The acronym CADD stands for _____.

   A. Computer-Aided Drafting and Design
   B. Coded Architectural Drafting and Design
   C. Cost Analysis Design Differences
   D. Computer-Assisted Detail Drawing

Short Answer

Provide brief answers to the following questions.

1. List three types of scales used by architectural drafters in manual drafting. _____

_____

_____

2. List the four steps used to sketch a horizontal line. _____

_____

_____

_____

3. List four typical hard copy output devices. _____

_____

_____

_____

4. List the three principal views in orthographic projection. _____

_____

5. List the four basic types of hardware devices used in most CADD workstations.

_____

_____

_____

Name _____

Matching

Select the answer that correctly matches each term. Place your answer in the space provided.

A. Very light lines used in the drawing process.
B. Used to form a boundary.
C. Freehand lines used to reveal an underlying feature or part of the object removed.
D. Used to indicate the center of symmetrical objects.

E. Used for interior walls, steps, and doors.
F. Used for objects that are not visible.
G. Heavy lines used to show where the object is to be sectioned.
H. Used in lettering.
I. Used to show size and location.

_____ 1. Construction lines

_____ 2. Cutting-plane lines

_____ 3. Centerlines

_____ 4. Dimension lines

_____ 5. Border lines

_____ 6. Hidden lines

_____ 7. Guidelines

_____ 8. Short break lines

_____ 9. Object lines

Chapter 4 Posttest
Drawing Instruments
and Techniques

Name _____

Period _____**Date** _____**Score** _____

Completion

Complete each sentence with the proper response. Place your answer on the space provided.

1. In orthographic projection, projection lines are _____ to each other.

1. _____

2. The _____ view is used as the basis for most of the other views in a set of drawings for a house.

2. _____

3. Architectural drawing sheets measuring 11″ × 17″ are designated with the letter _____.

3. _____

4. The divisions on an engineer's scale are based on _____ units to the inch.

4. _____

5. A drawing of an object made at 1/2 size will be _____ than a drawing made at 1/8 scale.

5. _____

Multiple Choice

Choose the answer that correctly completes the statement. Write the corresponding letter in the space provided.

_____ 1. The front view of an object in mechanical drawing is the same as the _____ elevation in architectural drawing.

    A. right side
    B. left side
    C. front
    D. rear

_____ 2. The size of a standard architectural drawing C-size sheet is _____.

    A. 11″ × 17″
    B. 17″ × 22″
    C. 22″ × 34″
    D. 24″ × 36″

_____ 3. A traditional drafting device that allows the drafter to draw a line at any angle is a(n) _____.

    A. straightedge
    B. adjustable triangle
    C. scale
    D. protractor

Name _____

_____ 4. The _____ is used to draw circles and arcs.

    A. T-square
    B. protractor
    C. compass
    D. triangle

_____ 5. The acronym CADD stands for _____.

    A. Computer-Aided Drafting and Design
    B. Coded Architectural Drafting and Design
    C. Cost Analysis Design Differences
    D. Computer-Assisted Detail Drawing

_____ 6. A _____ is an example of an output device used by a CADD system.

    A. mouse
    B. keyboard
    C. digitizing tablet
    D. monitor

Short Answer

Provide brief answers to the following questions.

1. List the three principal views in orthographic projection. _____

_____

2. List the four steps used to sketch a horizontal line. _____

_____

_____

_____

_____

3. List the four basic types of hardware devices used in most CADD workstations.

_____

_____

_____

4. List four typical hard copy output devices. _____

_____

_____

_____

5. List three types of scales used by architectural drafters in manual drafting. _____

_____

_____

Matching

Select the answer that correctly matches each term. Place your answer in the space provided.

A. Used for objects that are not visible.
B. Used to show size and location.
C. Freehand lines used to reveal an underlying feature or part of the object removed.
D. Used to form a boundary.
E. Used to indicate the center of symmetrical objects.

F. Used for interior walls, steps, and doors.
G. Very light lines used in the drawing process.
H. Heavy lines used to show where the object is to be sectioned.
I. Used in lettering.

_____ 1. Border lines

_____ 2. Object lines

_____ 3. Cutting-plane lines

_____ 4. Short break lines

_____ 5. Hidden lines

_____ 6. Centerlines

_____ 7. Guidelines

_____ 8. Construction lines

_____ 9. Dimension lines

Introduction to Computer-Aided Drafting and Design

Objectives

After studying this chapter, the student will be able to:

- Explain computer-aided drafting and design.
- Identify common applications for CADD in architecture.
- List the components of a typical CADD workstation.
- Identify features of CADD software and how they should be evaluated when selecting a program.
- Explain the advantages of AEC specific CADD software.

Displays

1. **CADD System.** Secure photos of the components of a modern CADD system. Attach the photos to the bulletin board using a residential CADD drawing as a background. Identify each of the CADD system components.
2. **Computer Applications.** Create a bulletin board display that shows several typical computer applications that are related to architecture and/or construction.
3. **Architecture/Construction Software.** Prepare a bulletin board display using specification sheets from an AEC software package. Highlight outstanding features. Include drawings, schedules, etc., produced with the package.
4. **Student Work.** Display examples of student work. Use problems from the textbook and workbook.

Instructional Materials

Text: Pages 91–108
   Review Questions, Suggested Activities
Workbook: Pages 35–42
   Review Questions, Problems/Activities
Teacher's Resources:
   Chapter 5 Pretest
   Chapter 5 Teaching Strategy
   Chapter 5 Posttest

Teaching Strategy

- **Knowledge Assessment.** Administer the Chapter 5 Pretest. Correct the test and return. Highlight topics in which the individual student is deficient.
- Prepare Display #1.
- Review the chapter objectives.
- Present an overview of the chapter.
- Assign one of the Suggested Activities in the text.
- Discuss the importance of CADD.
- Assign workbook Activity/Problem 5-1.
- Introduce architectural CADD applications.
- Prepare Display #2.
- Present CADD workstation.
- Assign workbook Activity/Problem 5-2.
- Assign one of the Suggested Activities in the text.
- Discuss selecting a CADD package.
- **Chapter Review.** Assign the Review Questions in the text. Discuss the correct answers. Assign the questions in the workbook. Have students check their own answers.
- **Evaluation.** Administer the Chapter 5 Posttest. Correct the test and return. Return graded problems with comments.

Answers to Review Questions, Text

Page 108

1. Computer-aided drafting and design.
2. CADD saves time and money.
3. A collection of standard shapes and symbols typically grouped by application.
4. Answer may include any three: Floor plans, elevations, plot plans, schedules, renderings, and animations.
5. A computer or processor, monitor, graphics adapter, input and pointing device, and hard copy device.
6. A graphics or display adapter that transmits data from the CPU to the monitor.
7. Answer may include any three: Monitor, pen plotter, laser printer, inkjet printer.

8. Usually designed for making typical mechanical drawings and other general drafting applications.
9. Architectural, engineering, and construction.
10. They typically have most, if not all, of the same functions as a general purpose program, but also have functions that would typically only be useful to an architect or construction technologist/engineer.

Answers to Workbook Questions

Page 35

Part I: Multiple Choice

1. D. symbols library
2. B. Central processing unit.
3. A. General purpose CADD package.
4. C. Keyboard.
5. B. Networking.
6. D. Storage device.
7. C. Cathode ray tube (CRT)
8. B. light pen
9. A. vectors
10. B. What you want to accomplish.

Part II: Completion

1. CADD
2. software
3. digitizer puck
4. Layers
5. animation
6. input
7. video card
8. true (or full)
9. attributes
10. rendering

Part III: Short Answer/Listing

1. Modify the design; call up symbols or base drawings from storage; automatically duplicate forms and shapes; produce schedules or analyses; and produce hard copies.
2. CADD saves time and money.
3. Display controls.
4. Window and door schedules, kitchen cabinet schedules, plumbing fixture schedules, and lighting fixture schedules.
5. Answer may include any four: Lines, points, circles, arcs, boxes, polylines, fillets, chamfers, and freehand sketching.

6. Architectural (fractional), engineering, scientific, and decimal.
7. Answer may include any four: Meridian (north) arrow, revision triangle, drawing title, scale, and tags.
8. From space diagrams, as continuous walls, and from dimensions.

Part V: Problems/Activities

1. Solution on page 124 of this manual.
2. Solution on page 125 of this manual.

Answers to Chapter 5 Pretest

Completion

1. animation
2. full
3. CADD
4. CPU
5. monitor (or screen)

Multiple Choice

1. A. output
2. B. Revising drawings.
3. C. video card
4. D. monitor
5. C. 17"
6. B. keyboard
7. A. trackball
8. B. digitizer puck
9. D. stylus wheel
10. B. vectors
11. D. pen plotter
12. A. laser printer

Short Answer

1. Computer or processor, monitor, graphics adapter, input and pointing device, and a hard copy device.
2. A symbols library is a collection of standard shapes and symbols typically grouped by application. These symbols can be inserted into drawings, thus eliminating the need to draw the symbols over and over.
3. Answer may contain any four: Lines, points, circles, arcs, and boxes.
4. By size and screen properties.
5. Architectural (fractional), engineering, scientific, and decimal.
6. From space diagrams, as continuous walls, and from dimensions.

Matching

1. A. Central processing unit
2. C. Symbols library
3. F. Most common input device
4. B. Input device to identify points on the screen; not used with a menu tablet
5. G. Used with a tablet menu
6. D. Memory
7. E. Computer hard drive

Answers to Chapter 5 Posttest

Completion

1. CADD
2. animation
3. monitor (or screen)
4. full
5. CPU

Multiple Choice

1. B. Revising drawings.
2. A. output
3. C. video card
4. D. monitor
5. B. keyboard
6. C. 17"
7. A. trackball
8. D. stylus wheel
9. B. digitizer puck
10. D. pen plotter
11. B. vectors
12. A. laser printer

Short Answer

1. A symbols library is a collection of standard shapes and symbols typically grouped by application. These symbols can be inserted into drawings, thus eliminating the need to draw the symbols over and over.
2. Computer or processor, monitor, graphics adapter, input and pointing device, and a hard copy device.
3. Answer may contain any four: Lines, points, circles, arcs, and boxes.
4. Architectural (fractional), engineering, scientific, and decimal.
5. By size and screen properties.
6. From space diagrams, as continuous walls, and from dimensions.

Matching

1. E. Computer hard drive
2. D. Memory
3. C. Symbols library
4. A. Central processing unit
5. F. Most common input device
6. B. Input device to identify points on the screen; not used with a menu tablet
7. G. Used with a tablet menu

Workbook Solution

1.

Directions:
Connect each of the general purpose CADD characteristics on the left with the appropriate example on the right.

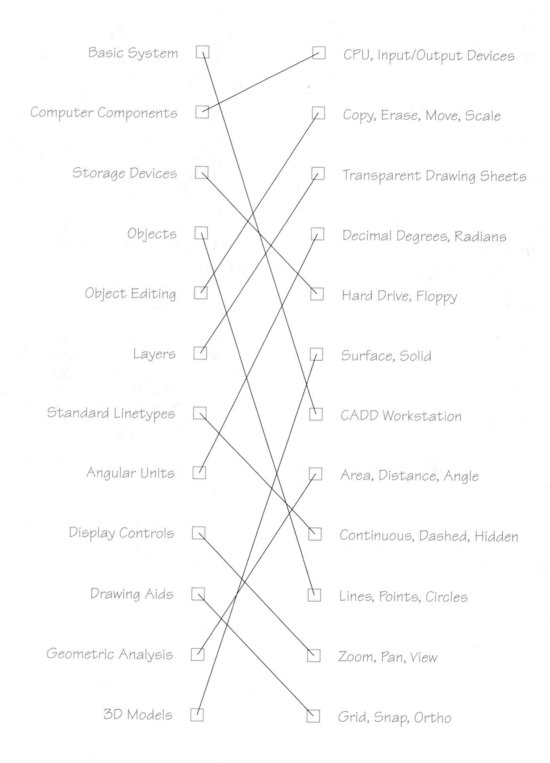

Basic System	CPU, Input/Output Devices
Computer Components	Copy, Erase, Move, Scale
Storage Devices	Transparent Drawing Sheets
Objects	Decimal Degrees, Radians
Object Editing	Hard Drive, Floppy
Layers	Surface, Solid
Standard Linetypes	CADD Workstation
Angular Units	Area, Distance, Angle
Display Controls	Continuous, Dashed, Hidden
Drawing Aids	Lines, Points, Circles
Geometric Analysis	Zoom, Pan, View
3D Models	Grid, Snap, Ortho

GENERAL PURPOSE CADD   NAME: 5-

Workbook Solution

Directions:
Draw a line from each of the AEC CADD characteristics on the left to the matching example on the right.

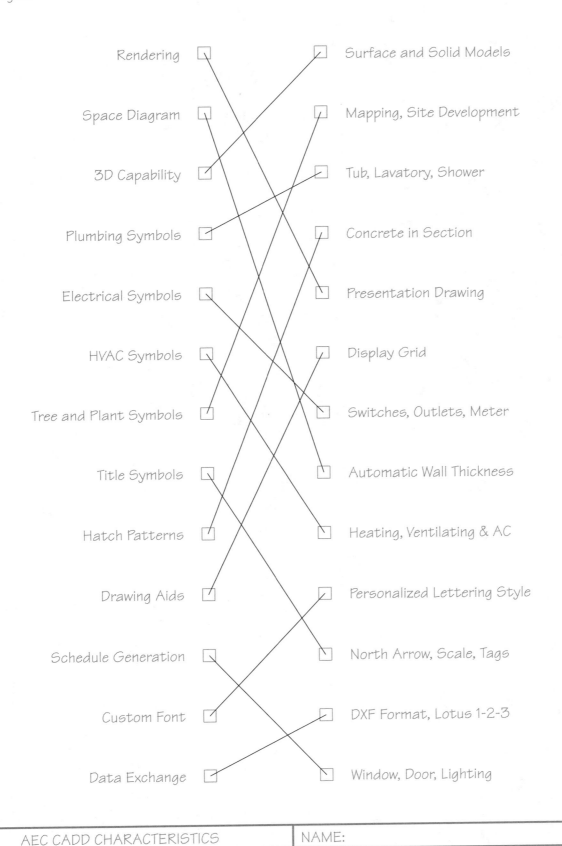

Left	Right
Rendering	Surface and Solid Models
Space Diagram	Mapping, Site Development
3D Capability	Tub, Lavatory, Shower
Plumbing Symbols	Concrete in Section
Electrical Symbols	Presentation Drawing
HVAC Symbols	Display Grid
Tree and Plant Symbols	Switches, Outlets, Meter
Title Symbols	Automatic Wall Thickness
Hatch Patterns	Heating, Ventilating & AC
Drawing Aids	Personalized Lettering Style
Schedule Generation	North Arrow, Scale, Tags
Custom Font	DXF Format, Lotus 1-2-3
Data Exchange	Window, Door, Lighting

AEC CADD CHARACTERISTICS	NAME:	5-2

Chapter 5 Pretest
Introduction to Computer-Aided Drafting and Design

Name _____

Period _____ **Date** _____ **Score** _____

Completion

Complete each sentence with the proper response. Place your answer on the space provided.

1. A(n) _____ is a type of presentation that shows motion.

2. Drawings in CADD should be drawn at _____ scale.

3. _____ is an acronym for computer-aided drafting and design.

4. The _____ contains the processor, RAM, and input/output devices.

5. The display device is typically referred to as the _____.

1. _____

2. _____

3. _____

4. _____

5. _____

Multiple Choice

Choose the answer that correctly completes the statement. Write the corresponding letter in the space provided.

_____ 1. Devices such as plotters, printers, and monitors are called _____ devices.

    A. output
    B. dedicated
    C. serial
    D. optional

_____ 2. In which area does CADD drawing provide true time savings?

    A. Making original drawings.
    B. Revising drawings.
    C. Working with a client.
    D. None of the above.

_____ 3. The _____ is the device that transmits data from the CPU to the monitor.

    A. network card
    B. mouse card
    C. video card
    D. output card

_____ 4. The _____ provides visual feedback on what the computer is doing and what you are doing with the computer.

    A. mouse
    B. sound card
    C. digitizing tablet
    D. monitor

_____ 5. In general, a CADD monitor should be at least _____ in size.

    A. 12″
    B. 15″
    C. 17″
    D. 21″

_____ 6. The most common input device is a _____.

    A. mouse
    B. keyboard
    C. puck
    D. digitizing tablet

_____ 7. A(n) _____ is like an upside-down mouse.

    A. trackball
    B. digitizing tablet
    C. light pen
    D. All of the above.

_____ 8. Tablet menus are generally used with a _____.

    A. graphics adapter
    B. digitizer puck
    C. mouse
    D. None of the above.

_____ 9. Which of the following is *not* an input device?

    A. Keyboard
    B. Digitizing tablet
    C. Trackball
    D. Stylus wheel

_____ 10. Pen plotters draw lines as _____.

    A. raster images
    B. vectors
    C. clusters
    D. small dots

_____ 11. The _____ is the most popular traditional device for producing high-quality CADD line drawings.

    A. laser printer
    B. thermal plotter
    C. color impact printer
    D. pen plotter

_____ 12. The _____ is very popular where line drawings and text material are integrated together.

    A. laser printer
    B. pen plotter
    C. film recorder
    D. daisy wheel printer

Name _____

Short Answer

Answer the following questions.

1. List the five basic components of a typical CADD system. _____

_____

_____

_____

2. Explain what a symbols library is and its advantages. _____

_____

_____

_____

_____

3. Name four objects (basic elements) that are used to create drawings. _____

_____

_____

_____

4. How are monitors generally described? _____

_____

5. List four units of measure that most CADD systems support. _____

_____

_____

_____

6. Name three methods of generating walls that are used by typical AEC CADD packages. ___

_____

_____

Matching

Select the answer that correctly matches each term. Place your answer in the space provided.

A. Central processing unit
B. Input device to identify points on the screen; not used with a menu tablet
C. Symbols library
D. Memory
E. Computer hard drive
F. Most common input device
G. Used with a tablet menu

_____ 1. CPU

_____ 2. Collection of plant symbols

_____ 3. Keyboard

_____ 4. Mouse

_____ 5. Digitizing puck

_____ 6. RAM

_____ 7. Storage device

Chapter 5 Posttest
Introduction to Computer-Aided Drafting and Design

Name _____

Period _____ **Date** _____ **Score** _____

Completion

Complete each sentence with the proper response. Place your answer on the space provided.

1. _____ is an acronym for computer-aided drafting and design.

2. A(n) _____ is a type of presentation that shows motion.

3. The display device is typically referred to as the _____.

4. Drawings in CADD should be drawn at _____ scale.

5. The _____ contains the processor, RAM, and input/output devices.

1. _____

2. _____

3. _____

4. _____

5. _____

Multiple Choice

Choose the answer that correctly completes the statement. Write the corresponding letter in the space provided.

_____ 1. In which area does CADD drawing provide true time savings?

    A. Making original drawings.
    B. Revising drawings.
    C. Working with a client.
    D. None of the above.

_____ 2. Devices such as plotters, printers, and monitors are called _____ devices.

    A. output
    B. dedicated
    C. serial
    D. optional

_____ 3. The _____ is the device that transmits data from the CPU to the monitor.

    A. network card
    B. mouse card
    C. video card
    D. output card

_____ 4. The _____ provides visual feedback on what the computer is doing and what you are doing with the computer.

    A. mouse
    B. sound card
    C. digitizing tablet
    D. monitor

Name _____

_____ 5. The most common input device is a _____.

    A. mouse
    B. keyboard
    C. puck
    D. digitizing tablet

_____ 6. In general, a CADD monitor should be at least _____ in size.

    A. 12″
    B. 15″
    C. 17″
    D. 21″

_____ 7. A(n) _____ is like an upside-down mouse.

    A. trackball
    B. digitizing tablet
    C. light pen
    D. All of the above.

_____ 8. Which of the following is *not* an input device?

    A. Keyboard
    B. Digitizing tablet
    C. Trackball
    D. Stylus wheel

_____ 9. Tablet menus are generally used with a _____.

    A. graphics adapter
    B. digitizer puck
    C. mouse
    D. None of the above.

_____ 10. The _____ is the most popular traditional device for producing high-quality CADD line drawings.

    A. laser printer
    B. thermal plotter
    C. color impact printer
    D. pen plotter

_____ 11. Pen plotters draw lines as _____.

    A. raster images
    B. vectors
    C. clusters
    D. small dots

_____ 12. The _____ is very popular where line drawings and text material are integrated together.

    A. laser printer
    B. pen plotter
    C. film recorder
    D. daisy wheel printer

Name _____

Short Answer

Answer the following questions.

1. Explain what a symbols library is and its advantages. _____

_____

_____

_____

_____

2. List the five basic components of a typical CADD system. _____

_____

_____

_____

3. Name four objects (basic elements) that are used to create drawings. _____

_____

_____

_____

4. List four units of measure that most CADD systems support. _____

_____

_____

_____

5. How are monitors generally described?_____

_____

6. Name three methods of generating walls that are used by typical AEC CADD packages. ____

_____

_____

Matching

Select the answer that correctly matches each term. Place your answer in the space provided.

A. Central processing unit
B. Input device to identify points on the screen; not used with a menu tablet
C. Symbols library
D. Memory
E. Computer hard drive
F. Most common input device
G. Used with a tablet menu

_____ 1. CPU

_____ 2. Collection of plant symbols

_____ 3. Keyboard

_____ 4. Mouse

_____ 5. Digitizing puck

_____ 6. RAM

_____ 7. Storage device

CADD Commands and Functions

Objectives

After studying this chapter, the student will be able to:

- List several general categories of commands used in popular CADD programs.
- Sketch an example of linear, angular, and leader dimensioning.
- Explain drawing aids.
- Discuss the purposes of colors, linetypes, and layers in typical CADD programs.
- Explain layer naming conventions as related to architectural drawings.
- Describe 3D drawing.
- Explain rendering.
- Explain animation.

Displays

1. **Commands and Functions.** Prepare a bulletin board display that consists of CADD commands and functions. List each command or function and show an example as related to architecture or construction drawing.
2. **3D Functions.** Prepare a bulletin board display of 3D functions. Provide a written description as well as an illustration.

Instructional Materials

Text: Pages 109–127
　　Review Questions, Suggested Activities
Workbook: Pages 43–56
　　Review Questions, Problems/Activities
Teacher's Resources:
　　Chapter 6 Pretest
　　Chapter 6 Teaching Strategy
　　Chapter 6 Posttest

Teaching Strategy

- **Knowledge Assessment.** Administer the Chapter 6 Pretest. Correct the test and return. Highlight topics in which the individual student is deficient.
- Prepare Display #1.
- Review the chapter objectives.
- Introduce CADD commands and functions.
- Discuss and illustrate drawing commands.
- Assign workbook Problem/Activity 6-1.
- Discuss editing and inquiry commands.
- Assign workbook Problem/Activity 6-2.
- Present display control commands.
- Discuss dimensioning commands.
- Assign workbook Problem/Activity 6-3.
- Cover drawing aids.
- Discuss layers, colors, and linetypes.
- Discuss blocks and attributes.
- Prepare Display #2.
- Discuss 3D drawing and viewing commands.
- Discuss 3D animation and rendering commands.
- Assign one or more of the Suggested Activities in the text.
- **Chapter Review.** Assign the Review Questions in the text. Discuss the correct answers. Assign the questions in the workbook. Have students check their own answers. Make a transparency of Figure 6-1 in the chapter and use for review.
- **Evaluation.** Administer the Chapter 6 Posttest. Correct the test and return. Return graded problems with comments.

Answers to Review Questions, Text

Page 127

1. Commands are the instructions you provide to CADD software to achieve the end result.
2. Drawing commands, editing commands, display control commands, dimensioning commands, and drawing aid commands.
3. Pull-down menus, toolbars, and a command line.
4. Drawing
5. Answer may include any three: **LINE, DOUBLE LINE, CIRCLE, ARC, RECTANGLE, POLYGON, TEXT, HATCH.**
6. Modify drawings.
7. Inquiry
8. The command is used to reverse the action of the previous commands in sequence;

you cannot "jump" a command in the sequence.

9. (Student answers will vary, many are acceptable.) Drawing one side of ornate scroll work on a door and identically reflecting the scroll work to the other side of the door.

10. A fillet is a smoothly fitted internal arc of a specified radius between two lines, arcs, or circles.

11. A round is just like a fillet except it is an exterior arc.

12. To control how a drawing is displayed on the screen.

13. Answer may include any three: **ZOOM, PAN, VIEW,** and **REDRAW/ REGENERATE.**

14. **LINEAR, ANGULAR, DIAMETER, RADIUS,** and **LEADER.**

15. Drawing aids are designed to speed up the drawing process and, at the same time, maintain accuracy.

16. A layer is a virtual piece of paper on which CADD objects are placed. All objects on all layers, or sheets of paper, are visible on top of each other.

17. Layer naming convention, object display color usage, and line type usage (always follow the Alphabet of Lines).

18. Blocks are special objects that can best be thought of as symbols inserted into a drawing. An attribute is text information saved with the block when it is inserted into a drawing.

19. two dimensions

20. Surface models

21. Solid models

22. To remove those lines from the display that would normally be hidden.

23. Rendering is shading or coloring the drawing, either by traditional means or a CADD system.

24. Add surface textures to a 3D model.

25. An animation is a series of still images played sequentially at a very fast rate, such as 30 frames per second. There are very small differences between each frame and when viewed quickly, the brain "mistakes" these differences as movement.

Answers to Workbook Questions
Page 43
Part I: Short Answer/Listing

1. They allow you to create objects on the screen.

2. They may be selected from a pull-down menu, picked from a toolbar, typed at a command line, or selected from a tablet with a puck.

3. Answer may include any five: **LINE, DOUBLE LINE, CIRCLE, ARC, RECTANGLE, POLYGON, TEXT,** and **HATCH.**

4. When drawings need to be modified.

5. **ERASE**

6. The **MOVE** command allows one or more objects to be moved from the present location to a new one without changing their orientation or size. The **COPY** command usually functions in much the same way as the **MOVE** command; however, it is used to place copies of the selected objects at the specified location without altering the original objects.

7. Creating walls on floor plans and similar applications where parallel lines are required.

8. These commands control the position and magnification of the screen window, save views for later use, and redraw or "clean up" the screen.

9. **ZOOM, PAN, VIEW, REDRAW,** and **REGENERATE.**

10. **LINEAR, ANGULAR, DIAMETER, RADIUS,** and **LEADER**.

11. **CHANGE, COLOR,** and **PROPERTIES**.

12. It is a visual guideline in the viewport, much like the lines on graph paper.

13. Drawing commands, editing commands, display control commands, dimensioning commands, drawing aid commands.

14. **HELP**

15. List the database records for selected objects; calculate distances, areas, and perimeters; and convert points on the screen to absolute coordinates (or the reverse).

Part II: Multiple Choice

1. D. None of the above.
2. C. Arc.
3. B. width and height
4. A. relative displacement
5. B. Alter the orientation of objects on a drawing.
6. B. **CHAMFER**
7. A. Show the data related to an object.
8. C. **ZOOM**
9. C. Dimensioning.
10. C. Add a specific or local note.
11. D. Objects can be drawn on different layers.
12. C. **SNAP**
13. A. Solid model.
14. D. **SAVE**

Part III: Completion

1. attributes
2. center
3. inquiry
4. **EXTEND**
5. **ARRAY**
6. **VIEW**
7. **REDRAW** (or **REGENERATE**)
8. dimensioning
9. Drawing aids
10. **HIDE**
11. **UNDO**

Part IV: Matching

1. G. **LINE**
2. B. **ARC**
3. J. Regular polygon
4. F. **HATCH**
5. K. **SCALE**
6. E. **FILLET**
7. I. **PAN**
8. A. **ANGULAR**
9. D. **DIAMETER**
10. L. Surface modeling
11. C. Blocks
12. H. Object snap

Part V: Problems/Activities

1. Student activity.
2. Solution on page 137 of this manual.
3. Solution on page 138 of this manual.
4. Solution on page 139 of this manual.

Answers to Chapter 6 Pretest

Completion

1. Editing
2. **ZOOM**
3. Drawing aids
4. Drawing
5. **LINE**

Multiple Choice

1. C. shows data stored for an object
2. B. fonts
3. A. automated
4. A. **MOVE**
5. D. drawing
6. D. **ZOOM**
7. A. **ERASE**, **MOVE**, **COPY**
8. B. Starting point, center, and endpoint

Short Answer

1. Answer may include any five: Three points on the arc; starting point, center, and endpoint; starting point, center, and included angle; starting point, center, and length of chord; starting point, endpoint, and radius; starting point, endpoint, and included angle; starting point, endpoint, and a starting direction.
2. They may be selected from a pull-down menu, picked from a toolbar, typed at a command line, or selected from a tablet with a puck.
3. It clears up the display by removing marker blips, etc.
4. To draw a rectangle, generally you can pick opposite corners or specify the width and height.
5. **LINEAR**, **ANGULAR**, **DIAMETER**, **RADIUS**, and **LEADER**.
6. To provide a specific or local note.
7. Ensures that all lines and traces drawn using a pointing device are orthogonal (vertical or horizontal) with respect to the current drawing plane.
8. Grid, snap, and ortho.

Matching

1. F. Creates a rectangular or circular pattern of objects.
2. E. Linetype, width, and color.
3. G. Measures the distance between two points.

4. L. Parallel lines useful in creating walls on a floor plan.
5. C. Generates a smoothly fitted arc of a specified radius between two lines, arcs, or circles.
6. K. Siding, bricks, ground coverings, masonry features, and water.
7. J. New location without changing the orientation or size.
8. H. Moves the drawing in the display window from one location to another.
9. A. An object with equal sides and included angles.
10. B. Can be used to alter the orientation of objects.
11. I. Placement can be justified left, right, or centered.
12. D. Increases or decreases the apparent size of objects on the screen without changing their actual size.

Answers to Chapter 6 Posttest

Completion
1. Drawing
2. Drawing aids
3. **LINE**
4. **ZOOM**
5. Editing

Multiple Choice
1. A. **ERASE, MOVE, COPY**
2. D. drawing
3. B. Starting point, center, and endpoint
4. B. fonts
5. D. **ZOOM**
6. A. **MOVE**
7. C. shows data stored for an object
8. A. automated

Short Answer
1. They may be selected from a pull-down menu, picked from a toolbar, typed at a command line, or selected from a tablet with a puck.
2. Answer may include any five: Three points on the arc; starting point, center, and endpoint; starting point, center, and included angle; starting point, center, and length of chord; starting point, endpoint, and radius; starting point, endpoint, and included angle; starting point, endpoint, and a starting direction.
3. To draw a rectangle, generally you can pick opposite corners or specify the width and height.
4. It clears up the display by removing marker blips, etc.
5. **LINEAR, ANGULAR, DIAMETER, RADIUS,** and **LEADER**.
6. To provide a specific or local note.
7. Grid, snap, and ortho.
8. Ensures that all lines and traces drawn using a pointing device are orthogonal (vertical or horizontal) with respect to the current drawing plane.

Matching
1. E. Linetype, width, and color.
2. A. An object with equal sides and included angles.
3. L. Parallel lines useful in creating walls on a floor plan.
4. I. Placement can be justified left, right, or centered.
5. K. Siding, bricks, ground coverings, masonry features, and water.
6. J. New location without changing the orientation or size.
7. B. Can be used to alter the orientation of objects.
8. C. Generates a smoothly fitted arc of a specified radius between two lines, arcs, or circles.
9. F. Creates a rectangular or circular pattern of objects.
10. G. Measures the distance between two points.
11. D. Increases or decreases the apparent size of objects on the screen without changing their actual size.
12. H. Moves the drawing in the display window from one location to another.

Workbook Solution

Directions:
This assignment requires the use of a CADD system. Using a scale of 1/4" = 1'-0" and an A-, B-, or C-size drawing sheet, draw a border line 480"@90°, 348"@0°, 480"@270°, and 348"@180°. The title block is 12" high and the plate number box is 36" wide. This matches the border shown here. Then, use the following drawing commands (or your software's equivalent) to draw the lines and shapes indicated.

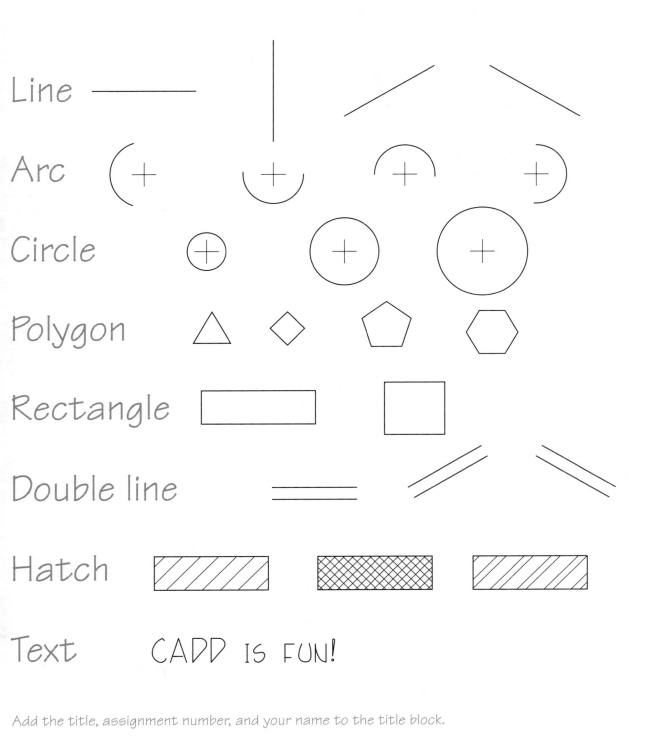

Add the title, assignment number, and your name to the title block.

3.

Directions:
This assignment requires the use of a CADD system. Using a scale of 1/4" = 1'-0", prepare a drawing sheet identical to the one required for Problem/Assignment 6-2. This assignment deals with selected editing and inquiry commands. Practice using all of the commands that your CADD software provides, but demonstrate the use of the following.

Draw a circle at one location and move it to another.

◯ FIRST LOCATION   ◯ SECOND LOCATION

Draw a rectangle and make two copies of it.

| ORIGINAL | COPY 1 | COPY 2 |

Draw one-half of a geometric shape and mirror the other side to complete the shape.

Draw a shape and rotate it 15°.

Draw a box and use the FILLET command to round the corners.

Draw a three-sided figure as shown and extend it to twice its original length.

Use the ARRAY command to create five circles around a center point.

Use the SCALE command to change the size of a circle to half of its original size.

Draw a rectangle and use the AREA command to determine its area.

16 SQUARE FEET

Workbook Solution

Directions:
This assignment requires the use of a CADD system. Using a scale of 1/4″ = 1′-0″, prepare a drawing sheet identical to the one required for Problem/Assignment 6-2. Draw a series of rectangles within the border leaving room for dimensions. Using the appropriate dimensioning commands, dimension the length and width of each rectangle. You may wish to add other shapes to show angular, diameter, radius, and leader dimensions as well.

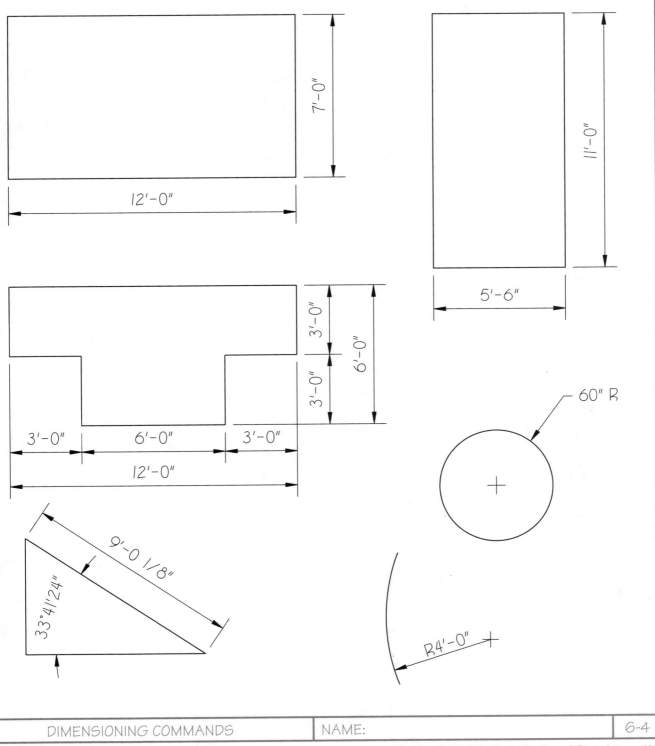

DIMENSIONING COMMANDS | NAME: | 6-4

Chapter 6 CADD Commands and Functions **139**

Chapter 6 Pretest
CADD Commands and Functions

Name _____

Period _____**Date** _____**Score** _____

Completion

Complete each sentence with the proper response. Place your answer on the space provided.

1. _____ commands allow you to modify a drawing in several ways.

2. The _____ command increases or decreases the magnification factor.

3. _____ are designed to speed up the drawing process and, at the same time, maintain accuracy.

4. _____ commands tell the computer which objects to create.

5. The _____ command is the most basic command in a CADD program.

1. _____

2. _____

3. _____

4. _____

5. _____

Multiple Choice

Choose the answer that correctly completes the statement. Write the corresponding letter in the space provided.

_____ 1. The **LIST** command _____.

    A. displays the files on the hard drive
    B. compiles a list of objects used
    C. shows data stored for an object
    D. None of the above.

_____ 2. Most CADD packages provide several standard text _____.

    A. line symbols
    B. fonts
    C. spacings
    D. None of the above.

_____ 3. Most CADD packages provide for _____ dimensioning.

    A. automated
    B. semiautomated
    C. nonautomated
    D. None of the above.

_____ 4. The **COPY** command functions in a similar manner to the _____ command except that it places a copy of the selected objects at the specified location.

    A. **MOVE**
    B. **ARRAY**
    C. **ROTATE**
    D. **SCALE**

_____ 5. **LINE**, **ARC**, and **CIRCLE** are _____ commands.

    A. editing and inquiry
    B. display control
    C. dimensioning
    D. drawing

_____ 6. _____ is *not* an editing or inquiry command.

    A. **ERASE**
    B. **MOVE**
    C. **LIST**
    D. **ZOOM**

_____ 7. Commands that provide for the modification of a drawing include _____.

    A. **ERASE, MOVE, COPY**
    B. **TEXT, ERASE, MOVE**
    C. **MOVE, PLOT, COPY**
    D. **COPY, ERASE, TEXT**

_____ 8. Which of the following is *not* a method of drawing a circle?

    A. Center and radius
    B. Starting point, center, and endpoint
    C. Center and diameter
    D. Two points on the circle

Short Answer

Provide brief answers to the following questions.

1. The **ARC** command draws partial circles. Several methods of drawing arcs are usually provided. Give five examples. _____

_____

_____

_____

_____

_____

2. List four different ways of entering CADD commands. _____

_____

_____

_____

_____

3. What is the function of the **REDRAW** command? _____

_____

4. What are the two methods generally provided for drawing rectangles? _____

_____

_____

5. List five basic dimensioning commands. _____

_____

_____

_____

_____

6. What is the purpose of a leader? _____

_____

7. What does the **ORTHO** command or mode ensure? _____

_____

8. List three drawing aids commonly provided in CADD software. _____

_____

_____

Matching

Select the answer that correctly matches each term. Place your answer in the space provided.

A. An object with equal sides and included angles.
B. Can be used to alter the orientation of objects.
C. Generates a smoothly fitted arc of a specified radius between two lines, arcs, or circles.
D. Increases or decreases the apparent size of objects on the screen without changing their actual size.
E. Linetype, width, and color.
F. Creates a rectangular or circular pattern of objects.
G. Measures the distance between two points.
H. Moves the drawing in the display window from one location to another.
I. Placement can be justified left, right, or centered.
J. New location without changing the orientation or size.
K. Siding, bricks, ground coverings, masonry features, and water.
L. Parallel lines useful in creating walls on a floor plan.

_____ 1. **ARRAY**

_____ 2. Attributes

_____ 3. **DISTANCE**

_____ 4. **DOUBLE LINE**

_____ 5. **FILLET**

_____ 6. **HATCH**

_____ 7. **MOVE**

_____ 8. **PAN**

_____ 9. Regular polygon

_____ 10. **ROTATE**

_____ 11. **TEXT**

_____ 12. **ZOOM**

Chapter 6 Posttest
CADD Commands and Functions

Name _____

Period _____ Date _____ Score _____

Completion
Complete each sentence with the proper response. Place your answer on the space provided.

1. _____ commands tell the computer which objects to create.

2. _____ are designed to speed up the drawing process and, at the same time, maintain accuracy.

3. The _____ command is the most basic command in a CADD program.

4. The _____ command increases or decreases the magnification factor.

5. _____ commands allow you to modify a drawing in several ways.

1. _____

2. _____

3. _____

4. _____

5. _____

Multiple Choice
Choose the answer that correctly completes the statement. Write the corresponding letter in the space provided.

_____ 1. Commands that provide for the modification of a drawing include _____.

    A. **ERASE, MOVE, COPY**
    B. **TEXT, ERASE, MOVE**
    C. **MOVE, PLOT, COPY**
    D. **COPY, ERASE, TEXT**

_____ 2. **LINE**, **ARC**, and **CIRCLE** are _____ commands.

    A. editing and inquiry
    B. display control
    C. dimensioning
    D. drawing

_____ 3. Which of the following is *not* a method of drawing a circle?

    A. Center and radius
    B. Starting point, center, and endpoint
    C. Center and diameter
    D. Two points on the circle

_____ 4. Most CADD packages provide several standard text _____.

    A. line symbols
    B. fonts
    C. spacings
    D. None of the above.

_____ 5. _____ is *not* an editing or inquiry command.

    A. **ERASE**
    B. **MOVE**
    C. **LIST**
    D. **ZOOM**

_____ 6. The **COPY** command functions in a similar manner to the _____ command except that it places a copy of the selected objects at the specified location.

    A. **MOVE**
    B. **ARRAY**
    C. **ROTATE**
    D. **SCALE**

_____ 7. The **LIST** command _____.

    A. displays the files on the hard drive
    B. compiles a list of objects used
    C. shows data stored for an object
    D. None of the above.

_____ 8. Most CADD packages provide for _____ dimensioning.

    A. automated
    B. semiautomated
    C. nonautomated
    D. None of the above.

Short Answer

Answer the following questions.

1. List four different ways of entering CADD commands. _____

_____

_____

_____

2. The **ARC** command draws partial circles. Several methods of drawing arcs are usually provided. Give five examples. _____

_____

_____

_____

_____

3. What are the two methods generally provided for drawing rectangles? _____

_____

_____

Name _____

4. What is the function of the **REDRAW** command? _____
_____

5. List five basic dimensioning commands. _____
_____
_____
_____
_____

6. What is the purpose of a leader? _____
_____

7. List three drawing aids commonly provided in CADD software. _____
_____
_____

8. What does the **ORTHO** command or mode ensure? _____
_____

Matching

Select the answer that correctly matches each term. Place your answer in the space provided.

A. An object with equal sides and included angles.
B. Can be used to alter the orientation of objects.
C. Generates a smoothly fitted arc of a specified radius between two lines, arcs, or circles.
D. Increases or decreases the apparent size of objects on the screen without changing their actual size.
E. Linetype, width, and color.
F. Creates a rectangular or circular pattern of objects.
G. Measures the distance between two points.
H. Moves the drawing in the display window from one location to another.
I. Placement can be justified left, right, or centered.
J. New location without changing the orientation or size.
K. Siding, bricks, ground coverings, masonry features, and water.
L. Parallel lines useful in creating walls on a floor plan.

_____ 1. Attributes

_____ 2. Regular polygon

_____ 3. **DOUBLE LINE**

_____ 4. **TEXT**

_____ 5. **HATCH**

_____ 6. **MOVE**

_____ 7. **ROTATE**

_____ 8. **FILLET**

_____ 9. **ARRAY**

_____ 10. **DISTANCE**

_____ 11. **ZOOM**

_____ 12. **PAN**

Room Planning—Sleeping Area and Bath Facilities

Objectives

After studying this chapter, the student will be able to:

- Discuss factors that are important in the design of bedrooms.
- Plan the size and location of closets for a typical residence.
- Plan a furniture arrangement for a room.
- List requirements to make a bedroom accessible to the disabled.
- Implement important design considerations for bathrooms.
- Plan a bathroom that follows solid design principles.
- List the requirements to make a bathroom accessible to the disabled.

Displays

1. **Bedrooms**. Select several examples (floor plans) of well-designed bedrooms that represent a broad range in size, complexity, and furniture arrangement. Display them in an attractive arrangement for the class to study.
2. **Bedroom Furniture Arrangement**. Obtain several 8 × 10 black-and-white glossy photos of bedroom arrangements from furniture manufacturers to illustrate the importance of planning a furniture arrangement in the bedroom.
3. **Bathrooms**. Obtain several 8 × 10 black-and-white glossy photos of bathroom arrangements from fixture manufacturers to illustrate the importance of planning a fixture arrangement in the bathroom.

Instructional Materials

Text: Pages 129–147
   Review Questions, Suggested Activities
Workbook: Pages 57–70
   Questions, Problems/Activities
Teacher's Resources:
   Chapter 7 Pretest
   Chapter 7 Teaching Strategy
   Chapter 7 Posttest

Teaching Strategy

- **Knowledge Assessment:** Administer the Chapter 7 Pretest. Correct the test and return. Highlight the topics in which the individual student is deficient.
- Prepare Display #1 for class members to study.
- Review the chapter objectives.
- Discuss bedrooms in relation to sizes, groupings, furnishings, and arrangements.
- Assign Problem 7-1 in the workbook.
- Prepare Display #2.
- Assign Problem 7-2 in the workbook.
- Discuss bathrooms in relation to sizes, fixtures, and arrangements.
- Assign Problems 7-3 and 7-4 in the workbook.
- Assign one or more of the Suggested Activities in the text.
- **Chapter Review:** Assign the Review Questions in the text. Discuss the correct answers. Assign the questions in the workbook. Have students check their own answers.
- **Evaluation:** Administer the Chapter 7 Posttest. Correct the test and return. Return graded problems with comments.

Answers to Review Questions, Text

Page 146

1. Electrical switches should not be accessible from the tub or shower, and ground fault circuit interrupter (GFCI) receptacles must be used.
2. Sleeping area, living area, and service area.
3. door (or pocket door)
4. Ceramic tile, terrazzo, or marble.
5. Metal, fiberglass, or plastic.

6. corner
7. six, four
8. A. 100 square feet.
9. 5′ × 8′
10. 30″ × 60″
11. Sliding, bifold, accordion, or flush.
12. lavatory, water closet, shower
13. 26″ to 30″
14. It is easier to clean and more accessible for persons in wheelchairs.
15. Grab bars

Answers to Workbook Questions
Page 57
Part I: Multiple Choice
1. C. 1/3
2. A. size of the family
3. C. three-bedroom
4. D. master bedroom
5. B. 100
6. B. 5′
7. C. 24″
8. C. near the bedroom entrance
9. D. accordion
10. A. on two walls
11. D. 3′-0″
12. B. near a corner

Part II: Completion
1. 1-1/2
2. 1/2
3. 3/4
4. 5′
5. master
6. mirror
7. 30″
8. 30″ × 60″
9. fiberglass
10. ceramic tile
11. vanities
12. Jacuzzis™
13. water closet
14. tub
15. Ground fault circuit interrupter
16. 2′-8″

Part III: Short Answer/Listing
1. Determine the size of furniture to be used. Draw the plan view of each item to the same scale as that used on the floor plan. Move and rotate the symbols to create the desired arrangement. Assign the appropriate linetypes and colors.
2. The decor of a bathroom should be well-planned so that it provides for ease of cleaning, resistance to moisture, and a pleasing atmosphere.
3. Answer may include any three of the following: Flooring materials should not become slick when wet, grab bars may be installed around shower stalls and tubs, devices can be installed in faucets to thermostatically control water temperatures, devices can be installed to control the hot water pressure when the cold water pressure is reduced, and nonshatter or safety glass can be used in tub and shower enclosures.
4. Dressing and exercising.
5. Sleeping, living, and service.
6. 30″ to 34″
7. 20″

Part IV: Problems/Activities
1. Solution on page 152 of this manual.
2. Solution on page 153 of this manual.
3. Solution on page 154 of this manual.
4. Evaluate plan designs based on the design principles discussed in the text.

Answers to Chapter 7 Pretest
Completion
1. swing
2. purpose
3. master
4. three
5. 2′-8″
6. six
7. south, southwest

Multiple Choice
1. A. 30″
2. C. 1/3
3. A. small
4. A. 18″
5. D. ground fault circuit interrupter
6. C. 24″
7. B. 30″
8. C. living area
9. D. 6′-8″
10. C. 30″ × 60″
11. A. 100
12. B. water closet and lavatory

Answers to Chapter 7 Posttest

Completion

1. three
2. purpose
3. south, southwest
4. master
5. six
6. swing
7. 2'-8"

Multiple Choice

1. C. living area
2. C. 1/3
3. A. 100
4. A. 18"
5. C. 24"
6. D. 6'-8"
7. B. water closet and lavatory
8. A. small
9. B. 30"
10. C. 30" × 60"
11. A. 30"
12. D. ground fault circuit interrupter

1.

Directions:
Using colored pencils, crayons, felt-tipped pens, or adhesive-backed (semitransparent) overlays, shade each of the three basic areas of the house using three colors. Include a legend for clarity.

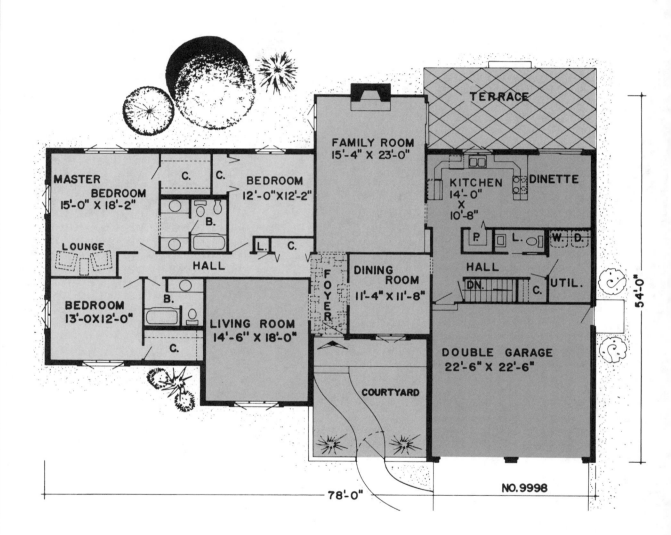

SLEEPING
LIVING
SERVICE

Workbook Solution

Directions:

Remove the Furniture Cutouts page from your workbook and carefully cut out furniture pieces for use in this assignment or use a furniture template. Plan a functional arrangement for each of the bedrooms below using the cutouts or template. Observe the spacing shown in the examples in the text. Trace the location of each item and label.

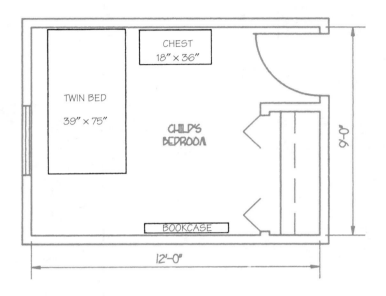

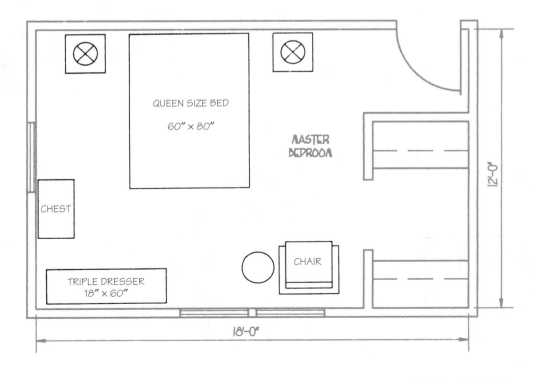

SCALE: 1/4"=1'-0"

BEDROOM PLANNING	NAME:	7-2

Workbook Solution

3.

Directions:

Plan a functional arrangement of fixtures for each of the baths shown below. Study Figures 7-16 through 7-21 in your text for arrangement ideas and clearances. Use a template to draw the fixtures.

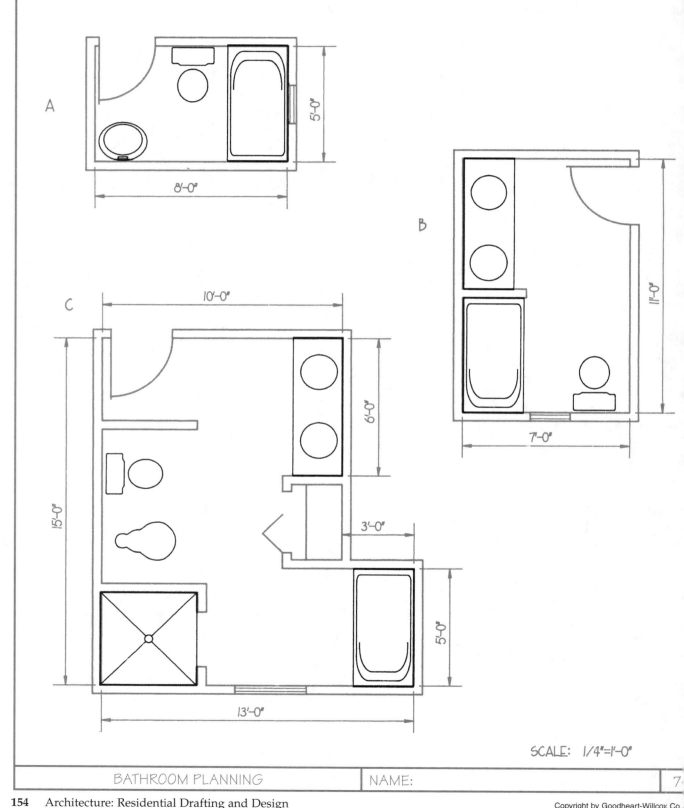

SCALE: 1/4"=1'-0"

BATHROOM PLANNING   NAME: 7

Chapter 7 Pretest
Room Planning—Sleeping Area and Bath Facilities

Name _____

Period _____**Date** _____**Score** _____

Completion

Complete each sentence with the proper response. Place your answer on the space provided.

1. An interior door should _____ into the bedroom.

1. _____

2. The _____ for each room must be understood by the house designer if a functional plan is to be developed.

2. _____

3. The largest bedroom is usually considered to be the _____ bedroom.

3. _____

4. A residential structure may be divided into _____ basic areas.

4. _____

5. If provisions are being made for wheelchair use, a bathroom door should be a minimum of _____ wide.

5. _____

6. The FHA recommends a minimum of four linear feet of rod space in a closet for a man and _____ feet for a woman.

6. _____

7. If possible, the sleeping area should have a _____ or _____ orientation.

7. _____

_____

Multiple Choice

Choose the answer that correctly completes the statement. Write the corresponding letter in the space provided.

_____ 1. Standard bathroom vanity base unit sizes are 21″ deep by _____ high.

   A. 30″
   B. 32″
   C. 34″
   D. 36″

_____ 2. Usually about _____ of the house is dedicated to the sleeping area.

   A. 1/8
   B. 1/4
   C. 1/3
   D. 1/2

_____ 3. A 5′ × 8′ bath would be considered a(n) _____ bath.

    A. small
    B. average
    C. large
    D. very large

_____ 4. For wheelchair access to a bathtub, the bathtub rims should not be lower than _____ from the floor.

    A. 18″
    B. 20″
    C. 22″
    D. 24″

_____ 5. A _____ receptacle should be used in the bathroom.

    A. shielded
    B. grounded
    C. waterproof
    D. ground fault circuit interrupter

_____ 6. The minimum depth of a clothes closet is _____.

    A. 12″
    B. 18″
    C. 24″
    D. 30″

_____ 7. Most water closets require a space at least _____ wide for installation.

    A. 24″
    B. 30″
    C. 36″
    D. 42″

_____ 8. The _____ is where the family relaxes, entertains guests, dines, and meets together.

    A. planning area
    B. entertaining area
    C. living area
    D. service area

_____ 9. The usual height of an interior door is _____.

    A. 6′-2″
    B. 6′-4″
    C. 6′-6″
    D. 6′-8″

_____ 10. The most common size bathtub is _____.

    A. 26″ × 48″
    B. 30″ × 50″
    C. 30″ × 60″
    D. 32″ × 72″

_____ 11. The Federal Housing Administration recommends _____ square feet as the minimum size for a bedroom.

    A. 100

    B. 150

    C. 200

    D. 250

_____ 12. A 1/2 bath is one that usually has only a _____.

    A. water closet and bidet

    B. water closet and lavatory

    C. water closet and shower

    D. water closet and tub

Chapter 7 Posttest
Room Planning—Sleeping Area and Bath Facilities

Name _____

Period _____**Date** _____**Score** _____

Completion

Complete each sentence with the proper response. Place your answer on the space provided.

1. A residential structure may be divided into _____ basic areas.

2. The _____ for each room must be understood by the house designer if a functional plan is to be developed.

3. If possible, the sleeping area should have a _____ or _____ orientation.

4. The largest bedroom is usually considered to be the _____ bedroom.

5. The FHA recommends a minimum of four linear feet of rod space in a closet for a man and _____ feet for a woman.

6. An interior door should _____ into the bedroom.

7. If provisions are being made for wheelchair use, a bathroom door should be a minimum of _____ wide.

1. _____

2. _____

3. _____
   _____

4. _____

5. _____

6. _____

7. _____

Multiple Choice

Choose the answer that correctly completes the statement. Write the corresponding letter in the space provided.

_____ 1. The _____ is where the family relaxes, entertains guests, dines, and meets together.
   A. planning area
   B. entertaining area
   C. living area
   D. service area

_____ 2. Usually about _____ of the house is dedicated to the sleeping area.
   A. 1/8
   B. 1/4
   C. 1/3
   D. 1/2

_____ 3. The Federal Housing Administration recommends _____ square feet as the minimum size for a bedroom.

    A. 100
    B. 150
    C. 200
    D. 250

_____ 4. For wheelchair access to a bathtub, the bathtub rims should not be lower than _____ from the floor.

    A. 18″
    B. 20″
    C. 22″
    D. 24″

_____ 5. The minimum depth of a clothes closet is _____.

    A. 12″
    B. 18″
    C. 24″
    D. 30″

_____ 6. The usual height of an interior door is _____.

    A. 6′-2″
    B. 6′-4″
    C. 6′-6″
    D. 6′-8″

_____ 7. A 1/2 bath is one that usually has only a _____.

    A. water closet and bidet
    B. water closet and lavatory
    C. water closet and shower
    D. water closet and tub

_____ 8. A 5′ × 8′ bath would be considered a(n) _____ bath.

    A. small
    B. average
    C. large
    D. very large

_____ 9. Most water closets require a space at least _____ wide for installation.

    A. 24″
    B. 30″
    C. 36″
    D. 42″

_____ 10. The most common size bathtub is _____.

    A. 26″ × 48″
    B. 30″ × 50″
    C. 30″ × 60″
    D. 32″ × 72″

_____ 11. Standard bathroom vanity base unit sizes are 21″ deep by _____ high.

    A. 30″
    B. 32″
    C. 34″
    D. 36″

_____ 12. A _____ receptacle should be used in the bathroom.

    A. shielded
    B. grounded
    C. waterproof
    D. ground fault circuit interrupter

Room Planning—Living Area

Objectives

After studying this chapter, the student will be able to:

- Identify the rooms and areas that comprise the living area.
- Apply design principles to planning a living room.
- Integrate the furniture in a living room plan.
- Analyze a dining room using good design principles.
- Design a functional entry and foyer.
- Communicate the primary design considerations for a recreation room.
- Integrate patios, porches, and courts into the total floor plan of a dwelling.

Displays

1. **Living Area**. Select a floor plan of a residence that has a well-designed living area. Shade the living area on the plan using colored pencils, felt-tipped pens, or transparent, adhesive-backed overlay material. Display the floor plan while the class is studying living areas of the home.
2. **Living Rooms**. Display several of the living room presentation plans prepared by students for Activity #1 in the Suggested Activities in the text. Change the display to show presentation plans of dining rooms, foyers, recreation rooms, and outdoor living areas as the class completes each activity.

Instructional Materials

Text: Pages 149–187
   Review Questions, Suggested Activities
Workbook: Pages 71–86
   Questions, Problems/Activities
Teacher's Resources:
   Chapter 8 Pretest
   Chapter 8 Teaching Strategy
   Chapter 8 Posttest

Teaching Strategy

- **Knowledge Assessment:** Administer the Chapter 8 Pretest. Correct the test and return. Highlight the topics in which the individual student is deficient.
- Prepare Display #1.
- Review the chapter objectives.
- Discuss living rooms in relation to shapes, sizes, furniture, arrangement, and locations.
- Prepare Display #2.
- Assign Problem 8-1 in the workbook.
- Discuss dining rooms in relation to shapes, sizes, furniture, arrangement, and locations.
- Assign Problem 8-2 in the workbook.
- Discuss entryways and foyers in relation to common types, features, placement, and provisions. Study the examples in the text with the students.
- Assign Problem 8-3 in the workbook.
- Discuss family recreation rooms and special-purpose rooms.
- Assign Problem 8-4 in the workbook.
- Discuss patios, porches, and courts.
- Assign Problem 8-5 in the workbook.
- Assign one or more of the Suggested Activities in the text.
- **Chapter Review:** Assign the Review Questions in the text. Discuss the correct answers. Assign the questions in the workbook. Have students check their own answers.
- **Evaluation:** Administer the Chapter 8 Posttest. Correct the test and return. Return graded problems with comments.

Answers to Review Questions, Text

Page 187

1. 3'-0"
2. It functions as a place to greet guests and, in colder climates, remove overcoats and boots.

3. large
4. Flower planters, screens, dividers, partial walls, furniture, and area rugs can define the boundaries of the dining area.
5. (1) What furniture is planned for this particular room? (2) How often will the room be used? (3) How many people are expected to use the room at any one time? (4) How many functions are combined in this one room? Is it a multipurpose room? (5) Is the living room size in proportion to the remainder of the house?
6. 1/3
7. Porches are generally structurally connected to the house, raised above grade level, and covered. They are typically smaller than patios, but they can be larger.
8. Main entry, service entry, and special-purpose entry.
9. 6'-8"
10. The living room, dining room, foyer, recreation or family room, and special-purpose rooms.
11. Answer may include any three of the following: Dedicated home office, sunroom or atrium, greenhouse, and ham radio room. (Other answers may be correct.)
12. deck

Answers to Workbook Questions
Page 71

Part I: Completion
1. 250
2. furniture
3. level
4. patios
5. foyer
6. north
7. sliding
8. dining
9. divider
10. texture

Part II: Multiple Choice
1. B. 120
2. A. 6 to 8
3. B. 2'-0"
4. C. living room
5. D. open plan
6. A. living room
7. C. 32"
8. B. main
9. D. 34"

Part III: Matching
1. D. Entry
2. C. Double doors
3. G. Mudroom
4. K. Sliding doors
5. F. Foyer
6. E. Recreation room
7. H. Patio
8. I. Play patio
9. J. Porch
10. B. Deck
11. A. Court

Part IV: Short Answer/Listing
1. Answer may include any five of the following: Living room, dining room, foyer, recreation or family room, sunroom, home office, patio, deck, and court.
2. (1) What furniture is planned for this particular room? (2) How often will the room be used? (3) How many people are expected to use the room at any one time? (4) How many functions are combined in this one room? Is it a multipurpose room? (5) Is the living room size in proportion to the remainder of the house?
3. The number of people who will use the room at any one time, the furniture to be included in the room, and clearance allowed for traffic through the room.
4. The table, chairs, buffet, china closet, and server or cart.
5. Either a large overhang may be provided or the entry may be recessed.
6. The size of the house, the cost of the house, the location, and personal preference.
7. It can be located near the dining or living room, between the kitchen and the garage, adjacent to a patio, or in the basement.
8. When persons in wheelchairs will be using the room.
9. Answer may include any four of the following: Home office, sunroom or atrium, greenhouse, ham radio room, and music room.

10. Privacy, storage, lighting, ventilation, plumbing, and electrical facilities.
11. Answer may include any three of the following: Relaxing, playing, entertaining, and living.
12. Answer may include any four of the following: Concrete, brick, stone, redwood, pressure-treated wood, and synthetic decking.
13. On a quiet side of the home near bedrooms where there is privacy.
14. To the back of the house.
15. Screens or glass.

Part V: Problems/Activities

1. Solution on page 165 of this manual.
2. Solution on page 166 of this manual.
3. Solution on page 167 of this manual.
4. Solution on page 168 of this manual.
5. Solution on page 169 of this manual.

Answers to Chapter 8 Pretest

Completion

1. kitchen
2. traffic
3. foyer
4. 34"
5. living area

Multiple Choice

1. A. 120
2. A. foyer
3. A. Atrium, greenhouse, ham radio room.
4. C. 4' to 5'
5. D. 250
6. C. main

Matching

1. E. Should be adjacent to the kitchen and living room.
2. G. A good place to try out decorating ideas.
3. D. In colder climates, a place to remove overcoats and boots.
4. A. Classified as one of three basic types: Main, service, or special-purpose.
5. C. The center of activity in the living area.
6. F. Types include a home office and music room.
7. B. Extends the living space to the outside.

Short Answer

1. Answer may include any three of the following: Patios, porches or decks, courts, and gazebos.
2. Main entry, service entry, and special-purpose entry.
3. (1) What furniture is planned for the room? (2) How often will the room be used? (3) How many people are expected to use the room at any one time? (4) How many functions are combined in the room? Is it a multipurpose room? (5) Is the room size in proportion to the remainder of the house?
4. The time required to develop a suitable solution is greatly reduced, and computer-generated renderings can be used as presentation drawings to show clients how the space will look when complete.

Answers to Chapter 8 Posttest

Completion

1. living area
2. traffic
3. foyer
4. kitchen
5. 34"

Multiple Choice

1. D. 250
2. A. 120
3. C. main
4. C. 4' to 5'
5. A. foyer
6. A. Atrium, greenhouse, ham radio room.

Matching

1. F. Types include a home office and music room.
2. G. A good place to try out decorating ideas.
3. C. The center of activity in the living area.
4. D. In colder climates, a place to remove overcoats and boots.
5. B. Extends the living space to the outside.
6. E. Should be adjacent to the kitchen and living room.
7. A. Classified as one of three basic types: Main, service, or special-purpose.

Short Answer

1. (1) What furniture is planned for the room? (2) How often will the room be used? (3) How many people are expected to use the room at any one time? (4) How many functions are combined in the room? Is it a multipurpose room? (5) Is the room size in proportion to the remainder of the house?

2. Main entry, service entry, and special-purpose entry.

3. Answer may include any three of the following: Patios, porches or decks, courts, and gazebos.

4. The time required to develop a suitable solution is greatly reduced, and computer-generated renderings can be used as presentation drawings to show clients how the space will look when complete.

Workbook Solution

ght by Goodheart-Willcox Co., Inc.

Directions:
Plan the furniture arrangement in Living Room "A" around a music center. The room should provide seating for five people. Living Room "B" may be planned around a theme of your choice. Use standard size furniture from Figure 8-6 in your text for both rooms.

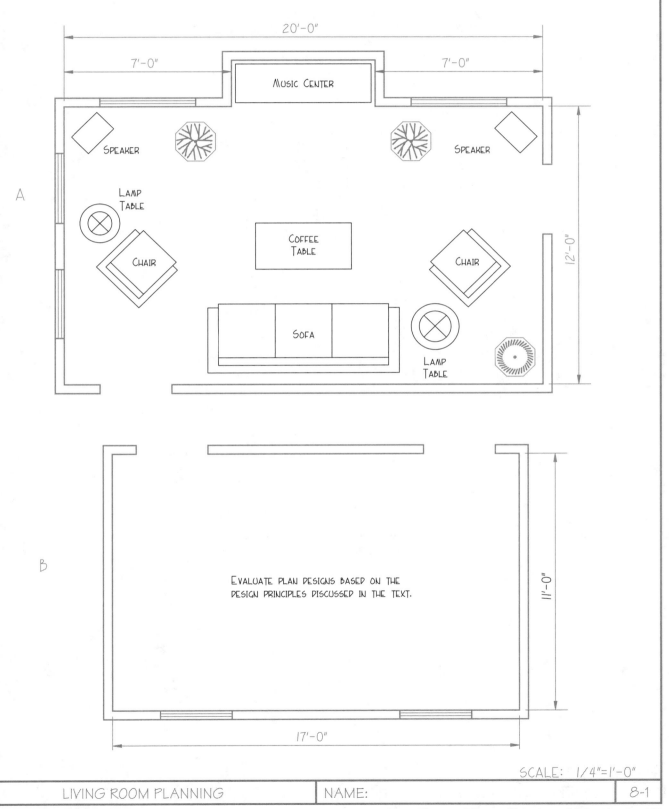

SCALE: 1/4"=1'-0"

LIVING ROOM PLANNING | NAME: | 8-1

Workbook Solution

2.

Directions:
Plan an arrangement of furniture pieces including a table with 6 chairs and a buffet or china cabinet in the dining room below. In the remaining space, design a medium-size dining room (180 square feet to 200 square feet) that provides seating for 8 and storage for dishes, table linens, silverware, and accessories.

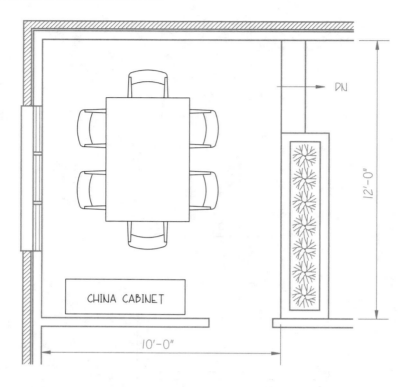

EVALUATE PLAN DESIGNS BASED ON THE
DESIGN PRINCIPLES DISCUSSED IN THE TEXT.

SCALE: 1/4"=1'-0"

DINING ROOM PLANNING   NAME: 8-

Workbook Solution

Directions:
Complete the entry/foyer below by adding a slate floor, a brick veneer exterior, an entry arrow, a plant in the foyer, and a closet shelf and rod.

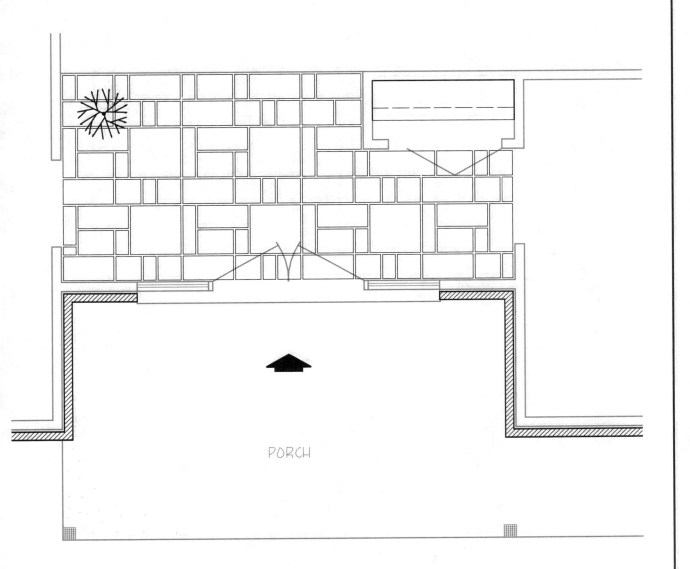

PORCH

SCALE: 1/4"=1'-0"

ENTRY/FOYER PLANNING NAME: 8-3

Workbook Solution

4.

Directions:
Plan a functional arrangement of furniture in the family recreation room below. Include a sofa, upholstered chair, coffee table, lamp table and lamp, and built-in cabinets along the wall opposite the fireplace. Draw an elevation view of the storage units in the space provided.

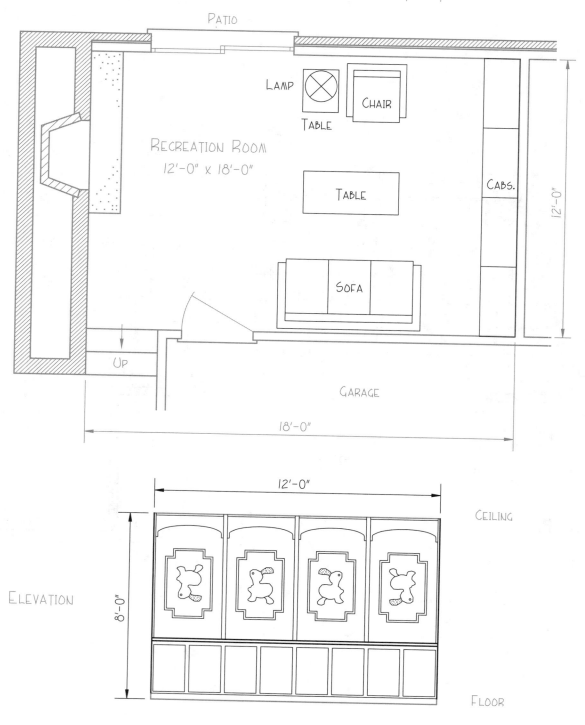

PATIO

LAMP

TABLE

CHAIR

RECREATION ROOM
12'-0" x 18'-0"

TABLE

CABS.

12'-0"

SOFA

UP

GARAGE

18'-0"

12'-0"

CEILING

ELEVATION

8'-0"

FLOOR

TYPICAL SOLUTION

SCALE: 1/4"=1'-0"

RECREATION ROOM PLANNING

NAME:

8-4

Directions:
Using the plan below, complete the covered porch on the right and patio on the left. Include clay tile pavers on the porch, a concrete patio divided into a 4'-0" square grid, seating along the long porch wall, two lounge chairs and a round table on the patio, plants along the front privacy wall, a hedge between the living room and patio, and several plants in pots on the patio and porch.

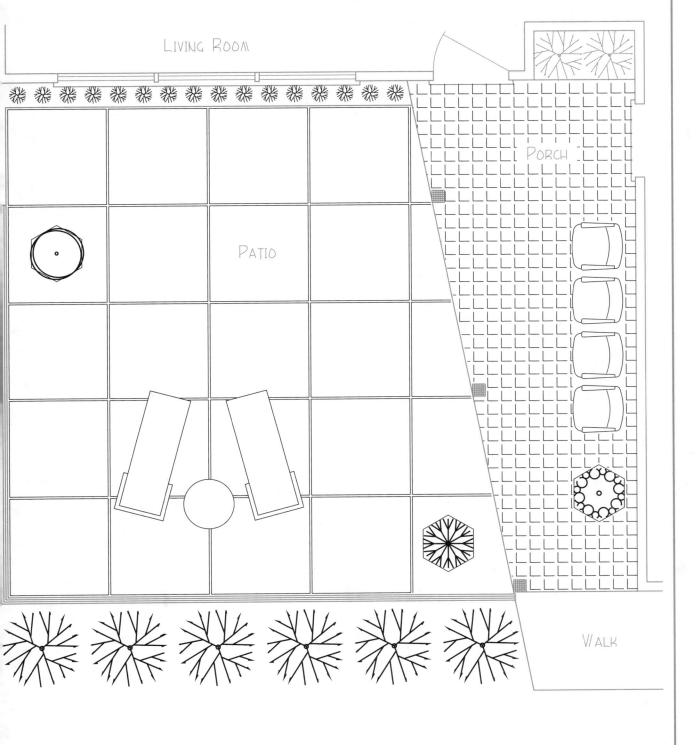

LIVING ROOM

PATIO

PORCH

WALK

SCALE: 1/4"=1'-0"

PATIO AND PORCH PLANNING | NAME: | 8-5

Chapter 8 Pretest
Room Planning—Living Area

Name _____

Period _____**Date** _____**Score** _____

Completion

Complete each sentence with the proper response. Place your answer on the space provided.

1. For efficient use, the dining room should be adjacent to the _____ and living room.

2. The living room should be located so that natural _____ patterns to other parts of the house do not pass through it.

3. The main outside entry should not open directly into the living room, rather into a hallway or _____.

4. In wheelchair-accessible homes, the entry door should have a clearing space of _____ around it.

5. The _____ of the home is designed for all activities that do not take place in the sleeping and service areas.

1. _____

2. _____

3. _____

4. _____

5. _____

Multiple Choice

Choose the answer that correctly completes the statement. Write the corresponding letter in the space provided.

_____ 1. A small dining room capable of seating four people around a table and providing space for a buffet would require about _____ square feet of space.

   A. 120
   B. 180
   C. 240
   D. 300

_____ 2. The _____ functions as a place to greet guests and remove overcoats and overshoes.

   A. foyer
   B. mudroom
   C. entryway
   D. living room

_____ 3. The following are examples of special-purpose rooms.

   A. Atrium, greenhouse, ham radio room.
   B. Darkroom, family recreation room, greenhouse.
   C. Shop, darkroom, living room.
   D. Kitchen, atrium, ham radio room.

_____ 4. To accommodate a person using a wheelchair, a space of _____ wide should be provided around furniture.

    A. 2′ to 3′
    B. 3′ to 4′
    C. 4′ to 5′
    D. 5′ to 6′

_____ 5. An average-size living room is about _____ square feet.

    A. 100
    B. 150
    C. 200
    D. 250

_____ 6. The _____ entry should be centrally located to provide easy access to various parts of the house.

    A. service
    B. special-purpose
    C. main
    D. side

Matching

Select the answer that correctly matches each term. Place your answer in the space provided.

A. Classified as one of three basic types: Main, service, or special-purpose.
B. Extends the living space to the outside.
C. The center of activity in the living area.
D. In colder climates, a place to remove overcoats and boots.
E. Should be adjacent to the kitchen and living room.
F. Types include a home office and music room.
G. A good place to try out decorating ideas.

_____ 1. Dining room

_____ 2. Family recreation room

_____ 3. Foyer

_____ 4. Entryway

_____ 5. Living room

_____ 6. Special-purpose room

_____ 7. Patio, deck, porch, or court

Short Answer

Provide brief answers to the following questions.

1. List three separate but similar living areas of the home that extend living to the outside.

_____

_____

2. List the three basic types of entryways. _____

_____

3. List five important questions to ask regarding the size and design of a living room.

_____

_____

_____

_____

_____

4. The design of living space may be facilitated through the use of a CADD system. List two reasons to use a CADD system for this purpose. _____

_____

_____

Chapter 8 Posttest
Room Planning—Living Area

Name _____

Period _____**Date** _____**Score** _____

Completion

Complete each sentence with the proper response. Place your answer on the space provided.

1. The _____ of the home is designed for all activities that do not take place in the sleeping and service areas.

   1. _____

2. The living room should be located so that natural _____ patterns to other parts of the house do not pass through it.

   2. _____

3. The main outside entry should not open directly into the living room, rather into a hallway or _____.

   3. _____

4. For efficient use, the dining room should be adjacent to the _____ and living room.

   4. _____

5. In wheelchair-accessible homes, the entry door should have a clearing space of _____ around it.

   5. _____

Multiple Choice

Choose the answer that correctly completes the statement. Write the corresponding letter in the space provided.

_____ 1. An average-size living room is about _____ square feet.

   A. 100
   B. 150
   C. 200
   D. 250

_____ 2. A small dining room capable of seating four people around a table and providing space for a buffet would require about _____ square feet of space.

   A. 120
   B. 180
   C. 240
   D. 300

_____ 3. The _____ entry should be centrally located to provide easy access to various parts of the house.

   A. service
   B. special-purpose
   C. main
   D. side

_____ 4. To accommodate a person using a wheelchair, a space of _____ wide should be provided around furniture.

    A. 2′ to 3′
    B. 3′ to 4′
    C. 4′ to 5′
    D. 5′ to 6′

_____ 5. The _____ functions as a place to greet guests and remove overcoats and overshoes.

    A. foyer
    B. mudroom
    C. entryway
    D. living room

_____ 6. The following are examples of special-purpose rooms.

    A. Atrium, greenhouse, ham radio room.
    B. Darkroom, family recreation room, greenhouse.
    C. Shop, darkroom, living room.
    D. Kitchen, atrium, ham radio room.

Matching

Select the answer that correctly matches each term. Place your answer in the space provided.

A. Classified as one of three basic types: Main, service, or special-purpose.
B. Extends the living space to the outside.
C. The center of activity in the living area.
D. In colder climates, a place to remove overcoats and boots.
E. Should be adjacent to the kitchen and living room.
F. Types include a home office and music room.
G. A good place to try out decorating ideas.

_____ 1. Special-purpose room

_____ 2. Family recreation room

_____ 3. Living room

_____ 4. Foyer

_____ 5. Patio, deck, porch, or court

_____ 6. Dining room

_____ 7. Entryway

Name _____

Short Answer

Provide brief answers to the following questions.

1. List five important questions to ask regarding the size and design of a living room.

   _____

   _____

   _____

   _____

   _____

   _____

2. List the three basic types of entryways. _____

   _____

3. List three separate but similar living areas of the home that extend living to the outside. ___

   _____

   _____

4. The design of living space may be facilitated through the use of a CADD system. List two reasons to use a CADD system for this purpose. _____

   _____

   _____

   _____

Room Planning—Service Area

Objectives

After studying this chapter, the student will be able to:

- Plan the service area of a home by applying good design principles.
- Design a functional kitchen to meet a family's needs.
- Select kitchen appliances that are appropriate for a design.
- Plan an efficient clothes care center.
- Describe appropriate dimensions for garage space.

Displays

1. **Service Area.** Obtain pictures from magazines or actual photos of various service areas of the home and display them in an attractive arrangement on your bulletin board.
2. **Student Work.** Display outstanding student work to encourage better work from all students in the class. Problem 9-3 in the workbook, Kitchen Design, is a possible choice for the bulletin board display.

Instructional Materials

Text: Pages 189–214
  Review Questions, Suggested Activities
Workbook: Pages 87–102
  Questions, Problems/Activities
Teacher's Resources:
  Chapter 9 Pretest
  Chapter 9 Teaching Strategy
  Chapter 9 Posttest

Teaching Strategy

- **Knowledge Assessment:** Administer the Chapter 9 Pretest. Correct the test and return. Highlight the topics in which the individual student is deficient.
- Prepare Display #1.
- Review the chapter objectives.
- Discuss the service area of the home.
- Discuss the kitchen in terms of styles, sizes, the work triangle, appliances, cabinets, and location.
- Discuss drawing symbols and common dimensions used for appliances.
- Assign Problems 9-1, 9-2, and 9-3 in the workbook.
- Prepare Display #2.
- Assign one or more of the Suggested Activities in the text.
- Discuss clothes care centers in relation to appliances, sizes, and operations.
- Assign Problem 9-4 in the workbook.
- Discuss garages and carports in terms of size, arrangement, doors, and turnarounds.
- Assign Problems 9-5 and 9-6 in the workbook.
- **Chapter Review:** Assign the Review Questions in the text. Discuss the correct answers. Assign the questions in the workbook. Have students check their own answers. Make a transparency of Problem 9-6 in the workbook to use for review with the class.
- **Evaluation:** Administer the Chapter 9 Posttest. Correct the test and return. Return graded problems with comments.

Answers to Review Questions, Text

Page 214

1. 3"
2. From $11' \times 19'$ to $16' \times 25'$.
3. 10'
4. Washing, drying, pressing, folding, storing, and mending clothes.
5. Straight line, L-shaped, corridor, island, U-shaped, and peninsula.
6. 22'
7. Kitchen, clothes care center, garage or carport, utility, and storage.

8. 34-1/2"
9. attic or crawl space
10. Wood, fiberglass, plastic or vinyl, aluminum, and steel.
11. 24"
12. 26"

Answers to Workbook Questions

Page 87

Part I: Matching
1. E. Straight-line kitchen
2. D. Peninsula kitchen
3. B. Island kitchen
4. F. U-shaped kitchen
5. C. L-shaped kitchen
6. A. Corridor kitchen

Part II: Multiple Choice
1. D. 34-1/2" high and 24" deep with a width in 3" increments
2. B. 6"
3. B. 20' × 20' to 25' × 25'
4. C. 12' to 14-1/2'
5. A. 16' wide and 7' high

Part III: Completion
1. most
2. 22
3. cooking
4. lower
5. cabinets
6. hidden lines
7. food preparation
8. 26
9. Carports
10. service
11. 7 or 8
12. 10
13. turnaround

Part IV: Short Answer/Listing
1. Kitchen, clothes care center, garage or carport, utility, and storage.
2. Food preparation center, cleanup center, and cooking center.
3. Measure from the front-center of the range to the refrigerator to the sink and back to the range. The lengths of these three lines are added together to determine the work triangle.
4. There should be a main ceiling fixture or fixtures in addition to lighting over the sink, cooking center, and food preparation areas.
5. To provide the location and facilities for washing, drying, pressing, folding, storing, and mending clothes.
6. The number of automobiles to be housed, the size and layout of the house, and the space available.
7. Evaluate responses individually.

Part V: Problems/Activities
1. Solution on page 180 of this manual.
2. Solution on page 181 of this manual.
3. Solution on pages 182–188 of this manual.
4. Solution on page 189 of this manual.
5. Solution on page 190 of this manual.
6. Solution on page 191 of this manual.

Answers to Chapter 9 Pretest

Completion
1. attic
2. apartments
3. larger
4. lower
5. refrigerator

Multiple Choice
1. D. adjacent
2. C. 20' × 20'
3. C. 4'
4. C. 22'
5. D. 24'
6. B. 4"
7. D. U-shaped

Short Answer
1. It provides plenty of work space, it is attractive, and it is easily joined to the dining room using the peninsula as a divider.
2. Straight-line, L-shaped, corridor, U-shaped, peninsula, and island.
3. Answer may include any four of the following: Kitchen, clothes care center, garage or carport, utility, and storage.
4. Washing, drying, pressing, folding, storing, and mending clothes.

Matching
1. D. 34-1/2"
2. C. 24"

3. B. 12″ to 36″ in increments of 3″
4. A. 12″ to 30″ in increments of 3″
5. F. 10′
6. E. 7′

Answers to Chapter 9 Posttest

Completion

1. refrigerator
2. apartments
3. lower
4. attic
5. larger

Multiple Choice

1. C. 22′
2. D. adjacent
3. D. U-shaped
4. C. 4′
5. D. 24′
6. C. 20′ × 20′
7. B. 4″

Short Answer

1. Answer may include any four of the following: Kitchen, clothes care center, garage or carport, utility, and storage.
2. Straight-line, L-shaped, corridor, U-shaped, peninsula, and island.
3. It provides plenty of work space, it is attractive, and it is easily joined to the dining room using the peninsula as a divider.
4. Washing, drying, pressing, folding, storing, and mending clothes.

Matching

1. C. 12″ to 30″ in increments of 3″
2. D. 12″ to 36″ in increments of 3″
3. B. 34-1/2″
4. A. 24″
5. E. 7′
6. F. 10′

Workbook Solution

1.

Directions:
Draw the base and wall cabinets, appliances, and work triangle for each of the kitchens below. Use standard size units.
U-Shaped Kitchen: The available space is 12′ × 12′. Include a 36″ wide range on the right-side wall, a 36″ wide refrigerator on the left-side wall, and a sink under the window. Label appliances.
Peninsula Kitchen: The available space is 12′ × 16′. The peninsula is designed to accommodate four stools. The range is to be located on the right, the refrigerator on the left, and the sink below the window.

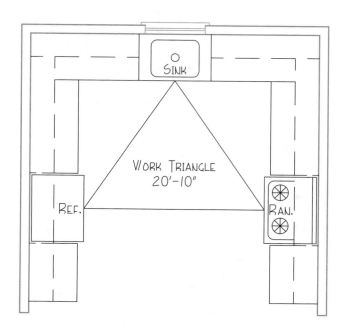

U-SHAPED
KITCHEN

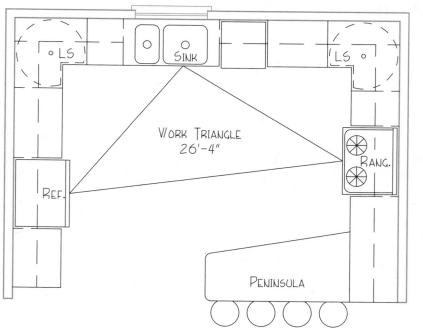

PENINSULA
KITCHEN

SCALE: 1/4″=1′-0″

KITCHEN PLANNING   NAME: 9-1

Directions:
Study the configuration of this large, complex kitchen to determine the most functional layout.
Include a refrigerator, range, dishwasher, planning desk, sink, and breakfast bar with cabinets
above and stools below. Show a ceramic tile floor as a 12" square grid. Label appliances.

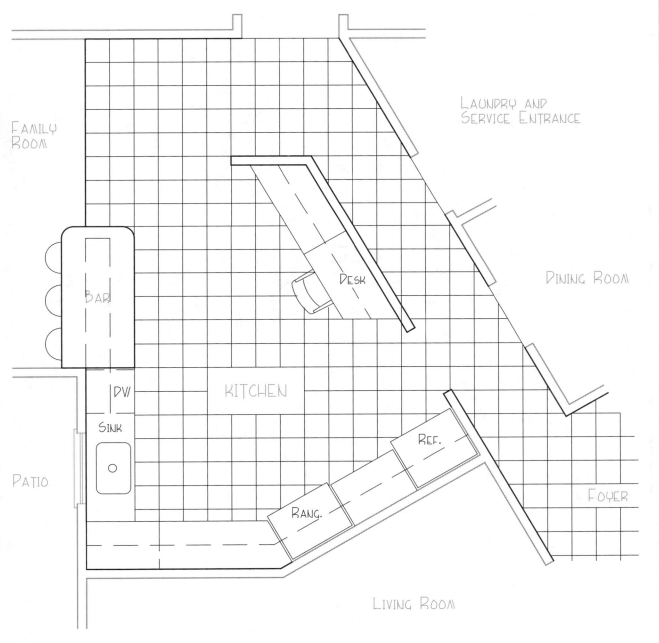

BEDROOMS AND STUDY

FAMILY
ROOM

LAUNDRY AND
SERVICE ENTRANCE

DINING ROOM

BAR

DESK

KITCHEN

DW

SINK

PATIO

REF.

FOYER

RANG.

LIVING ROOM

SCALE: 1/4"=1'-0"

KITCHEN PLANNING   NAME: 9-2

3a.

TYPICAL SOLUTION

KITCHEN
DESIGN

BY: JOHN Q. STUDENT

ASSIGNMENT 9-3

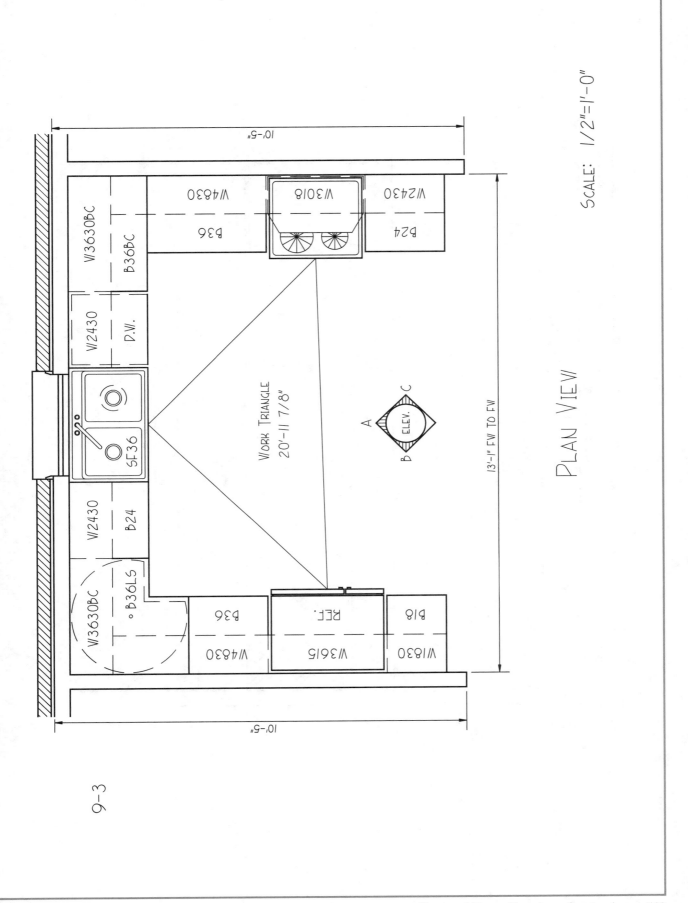

PLAN VIEW

SCALE: 1/2"=1'-0"

9-3

3c.

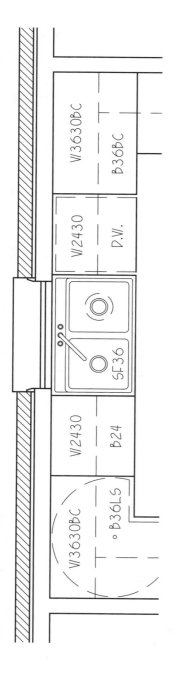

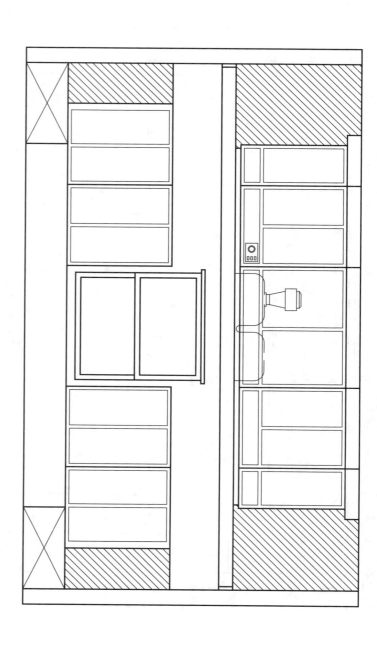

9-3

SCALE: 1/2"=1'-0"

ELEVATION A

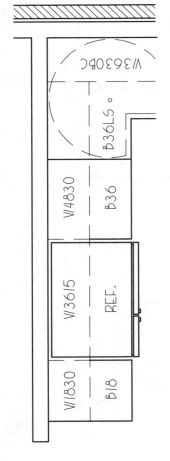

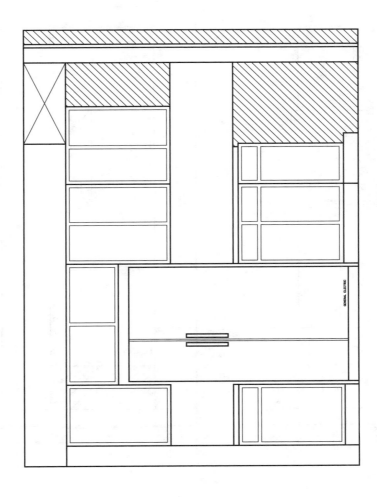

SCALE: 1/2"=1'-0"

ELEVATION B

9-3

3e.

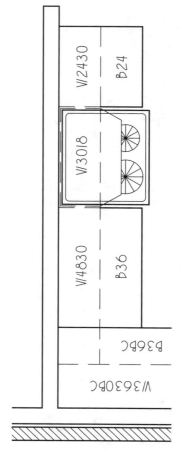

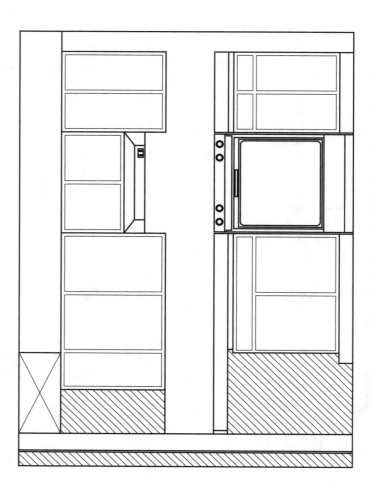

ELEVATION C

SCALE: 1/2"=1'-0"

9-3

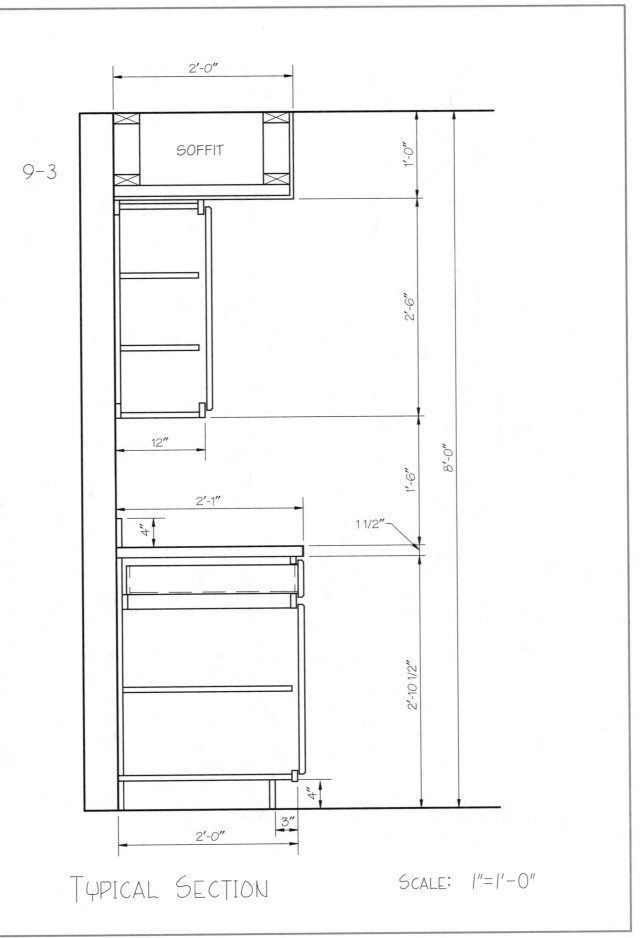

2'-0"

SOFFIT

1'-0"

2'-6"

12"

8'-0"

2'-1"

1 1/2"

4"

1'-6"

2'-10 1/2"

4"

3"

2'-0"

TYPICAL SECTION   SCALE: 1"=1'-0"

9-3

Cabinet & Appliance Schedule

Appliances

# Reqd.	Mfg. #	Manufacturer	Model	Remarks
1	46G5769IN	Sears Kenmore	Side by Side Ref./Freezer	58-7/8" H x 35-3/4" W x 30-5/8" D
1	22G16965N	Sears Kenmore	Dishwasher	34-1/2" H x 23-5/16" W x 25-1/2" D
1	22G45588N	Sears Kenmore	Cooktop Range/Oven	30-3/4" H x 30" W x 26-3/4" D
1	AH 133 791	Gaggenau	Hood	3-5/16" H x 35-1/16" W x 19-11/16" D
1	GC 430	Jenn-Air	Garbage Disposal	7-1/2" Dia. x 14" H
1	K 5924	Kohler	Double Sink	9-5/8" H x 33" W x 22" D

Cabinets

# Reqd.	Mfg. #	Manufacturer	Model	Remarks
1	B 18	Scheirich/Gardencourt	Base Cabinet	34-1/2" H x 18" W x 24" D
2	B 24	Scheirich/Gardencourt	Base Cabinet	34-1/2" H x 24" W x 24" D
2	B 36	Scheirich/Gardencourt	Base Cabinet	34-1/2" H x 36" W x 24" D
1	CB 36	Scheirich/Gardencourt	Base Cabinet	34-1/2" H x 36" W x 24" D
1	LSB 36	Scheirich/Gardencourt	Base Cabinet	34-1/2" H x 36" W x 36" D
1	SB 36	Scheirich/Gardencourt	Base Cabinet	34-1/2" H x 36" W x 24" D
1	W 30 18	Scheirich/Gardencourt	Wall Cabinet	30" H x 18" W x 12" D
1	W 36 15	Scheirich/Gardencourt	Wall Cabinet	15" H x 36" W x 12" D
2	W 48 30	Scheirich/Gardencourt	Wall Cabinet	30" H x 48" W x 12" D
2	CW 30 30	Scheirich/Gardencourt	Wall Cabinet	30" H x 30" W x 12" D
3	W 30 24	Scheirich/Gardencourt	Wall Cabinet	30" H x 24" W x 12" D
1	W 18 30	Scheirich/Gardencourt	Wall Cabinet	18" H x 30" W x 12" D

Workbook Solution

Directions:
Plan a functional arrangement for the clothes care center below. Include the following items: fold-down ironing board, washer, dryer, laundry tub, countertop space for folding and sewing with base cabinets below, wall cabinets for storage, and planning area. Draw an elevation of the wall with the window in the space provided. Label each component in the plan view.

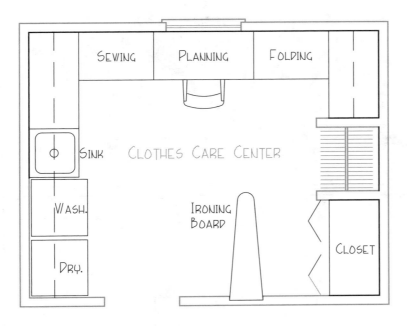

PLAN VIEW

In the plan view, the following components are labeled: SEWING, PLANNING, FOLDING, SINK, WASH., DRY., IRONING BOARD, CLOSET, CLOTHES CARE CENTER

ELEVATION

SCALE: 1/4"=1'-0"

CLOTHES CARE CENTER PLANNING	NAME:	9-4

5.

Directions:

The pictorial shows a detached garage of frame construction. Draw a plan view of this garage assuming the following: The garage is 22'-0" long by 20'-0" wide, the door is 16'-0" wide, a 3'-0" side door leads to the house, the garage has two windows on the left side, and shelves are located at the rear of the garage. The garage walls are 5 1/4" thick. Draw the garage at 1/4"=1'-0" scale.

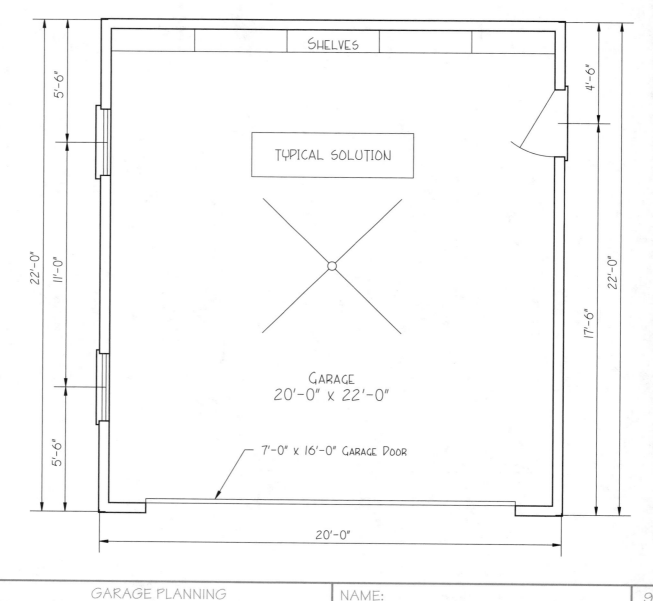

Workbook Solution

Directions:

Plan a driveway with a turnaround that meets the following criteria. The drive is 18'-0" wide at the garage with a turning radius beginning 6'-0" in front of the garage on the right side. The turnaround is 20'-0" wide and proceeds 6'-0" beyond the turning radius tangent point. The width of the drive between the turnaround and street is 10'-0". Show all tangent points, centers, and dimensions.

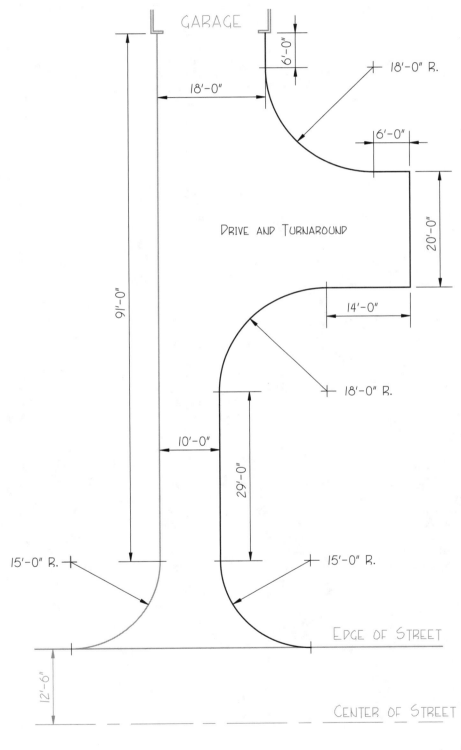

GARAGE

6'-0"

18'-0" R.

18'-0"

6'-0"

DRIVE AND TURNAROUND

20'-0"

14'-0"

91'-0"

18'-0" R.

10'-0"

29'-0"

15'-0" R.

15'-0" R.

EDGE OF STREET

12'-6"

CENTER OF STREET

SCALE: 1/16"=1'-0"

DRIVEWAY TURNAROUND PLANNING | NAME: | 9-6

Chapter 9 Pretest
Room Planning—Service Area

Name _____

Period _____ **Date** _____ **Score** _____

Completion

Complete each sentence with the proper response. Place your answer on the space provided.

1. Exhaust from the kitchen should not be expelled into the _____ or crawl space.

2. The straight-line kitchen is generally used in small houses, cottages, and _____.

3. A lowered ceiling makes a room appear _____.

4. Work surfaces for a kitchen that is handicapped accessible should be _____ than those designed for kitchens with different layouts.

5. The work triangle is determined by drawing a line from the front-center of the range to the _____ to the sink and back to the range.

1. _____

2. _____

3. _____

4. _____

5. _____

Multiple Choice

Choose the answer that correctly completes the statement. Write the corresponding letter in the space provided.

_____ 1. The L-shaped kitchen is located along two _____ walls.

    A. opposite
    B. outside
    C. interior
    D. adjacent

_____ 2. A garage designed for two cars may be as small as _____.

    A. $11' \times 19'$
    B. $16' \times 20'$
    C. $20' \times 20'$
    D. $24' \times 24'$

_____ 3. At least _____ clearance should be provided on all sides of the island in an island kitchen.

    A. $2'$
    B. $3'$
    C. $4'$
    D. $5'$

_____ 4. For practical kitchen design, the length of the work triangle should not exceed _____.

    A. 10'
    B. 16'
    C. 22'
    D. 28'

_____ 5. To be handicapped accessible, a garage or carport should be a minimum of _____ long.

    A. 18'
    B. 20'
    C. 22'
    D. 24'

_____ 6. The floor of a garage or carport should be at least _____ thick concrete reinforced with steel or wire mesh.

    A. 2"
    B. 4"
    C. 6"
    D. 8"

_____ 7. The most popular kitchen design is the _____ kitchen.

    A. L-shaped
    B. corridor
    C. straight-line
    D. U-shaped

Short Answer

Provide brief answers to the following questions.

1. List three reasons why the peninsula kitchen is popular. _____

_____

_____

_____

2. List the six basic styles of kitchens. _____

_____

_____

3. The service area houses equipment and space for maintenance, storage, and services. List four rooms of the home that are included in the service area. _____

_____

_____

4. List six functions performed in the clothes care center. _____

_____

_____

_____

Name _____

Matching

Select the answer that correctly matches each term. Place your answer in the space provided.

A. 12″ to 30″ in increments of 3″   D. 34-1/2″
B. 12″ to 36″ in increments of 3″   E. 7′
C. 24″   F. 10′

_____ 1. Standard base cabinet height

_____ 2. Standard base cabinet depth

_____ 3. Standard wall cabinet width

_____ 4. Standard wall cabinet height

_____ 5. Minimum driveway width (single-car garage)

_____ 6. Garage door height

Chapter 9 Posttest
Room Planning—Service Area

Name _____

Period _____ **Date** _____ **Score** _____

Completion
Complete each sentence with the proper response. Place your answer on the space provided.

1. The work triangle is determined by drawing a line from the front-center of the range to the _____ to the sink and back to the range.

1. _____

2. The straight-line kitchen is generally used in small houses, cottages, and _____.

2. _____

3. Work surfaces for a kitchen that is handicapped accessible should be _____ than those designed for kitchens with different layouts.

3. _____

4. Exhaust from the kitchen should not be expelled into the _____ or crawl space.

4. _____

5. A lowered ceiling makes a room appear _____.

5. _____

Multiple Choice
Choose the answer that correctly completes the statement. Write the corresponding letter in the space provided.

_____ 1. For practical kitchen design, the length of the work triangle should not exceed _____.

    A. 10′
    B. 16′
    C. 22′
    D. 28′

_____ 2. The L-shaped kitchen is located along two _____ walls.

    A. opposite
    B. outside
    C. interior
    D. adjacent

_____ 3. The most popular kitchen design is the _____ kitchen.

    A. L-shaped
    B. corridor
    C. straight-line
    D. U-shaped

_____ 4. At least _____ clearance should be provided on all sides of the island in an island kitchen.

    A. 2'
    B. 3'
    C. 4'
    D. 5'

_____ 5. To be handicapped accessible, a garage or carport should be a minimum of _____ long.

    A. 18'
    B. 20'
    C. 22'
    D. 24'

_____ 6. A garage designed for two cars may be as small as _____.

    A. 11' × 19'
    B. 16' × 20'
    C. 20' × 20'
    D. 24' × 24'

_____ 7. The floor of a garage or carport should be at least _____ thick concrete reinforced with steel or wire mesh.

    A. 2"
    B. 4"
    C. 6"
    D. 8"

Short Answer

Provide brief answers to the following questions.

1. The service area houses equipment and space for maintenance, storage, and services. List four rooms of the home that are included in the service area. _____
_____
_____

2. List the six basic styles of kitchens. _____
_____
_____

3. List three reasons why the peninsula kitchen is popular. _____
_____
_____
_____

4. List six functions performed in the clothes care center. _____
_____
_____
_____

Matching

Select the answer that correctly matches each term. Place your answer in the space provided.

A. 24″
B. 34-1/2″
C. 12″ to 30″ in increments of 3″

D. 12″ to 36″ in increments of 3″
E. 7′
F. 10′

_____ 1. Standard wall cabinet height

_____ 2. Standard wall cabinet width

_____ 3. Standard base cabinet height

_____ 4. Standard base cabinet depth

_____ 5. Garage door height

_____ 6. Minimum driveway width (single-car garage)

Plot Plans

10

Objectives

After studying this chapter, students will be able to:

- Identify the various features shown on a typical plot plan.
- Visualize land elevations from contour lines.
- Recognize typical topographical symbols and apply them to site considerations.
- Properly locate a building on a site.
- Draw a plot plan using correct symbols and conventions.
- Draw a plot plan using CADD.

Displays

1. **Plot Plan Elements.** Select examples of each of the elements typically included on a residential plot plan. Cut out the elements and display them with identification. Include all the items covered in this chapter.
2. **Site Topography.** Display a site plan that illustrates an interesting topography along with a model made from cardboard to the same scale represented on the drawing. Cut cardboard pieces to represent the various contours. See Figure 34-10A.

Instructional Materials

Text: Pages 217–232
   Review Questions, Suggested Activities
Workbook: Pages 103–118
   Review Questions, Problems/Activities
Teacher's Resources:
   Chapter 10 Pretest
   Chapter 10 Teaching Strategy
   Chapter 10 Posttest

Teaching Strategy

- **Knowledge Assessment:** Administer the Chapter 10 Pretest. Correct the test and return. Highlight the topics in which the individual student is deficient.
- Prepare Display #1.
- Review the chapter objectives.
- Discuss the definition and purpose of plot plans.
- Cover the elements of property lines.
- Discuss bearing angles.
- Discuss contour lines.
- Prepare Display #2.
- Assign one or more of the Suggested Activities in the text.
- Discuss topographical features.
- Assign Problem/Activity 10-1 in the workbook.
- Assign Problems/Activities 10-2, 10-3, and 10-4 in the workbook.
- Discuss location of a structure on the site.
- Present the procedure for drawing a plot plan.
- Assign Problems/Activities 10-5 and 10-6 in the workbook.
- Discuss landscape plot plans.
- **Chapter Review:** Assign the Review Questions in the text. Discuss the correct answers. Assign the questions in the workbook. Have students check their own answers. Make a transparency of the answers for workbook Problems/Activities 10-1, 10-2, and 10-3 to review principles taught in Chapter 10.
- **Evaluation:** Administer the Chapter 10 Posttest. Correct the test and return. Return graded problems with comments.

Answers to Review Questions, Text

Page 231

1. c) A contour line.
2. proposed construction
3. Answer may contain any five of the following: Natural contour, trees, view, surrounding houses, code restrictions, style of house to be built, solar orientation, winds, placement of well and septic system, and size and shape of the site.

4. scale
5. It shows the direction of north.
6. short dashes
7. Trees (green), shrubs (green), streams (blue), roads (black), utilities (black), and fences (black).
8. lot
9. bearing (or direction)
10. landscape
11. full
12. symbols

Answers to Workbook Questions
Page 103

Part I: Matching
1. K. Plot plan
2. L. Property lines
3. A. Bearing angles
4. B. Benchmark
5. F. Contour line
6. E. Contour interval
7. D. Closed contour lines
8. G. Estimated contours
9. M. Topographical features
10. C. Blue
11. H. Green
12. J. Meridian arrow
13. I. Landscape plan

Part II: Short Answer/Listing
1. Length and bearing of each property line; location, outline, and size of buildings on the site; contour of the land; elevation of property corners and contour lines; meridian arrow (north symbol); trees, shrubs, streams, and gardens; streets, driveways, sidewalks, and patios; location of utilities; easements for utilities and drainage, if any; well, septic tank, and field; fences and retaining walls; lot number or address of the site; and scale of the drawing.
2. Begin at a given corner; use the benchmark if one is given. Then, proceed in a clockwise manner until the beginning point is reached.
3. A series of long (1" to 2"), thin, freehand lines.
4. Lettering and man-made features such as roads, houses, and other structures.

5. Land forms such as contour lines.
6. Natural contour; trees; view; surrounding houses; code restrictions; style of house to be built; solar orientation; winds; placement of well; septic system; and size and shape of the site.
7. Draw the outside of exterior walls and shade or hatch the area covered by the house; draw the exterior walls as hidden lines with the roof shown as solid lines; and draw the exterior walls thickened.
8. Letter the elevation of each contour line and property corner.
9. After all topographical features have been drawn.
10. Boundary lines; meridian arrow; outline of the house; driveway; walks; patios; and contour lines.

Part III: Completion
1. surveyor
2. engineer's
3. Contour
4. Relative
5. steep
6. even
7. Irregular
8. different
9. right
10. overhang
11. outside
12. 1" = 30'-0".

Part IV: Problems/Activities
1. Solution on page 202 of this manual.
2. Solution on page 203 of this manual.
3. Solution on page 204 of this manual.
4. Solution on page 205 of this manual.
5. Solution on page 206 of this manual.
6. Solution on page 207 of this manual.

Answers to Chapter 10 Pretest
Completion
1. landscape
2. Property
3. Contour interval
4. plot plan
5. symbols
6. contour

Multiple Choice

1. C. N 90° E
2. D. topography
3. C. 1" = 30'-0"
4. B. the works of man
5. C. engineer's
6. D. one corner
7. A. benchmark

Identification

1. X Lot number or address of the site.
2. X Location of utilities.
3. X Elevation of property corners and contour lines.
4. X Streets, driveways, sidewalks, and patios.
5. —
6. X Fences and retaining walls.
7. X Location, outline, and size of buildings on the site.
8. X Trees, shrubs, streams, and gardens.
9. X Meridian arrow (north symbol).
10. —
11. X Easements for utilities and drainage (if any).
12. —
13. —
14. X Contour of the land.
15. —
16. —
17. X Well, septic tank, and field.
18. —
19. X Scale of the drawing.
20. X Length and bearing of each property line.

Short Answer

1. Show only exterior walls of the house and shade the space covered by the house; show the exterior walls as hidden lines and the roof as object lines (typical roof plan); and show exterior wall thickness with all interior walls without showing windows and doors.

Answers to Chapter 10 Posttest
Completion

1. plot plan
2. Property

3. contour
4. Contour interval
5. symbols
6. landscape

Multiple Choice

1. C. engineer's
2. C. N 90° E
3. A. benchmark
4. D. topography
5. B. the works of man
6. D. one corner
7. C. 1" = 30'-0"

Identification

1. X Scale of the drawing.
2. X Location of utilities.
3. —
4. X Elevation of property corners and contour lines.
5. X Length and bearing of each property line.
6. —
7. —
8. X Location, outline, and size of buildings on the site.
9. —
10. X Meridian arrow (north symbol).
11. —
12. X Streets, driveways, sidewalks, and patios.
13. X Contour of the land.
14. —
15. X Trees, shrubs, streams, and gardens.
16. X Well, septic tank, and field.
17. X Fences and retaining walls.
18. X Easements for utilities and drainage (if any).
19. —
20. X Lot number or address of the site.

Short Answer

1. Show only exterior walls of the house and shade the space covered by the house; show the exterior walls as hidden lines and the roof as object lines (typical roof plan); and show exterior wall thickness with all interior walls without showing windows and doors.

Workbook Solution

1.

Directions:
Draw the proper topographical symbol in the space provided.

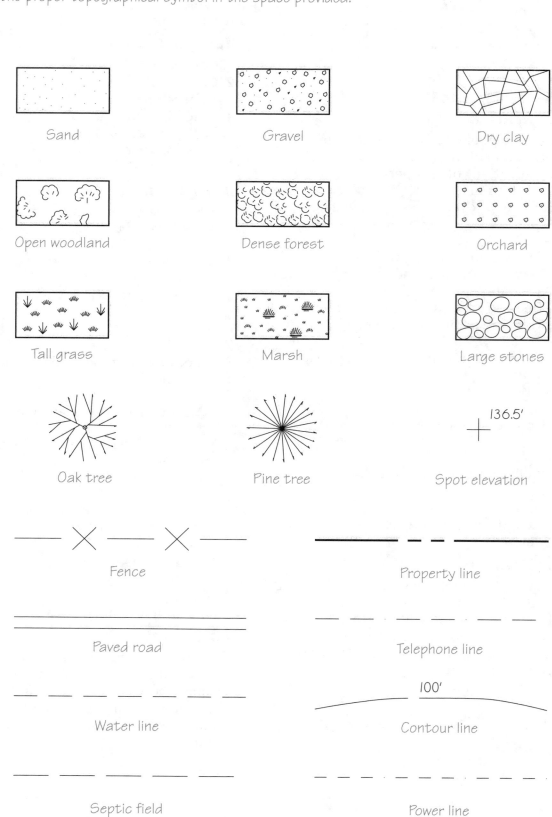

Sand

Gravel

Dry clay

Open woodland

Dense forest

Orchard

Tall grass

Marsh

Large stones

Oak tree

Pine tree

Spot elevation

Fence

Property line

Paved road

Telephone line

Water line

Contour line

Septic field

Power line

TOPOGRAPHICAL SYMBOLS   NAME:

Directions:
Plot the following property line directions (bearings) in the circle as shown. Note the direction of north is generally toward the top of the drawing, but this may be any direction desired. Label each line showing its bearing.

N 15° E
N 90° 0′ 0″ E
S 75° E
Due South

S 32° 30′ W
S 78° 15′ W
N 90° W
N 45° W

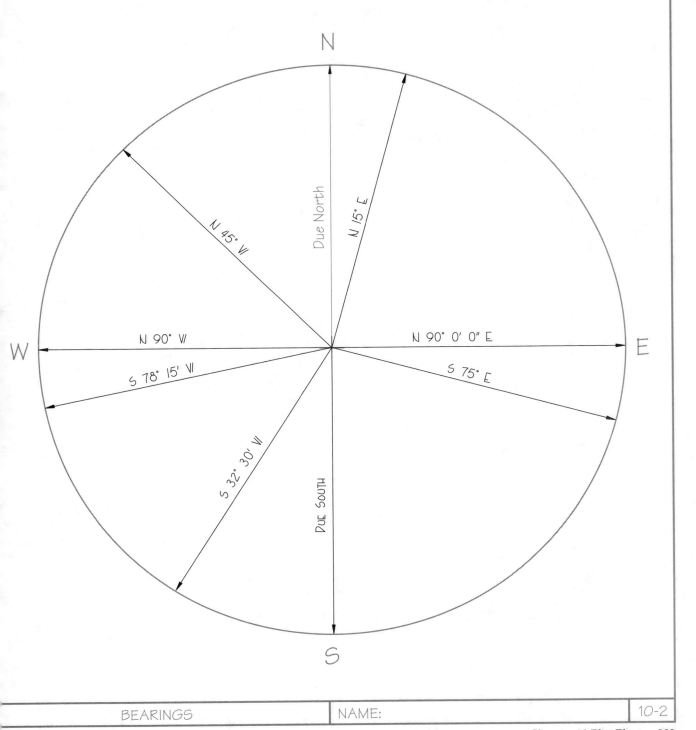

| BEARINGS | NAME: | 10-2 |

Workbook Solution

3.

Directions:

Using the property line symbol and format shown in the example below, locate the property boundaries described in the chart. Note the scale and direction of north.

- > Begin at point A.
- > Line AB bears Due North for a distance of 150.0′.
- > Line BC bears N 75° E for a distance of 112.5′.
- > Line CD bears S 56° E for a distance of 45.0′.
- > Line DE bears S 15° W for a distance of 142.5′.
- > Determine the bearing and length of line EA.
- > Label property lines and corners.

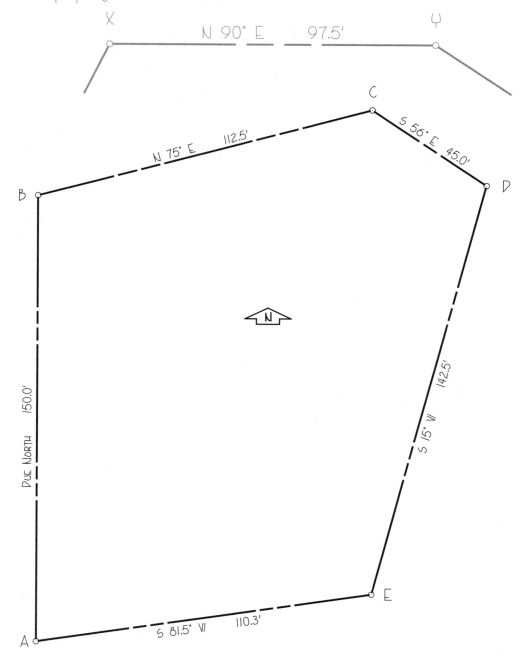

SCALE: 1″=30′-0″

Workbook Solution

Directions:
This assignment consists of two parts—plotting contour lines from an elevation grid and showing a profile section defined by a cutting plane. Using the elevation grid at the top of the page, plot the contour lines at elevations 5, 10, and 15 feet. Use the proper contour line symbol and label. Draw a profile section of the property defined by Section A1,1 in the space provided. Be sure to project the points from the grid above. Hatch the sectioned area in the profile.

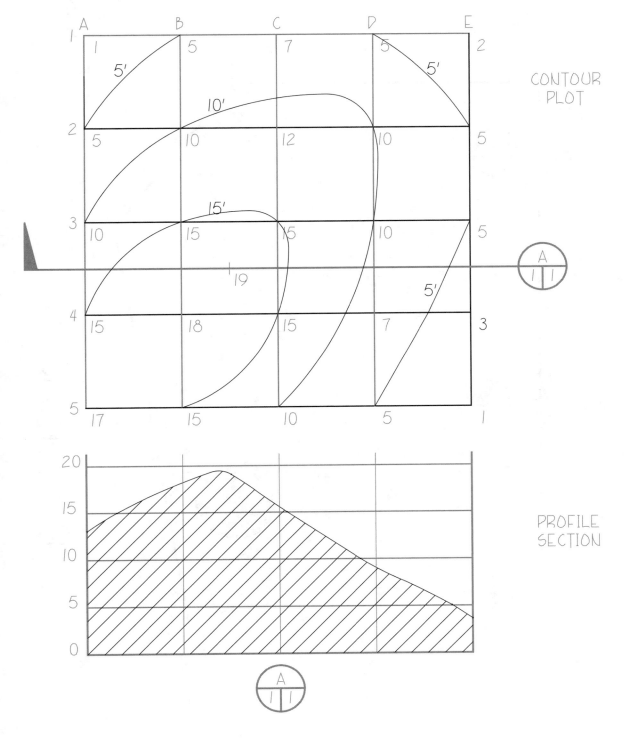

CONTOUR PLOT

PROFILE SECTION

SCALE: 1"=10'-0"

CONTOUR LINES   NAME: 10-4

5.

SCALE : 1" = 20'-0"

PLOT PLAN

SANDY LAKE

CHORD EA = 129.0'
BEARING N 12° W

EL. 106.4'
B

112.0'
S 15° E

C EL. 108.6'

EL. 107.9'
D

S 86° W 100.0'

EL. 100.0'
A

N 75° E 200.0'

S 85° W 154.0'

E EL. 100.0'

108

100'
101'
102'
103'
104'
105'
106'
107'
108'
109'

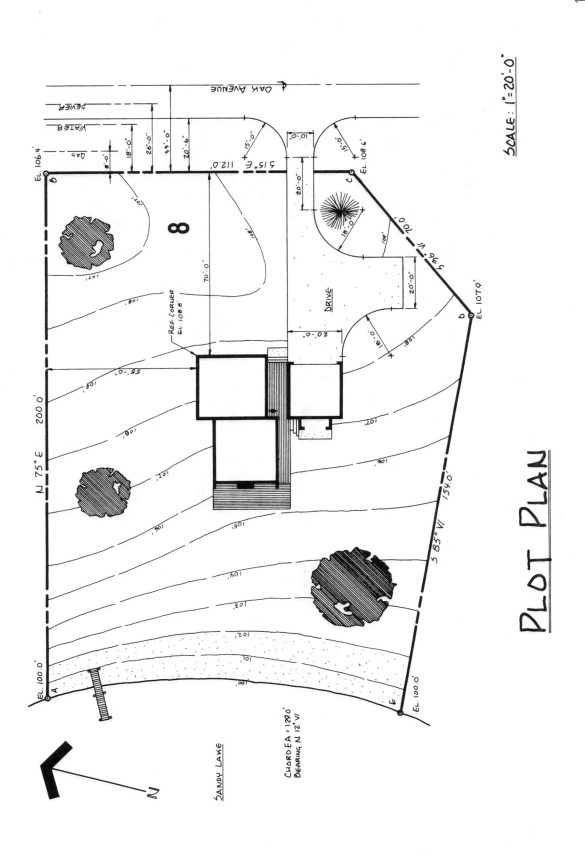

PLOT PLAN

SCALE : 1" = 20'-0"

Chapter 10 Pretest
Plot Plans

Name _____

Period _____ **Date** _____ **Score** _____

Completion
Complete each sentence with the proper response. Place your answer on the space provided.

1. A(n) _____ plan is designed to show the type and placement of trees, shrubs, flowers, gardens, and pools on the site.

2. _____ lines define the site boundaries.

3. _____ is the vertical distance between two adjacent contours.

4. A(n) _____ shows the site and location of the buildings on the property.

5. Topographical features are represented by _____.

6. A(n) _____ is a line connecting points that have the same elevation.

1. _____

2. _____

3. _____

4. _____

5. _____

6. _____

Multiple Choice
Choose the answer that correctly completes the statement. Write the corresponding letter in the space provided.

_____ 1. The proper format for describing the bearing of a property line is _____.

    A. S 45° N
    B. N 45° 60′ 15″ E
    C. N 90° E
    D. S 75° 30′ 62″ W

_____ 2. Contour lines help describe the _____ of a site by depicting shape and elevation of the land.

    A. view
    B. entourage
    C. value
    D. topography

_____ 3. A typical scale used for plot plans is _____.

    A. 1″ = 1′-0″
    B. 1/4″ = 1′-0″
    C. 1″ = 30′-0″
    D. 10′ = 1′-0″

_____ 4. When color is used on a topographical drawing, black is used to represent _____.

    A. all land forms
    B. the works of man
    C. streams, lakes, marsh, and ponds
    D. vegetation

_____ 5. Property lines are measured with a(n) _____ scale to the nearest 1/100 foot.

    A. architect's
    B. combination
    C. engineer's
    D. metric

_____ 6. The standard procedure for dimensioning the location of a house on a site is to dimension _____ of the house from adjacent lot lines.

    A. one side
    B. two sides
    C. two corners
    D. one corner

_____ 7. If a property corner begins or ends on a _____, it is usually identified with a special symbol.

    A. benchmark
    B. contour line
    C. bearing line
    D. meridian arrow

Identification

Place a check in the space provided next to those features that are generally shown on a plot plan.

_____ 1. Lot number or address of the site.

_____ 2. Location of utilities.

_____ 3. Elevation of property corners and contour lines.

_____ 4. Streets, driveways, sidewalks, and patios.

_____ 5. Room layout.

_____ 6. Fences and retaining walls.

_____ 7. Location, outline, and size of buildings on the site.

_____ 8. Trees, shrubs, streams, and gardens.

_____ 9. Meridian arrow (north symbol).

_____ 10. Window wells and areaways.

_____ 11. Easements for utilities and drainage (if any).

Identification (continued)

_____ 12. Height of windows and doors.

_____ 13. Ornamental plant list.

_____ 14. Contour of the land.

_____ 15. Cut and fill calculations.

_____ 16. Footings for buildings on the site.

_____ 17. Well, septic tank, and field.

_____ 18. Electrical distribution panel.

_____ 19. Scale of the drawing.

_____ 20. Length and bearing of each property line.

Short Answer

Provide a brief answer to the following question.

1. Briefly describe the three commonly accepted methods of representing the house on the site.

_____

_____

_____

_____

_____

Chapter 10 Posttest
Plot Plans

Name _____

Period _____**Date** _____**Score** _____

Completion

Complete each sentence with the proper response. Place your answer on the space provided.

1. A(n) _____ shows the site and location of the buildings on the property.

2. _____ lines define the site boundaries.

3. A(n) _____ is a line connecting points that have the same elevation.

4. _____ is the vertical distance between two adjacent contours.

5. Topographical features are represented by _____.

6. A(n) _____ plan is designed to show the type and placement of trees, shrubs, flowers, gardens, and pools on the site.

1. _____

2. _____

3. _____

4. _____

5. _____

6. _____

Multiple Choice

Choose the answer that correctly completes the statement. Write the corresponding letter in the space provided.

_____ 1. Property lines are measured with a(n) _____ scale to the nearest 1/100 foot.

    A. architect's
    B. combination
    C. engineer's
    D. metric

_____ 2. The proper format for describing the bearing of a property line is _____.

    A. S 45° N
    B. N 45° 60′ 15″ E
    C. N 90° E
    D. S 75° 30′ 62″ W

_____ 3. If a property corner begins or ends on a _____, it is usually identified with a special symbol.

    A. benchmark
    B. contour line
    C. bearing line
    D. meridian arrow

_____ 4. Contour lines help describe the _____ of a site by depicting shape and elevation of the land.

    A. view
    B. entourage
    C. value
    D. topography

_____ 5. When color is used on a topographical drawing, black is used to represent _____.

    A. all land forms
    B. the works of man
    C. streams, lakes, marsh, and ponds
    D. vegetation

_____ 6. The standard procedure for dimensioning the location of a house on a site is to dimension _____ of the house from adjacent lot lines.

    A. one side
    B. two sides
    C. two corners
    D. one corner

_____ 7. A typical scale used for plot plans is _____.

    A. 1″ = 1′-0″
    B. 1/4″ = 1′-0″
    C. 1″ = 30′-0″
    D. 10′ = 1′-0″

Identification

Place a check in the space provided next to those features that are generally shown on a plot plan.

_____ 1. Scale of the drawing.

_____ 2. Location of utilities.

_____ 3. Window wells and areaways.

_____ 4. Elevation of property corners and contour lines.

_____ 5. Length and bearing of each property line.

_____ 6. Room layout.

_____ 7. Cut and fill calculations.

_____ 8. Location, outline, and size of buildings on the site.

_____ 9. Ornamental plant list.

_____ 10. Meridian arrow (north symbol).

_____ 11. Height of windows and doors.

Identification (continued)

_____ 12. Streets, driveways, sidewalks, and patios.

_____ 13. Contour of the land.

_____ 14. Footings for buildings on the site.

_____ 15. Trees, shrubs, streams, and gardens.

_____ 16. Well, septic tank, and field.

_____ 17. Fences and retaining walls.

_____ 18. Easements for utilities and drainage (if any).

_____ 19. Electrical distribution panel.

_____ 20. Lot number or address of the site.

Short Answer

Provide a brief answer to the following question.

1. Briefly describe the three commonly accepted methods of representing the house on the site.

_____

_____

_____

_____

_____

Footings, Foundations, and Concrete

Objectives

After studying this chapter, the student will be able to:
- Describe the procedure for staking out a house location.
- List the major considerations when designing a footing for a residential foundation.
- Analyze a typical floor plan to determine the appropriate foundation.
- Discuss the design considerations for wood, concrete, and masonry foundation walls.
- Calculate the load to be supported by a beam.
- Explain the purpose of a lintel.

Displays

1. **Residential Foundations**. Select a floor plan which includes several types of footings and foundations. Display the plan with appropriate details to communicate the construction techniques. Connect each detail with the proper location on the plan view using a string and tack.
2. **Wood Foundations**. Display an assortment of design materials and ideas related to all-weather wood foundations. Literature which includes specifications, building techniques, and code requirements can be secured from the American Plywood Association as well as companies that produce pressure-treated wood products.

Instructional Materials

Text: Pages 233–258
  Review Questions, Suggested Activities
Workbook: Pages 119–136
  Review Questions, Problems/Activities
Teacher's Resources:
  Chapter 11 Pretest
  Chapter 11 Teaching Strategy
  Chapter 11 Posttest

Teaching Strategy

- **Knowledge Assessment:** Administer the Chapter 11 Pretest. Correct the test and return. Highlight the topics in which the individual student is deficient.
- Prepare Display #1.
- Review chapter objectives.
- Discuss staking out the house location.
- Present excavation.
- Discuss the average maximum frost penetration in various areas of the United States.
- Discuss footing shapes and specifications and foundation walls.
- Cover slab foundations.
- Assign Problem 11-1 in the workbook.
- Present pier and post foundations.
- Prepare Display #2.
- Present wood foundations.
- Discuss concrete masonry basement walls.
- Assign workbook Problems 11-2 and 11-3.
- Discuss beams and girders.
- Assign workbook Problem 11-4.
- Discuss lintels, concrete, and masonry.
- Assign one or more of the Suggested Activities in the text.
- **Chapter Review:** Assign the Review Questions in the text. Discuss the correct answers. Assign Review Questions in the workbook. Have students check their own answers.
- **Evaluation:** Administer the Chapter 11 Posttest. Correct the test and return. Return graded problems with comments.

Answers to Review Questions, Text

Page 257
1. plot
2. 9-12-15 method or by comparing diagonal measurements.
3. To retain the location of the foundation during excavation and construction.
4. 6"

5. weight
6. foundation wall
7. slopped or hilly terrain
8. 1/2"
9. T- foundation
10. Answer may include any two of the following: Requires less time, expense, labor, and excavation.
11. height
12. Wood foundation.
13. Pressure treating with chemical solutions.
14. To ensure that the top plate of the foundation unit is level and accurately located.
15. Silicon bronze, copper, or hot-dipped zinc-coated steel.
16. 7
17. pilaster
18. hot tar, cement-base paint.
19. beam or girder
20. S-beam and W-beam.
21. live
22. kips
23. lintel
24. Cement, sand, aggregate, and water.
25. increases
26. screed
27. contraction joints
28. 7-5/8" × 7-5/8" × 15-5/8"

Answers to Workbook Questions

Page 119

Part I: Completion

1. 90
2. plot
3. 15
4. Diagonal
5. batter boards
6. 4'
7. plumb bob
8. control
9. 8"
10. 6"
11. building codes
12. 6"
13. footings
14. sandy
15. clay
16. wood
17. bottom
18. 4"
19. three
20. tamping
21. 12" × 10"

Part II: Short Answer/Listing

1. To increase the supporting capacity of the foundation wall by spreading the load over a larger area.
2. Poured concrete.
3. The thickness should be the same as the foundation wall and the width should be two times the foundation wall thickness.
4. The different subsoils may have unequal compressibilities.
5. The footing size can be increased to minimize any differences in settlement to reduce cracking.
6. When footings are located over soft or poorly drained soils, soils that are not uniform, or over backfilled utility trenches.
7. 12"
8. The use of two 1/2" steel rods in the horizontal and vertical footings where the steps are located.
9. The foundation walls extend from the first floor to the footing.
10. Cast concrete, concrete block, pressure-treated wood, and brick. Stone was once common but not used anymore.
11. T-foundation, slab foundation; pier or post foundation, and permanent wood foundation.
12. Weight to be supported; load bearing capacity of the soil; location of the foundation in the building; climate; local building codes; and preferred building practice.
13. Form boards are made from construction lumber and are used to provide a form for the cast footing used with the T-foundation.
14. Yes.
15. Requires less time, expense, and labor to construct; excavation is simpler than for the T-foundation since a separate footing is not required; casting the foundation and floor in one operation uses less time.
16. They are easier to handle, more readily available, and do not check as much as solid beams.

17. Stronger and more fire resistant than built-up beams.
18. Wide-flange beam (W-beam) will support more weight and is more stable.
19. Live loads are those that move or fixed weights that are not structural elements of the house; examples include furniture, occupants, snow on the roof, wind, etc.
20. Dead loads are those that are static or fixed weights of the building itself; examples include the weight of roofing, foundation walls, siding, joists, etc.
21. Precast concrete, cast-in-place concrete, lintel blocks, and steel angle.
22. In line with interior columns; where the slab changes in width; or at a maximum spacing of 20'.
23. A. T-foundation.
    B. Slab foundation.
    C. Pier foundation.
    D. Post foundation.
    E. Wood foundation.
24. A. Header.
    B. Sill.
    C. Drain tile.
    D. Expansion joint.

Part III: Multiple Choice

1. D. All of the above.
2. C. Warmer climates where freezing of the ground is infrequent.
3. B. at least 12"
4. B. A basement sump is installed in poorly drained soils.
5. D. All of the above.
6. A. Double top plate of the foundation wall.
7. C. After the basement floor has cured and the first floor is installed.
8. A. Support from crosswalls.
9. C. 7'
10. A. Metal tie bars.
11. B. Capping may be omitted.
12. C. Applying two 1/4" thick coats of cement-mortar or plaster, then a coat of hot tar or similar waterproofing material.
13. D. All of the above.
14. C. 4" × 4" × 3/8"
15. D. All of the above.
16. B. 25

17. A. 4" to 6"
18. A. 7-5/8" × 7-5/8" × 15-5/8"

Part IV: Matching

1. N. Plot plan.
2. P. Saw kerf.
3. S. T-foundation.
4. R. Slab foundation.
5. M. Pier foundation.
6. L. PWF.
7. C. AWWF.
8. A. ACA or CCA.
9. D. Bearing wall.
10. O. S-beam.
11. J. Kip.
12. K. Lintel.
13. F. Concrete.
14. E. Cement.
15. B. Aggregate.
16. Q. Screed.
17. H. Float.
18. T. Trowel.
19. G. Contraction joints.
20. I. Jointing tool.

Part V: Problems/Activities

1. Solution on page 219 of this manual.
2. Solution on page 220 of this manual.
3. Solution on page 221 of this manual.
4. Solution on page 222 of this manual.

Answers to Chapter 11 Pretest

Completion

1. 8"
2. 12"
3. clay
4. 9-12-15
5. cast concrete
6. 6"

Multiple Choice

1. A. vertical load to be supported
2. D. staking out the location of the house on the site
3. D. control
4. C. silicon bronze, copper, or hot-dipped zinc-coated steel
5. C. 6
6. D. 16"
7. B. building on hilly terrain

8. C. located over soft or poorly drained soils.
9. A. from the first floor to the footing
10. B. waterborne preservative salts
11. B. batter boards
12. B. footing

Matching

1. C. Support for the foundation walls
2. B. Pressure-treated wood is used
3. E. Used to support a beam
4. A. Extension of a slab floor
5. D. The most common foundation type

Short Answer

1. Cement, sand, coarse aggregate, and water.
2. Use pilasters, wall stiffeners, or continuous horizontal steel joint reinforcement.
3. Live loads and dead loads.
4. A heavy coat of hot tar or two coats of cement-based paint designed for this purpose.
5. Precast concrete, cast-in-place concrete, lintel blocks, and steel angle.
6. 7-5/8″ × 7-5/8″ × 15-5/8″
7. S-beams and W-beams.

Answers to Chapter 11 Posttest

Completion

1. 9-12-15
2. 8″
3. 6″
4. clay
5. cast concrete
6. 12″

Multiple Choice

1. D. staking out the location of the house on the site
2. B. batter boards
3. D. control
4. C. 6″
5. B. footing
6. D. 16″
7. C. located over soft or poorly drained soils.
8. B. building on hilly terrain
9. A. from the first floor to the footing
10. C. silicon bronze, copper, or hot-dipped zinc-coated steel
11. B. waterborne preservative salts
12. A. vertical load to be supported

Matching

1. B. Pressure-treated wood is used
2. A. Extension of a slab floor
3. D. The most common foundation type
4. E. Used to support a beam
5. C. Support for the foundation walls

Short Answer

1. Use pilasters, wall stiffeners, or continuous horizontal steel joint reinforcement.
2. A heavy coat of hot tar or two coats of cement-based paint designed for this purpose.
3. S-beams and W-beams.
4. Live loads and dead loads.
5. Precast concrete, cast-in-place concrete, lintel blocks, and steel angle.
6. Cement, sand, coarse aggregate, and water.
7. 7-5/8″ × 7-5/8″ × 15-5/8″

Workbook Solution

Directions:

Draw a typical foundation wall section for a thickened-edge slab that includes the following elements:

> Scale: 3/4" = 1'-0"
> Foundation 10" thick and 48" from top of slab to bottom of foundation (no footing). Thickness and depth should conform to code.
> Welded wire fabric in foundation and slab.
> Slab 4" thick on 1" RF insulation and 4" compacted sand.
> Wall on foundation of 8" concrete block with 3/4" RF insulation outside extending 24" below the grade. Use wood siding over insulation to 2" above the grade. Flash exposed insulation with aluminum.
> Label and dimension. Add scale.

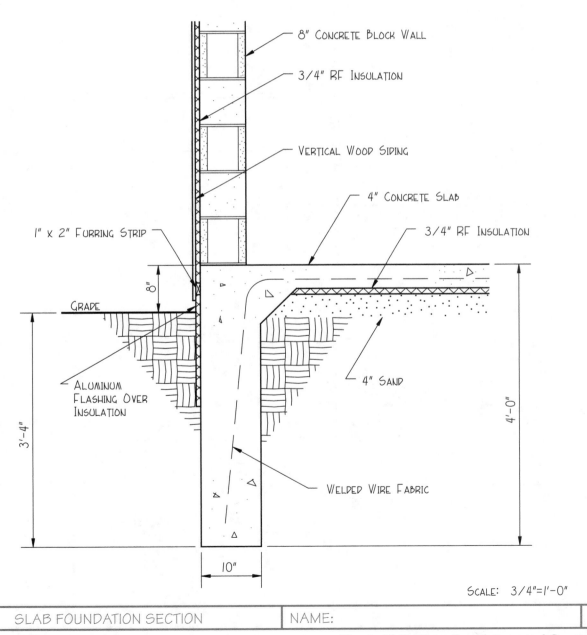

| SLAB FOUNDATION SECTION | NAME: | 11-1 |

SCALE: 3/4"=1'-0"

Workbook Solution

2.

Directions:
Draw a typical foundation wall section for a frame structure with siding that has a crawl space.
Include the following elements in your drawing:

> Scale: 3/4″ = 1′-0″
> Continuous footing 8″ × 16″ with 2-1/2″ rebar and 4″ perforated drain tile in pea gravel.
> 8″ concrete block foundation wall (6 courses high or code) with 1/2″ parge coat for moisture
  protection. Grade 8″ below top of foundation and crawl space from top of footing to bottom
  of joists.
> 2″ × 8″ treated sill plate with 1/2″ × 16″ anchor bolts and sill sealer.
> 2″ × 10″ floor joist with 3/4″ T&G P.W. glued and nailed.
> Frame wall with 3/4″ RF insulation to top of foundation with horizontal siding, 3-1/2″ batt
  insulation, and 1/2″ drywall.
> Label and dimension. Add scale.

3 1/2″ Batt Insulation

1/2″ Drywall

3/4″ T&G Plywood

2″ x 10″ Joist

1/2″ x 16″ Anchor Bolt

Grade

Sand

Crawl Space

4′-1 1/2″

Pea Gravel

1/2″ Parge Coat

4″ Drain Tile

4′-0″

8″

16″

1/2″ Rebar

Scale: 3/4″=1′-0″

FOUNDATION WITH CRAWL SPACE   NAME: 11-

Workbook Solution

Directions:
Draw a typical foundation/basement wall section for a brick veneer on a frame residential structure. Include the following elements in your drawing:

> Scale: 3/4" = 1'-0"
> Continuous footing 12" × 24" with 2-1/2" rebar and 4" perforated drain tile in pea gravel.
> 12" thick basement wall with 4" brick ledge and damp-proofing. Basement floor to ceiling should be 7'-10" to 8'-0".
> 4" basement floor slab with welded wire fabric and 4" compacted sand with vapor barrier.
> 2" × 8" treated sill plate with sill sealer and 1/2" × 8" anchor bolts.
> Floor system is 14" wood floor trusses to span 24'-0" with 3/4" T&G P.W. panels glued and nailed. See Reference Section in text.
> First floor frame wall has 3/4" RF insulation, 3-1/2" batt insulation, and 1/2" drywall inside. Veneer is common brick with 1" air space, wall ties, and flashing.
> Label and dimension. Add scale.

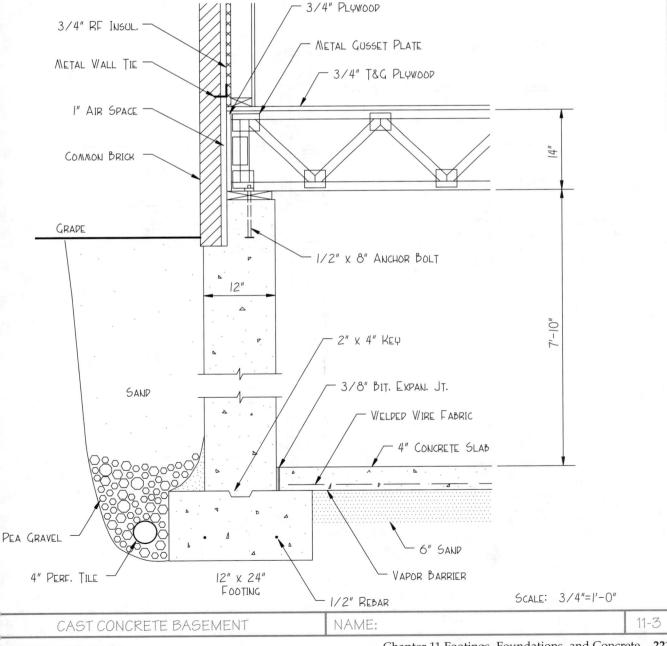

CAST CONCRETE BASEMENT | NAME: | 11-3

4.

Directions:

Draw a typical foundation/basement wall section for a residential structure that requires a wood foundation. Include the following elements:

> Scale: 3/4" = 1'-0"
> Base for foundation is 8" of crushed stone or gravel.
> Foundation/basement wall is 2" × 6" frame with 2" × 10" footing plate and 3/4" P.W. sheathing covered with polyethylene film. All wood materials are specially treated for this application.
> Include protection strip at grade, double top plate, and 1" × 4" screed.
> Basement floor is 4" thick with welded wire fabric and moisture barrier. Include drain tiles where ground water is a problem.
> First floor system is 2" × 10" joists with 3/4" T&G P.W. glued and nailed.
> Exterior wall is 2" × 4" stud, 3/4" RF insulation, siding, and 1/2" drywall.
> Label and dimension. Add scale.

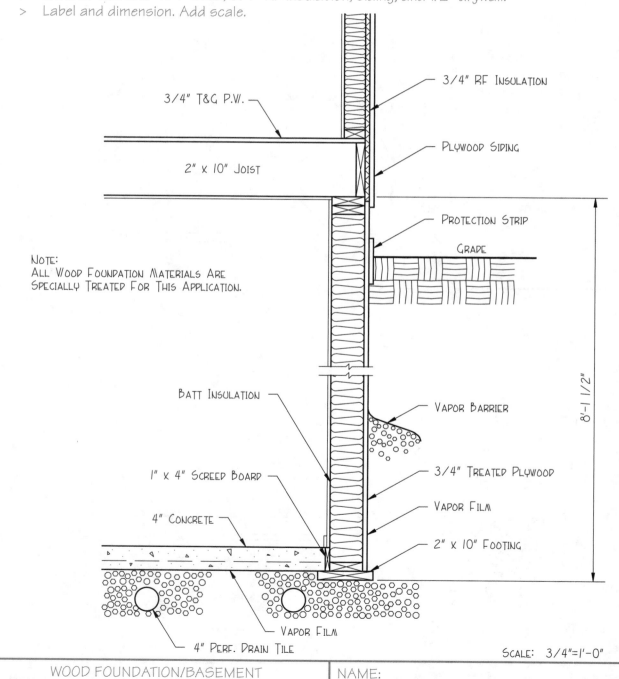

NOTE:
ALL WOOD FOUNDATION MATERIALS ARE SPECIALLY TREATED FOR THIS APPLICATION.

3/4" T&G P.W.

2" x 10" JOIST

3/4" RF INSULATION

PLYWOOD SIDING

PROTECTION STRIP

GRADE

BATT INSULATION

VAPOR BARRIER

1" x 4" SCREED BOARD

3/4" TREATED PLYWOOD

VAPOR FILM

4" CONCRETE

2" x 10" FOOTING

VAPOR FILM

4" PERF. DRAIN TILE

8'-1 1/2"

SCALE: 3/4"=1'-0"

| WOOD FOUNDATION/BASEMENT | NAME: | 11- |

Chapter 11 Pretest
Footings, Foundations, and Concrete

Name _____

Period _____**Date** _____**Score** _____

Completion

Complete each sentence with the proper response. Place your answer on the space provided.

1. The finished floor of a house should be at least _____ above the grade.

1. _____

2. The footing for a chimney is generally _____ thick.

2. _____

3. Excavating in _____ may be nearly vertical.

3. _____

4. Square corners of a rectangle may be laid out using the _____ unit method.

4. _____

5. Footings for most residential structures are made from _____.

5. _____

6. Residential footings should be at least _____ below the average maximum frost penetration.

6. _____

Multiple Choice

Choose the answer that correctly completes the statement. Write the corresponding letter in the space provided.

_____ 1. Concrete and masonry basement wall thickness depends on lateral earth pressure and _____.

    A. vertical load to be supported
    B. wishes of the builder
    C. weight of the foundation material
    D. None of the above.

_____ 2. The plot plan provides the necessary dimensions required for _____.

    A. locating all windows and doors on the plan
    B. building the house foundation
    C. securing a building permit
    D. staking out the location of the house on the site

_____ 3. A _____ point is needed to determine the depth of excavation and foundation wall height.

    A. rod
    B. stake
    C. clearance
    D. control

_____ 4. Nails and other fasteners used in an all-weather wood foundation should be made from _____.

    A. aluminum, silicon bronze, or copper
    B. brass, copper, or aluminum
    C. silicon bronze, copper, or hot-dipped zinc-coated steel
    D. copper, brass, or hot-dipped zinc-coated steel

_____ 5. Excavation for residential footings should extend down to a minimum of _____ into undisturbed earth.

    A. 2″
    B. 4″
    C. 6″
    D. 12″

_____ 6. The footing for a residential structure is generally _____ wide when the foundation wall is 8″ thick.

    A. 8″
    B. 10″
    C. 14″
    D. 16″

_____ 7. Stepped footings are frequently necessary when _____.

    A. the house has more than one floor level
    B. building on hilly terrain
    C. brick veneer is used
    D. two different materials are used

_____ 8. Steel reinforcing bar is required in footings:

    A. for all residential structures.
    B. when the house is built in the 100 year floodplain.
    C. located over soft or poorly drained soils.
    D. to prevent frost heave.

_____ 9. Foundation walls are the part of the house that extends _____.

    A. from the first floor to the footing
    B. from the first floor to the soffit
    C. from the frost line to the grade
    D. from the footing to the eaves line

_____ 10. In an AWWF foundation, all lumber and plywood that comes in contact with the ground should be pressure treated with _____.

    A. tar or other rot-resistant material
    B. waterborne preservative salts
    C. special caulking compounds
    D. kerosene

_____ 11. The exact location of a proposed house foundation is maintained through the use of _____.

    A. angle boards
    B. batter boards
    C. construction boards
    D. building boards

_____ 12. The _____ spreads the weight of a building over a broad area.

    A. floating slab
    B. footing
    C. site foundation
    D. reinforcing rod

Matching

Select the answer that correctly matches each term. Place your answer in the space provided.

A. Extension of a slab floor
B. Pressure-treated wood is used
C. Support for the foundation walls

D. The most common foundation type
E. Used to support a beam

_____ 1. Footings

_____ 2. All weather wood foundation

_____ 3. Pier and post foundations

_____ 4. Slab foundation

_____ 5. T-foundation

Short Answer

Answer the following questions.

1. What are the common ingredients in concrete? _____

_____

2. List three methods that might be used to strengthen a block foundation wall against strong earth pressures. _____

_____

3. Name the two basic types of loads that are imposed on a structure. _____

_____

4. Identify two methods for damp-proofing a cast concrete basement wall. _____

_____

5. Name the four types of lintels generally used in residential building construction.

_____

_____

_____

6. What are the actual dimensions of an 8″ × 8″ × 16″ concrete block? _____

_____

7. Which two types of steel beams are commonly used in residential construction?

_____

_____

Chapter 11 Posttest
Footings, Foundations, and Concrete

Name _____

Period _____**Date** _____**Score** _____

Completion
Complete each sentence with the proper response. Place your answer on the space provided.

1. Square corners of a rectangle may be laid out using the _____ unit method.

1. _____

2. The finished floor of a house should be at least _____ above the grade.

2. _____

3. Residential footings should be at least _____ below the average maximum frost penetration.

3. _____

4. Excavating in _____ may be nearly vertical.

4. _____

5. Footings for most residential structures are made from _____.

5. _____

6. The footing for a chimney is generally _____ thick.

6. _____

Multiple Choice
Choose the answer that correctly completes the statement. Write the corresponding letter in the space provided.

_____ 1. The plot plan provides the necessary dimensions required for _____.

    A. locating all windows and doors on the plan
    B. building the house foundation
    C. securing a building permit
    D. staking out the location of the house on the site

_____ 2. The exact location of a proposed house foundation is maintained through the use of _____.

    A. angle boards
    B. batter boards
    C. construction boards
    D. building boards

_____ 3. A _____ point is needed to determine the depth of excavation and foundation wall height.

    A. rod
    B. stake
    C. clearance
    D. control

_____ 4. Excavation for residential footings should extend down to a minimum of _____ into undisturbed earth.

    A. 2″
    B. 4″
    C. 6″
    D. 12″

_____ 5. The _____ spreads the weight of a building over a broad area.

    A. floating slab
    B. footing
    C. site foundation
    D. reinforcing rod

_____ 6. The footing for a residential structure is generally _____ wide when the foundation wall is 8″ thick.

    A. 8″
    B. 10″
    C. 14″
    D. 16″

_____ 7. Steel reinforcing bar is required in footings:

    A. for all residential structures.
    B. when the house is built in the 100 year floodplain.
    C. located over soft or poorly drained soils.
    D. to prevent frost heave.

_____ 8. Stepped footings are frequently necessary when _____.

    A. the house has more than one floor level
    B. building on hilly terrain
    C. brick veneer is used
    D. two different materials are used

_____ 9. Foundation walls are the part of the house that extends _____.

    A. from the first floor to the footing
    B. from the first floor to the soffit
    C. from the frost line to the grade
    D. from the footing to the eaves line

_____ 10. Nails and other fasteners used in an all-weather wood foundation should be made from _____.

    A. aluminum, silicon bronze, or copper
    B. brass, copper, or aluminum
    C. silicon bronze, copper, or hot-dipped zinc-coated steel
    D. copper, brass, or hot-dipped zinc-coated steel

_____ 11. In an AWWF foundation, all lumber and plywood that comes in contact with the ground should be pressure treated with _____.

    A. tar or other rot-resistant material
    B. waterborne preservative salts
    C. special caulking compounds
    D. kerosene

_____ 12. Concrete and masonry basement wall thickness depends on lateral earth pressure and _____.

    A. vertical load to be supported
    B. wishes of the builder
    C. weight of the foundation material
    D. None of the above.

Matching

Select the answer that correctly matches each term. Place your answer in the space provided.

A. Extension of a slab floor
B. Pressure-treated wood is used
C. Support for the foundation walls

D. The most common foundation type
E. Used to support a beam

_____ 1. All weather wood foundation

_____ 2. Slab foundation

_____ 3. T-foundation

_____ 4. Pier and post foundations

_____ 5. Footings

Short Answer

Answer the following questions.

1. List three methods that might be used to strengthen a block foundation wall against strong earth pressures. _____

_____

_____

2. Identify two methods for damp-proofing a cast concrete basement wall. _____

_____

3. Which two types of steel beams are commonly used in residential construction?

_____

_____

4. Name the two basic types of loads that are imposed on a structure. _____

_____

5. Name the four types of lintels generally used in residential building construction.

_____

_____

_____

6. What are the common ingredients in concrete? _____

_____

_____

7. What are the actual dimensions of an 8″ × 8″ × 16″ concrete block? _____

_____

The Foundation Plan

12

Objectives

After studying this chapter, the student will be able to:

- Identify the primary features included in a foundation plan.
- Discuss the difference between a foundation plan and a basement plan.
- Design and draw a foundation plan for a typical residential structure using traditional or CADD methods.

Displays

1. **Types of Foundations.** Select a foundation plan that includes a basement, crawl space, and slab construction for display on the bulletin board. Emphasize the different types of foundation construction through the use of titles and different colors.
2. **Types of Framing.** Display foundation wall details of for both platform framing and solid sill and balloon framing construction. Label each detail as to the type of framing and sill construction.

Instructional Materials

Text: Pages 259–271
    Review Questions, Suggested Activities
Workbook: Pages 137–146
    Review Questions, Problems/Activities
Teacher's Resources:
    Chapter 12 Pretest
    Chapter 12 Teaching Strategy
    Chapter 12 Posttest

Teaching Strategy

- **Knowledge Assessment:** Administer the Chapter 12 Pretest. Correct the test and return. Highlight the topics in which the individual student is deficient.
- Prepare Display #1.
- Review the chapter objectives.
- Discuss the definition and purpose of the foundation plan.
- Display symbols commonly used on a foundation plan.
- Present the preliminary steps to drawing a foundation plan.
- Discuss drawing a foundation plan.
- Prepare Display #2.
- Assign workbook Problems/Activities 12-1 and 12-2.
- Assign one or more of the Suggested Activities in the text.
- **Chapter Review:** Assign the Review Questions in the text. Discuss the correct answers. Assign the Review Questions in the workbook. Have students check their own answers. Make a transparency of solution to Problem/Activity 12-1 and use for review.
- **Evaluation:** Administer Chapter 12 Posttest. Correct the test and return. Return graded problems with comments.

Answers to Review Questions, Text

Page 271

1. It is a plan view drawing, in section, that provides all of the information necessary to construct the foundation.
2. 1/4″ = 1′-0″
3. Answer may contain any eight of the following: Footings for foundation walls; foundation walls; piers for posts and columns; posts and columns; dwarf walls; partial walls, doors, and bath fixtures in the basement; openings in the foundation wall, such as for windows, doors, and vents; beams and pilasters; direction, size, and spacing of floor joists or trusses; drains and sump; details of foundation and footing construction; complete dimensions and notes; scale of the drawing.
4. Excavators, masons, carpenters, and cement workers who build the foundation.
5. floor plan; plot plan; elevations
6. 4″

7. Type of exterior walls for the structure, maximum frost penetration depth, and soil bearing capacity.
8. centerline
9. different materials
10. It is a combination foundation and floor plan that shows interior walls, stairs, windows, and doors in the basement in addition to the foundation details.
11. Because the depth of frost penetration is so great and footings must be below that depth, not much additional cost is required to excavate to the depth required for a basement.
12. By making a copy of the floor plan on the foundation plan layer and then turning off the floor plan layer.
13. By inserting symbols.
14. The plan is drawn at full scale; objects are always drawn at full scale in CADD and then plotted at the required scale.
15. foundation plan; basement floor plan

Answers to Workbook Questions
Page 137

Part I: Short Answer/Listing

1. Floor plan, plot plan, and elevations.
2. Answer may include any five: Footings for foundation walls, piers, and columns; foundation walls; piers and columns (posts); dwarf walls; partial walls, doors, and bath fixtures in the basement; openings in the foundation wall, such as for windows, doors, and vents; beams and pilasters; direction, size, and spacing of floor joists or trusses; drains and sump; details of foundation and footing construction; complete dimensions and notes; and scale of the drawing.
3. Because the dimensions of the foundation may not be the same for different types of exterior walls.
4. Select the scale to be used.
5. Foundation plan and floor plan.
6. A. Concrete block.
   B. Cast concrete.
   C. Cinder concrete.
   D. Common brick.
   E. Face brick.
   F. Firebrick.
   G. Cut stone.
   H. Rubble.
   I. Slate.
   J. Structural clay tile.
   K. Gravel.
   L. Sand.
   M. Earth.
   N. Rock.
   O. Flashing.
7. It reduces both errors and the time required to make the drawing.
8. C.
9. To their centers.
10. The basement/foundation plan shows interior walls, stairs, windows, and doors in the basement.
11. Check the drawing to see that all necessary information is included.
12. If a separate basement electrical plan is not drawn.

Part II: Completion

1. split-level
2. columns (posts)
3. masons
4. basements
5. floor
6. 1/4" = 1'-0"
7. hidden
8. centers
9. edge
10. plot
11. less

Part III: Multiple Choice

1. B. Mr. Jones's foundation will be 8" longer and wider than Ms. Smith's because a brick veneer house needs a 4" ledge on all four sides.
2. D. All of the above.
3. A. The drawing is created at full scale.
4. D. Look over the plan to be sure it is complete.

Part IV: Matching

1. E. Soil bearing test.
2. C. Foundation details.
3. D. Material symbols.
4. A. Dwarf walls.
5. F. Windows or doors.
6. B. Concrete block symbol.

Part V: Problems/Activities
1. Solution on page 234 of this manual.
2. Solution on page 235 of this manual.

Answers to Chapter 12 Pretest
Completion
1. foundation plan
2. hatch patterns (section symbols)
3. hidden
4. 1/4″ = 1′-0″
5. Dwarf

Multiple Choice
1. B. 24″
2. D. All of the above.
3. C. 4″
4. A. footings, piers, columns, foundation walls, and supporting beams
5. D. sump
6. A. a combination foundation plan and floor plan
7. C. outside of the rough stud wall
8. B. basements are popular in areas where space is crowded and sites are small

Answers to Chapter 12 Posttest
Completion
1. 1/4″ = 1′-0″
2. hatch patterns (section symbols)
3. Dwarf
4. foundation plan
5. hidden

Multiple Choice
1. A. footings, piers, columns, foundation walls, and supporting beams
2. D. All of the above.
3. D. sump
4. C. 4″
5. C. outside of the rough stud wall
6. B. 24″
7. B. basements are popular in areas where space is crowded and sites are small
8. A. a combination foundation plan and floor plan

1.

12-1

Directions:

Use the floor plan of the garden house below to construct a thickened-edge slab foundation in the space provided. Scale is 1/4″ = 1′-0″. Include the following elements in your drawing:

> Thickness of foundation wall (8″) and slab floor (4″).
> Anchor bolts (1/2″ × 8″) at least every 4 feet along perimeter.
> Cutting plane through one foundation wall. Draw the section and dimension it. Foundation depth should be at least 24″ or frost depth for your area.

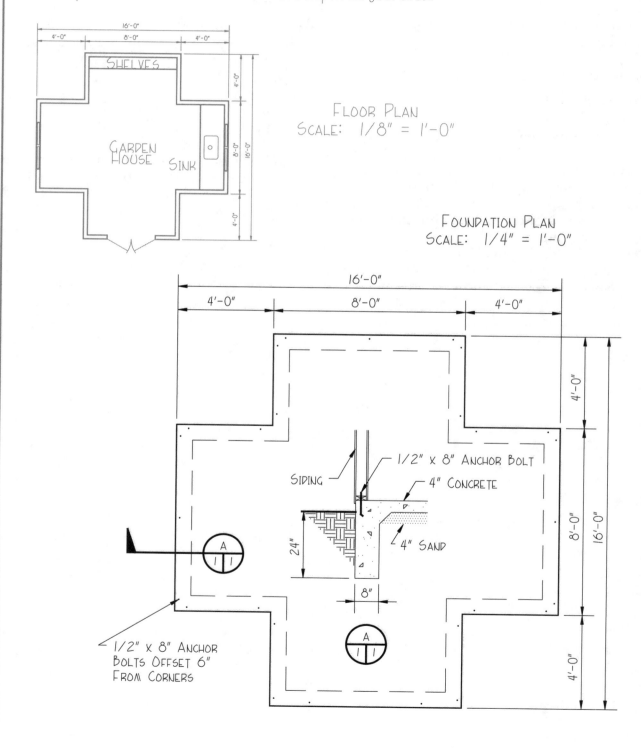

FLOOR PLAN
SCALE: 1/8″ = 1′-0″

FOUNDATION PLAN
SCALE: 1/4″ = 1′-0″

FOUNDATION PLAN   NAME:

26'-0"
5'-0"
4'-0"
17'-0"
2'-0"
6'-0"
4'-0"
3'-0"
36'-0"
21'-0"
56'-0"
20'-0"

8" x 8" W BEAM
31#/FT.

8" x 8" BEAM NOTCH

RECREATION ROOM
16'-2" X 24'-4"
15'-2"

11'-2"
13'-2"
11'-2"

3'-6"
2'-0"
3'-3 1/2"
4'-2 1/2"

WATER
W.H.

DRYER
WASHER
TUB
CABINETS

UTILITY/STORAGE
11'-2" X 19'-2"
DRAIN/SUMP

FURNACE

24" SQ. FOOTING

3" STEEL COLUMN

HOBBY ROOM
13'-2" X 19'-2"

ELECTRICAL PANEL

UP

8'-0"

2'-2"
10"
2'-0"

16" O.C.
2" x 10" FLOOR JOISTS

PORCH
UNEXCAVATED

10"

5'-0"
14'-0"
56'-0"
10'-0"
3'-0"
4'-0"
3'-0"
3'-0"

4" CONCRETE WITH REINFORCING

FLOOR DRAIN

GARAGE
20'-0" x 26'-0"

UNEXCAVATED

19'-0"
26'-0"
10"

SCALE: 1/4" = 1'-0"

12-2

BASEMENT/FOUNDATION PLAN

Chapter 12 Pretest
The Foundation Plan

Name _____

Period _____**Date** _____**Score** _____

Completion
Complete each sentence with the proper response. Place your answer on the space provided.

1. The direction of floor joists or trusses is shown on the _____.

1. _____

2. Various materials are shown on a foundation plan using different _____.

2. _____

3. Footings are represented on the foundation plan using a(n) _____ line.

3. _____

4. The scale of most residential floor plans is _____.

4. _____

5. _____ walls are built to retain an excavation or embankment.

5. _____

Multiple Choice
Choose the answer that correctly completes the statement. Write the corresponding letter in the space provided.

_____ 1. Floor trusses are generally spaced _____ OC.

    A. 12"
    B. 24"
    C. 16"
    D. 30"

_____ 2. The foundation plan is drawn from information presented on the _____.

    A. floor plan
    B. plot plan
    C. elevations
    D. All of the above.

_____ 3. The brick ledge is generally _____ wide.

    A. 1"
    B. 2"
    C. 4"
    D. 6"

_____ 4. The foundation plan is a plan view drawing, in section, that shows the location and size of _____.

    A. footings, piers, columns, foundation walls, and supporting beams
    B. supporting beams, footings, piers, first floor walls, and columns
    C. all parts of the structure above the grade
    D. All of the above.

_____ 5. When groundwater is present, a _____ is generally required to prevent water in the basement.

    A. dry well
    B. tight basement wall
    C. thicker footing
    D. sump

_____ 6. The basement plan is _____.

    A. a combination foundation plan and floor plan
    B. no different than a foundation plan
    C. easier to draw than a foundation plan
    D. required for all houses

_____ 7. A brick veneer structure is dimensioned to the _____.

    A. outside of the brick veneer
    B. inside of the brick veneer
    C. outside of the rough stud wall
    D. inside of the rough stud wall

_____ 8. One reason why a house may have a basement is that _____.

    A. basements add no cost to price of a house
    B. basements are popular in areas where space is crowded and sites are small
    C. some codes require each house to have a basement
    D. heat loss is reduced

Chapter 12 Posttest
The Foundation Plan

Name _____

Period _____ **Date** _____ **Score** _____

Completion

Complete each sentence with the proper response. Place your answer on the space provided.

1. The scale of most residential floor plans is _____.

    1. _____

2. Various materials are shown on a foundation plan using different _____.

    2. _____

3. _____ walls are built to retain an excavation or embankment.

    3. _____

4. The direction of floor joists or trusses is shown on the _____.

    4. _____

5. Footings are represented on the foundation plan using a(n) _____ line.

    5. _____

Multiple Choice

Choose the answer that correctly completes the statement. Write the corresponding letter in the space provided.

_____ 1. The foundation plan is a plan view drawing, in section, that shows the location and size of _____.

    A. footings, piers, columns, foundation walls, and supporting beams
    B. supporting beams, footings, piers, first floor walls, and columns
    C. all parts of the structure above the grade
    D. All of the above.

_____ 2. The foundation plan is drawn from information presented on the _____.

    A. floor plan
    B. plot plan
    C. elevations
    D. All of the above.

_____ 3. When groundwater is present, a _____ is generally required to prevent water in the basement.

    A. dry well
    B. tight basement wall
    C. thicker footing
    D. sump

_____ 4. The brick ledge is generally _____ wide.

    A. 1″
    B. 2″
    C. 4″
    D. 6″

_____ 5. A brick veneer structure is dimensioned to the _____.

    A. outside of the brick veneer
    B. inside of the brick veneer
    C. outside of the rough stud wall
    D. inside of the rough stud wall

_____ 6. Floor trusses are generally spaced _____ OC.

    A. 12″
    B. 24″
    C. 16″
    D. 30″

_____ 7. One reason why a house may have a basement is that _____.

    A. basements add no cost to price of a house
    B. basements are popular in areas where space is crowded and sites are small
    C. some codes require each house to have a basement
    D. heat loss is reduced

_____ 8. The basement plan is _____.

    A. a combination foundation plan and floor plan
    B. no different than a foundation plan
    C. easier to draw than a foundation plan
    D. required for all houses

Sill and Floor Construction

Objectives

After studying this chapter, the student will be able to:
- Explain the difference between platform and balloon framing.
- Plan the appropriate floor support using joists or trusses for a structure.
- Determine proper joist sizes using a typical span data chart.
- Describe the components of a floor system.
- Explain the principles of post and beam construction.
- Select the appropriate engineered wood products for specific applications in residential construction.

Displays

1. **Sill Construction**. Build a scale model of each of the following types of sill construction: Box sill, solid sill, and T-sill. Use a 1″ = 1′-0″ scale. Refer to Figures 13-1 and 13-4 in the text.
2. **Definition of Terms**. Prepare a bulletin board display consisting of terms pertaining to sill and floor construction. Use the terms identified in Activity #2 in the Suggested Activities in the text.

Instructional Materials

Text: Pages 273–296
   Review Questions, Suggested Activities
Workbook: Pages 147–158
   Questions, Problems/Activities
Teacher's Resources:
   Chapter 13 Pretest
   Chapter 13 Teaching Strategy
   Chapter 13 Posttest

Teaching Strategy

- **Knowledge Assessment:** Administer the Chapter 13 Pretest. Correct the test and return. Highlight the topics in which the individual student is deficient.
- Prepare Display #1.
- Review the chapter objectives.
- Discuss platform and balloon framing.
- Assign Problem 13-1 in the workbook.
- Prepare Display #2.
- Discuss joists and beams.
- Assign Problem 13-2 in the workbook.
- Discuss floor trusses.
- Discuss subfloors, cantilevered joists, and framing under slate or tile.
- Assign Problem 13-3 in the workbook.
- Discuss post and beam construction.
- Assign one or more of the Suggested Activities in the text.
- Review new terms presented in the chapter.
- **Chapter Review:** Assign the Review Questions in the text. Discuss the correct answers. Assign the questions in the workbook. Have students check their own answers. Make a transparency of the solution to Problem 13-1 in the workbook and use for review.
- **Evaluation:** Administer the Chapter 13 Posttest. Correct the test and return. Return graded problems with comments.

Answers to Review Questions, Text

Page 294

1. platform, balloon
2. sill
3. 1-1/2″ × 5-1/2″
4. box
5. solid (standard) sill, T-sill
6. Small potential for shrinkage and good vertical stability.
7. joists
8. Answer may include any three of the following: Southern yellow pine, fir, larch, hemlock, and spruce.
9. 16″
10. 15 percent to 19 percent
11. 2″ × 8″
12. spread the load over a larger area

13. 1/2" (or 5/8")
14. Plywood, composite board, waferboard, oriented strand board, and structural particleboard.
15. Answer may include any four of the following: They provide clear spans with a minimum of depth; they have a lightweight assembly; they are easy to handle; they reduce sound transmission through the floor/ceiling assemblies; and they make the installation of plumbing, heating, and electrical systems easy.
16. So that the floor/ceiling will be level once the load of the house is applied.
17. cantilever
18. Posts, beams, and planks.
19. Solid, laminated, reinforced with steel, and plywood box.
20. longitudinal, transverse
21. 2", 3", and 4"
22. Ridge-type insulation.
23. There is a lack of industry standards.
24. swelling
25. Beams, columns, and headers.
26. 66
27. The plies in LVL are parallel rather than perpendicular.
28. Industrial, architectural, and premium.
29. 66

Answers to Workbook Questions
Page 147

Part I: Short Answer/Listing

1. Plates, joists, and studs.
2. Answer may include any three of the following: It is compatible for both one- and two-story buildings, it is easy and fast to construct, shrinkage is uniform throughout the structure, the platform automatically provides a fire-stop between floors, and construction is safe because the work is performed on solid surfaces.
3. The sill.
4. Joists.
5. Stairs and chimneys.
6. A less-than-desirable surface on which to work during construction and the need to add fire-stops.
7. The wall studs rest directly on the sill plate.

8. Solid or standard sill construction and T-sill construction.
9. The length of the span, the load to be supported, the species and grade of wood, and the distance the joists are spaced apart.
10. The allowable span is 21'-1".
11. The large size of the sheets and the comparatively short time required to nail the sheets.
12. Plywood, composite board, waferboard, oriented strand board, and structural particleboard.
13. Reduce the size of the joists and the spacing between joists or use one or more beams under the section.
14. The maximum allowable span is generally 7'-0".
15. A continuous wall or a series of piers on which each post is located.
16. A 5-1/4" × 13-1/2" beam is needed. It will support 316 pounds per linear foot over a span of 24'-0".
17. A. Solid beam.
    B. Horizontal laminated beam.
    C. Vertical laminated beam.
    D. Steel reinforced beam.
    E. Box beam.
18. Answer may include any two of the following: Southern yellow pine, fir, larch, hemlock, and spruce.
19. Trusses provide clear spans with a minimum of depth, they have a lightweight assembly, they are easy to handle, and the open web construction reduces sound transmission and makes the installation of plumbing, heating, and electrical systems easy.
20. There is a lack of industry standards.
21. The main difference between plywood and LVL is that the plies are parallel in LVL, rather than perpendicular, to maximize strength.

Part II: Completion

1. right angles
2. wall
3. floor
4. box
5. header
6. 1-1/2" × 9-1/4"
7. header

8. 4'
9. header
10. vertical
11. 3/4" × 5-1/2"
12. trusses
13. frame
14. solid blocking
15. stress
16. 2" × 4"
17. supported
18. underlayment
19. expansion
20. beams
21. 4"
22. planks

Part III: Multiple Choice
1. A. 1-1/2" × 5-1/2"
2. B. Headers are not required.
3. C. 16"
4. D. All of the above.
5. C. 24"
6. A. 25
7. D. All of the above.
8. C. posts
9. B. soil bearing capacity

Part IV: Matching
1. D. Engineered wood floor trusses
2. B. Built-in camber
3. C. Cantilevered joists
4. A. A special type of concrete
5. F. Post and beam construction
6. G. Transverse method
7. E. Metal plates

Part V: Problems/Activities
1. Solution on page 245 of this manual.
2. Solution on page 246 of this manual.
3. Solution on page 247 of this manual.

Answers to Chapter 13 Pretest
Completion
1. sill
2. softwood
3. platform
4. 24"
5. Balloon

Multiple Choice
1. B. twice
2. C. box sill

3. C. 1-1/2" × 11-1/4"
4. D. All of the above.
5. A. 1/360th
6. B. 2 to 4
7. A. doubled
8. B. 2" × 6"
9. C. camber
10. D. stress-graded
11. C. balloon
12. C. 24"
13. A. posts

Short Answer
1. Small potential shrinkage and good vertical stability.
2. Posts, beams, and planks.
3. Platform framing and balloon framing.
4. Ceramic tile, slate, and stone.
5. Plates, joists, and studs.
6. To stiffen the floor and to spread the load over a broader area.
7. The length of the span, the load to be supported, the species and grade of wood, and the distance the joists are spaced apart.

Answers to Chapter 13 Posttest
Completion
1. platform
2. sill
3. Balloon
4. softwood
5. 24"

Multiple Choice
1. D. All of the above.
2. B. 2" × 6"
3. C. box sill
4. C. balloon
5. C. 1-1/2" × 11-1/4"
6. A. 1/360th
7. A. doubled
8. C. camber
9. D. stress-graded
10. C. 24"
11. B. twice
12. A. posts
13. B. 2 to 4

Short Answer
1. Platform framing and balloon framing.
2. Plates, joists, and studs.

3. Small potential shrinkage and good vertical stability.
4. The length of the span, the load to be supported, the species and grade of wood, and the distance the joists are spaced apart.
5. To stiffen the floor and to spread the load over a broader area.
6. Ceramic tile, slate, and stone.
7. Posts, beams, and planks.

Workbook Solution

Directions:
Using guidelines and proper form, label and dimension the basement wall section below using the following information:

> Footing is 12″ × 24″ with two 1/2″ rebars and drain tile in pea gravel.
> Basement floor is 4″ thick with a 4″ sand base and 3/8″ expansion joint.
> Basement wall is 12″ concrete block with a 1/2″ parge coat outside.
> Distance from the top of the footing to grade (224.2′ elevation) is 8′-8″.
> Distance from the floor to the underside of 24″ trusses is 8′-2″.
> Anchor bolts are 1/2″ × 16″ spaced 8′-0″ apart.
> Flooring material on the first floor is 3/4″ T&G P.W.
> Stud wall is covered with 3/4″ RF insulation and panel siding.

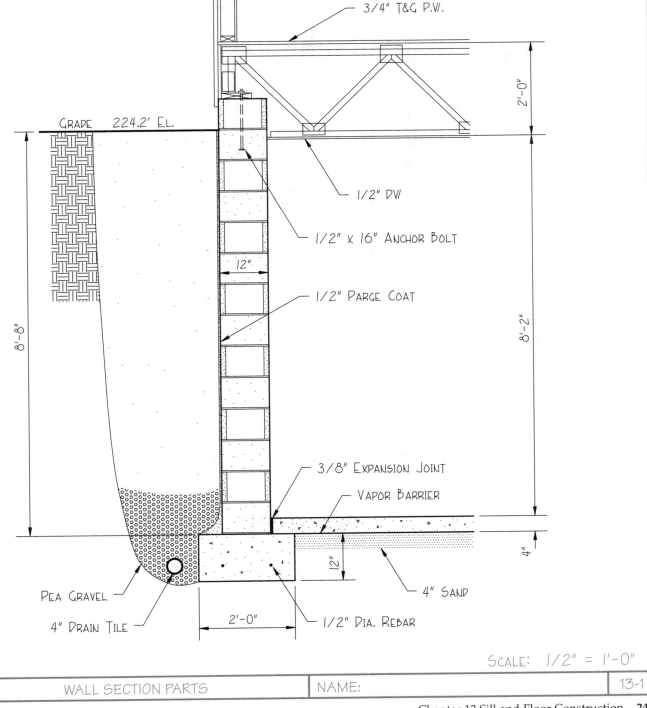

SCALE: 1/2″ = 1′-0″

WALL SECTION PARTS	NAME:	13-1

Workbook Solution

2.

Directions:
Complete the floor framing problems below as indicated.

A. Draw the framing to allow for an opening 40″ × 36″ centered in the floor area. The shortest dimension is parallel to the joist direction. Use double headers and double trimmers. Dimension the opening and label the joists.

B. Plan the joist layout (16″ OC) for the area between existing joists and 2′ beyond the foundation wall. Label parts and show the dimensions.

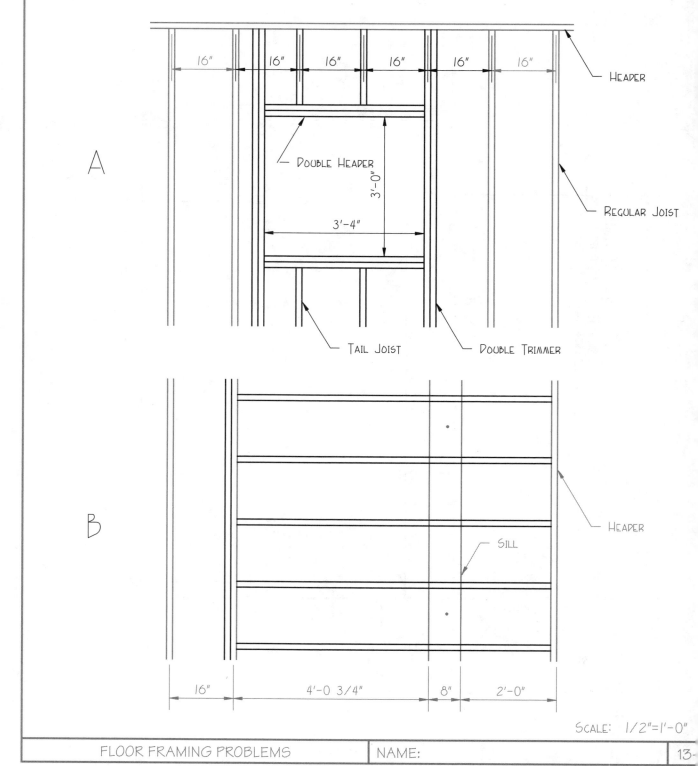

A

16″ 16″ 16″ 16″ 16″ 16″

HEADER

DOUBLE HEADER

3′-0″

3′-4″

REGULAR JOIST

TAIL JOIST

DOUBLE TRIMMER

B

HEADER

SILL

16″ 4′-0 3/4″ 8″ 2′-0″

SCALE: 1/2″=1′-0″

FLOOR FRAMING PROBLEMS   NAME: 13-

ASSIGNMENT 13-3

3/4" R.F. INSULATION

1/2" DRYWALL

4" GARAGE FLOOR

4" SAND

3/4" T&G P.W.

SCALE: 1/2"=1'-0"

1/2" x 8" ANCHOR BOLT

FLOATING SLAB FLOOR

2" x 8" TREATED SILL

2" x 10" JOIST 16" O.C.

8'-8 1/2"
STAIRWELL OPENING

36"

2" CLEARANCE

4" x 8" S BEAM

2'-8" x 10'-4"
CHIMNEY OPENING

NOTE: FRAMING MATERIALS ARE #2 DOUGLAS FIR

FLOOR FRAMING PLAN

SCALE: 1/4"=1'-0"

Chapter 13 Pretest
Sill and Floor Construction

Name _____

Period _____ **Date** _____ **Score** _____

Completion
Complete each sentence with the proper response. Place your answer on the space provided.

1. A(n) _____ is the lowest member of the frame of a structure.

2. Floor joists are generally made from a common _____.

3. Shrinkage is uniform throughout the structure when _____ framing is used.

4. Floor joists are usually spaced 12", 16", or _____ on center (OC).

5. _____ framing was once used extensively, but in recent years has diminished in importance.

1. _____

2. _____

3. _____

4. _____

5. _____

Multiple Choice
Choose the answer that correctly completes the statement. Write the corresponding letter in the space provided.

_____ 1. A rule of thumb to follow in determining the necessary length of cantilevered joists is to extend the joists inside at least _____ the distance they overhang outside.

    A. the same length as
    B. twice
    C. three times
    D. four times

_____ 2. Platform framing utilizes a method of sill construction known as _____ construction.

    A. solid sill
    B. T-sill
    C. box sill
    D. standard sill

_____ 3. The actual size of a 2" × 12" floor joist is _____.

    A. 1-5/8" × 11-5/8"
    B. 1-1/2" × 11-1/2"
    C. 1-1/2" × 11-1/4"
    D. 2" × 12"

_____ 4. One advantage of platform framing is _____.

    A. a fire-stop is automatically provided
    B. construction is safe because the work is performed on solid surfaces
    C. it is easy and fast to construct
    D. All of the above.

_____ 5. A maximum allowable deflection of _____ the span (with a normal live load) is specified for floor joists.

    A. 1/360th
    B. 1/280th
    C. 1/100th
    D. 1/10th

_____ 6. Decking planks for the roof and floor of a post and beam structure range in thickness from _____ inches.

    A. 1 to 2
    B. 2 to 4
    C. 4 to 6
    D. 6 to 8

_____ 7. Floor joists should be _____ under partition walls that run parallel to the joists.

    A. doubled
    B. tripled
    C. turned on their sides
    D. None of the above.

_____ 8. The sill plate in most residential construction is _____.

    A. $2'' \times 4''$
    B. $2'' \times 6''$
    C. $2'' \times 8''$
    D. $2'' \times 10''$

_____ 9. Wood floor trusses have a built-in _____ so that the floor will be level when the load is applied.

    A. bow
    B. twist
    C. camber
    D. wind

_____ 10. Wood floor trusses use _____ lumber so that a minimum of material may be used.

    A. hardwood
    B. construction grade
    C. air-dried
    D. stress-graded

_____ 11. T-sill construction is used with _____ framing.

    A. platform
    B. barn
    C. balloon
    D. All of the above.

_____ 12. Wood floor trusses are usually spaced _____ on center (OC).

    A. 12"
    B. 16"
    C. 24"
    D. 36"

_____ 13. Most of the weight of a post and beam building is carried by the _____.
    A. posts
    B. beams
    C. sills
    D. curtain walls

Short Answer

Provide brief answers to the following questions.

1. List two advantages of balloon framing. _____
_____
_____

2. Identify the three large framing members used in post and beam construction.
_____
_____

3. List the two basic types of floor framing. _____
_____

4. List three floor materials that generally require a substantial base. _____
_____
_____

5. Identify the three structural components used in floor framing. _____
_____
_____

6. List two reasons why bridging is used with floor joists. _____
_____
_____

7. The size of floor joist required for a given situation will depend on four factors. Name them.
_____
_____
_____
_____

Chapter 13 Posttest
Sill and Floor Construction

Name _____

Period _____Date _____Score _____

Completion

Complete each sentence with the proper response. Place your answer on the space provided.

1. Shrinkage is uniform throughout the structure when _____ framing is used.

1. _____

2. A(n) _____ is the lowest member of the frame of a structure.

2. _____

3. _____ framing was once used extensively, but in recent years has diminished in importance.

3. _____

4. Floor joists are generally made from a common _____.

4. _____

5. Floor joists are usually spaced 12″, 16″, or _____ on center (OC).

5. _____

Multiple Choice

Choose the answer that correctly completes the statement. Write the corresponding letter in the space provided.

_____ 1. One advantage of platform framing is _____.

    A. a fire-stop is automatically provided
    B. construction is safe because the work is performed on solid surfaces
    C. it is easy and fast to construct
    D. All of the above.

_____ 2. The sill plate in most residential construction is _____.

    A. 2″ × 4″
    B. 2″ × 6″
    C. 2″ × 8″
    D. 2″ × 10″

_____ 3. Platform framing utilizes a method of sill construction known as _____ construction.

    A. solid sill
    B. T-sill
    C. box sill
    D. standard sill

_____ 4. T-sill construction is used with _____ framing.

    A. platform
    B. barn
    C. balloon
    D. All of the above.

_____ 5. The actual size of a 2″ × 12″ floor joist is _____.

    A. 1-5/8″ × 11-5/8″
    B. 1-1/2″ × 11-1/2″
    C. 1-1/2″ × 11-1/4″
    D. 2″ × 12″

_____ 6. A maximum allowable deflection of _____ the span (with a normal live load) is specified for floor joists.

    A. 1/360th
    B. 1/280th
    C. 1/100th
    D. 1/10th

_____ 7. Floor joists should be _____ under partition walls that run parallel to the joists.

    A. doubled
    B. tripled
    C. turned on their sides
    D. None of the above.

_____ 8. Wood floor trusses have a built-in _____ so that the floor will be level when the load is applied.

    A. bow
    B. twist
    C. camber
    D. wind

_____ 9. Wood floor trusses use _____ lumber so that a minimum of material may be used.

    A. hardwood
    B. construction grade
    C. air-dried
    D. stress-graded

_____ 10. Wood floor trusses are usually spaced _____ on center (OC).

    A. 12″
    B. 16″
    C. 24″
    D. 36″

_____ 11. A rule of thumb to follow in determining the necessary length of cantilevered joists is to extend the joists inside at least _____ the distance they overhang outside.

    A. the same length as
    B. twice
    C. three times
    D. four times

_____ 12. Most of the weight of a post and beam building is carried by the _____.

    A. posts
    B. beams
    C. sills
    D. curtain walls

_____ 13. Decking planks for the roof and floor of a post and beam structure range in thickness from _____ inches.

    A. 1 to 2
    B. 2 to 4
    C. 4 to 6
    D. 6 to 8

Short Answer

Provide brief answers to the following questions.

1. List the two basic types of floor framing. _____

2. Identify the three structural components used in floor framing. _____

3. List two advantages of balloon framing. _____

4. The size of floor joist required for a given situation will depend on four factors. Name them.

5. List two reasons why bridging is used with floor joists. _____

6. List three floor materials that generally require a substantial base. _____

7. Identify the three large framing members used in post and beam construction.

Wall and Ceiling Construction

Objectives

After studying this chapter, the student will be able to:
- List the members of a typical frame wall.
- Explain methods of frame wall construction.
- Explain information shown on a ceiling joist span data chart.
- Sketch the various types of exterior walls used in residential construction.
- Explain the applications, advantages, and disadvantages of steel framing in residential construction.
- Identify the basic processes used to produce a quality, three-coat stucco finish.

Displays

1. **Wall Construction Details**. Create a bulletin board arrangement of photos and/or details of frame wall construction showing construction members.
2. **Wall Sections**. Display student work from Suggested Activity #1 in the text.
3. **Construction Materials**. Display a collection of typical materials used in light frame wall and ceiling construction. Label each sample.
4. **Brick Bonds**. Prepare a bulletin board arrangement consisting of photos of brick bonds submitted by students for Suggested Activity #6 in the text.

Instructional Materials

Text: Pages 297–318
   Review Questions, Suggested Activities
Workbook: Pages 159–168
   Questions, Problems/Activities
Teacher's Resources:
   Chapter 14 Pretest
   Chapter 14 Teaching Strategy
   Chapter 14 Posttest

Teaching Strategy

- **Knowledge Assessment:** Administer the Chapter 14 Pretest. Correct the test and return. Highlight the topics in which the individual student is deficient.
- Prepare Display #1.
- Review the chapter objectives.
- Present frame wall construction. Compare and contrast platform framing and balloon framing. Assign one Suggested Activity in the text.
- Prepare Display #2 and/or #3.
- Assign Problem 14-1 in the workbook.
- Discuss ceiling construction.
- Discuss masonry wall construction.
- Assign Problem 14-2 in the workbook.
- Illustrate how the top plate is attached to a masonry wall.
- Prepare Display #4.
- Discuss brick names and sizes.
- Assign one or more of the remaining Suggested Activities in the text.
- **Chapter Review:** Assign the Review Questions in the text. Discuss the correct answers. Assign the questions in the workbook. Have students check their own answers. Make transparencies of the solutions to Problems 14-1 and 14-2 in the workbook and use for review.
- **Evaluation:** Administer the Chapter 14 Posttest. Correct the test and return. Return graded problems with comments.

Answers to Review Questions, Text

Page 317

1. The load to be supported, span, wood species, spacing of joists, and grade of lumber used.
2. Sole plate, top plates, studs, bracing, and headers.
3. It must have good stiffness and nail-holding properties, be free from warp, and be easy to work.

4. Answer may include any three of the following: Douglas fir, southern yellow pine, hemlock, spruce, and larch.
5. between 15% and 19%
6. 8'-0"
7. header, lintel
8. Reduced construction time.
9. cripple studs
10. 6'-10"
11. 2" × 10"
12. Openings for heating ducts, wall backing for various fixtures, and extra support for the bathtub. Also acceptable: Access hole and bay window.
13. bond multiple thicknesses of the wall together
14. 16", 32"
15. 8"
16. cavity
17. firecut
18. ashlar, rubble
19. 1"
20. anchor bolts and nuts
21. clay
22. face bricks, common bricks
23. common
24. The rising cost of construction lumber, the declining quality of construction lumber, the better performance of steel frame structures during hurricanes and earthquakes, and environmental concerns—steel is recyclable.
25. It is recyclable.
26. They are used for nonbearing interior partitions.
27. A coating applied to the outside of the structure.
28. 100
29. rigid
30. water
31. caulk

Answers to Workbook Questions
Page 159
Part I: Matching
1. G. Sole plate
2. H. Subfloor
3. D. Cripples
4. I. Trimmers
5. B. Ceiling joists
6. A. Ashlar stonework
7. F. Rubble stonework
8. K. Veneer
9. E. Flashing
10. C. Common brick
11. J. Stucco

Part II: Multiple Choice
1. A. southern yellow pine
2. B. sole plate
3. A. Fastening a 2" × 6" to cross blocking.
4. B. The size of the material used.
5. C. openings wider than 8'-0"
6. D. All of the above.
7. B. The veneer does not support the weight of the wall.
8. A. face brick

Part III: Completion
1. prefabrication
2. Number 2
3. nailer
4. 8'-0"
5. reduced
6. floor
7. header
8. slope
9. double
10. cantilevered
11. 32"
12. frame
13. shields
14. 100

Part IV: Short Answer/Listing
1. Frame, masonry, and combination frame and masonry.
2. 1" × 4" stock, metal strap, and plywood sheathing.
3. To allow for the thickness of sheathing, weatherboard, or rigid foam insulation.
4. In solid blocking construction.
5. The length is equal to the width of the opening plus the thickness of the two trimmers.
6. In ceiling joist construction, a header is not placed around the perimeter. Smaller lumber is also used in ceiling joist construction than in floor joist construction.
7. Advantages include relatively low expense to construct and the variety of

textures and designs possible. The disadvantage is the necessity of using furring strips for interior walls of drywall, plaster, or paneling.

8. Better insulation, less expensive to construct, and fewer construction problems.
9. A. Running bond
   B. Common bond
   C. Stack bond
   D. Flemish bond
10. The rising cost of construction lumber, the declining quality of construction lumber, the better performance of steel frame structures during destructive events such as hurricanes and earthquakes, and environmental concerns (steel is recyclable).

Part V: Problems/Activities

1. Solution on page 258 of this manual.
2. Solution on page 259 of this manual.

Answers to Chapter 14 Pretest

Completion

1. bracing
2. 15, 19
3. 8'-0"
4. sole
5. cripple

Multiple Choice

1. C. 8'-1 1/2"
2. B. access hole
3. C. 8"
4. C. 6'-10"
5. A. veneer
6. C. southern yellow pine
7. D. bonded

Short Answer

1. common bond
2. Answer may include any eight of the following: Flush, raked, extruded, weathered, beaded, struck, concave, V-shaped, and grapevine.
3. face brick, common brick

4. Stretcher, header, rowlock stretcher, soldier, rowlock, and sailor.
5. ashlar, rubble
6. The load to be supported, span distance, wood species, spacing of joists, and grade of lumber used.
7. The sole plate, top plates, studs, headers, and bracing.
8. Frame, masonry, and combination frame and masonry.

Answers to Chapter 14 Posttest

Completion

1. 15, 19
2. sole
3. cripple
4. bracing
5. 8'-0"

Multiple Choice

1. C. southern yellow pine
2. C. 8'-1 1/2"
3. C. 6'-10"
4. B. access hole
5. D. bonded
6. C. 8"
7. A. veneer

Short Answer

1. Frame, masonry, and combination frame and masonry.
2. The sole plate, top plates, studs, headers, and bracing.
3. The load to be supported, span distance, wood species, spacing of joists, and grade of lumber used.
4. ashlar, rubble
5. Stretcher, header, rowlock stretcher, soldier, rowlock, and sailor.
6. face brick, common brick
7. Answer may include any eight of the following: Flush, raked, extruded, weathered, beaded, struck, concave, V-shaped, and grapevine.
8. common bond

Workbook Solution

1.

Complete the wall framing in each of the problems below by applying the specific requirements.

A. Frame a rough opening that is 52" wide by 40" high. Use a solid (2" × 12") header. Label all framing members and dimension the rough opening and height from the floor to the top of the opening.

B. In these two problems, complete the plan view framing for a corner formed with three full studs (left) and a wall intersecting at a stud (right).

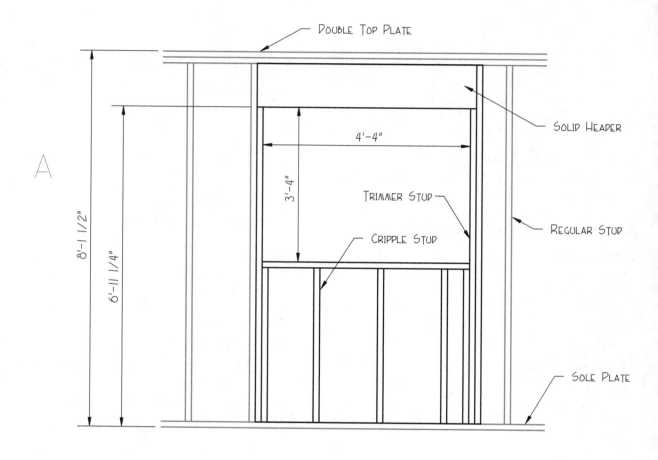

A

DOUBLE TOP PLATE

SOLID HEADER

4'-4"

3'-4"

TRIMMER STUD

CRIPPLE STUD

REGULAR STUD

8'-1 1/2"

6'-11 1/4"

SOLE PLATE

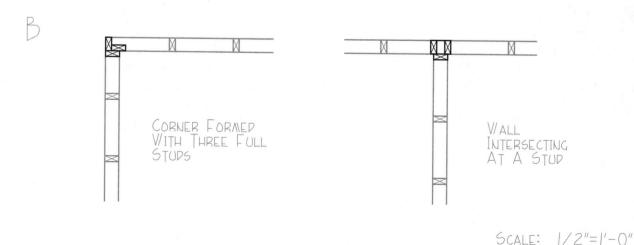

B

CORNER FORMED WITH THREE FULL STUDS

WALL INTERSECTING AT A STUD

SCALE: 1/2"=1'-0"

| WALL FRAMING DETAILS | NAME: | 14- |

Workbook Solution

Directions:
Draw a large scale symbol (elevation view at 1/2″ = 1′-0″) for each of the exterior masonry walls indicated below. Refer to the chapter and the reference section in the text. Fill the space provided.

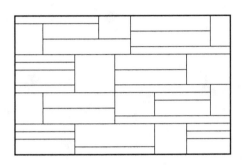

CONCRETE BLOCK

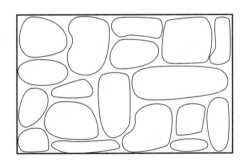

BRICK

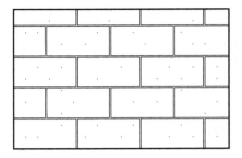

ASHLAR STONE

RANDOM RUBBLE STONE

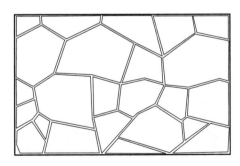

STUCCO

UNCOURSED COBWEB

SCALE: 1/2″=1′-0″

MASONRY WALL SYMBOLS | NAME: | 14-2

Chapter 14 Pretest
Wall and Ceiling Construction

Name _____

Period _____ **Date** _____ **Score** _____

Completion

Complete each sentence with the proper response. Place your answer on the space provided.

1. Corner _____ on frame walls is required by most codes.

1. _____

2. The recommended moisture content of construction lumber is between _____ percent and _____ percent.

2. _____

   _____

3. Trussed headers are generally required for openings wider than _____.

3. _____

4. Frame wall construction usually begins with the _____ plate.

4. _____

5. A(n) _____ wall stud may be found under a window opening.

5. _____

Multiple Choice

Choose the answer that correctly completes the statement. Write the corresponding letter in the space provided.

_____ 1. The distance from the top of the subfloor to the bottom of the ceiling joists is usually _____.

    A. 7'-6"
    B. 8'-0"
    C. 8'-1 1/2"
    D. 8'-6"

_____ 2. A(n) _____ must be provided in the ceiling to afford entry to the attic.

    A. stairway
    B. access hole
    C. door
    D. None of the above.

_____ 3. Solid masonry walls for residential construction are usually _____ thick.

    A. 4"
    B. 6"
    C. 8"
    D. 10"

_____ 4. The rough opening height of most doors in frame wall construction is _____.

    A. 6'-6"
    B. 6'-8"
    C. 6'-10"
    D. 7'-0"

_____ 5. The term _____ is commonly used to indicate that a less desirable or expensive material has been covered up with some type of facing material.

    A. veneer
    B. covering
    C. siding
    D. facing

_____ 6. Wall framing lumber is generally Douglas fir, hemlock, spruce, larch, and _____.

    A. oak
    B. beech
    C. southern yellow pine
    D. hickory

_____ 7. Walls that require more than one thickness of masonry must have all thicknesses _____ together.

    A. welded
    B. cemented
    C. nailed
    D. bonded

Short Answer

Provide brief answers to the following questions.

1. What is the most popular bond used in solid masonry walls? _____

_____

2. List eight types of mortar joints that are used in masonry construction. _____

_____

_____

_____

3. Identify the two types of brick used for wall construction. _____

_____

4. List the specific terms used for the six positions in which brick is laid. _____

_____

_____

_____

5. List the two basic types of stonework. _____

_____

6. The size of ceiling joists required will depend on what five factors? _____

_____

_____

_____

7. Name the basic parts of a conventional frame wall. _____

_____

_____

8. Identify the three usual types of residential wall construction. _____

_____

_____

Chapter 14 Posttest
Wall and Ceiling Construction

Name _____

Period _____ Date _____ Score _____

Completion

Complete each sentence with the proper response. Place your answer on the space provided.

1. The recommended moisture content of construction lumber is between _____ percent and _____ percent.

1. _____
_____

2. Frame wall construction usually begins with the _____ plate.

2. _____

3. A(n) _____ wall stud may be found under a window opening.

3. _____

4. Corner _____ on frame walls is required by most codes.

4. _____

5. Trussed headers are generally required for openings wider than _____.

5. _____

Multiple Choice

Choose the answer that correctly completes the statement. Write the corresponding letter in the space provided.

_____ 1. Wall framing lumber is generally Douglas fir, hemlock, spruce, larch, and _____.

    A. oak
    B. beech
    C. southern yellow pine
    D. hickory

_____ 2. The distance from the top of the subfloor to the bottom of the ceiling joists is usually _____.

    A. 7'-6"
    B. 8'-0"
    C. 8'-1 1/2"
    D. 8'-6"

_____ 3. The rough opening height of most doors in frame wall construction is _____.

    A. 6'-6"
    B. 6'-8"
    C. 6'-10"
    D. 7'-0"

_____ 4. A(n) _____ must be provided in the ceiling to afford entry to the attic.

    A. stairway
    B. access hole
    C. door
    D. None of the above.

_____ 5. Walls that require more than one thickness of masonry must have all thicknesses _____ together.

    A. welded
    B. cemented
    C. nailed
    D. bonded

_____ 6. Solid masonry walls for residential construction are usually _____ thick.

    A. 4″
    B. 6″
    C. 8″
    D. 10″

_____ 7. The term _____ is commonly used to indicate that a less desirable or expensive material has been covered up with some type of facing material.

    A. veneer
    B. covering
    C. siding
    D. facing

Short Answer

Provide brief answers to the following questions.

1. Identify the three usual types of residential wall construction. _____

_____

_____

2. Name the basic parts of a conventional frame wall. _____

_____

_____

3. The size of ceiling joists required will depend on what five factors? _____

_____

_____

_____

4. List the two basic types of stonework. _____

_____

5. List the specific terms used for the six positions in which brick is laid. _____

_____

_____

_____

6. Identify the two types of brick used for wall construction. _____

_____

7. List eight types of mortar joints that are used in masonry construction. _____

_____

_____

_____

8. What is the most popular bond used in solid masonry walls? _____

_____

Doors and Windows

Objectives

After studying this chapter, the student will be able to:
- List the functions that doors and windows perform.
- Compare the types of doors used in a residential dwelling.
- Draw proper door and window symbols on a typical floor plan.
- Explain the information shown in a window or door detail.
- Prepare window and door schedules.

Displays

1. **Door and Window Cutaways.** Assemble a collection of door and window cutaway models from door and window manufacturers. Display these models in the classroom.
2. **Door and Window Literature.** Create a bulletin board display using door and window literature to illustrate products that are available.
3. **Windows Add to the Design.** Arrange several photos of residential structures that make good design use of modern windows.

Instructional Materials

Text: Pages 319–351
Review Questions, Suggested Activities
Workbook: Pages 169–182
Review Questions, Problems/Activities
Teacher's Resources:
Chapter 15 Pretest
Chapter 15 Teaching Strategy
Chapter 15 Posttest

Teaching Strategy

- **Knowledge Assessment.** Administer the Chapter 15 Pretest. Correct the test and return. Highlight topics in which the individual student is deficient.
- Prepare Display #1.
- Review chapter objectives.
- Present interior and exterior doors. Draw typical door symbols.
- Prepare Display #2.
- Assign workbook Problem/Activity 15-1.
- Discuss door schedules.
- Assign workbook Problem/Activity 15-3.
- Present windows. Draw typical window symbols.
- Assign workbook Problem/Activity 15-2.
- Discuss window schedules.
- Prepare Display #3.
- Assign one or more of the Suggested Activities in the text.
- **Chapter Review.** Assign the Review Questions in the text. Discuss the correct answers. Assign Review Questions in the workbook. Have students check their own answers. Make transparencies of the solutions to Problem/Activities 15-1 and 15-2 and use for review.
- **Evaluation.** Administer Chapter 15 Posttest. Correct the test and return. Return graded problems with comments.

Answers to Review Questions, Text

Page 350

1. They shield an opening from the elements, add decoration, emphasize the overall design, provide light and ventilation, and expand visibility.
2. Answer may include any eight: Flush, panel, bi-fold, sliding, pocket, double-action, accordion, Dutch, and French.
3. 1-3/8"
4. rails; stiles
5. closets
6. 6'-8"
7. pocket
8. double-action
9. Answer may include any two: They are thicker, may have one or more glass panels to provide visibility, and are usually not hollow core.

10. 3'-0"
11. overhead sectional
12. head jamb; side jamb; sill
13. Placed over the top piece of trim in frame construction, it sheds water from the trim.
14. 20
15. Answer may include any one: Picture, circle top, and special-shape. ("fixed" may also be considered correct)
16. Sliding, swinging, fixed, and combination. A fifth type or category includes skylights and clerestory windows.
17. muntins
18. The rough framed space in a wall required to install the window.
19. casement window
20. hopper
21. window schedule

Answers to Workbook Questions
Page 169

Part I: Multiple Choice
1. B. Double-action.
2. A. 1"
3. A. Used frequently for large openings.
4. B. Hinged to swing through an arc of 180°.
5. D. All of the above.
6. C. Thicker than interior doors.
7. B. Composed of two side jambs and a head jamb.
8. C. Glass area equal to at least 20% of the floor area should provide adequate natural light.
9. D. All of the above.
10. B. Uniform specifications.
11. C. Rough opening.
12. D. All of the above.
13. A. Dashed line.
14. B. Hopper windows are more efficient when placed low on the wall because they direct air upward.
15. C. Be large fixed glass units used with other window types.
16. C. 45°
17. B. four to seven.
18. A. They are placed high on the wall.

Part II: Completion
1. birch
2. kitchen
3. fabric

4. Dutch
5. 6'-8"
6. oak
7. motor drive
8. manufacturers' literature
9. casing
10. sill
11. section
12. windows
13. wide
14. narrow
15. higher
16. larger
17. metal
18. friction
19. basic
20. jalousie
21. Circle top
22. Special-shape
23. 90
24. rectangular

Part III: Short Answer/Listing
1. Wood, glass, and metal.
2. The advantage is that they require no wall space along the wall when open. Two disadvantages include being difficult to operate and presenting problems if outlets or cabinets are planned for the wall space outside the pocket cavity.
3. As an opening to a patio or terrace; also between rooms.
4. Interior doors are usually hollow core, while exterior doors are usually solid. Exterior doors are usually thicker than interior doors and are more likely to have glass panels to provide visibility.
5. 8'-0" (single door width) and 16'-0" (double door width)
6. A door schedule would be found with the floor plan or elevations if space permits; otherwise, in the details section.
7. The door jamb is the frame that fits inside the rough opening.
8. To provide space for the jambs as well as leveling and squaring.
9. Wood, metal, concrete, and stone.
10. A large area of fixed glass provides clear viewing without obstructions; horizontal and vertical divisions in the window or between windows should be thin to minimize obstruction; and the sill height of

windows should be determined on the basis of furniture, room arrangement, and view.

11. Slightly vary the size, placement, and type of windows.

12. Sash opening is the size of the opening inside the frame or outside dimensions of the sash.

13. When several windows are placed together to form a unit.

14. Quarter circles, half circles, ellipses, and full circle.

15. Type of window, size, identifying symbol, manufacturer's number, and installation.

Part IV: Matching

1. L. Stiles.
2. K. Rails.
3. J. Prehung doors.
4. C. Drip cap.
5. B. Brick mold.
6. D. Double-hung.
7. I. Muntins.
8. H. Mullions.
9. F. Glass size.
10. G. Glider.
11. A. Awning.
12. E. Fixed.

Part V: Problems/Activities

1. Solution on page 271 of this manual.
2. Solution on page 272 of this manual.
3. Solution on page 273 of this manual.

Answers to Chapter 15 Pretest

Completion

1. 6'-8"
2. pocket
3. panel
4. Double-hung
5. more
6. sliding

Multiple Choice

1. B. hopper
2. D. glider windows
3. A. 20
4. C. 3'-0"
5. B. Dutch
6. A. sliding
7. C. flush
8. C. Both A and B.

9. C. Double-action
10. A. French
11. D. 8'-0" h × 9'-0" w
12. B. sashes
13. C. casement

Short Answer

1. Double-hung, casement, and fixed (or picture).
2. Interior and exterior.
3. 8'-0" (single door width) and 16'-0" (double door width)
4. They admit light from the outside; provide fresh air and ventilation to the various rooms; help to create an atmosphere inside by framing an exterior view; and add detail, balance, and design to the exterior of the house.
5. Double-hung and horizontal sliding.
6. Flush, panel, bi-fold, sliding, pocket, double-action, accordion, Dutch, and French.
7. Quarter circles, half circles, ellipses, and full circles.
8. Type of window, size, identifying symbol, manufacturer's number, and installation.
9. Sliding, swinging, and fixed windows; also combination.
10. To admit light into areas of the structure that receive little or no natural light.

Answers to Chapter 15 Posttest

Completion

1. panel
2. sliding
3. pocket
4. Double-hung
5. 6'-8"
6. more

Multiple Choice

1. C. flush
2. C. Both A and B.
3. A. sliding
4. C. Double-action
5. B. Dutch
6. A. French
7. C. 3'-0"
8. D. 8'-0" h × 9'-0" w
9. A. 20
10. B. sashes
11. D. glider windows

12. C. casement
13. B. hopper

Short Answer

1. They admit light from the outside; provide fresh air and ventilation to the various rooms; help to create an atmosphere inside by framing an exterior view; and add detail, balance, and design to the exterior of the house.
2. Interior and exterior.
3. Flush, panel, bi-fold, sliding, pocket, double-action, accordion, Dutch, and French.
4. 8'-0" (single door width) and 16'-0" (double door width)
5. Sliding, swinging, and fixed windows; also combination.
6. Double-hung and horizontal sliding.
7. Double-hung, casement, and fixed (or picture).
8. Quarter circles, half circles, ellipses, and full circles.
9. To admit light into areas of the structure that receive little or no natural light.
10. Type of window, size, identifying symbol, manufacturer's number, and installation.

Workbook Solution

Directions:
Draw a plan view symbol for each of the door types specified below.

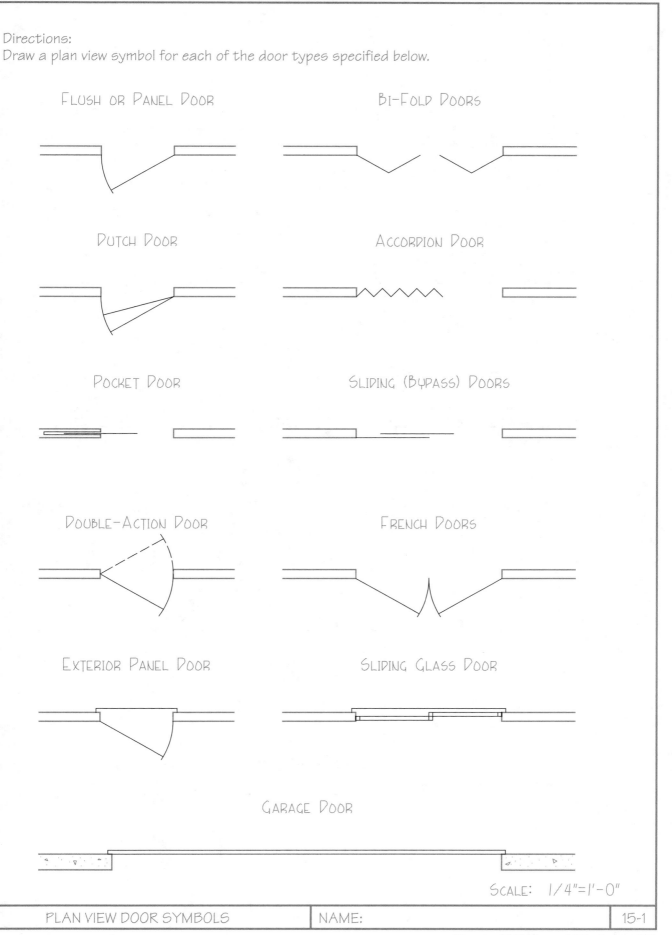

FLUSH OR PANEL DOOR

BI-FOLD DOORS

DUTCH DOOR

ACCORDION DOOR

POCKET DOOR

SLIDING (BYPASS) DOORS

DOUBLE-ACTION DOOR

FRENCH DOORS

EXTERIOR PANEL DOOR

SLIDING GLASS DOOR

GARAGE DOOR

SCALE: 1/4"=1'-0"

PLAN VIEW DOOR SYMBOLS

NAME:

15-1

Workbook Solution

2.

Directions:
Draw a plan view symbol for each of the window types specified below.

DOUBLE-HUNG WINDOW

AWNING WINDOW

CASEMENT WINDOW (TWO SASH)

FIXED WINDOW

HORIZONTAL SLIDING WINDOW

HOPPER WINDOW

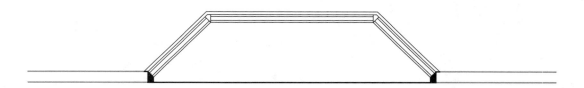

DOUBLE-HUNG 45° BAY WINDOW

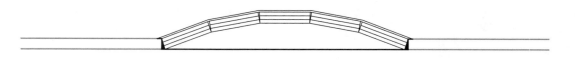

FIVE-UNIT CASEMENT BOW WINDOW

SCALE: 1/4"=1'-0"

PLAN VIEW WINDOW SYMBOLS	NAME:	15

Workbook Solution

Directions:
Label the parts indicated on the exterior door details below.

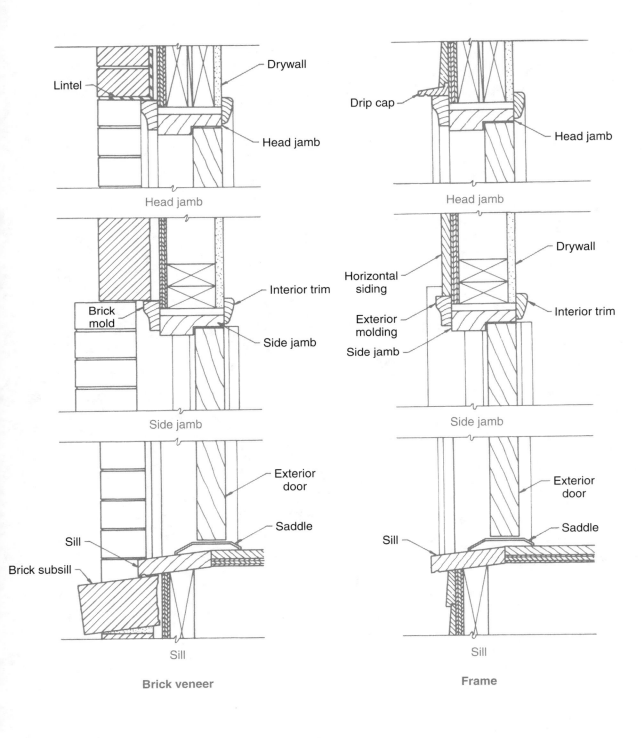

Brick veneer

Frame

Chapter 15 Pretest
Doors and Windows

Name _____

Period _____**Date** _____**Score** _____

Completion

Complete each sentence with the proper response. Place your answer on the space provided.

1. An exterior flush door is usually _____ high.

2. The chief advantage of the _____ door is that it requires no space along the wall when open.

3. A _____ door has a heavy frame around the outside and generally at least one cross member.

4. _____ windows have two sashes.

5. One large window opening will produce _____ contrast in brightness than several smaller openings.

6. The pocket door, generally a flush door, is a variation of the _____ door.

1. _____

2. _____

3. _____

4. _____

5. _____

6. _____

Multiple Choice

Choose the answer that correctly completes the statement. Write the corresponding letter in the space provided.

_____ 1. A(n) _____ window directs air upward and should be placed low on the wall for best ventilation.

    A. awning
    B. hopper
    C. jalousie
    D. casement

_____ 2. Horizontal sliding windows are also called _____.

    A. casements
    B. walk-throughs
    C. picture windows
    D. glider windows

_____ 3. An evenly lighted room will result if the glass area is at least _____ percent of the floor area of the room.

    A. 20
    B. 25
    C. 30
    D. 35

_____ 4. Exterior doors are generally _____ wide.

    A. 2′-6″
    B. 2′-10″
    C. 3′-0″
    D. 3′-6″

_____ 5. A _____ door is composed of two parts—an upper and lower half.

    A. French
    B. Dutch
    C. double-action
    D. bi-fold

_____ 6. A _____ door is used for a wide opening.

    A. sliding
    B. pocket
    C. French
    D. double-action

_____ 7. Doors that are smooth on both sides are called _____ doors and usually made of wood.

    A. French
    B. panel
    C. flush
    D. accordion

_____ 8. A _____ door has two parts to form the door.

    A. bi-fold
    B. Dutch
    C. Both A and B.
    D. None of the above

_____ 9. _____ doors are hinged in such a way that they may swing through an arc of 180°.

    A. Accordion
    B. Dutch
    C. Double-action
    D. By-pass

_____ 10. _____ doors have panels made of glass.

    A. French
    B. Dutch
    C. Panel
    D. Accordion

_____ 11. Which of the following is not a standard garage door size?

    A. 6′-6″ h × 8′-0″ w
    B. 8′-0″ h × 8′-0″ w
    C. 7′-0″ h × 10′-0″ w
    D. 8′-0″ h × 9′-0″ w

_____ 12. Double-hung windows have two _____.

    A. sills
    B. sashes
    C. muntins
    D. unit sizes

_____ 13. A _____ window may be opened or closed by using a crank, push-bar on the frame, or handle on the sash.

    A. double-hung
    B. horizontal sliding
    C. casement
    D. hopper

Short Answer

Answer the following questions.

1. Identify three types of windows that are frequently used for bay and bow windows.

_____

_____

_____

2. Name the two broad classifications of doors. _____

_____

3. Identify the two most common widths of garage doors. _____

4. List four functions that windows perform in a residential structure. _____

_____

_____

_____

5. List the two most common types of sliding windows. _____

6. List the nine types of interior doors. _____

_____

_____

_____

7. List the four types of circle top windows that are generally available. _____

_____

8. Identify the five categories usually included on a window schedule. _____

_____

_____

9. List three basic types of windows typically used in residential construction. _____

_____

10. Why are skylights and clerestory windows generally used? _____

_____

Chapter 15 Posttest
Doors and Windows

Name _____

Period _____ **Date** _____ **Score** _____

Completion

Complete each sentence with the proper response. Place your answer on the space provided.

1. A _____ door has a heavy frame around the outside and generally at least one cross member.

2. The pocket door, generally a flush door, is a variation of the _____ door.

3. The chief advantage of the _____ door is that it requires no space along the wall when open.

4. _____ windows have two sashes.

5. An exterior flush door is usually _____ high.

6. One large window opening will produce _____ contrast in brightness than several smaller openings.

1. _____

2. _____

3. _____

4. _____

5. _____

6. _____

Multiple Choice

Choose the answer that correctly completes the statement. Write the corresponding letter in the space provided.

_____ 1. Doors that are smooth on both sides are called _____ doors and usually made of wood.

    A. French
    B. panel
    C. flush
    D. accordion

_____ 2. A _____ door has two parts to form the door.

    A. bi-fold
    B. Dutch
    C. Both A and B.
    D. None of the above.

_____ 3. A _____ door is used for a wide opening.

    A. sliding
    B. pocket
    C. French
    D. double-action

_____ 4. _____ doors are hinged in such a way that they may swing through an arc of 180°.

    A. Accordion
    B. Dutch
    C. Double-action
    D. By-pass

_____ 5. A _____ door is composed of two parts—an upper and lower half.

    A. French
    B. Dutch
    C. double-action
    D. bi-fold

_____ 6. _____ doors have panels made of glass.

    A. French
    B. Dutch
    C. Panel
    D. Accordion

_____ 7. Exterior doors are generally _____ wide.

    A. 2'-6"
    B. 2'-10"
    C. 3'-0"
    D. 3'-6"

_____ 8. Which of the following is not a standard garage door size?

    A. 6'-6" h × 8'-0" w
    B. 8'-0" h × 8'-0" w
    C. 7'-0" h × 10'-0" w
    D. 8'-0" h × 9'-0" w

_____ 9. An evenly lighted room will result if the glass area is at least _____ percent of the floor area of the room.

    A. 20
    B. 25
    C. 30
    D. 35

_____ 10. Double-hung windows have two _____.

    A. sills
    B. sashes
    C. muntins
    D. unit sizes

_____ 11. Horizontal sliding windows are also called _____.

    A. casements
    B. walk-throughs
    C. picture windows
    D. glider windows

_____ 12. A _____ window may be opened or closed by using a crank, push-bar on the frame, or handle on the sash.

    A. double-hung
    B. horizontal sliding
    C. casement
    D. hopper

_____ 13. A(n) _____ window directs air upward and should be placed low on the wall for best ventilation.

    A. awning
    B. hopper
    C. jalousie
    D. casement

Short Answer

Answer the following questions.

1. List four functions that windows perform in a residential structure.

_____

_____

_____

_____

2. Name the two broad classifications of doors. _____

_____

_____

3. List the nine types of interior doors. _____

_____

_____

_____

_____

_____

4. Identify the two most common widths of garage doors. _____

_____

5. List three basic types of windows typically used in residential construction.

_____

_____

6. List the two most common types of sliding windows. _____

_____

7. Identify three types of windows that are frequently used for bay and bow windows. _____

_____

_____

_____

8. List the four types of circle top windows that are generally available. _____

_____

_____

9. Why are skylights and clerestory windows generally used? _____

_____

10. Identify the five categories usually included on a window schedule. _____

_____

_____

_____

Stairs

16

Objectives

After studying this chapter, the student will be able to:
- Define common stair terminology.
- Explain the appropriate use of the various stair designs.
- Design a stairway for a residential structure.
- Draw structural details for main stairs.
- Perform stair calculations for a residential stairway.
- Identify model code requirements for handrails and guardrails.

Displays

1. **Stairs, Stairs, Stairs.** Arrange a bulletin board display from photos of well-designed stairs to create interest in the subject.
2. **Stair Models.** Display scale models of stairs built by students for Suggested Activity #5 in the text.
3. **Student Work.** Put examples of outstanding student work on the bulletin board. Select examples from the workbook assignments.
4. **Stair Materials.** Display stair materials—tread, riser, stringer, handrail, etc. Label each part.

Instructional Materials

Text: Pages 353–368
   Review Questions, Suggested Activities
Workbook: Pages 183–192
   Review Questions, Problems/Activities
Teacher's Resources:
   Chapter 16 Pretest
   Chapter 16 Teaching Strategy
   Chapter 16 Posttest

Teaching Strategy

- **Knowledge Assessment.** Administer the Chapter 16 Pretest. Correct the test and return. Highlight topics in which the individual student is deficient.
- Prepare Display #1. Review chapter objectives. Present types of stairs. Compare and contrast the various types.
- Prepare Display #2.
- Assign workbook Problem 16-1. Discuss stair design.
- Prepare Display #3.
- Present stair calculations and drawing procedures.
- Prepare Display #4.
- Assign workbook Problem 16-2.
- Assign one or more of the Suggested Activities in the text.
- **Chapter Review.** Assign Review Questions in the text. Discuss the correct answers. Assign Review Questions in the workbook. Have students check their own answers. Make a transparency of the solution to Problem/Activity 16-1 and use for review.
- **Evaluation.** Administer the Chapter 16 Posttest. Correct the test and return. Return graded problems with comments.

Answers to Review Questions, Text

Page 367

1. main
2. Straight run, L, double-L, U, winder, and spiral.
3. Double-L
4. U
5. winder (also acceptable: spiral)
6. balusters
7. enclosed (also acceptable: closed, housed, or boxed)
8. 6'-6".
9. plain; housed
10. nosing
11. open
12. housed
13. The distance from the top surface of one tread to the same position on the next tread.
14. The distance from the face of one riser to the face of the next.

15. total rise
16. total run
17. 30; 35
18. 3'-0"
19. hardwood
20. 7-1/4"; 10-1/2"

Answers to Workbook Questions
Page 183
Part I: Matching
1. L. Stairway
2. N. Straight run
3. C. L
4. S. U
5. T. Winder
6. B. Circular
7. A. Balusters
8. D. Landing
9. E. Newel
10. F. Nosing
11. G. Open
12. H. Plain stringer
13. I. Rise
14. J. Riser
15. K. Run
16. M. Stairwell
17. O. Stringer
18. P. Total rise
19. Q. Total run
20. R. Tread

Part II: Completion
1. safety
2. Service
3. narrow
4. spiral
5. Circular
6. stringer
7. 3'-0"
8. stringer
9. nails
10. wedges

Part III: Short Answer/Listing
1. Long L
2. The midpoint width of the triangular steps in winder stairs should be equal to the tread width of the regular steps.
3. The stairs should support the required weight; they should be wide enough to provide ease of passage and movement of furniture; the slope of the stairs should be between 30° and 35°.
4. Place the third stringer at midpoint between the outside stringers and under the treads and risers.
5. The advantages are their sturdiness and low construction cost. Disadvantages include an unfinished appearance and they tend to squeak.
6. The stringers normally have 1/2" deep routed grooves to hold the treads and risers in place. Wedges are driven into the grooves to keep the treads and risers in place; all three components are nailed and glued.
7. 7" to 7-5/8"
8. Rule 1: The slope of the stairs (rise-run ratio) should be between 30° and 35°. Rule 2: The sum of two risers and one tread should equal 25". Rule 3: The product of the riser height multiplied by the tread should equal approximately 75". Rule 4: The sum of one riser and one tread should equal 17" to 18".
9. The upper floor serves as the top tread.
10. A. Straight run; B. L stairs; C. Double-L stairs; D. U stairs; E. Winder stairs; F. Spiral or circular stairs.
11. A. Baluster; B. Handrail; C. Newel.
12. Total run = 94.5"; Number of risers = 10; Riser height = 7.2"; Number of treads = 9; Run of a step = 10-1/2"

Part IV: Multiple Choice
1. D. All of the above.
2. B. Straight run.
3. C. Trapezoidal.
4. D. All of the above.
5. B. Service stairs.
6. D. All of the above.
7. C. 1-1/6"
8. A. 30" along the incline and 36" at the landing.
9. B. 6'-6".
10. C. All stairs and ramps.

Part V: Problems/Activities
1. Solution on page 287 of this manual.
2. Solution on page 288 of this manual.

Answers to Chapter 16 Pretest

Completion

1. 3'
2. two
3. housed
4. safety
5. wide U

Multiple Choice

1. C. L stairs
2. A. steel
3. B. main
4. D. 2" × 12"
5. C. 30°–35°
6. D. pie-shaped
7. B. stringers

Matching

1. A. Stairs that have no wall on one or both sides.
2. H. The distance from the top surface of one tread to the same spot on the next.
3. J. The distance from the face of one riser to the face of the next.
4. L. Vertical members that support the handrail on open stairs.
5. G. The shortest clear vertical distance measured between the nosing of the treads and the ceiling.
6. I. The rounded projection of the tread that extends past the face of the riser.
7. F. A stringer that has been cut or notched to fit the profile of the stairs.
8. K. The vertical face of a step.
9. B. The horizontal member of each step.
10. D. Stairs that have a wall on both sides.
11. C. A stringer that has been routed to receive the treads and risers.
12. E. The main posts of the handrail at the top, bottom, or points where the stairs change directions.
13. A. 1"
14. C. 7.15"
15. E. 10-1/2"
16. F. 11-1/2"
17. D. 8'-11 1/4"
18. G. 12'-3"
19. B. 1-1/16"

Short Answer

1. total rise
2. Landing: 36"; Along stairs: 30"

3. total run
4. Answer may include any six: Straight run stairs, L stairs, double-L stairs, U stairs, winder stairs, spiral stairs, and circular stairs.
5. 7-1/4" to 10-1/2"
6. 14

Answers to Chapter 16 Posttest

Completion

1. safety
2. two
3. wide U
4. 3'
5. housed

Multiple Choice

1. B. main
2. C. L stairs
3. D. pie-shaped
4. A. steel
5. C. 30°–35°
6. B. stringers
7. D. 2" × 12"

Matching

1. H. Vertical members that support the handrail on open stairs.
2. C. Stairs that have a wall on both sides.
3. J. The shortest clear vertical distance measured between the nosing of the treads and the ceiling.
4. A. A stringer that has been routed to receive the treads and risers.
5. E. The main posts of the handrail at the top, bottom, or points where the stairs change directions.
6. B. The rounded projection of the tread that extends past the face of the riser.
7. I. Stairs that have no wall on one or both sides.
8. G. A stringer that has been cut or notched to fit the profile of the stairs.
9. L. The distance from the top surface of one tread to the same spot on the next.
10. F. The vertical face of a step.
11. D. The distance from the face of one riser to the face of the next.
12. K. The horizontal member of each step.
13. E. 7.15"
14. A. 10-1/2"
15. G. 8'-11 1/4"

16. B. 12'-3"
17. D. 1"
18. F. 11-1/2"
19. C. 1-1/16"

Short Answer

1. Answer may include any six: Straight run stairs, L stairs,   double-L stairs, U stairs, winder stairs, spiral stairs, and circular stairs.

2. total rise
3. total run
4. 7-1/4" to 10-1/2"
5. Landing: 36"; Along stairs: 30"
6. 14

Workbook Solution

Directions:

Problem A—Draw the plan view and elevation in section of plain stringer stairs that meet the following specifications: width = 36″, tread width = 11-1/2″, riser height = 7-1/4″, nosing = 1″, stringer is 2″ × 12″, number of risers is 6, and the total run is 52.5″.

PLAN VIEW

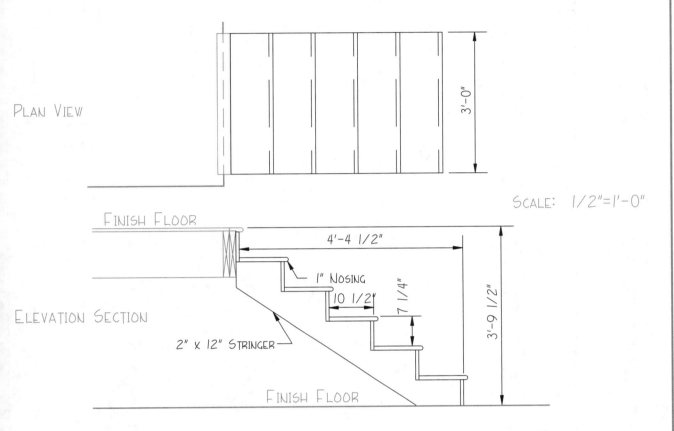

SCALE: 1/2″=1′-0″

ELEVATION SECTION

FINISH FLOOR

1″ NOSING

10 1/2″

7 1/4″

4′-4 1/2″

3′-0″

3′-9 1/2″

2″ × 12″ STRINGER

FINISH FLOOR

Problem B—Draw a detail (scale: 1″ = 1′-0″) of housed stringer stairs showing 5/4″ oak treads, 1″ pine risers, 2″ × 12″ vertical grain fir stringers, and wedges. Label and show dimensions.

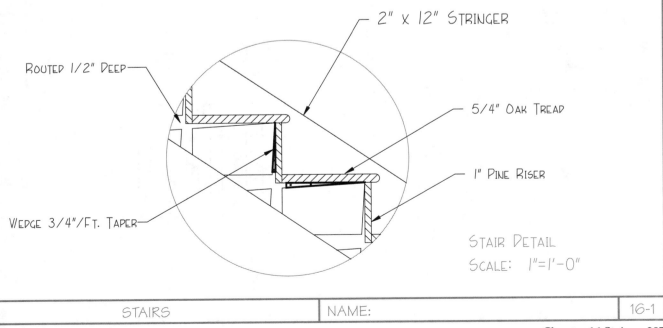

ROUTED 1/2″ DEEP

2″ × 12″ STRINGER

5/4″ OAK TREAD

1″ PINE RISER

WEDGE 3/4″/FT. TAPER

STAIR DETAIL
SCALE: 1″=1′-0″

| STAIRS | NAME: | 16-1 |

2.

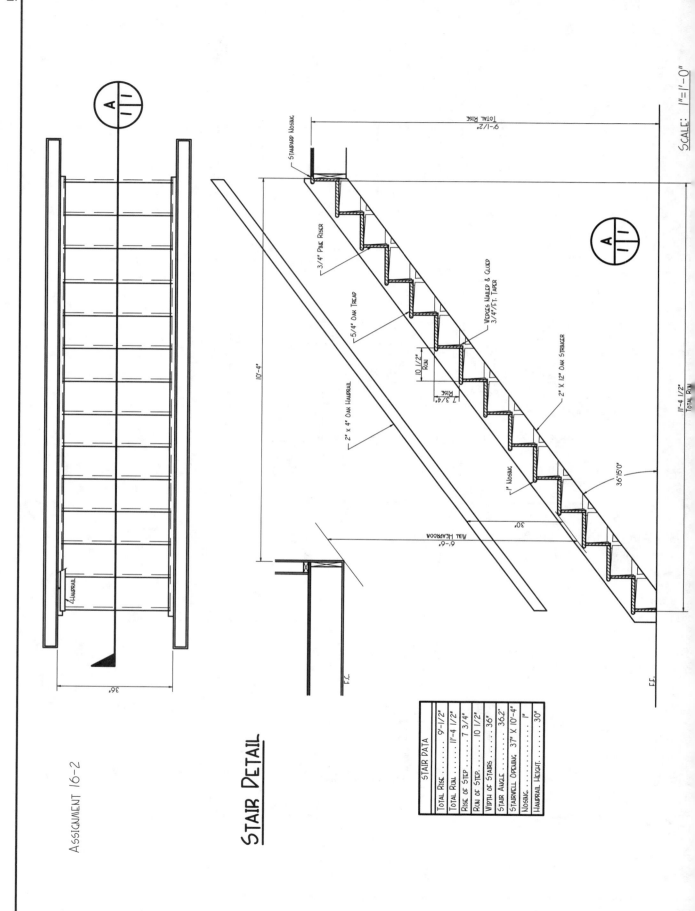

ASSIGNMENT 16-2

STAIR DETAIL

SCALE: 1"=1'-0"

STAIR DATA	
TOTAL RISE	9'-1/2"
TOTAL RUN	11'-4 1/2"
RISE OF STEP	7 3/4"
RUN OF STEP	10 1/2"
WIDTH OF STAIRS	36"
STAIR ANGLE	36.2°
STAIRWELL OPENING	37" X 10'-4"
NOSING	1"
HANDRAIL HEIGHT	30"

STANDARD NOSING

3/4" PINE RISER

5/4" OAK TREAD

2" X 4" OAK HANDRAIL

WEDGES NAILED & GLUED 3/4"/FT. TAPER

2" X 12" OAK STRINGER

1" NOSING

10 1/2" RUN

7 3/4" RISE

36°15'0"

30°

MIN. HEADROOM 6'-6"

TOTAL RISE 9'-1/2"

TOTAL RUN 11'-4 1/2"

10'-4"

F.F.

F.C.

4" HANDRAIL

36"

Chapter 16 Pretest
Stairs

Name _____

Period _____ Date _____ Score _____

Completion

Complete each sentence with the proper response. Place your answer on the space provided.

1. Two stringers are usually sufficient to support stairs that are _____ wide.

1. _____

2. Double-L stairs require _____ 90° turn(s) along the flight.

2. _____

3. Wedges are generally used with _____ stringer stairs.

3. _____

4. Prime considerations in stair design should be easy ascent or descent and _____.

4. _____

5. _____ stairs have a well hole.

5. _____

Multiple Choice

Choose the answer that correctly completes the statement. Write the corresponding letter in the space provided.

_____ 1. The type of stairs that has one landing at some point along the flight of steps (nonparallel flights) is a(n) _____.

    A. straight run stairs
    B. winder stairs
    C. L stairs
    D. U stairs

_____ 2. Most spiral stairs are made from _____.

    A. steel
    B. wood
    C. stone
    D. aluminum

_____ 3. The treads of _____ stairs are usually made of hardwoods such as oak, maple, or birch.

    A. service
    B. main
    C. side
    D. open stringer

_____ 4. Plain stringers are generally cut from _____ straight-grain fir.

    A. $2'' \times 4''$
    B. $2'' \times 6''$
    C. $2'' \times 8''$
    D. $2'' \times 12''$

_____ 5. A well-designed set of stairs should have a slope of between _____.

    A. 15°–20°
    B. 20°–30°
    C. 30°–35°
    D. 35°–40°

_____ 6. Winder stairs have _____ steps that are substituted for a landing.

    A. trapezoidal
    B. rectangular
    C. square
    D. pie-shaped

_____ 7. The main supporting members of the stairs are the _____.

    A. handrails
    B. stringers
    C. steps
    D. balusters

Matching

Select the answer that correctly matches each term. Place your answer in the space provided.

A. Stairs that have no wall on one or both sides.
B. The horizontal member of each step.
C. A stringer that has been routed to receive the treads and risers.
D. Stairs that have a wall on both sides.
E. The main posts of the handrail at the top, bottom, or points where the stairs change directions.
F. A stringer that has been cut or notched to fit the profile of the stairs.

G. The shortest clear vertical distance measured between the nosing of the treads and the ceiling.
H. The distance from the top surface of one tread to the same spot on the next.
I. The rounded projection of the tread that extends past the face of the riser.
J. The distance from the face of one riser to the face of the next.
K. The vertical face of a step.
L. Vertical members that support the handrail on open stairs.

_____ 1. Open stairs

_____ 2. Rise

_____ 3. Run

_____ 4. Balusters

_____ 5. Headroom

_____ 6. Nosing

_____ 7. Plain stringer

_____ 8. Riser

_____ 9. Tread

_____ 10. Enclosed stairs

_____ 11. Housed stringer

_____ 12. Newel

Name _____

Select the answer that correctly matches each term. Place your answer in the space provided.

A. 1"

B. 1-1/16"

C. 7.15"

D. 8'-11 1/4"

E. 10-1/2"

F. 11-1/2"

G. 12'-3"

_____ 13. Nosing

_____ 14. Rise of a step

_____ 15. Run of a step

_____ 16. Tread width (run + nosing)

_____ 17. Total rise

_____ 18. Total run

_____ 19. Tread thickness

Short Answer

Answer the following questions.

1. The total floor-to-floor vertical height of the stairs is the definition of _____.

2. What are the standard heights of a handrail at landing and along the stairs?

   Landing:_____

   Along stairs: _____

3. The total horizontal length of the stairs is the definition of_____.

4. List the six general types of stairs commonly used in residential construction.

   _____

   _____

   _____

   _____

   _____

   _____

5. What is the ideal ratio of rise to run for a stair step?_____

   _____

6. A stair that has 15 risers will have_____treads.

Chapter 16 Posttest
Stairs

Name _____

Period _____**Date** _____**Score** _____

Completion
Complete each sentence with the proper response. Place your answer on the space provided.

1. Prime considerations in stair design should be easy ascent or descent and _____.

2. Double-L stairs require _____ 90° turn(s) along the flight.

3. _____ stairs have a well hole.

4. Two stringers are usually sufficient to support stairs that are _____ wide.

5. Wedges are generally used with _____ stringer stairs.

1. _____

2. _____

3. _____

4. _____

5. _____

Multiple Choice
Choose the answer that correctly completes the statement. Write the corresponding letter in the space provided.

_____ 1. The treads of _____ stairs are usually made of hardwoods such as oak, maple, or birch.

    A. service
    B. main
    C. side
    D. open stringer

_____ 2. The type of stairs that has one landing at some point along the flight of steps (nonparallel flights) is a(n) _____.

    A. straight run stairs
    B. winder stairs
    C. L stairs
    D. U stairs

_____ 3. Winder stairs have _____ steps that are substituted for a landing.

    A. trapezoidal
    B. rectangular
    C. square
    D. pie-shaped

_____ 4. Most spiral stairs are made from _____.

    A. steel
    B. wood
    C. stone
    D. aluminum

_____ 5. A well-designed set of stairs should have a slope of between _____.

     A. 15°–20°
     B. 20°–30°
     C. 30°–35°
     D. 35°–40°

_____ 6. The main supporting members of the stairs are the _____.

     A. handrails
     B. stringers
     C. steps
     D. balusters

_____ 7. Plain stringers are generally cut from _____ straight-grain fir.

     A. 2″ × 4″
     B. 2″ × 6″
     C. 2″ × 8″
     D. 2″ × 12″

Matching

Select the answer that correctly matches each term. Place your answer in the space provided.

A. A stringer that has been routed to receive the treads and risers.
B. The rounded projection of the tread that extends past the face of the riser.
C. Stairs that have a wall on both sides.
D. The distance from the face of one riser to the face of the next.
E. The main posts of the handrail at the top, bottom, or points where the stairs change directions.
F. The vertical face of a step.

G. A stringer that has been cut or notched to fit the profile of the stairs.
H. Vertical members that support the handrail on open stairs.
I. Stairs that have no wall on one or both sides.
J. The shortest clear vertical distance measured between the nosing of the treads and the ceiling.
K. The horizontal member of each step.
L. The distance from the top surface of one tread to the same spot on the next.

_____ 1. Balusters

_____ 2. Enclosed stairs

_____ 3. Headroom

_____ 4. Housed stringer

_____ 5. Newel

_____ 6. Nosing

_____ 7. Open stairs

_____ 8. Plain stringer

_____ 9. Rise

_____ 10. Riser

_____ 11. Run

_____ 12. Tread

Name _____

Select the answer that correctly matches each term. Place your answer in the space provided.

A. 10-1/2"
B. 12'-3"
C. 1-1/16"
D. 1"

E. 7.15"
F. 11-1/2"
G. 8'-11 1/4"

_____ 13. Rise of a step

_____ 14. Run of a step

_____ 15. Total rise

_____ 16. Total run

_____ 17. Nosing

_____ 18. Tread width (run + nosing)

_____ 19. Tread thickness

Short Answer

Answer the following questions.

1. List the six general types of stairs commonly used in residential construction.

_____

_____

_____

_____

_____

_____

2. The total floor-to-floor vertical height of the stairs is the definition of _____.

3. The total horizontal length of the stairs is the definition of _____.

4. What is the ideal ratio of rise to run for a stair step? _____

_____

5. What are the standard heights of a handrail at landing and along the stairs?

   Landing: _____

   Along stairs: _____

6. A stair that has 15 risers will have_____treads.

Fireplaces, Chimneys, and Stoves

Objectives
After studying this chapter, the student will be able to:
- Compare various types of fireplaces that are appropriate for a residence.
- Identify the parts of a standard masonry fireplace and chimney.
- Apply the appropriate principles to design a typical fireplace.
- Use a fireplace design data chart.
- Explain the difference between a radiant and circulating stove.

Displays
1. **Fireplace Styles.** Collect photos of various fireplace styles. Create a bulletin board arrangement using the photos.
2. **Fireplace Materials and Parts.** Display typical fireplace materials and parts. Examples include a damper, firebrick, ash dump model, flue liner, etc.
3. **Fireplace Models.** Display the fireplace models built by students from past classes for Suggested Activity #2 in text.

Instructional Materials
Text: Pages 369–387
 Review Questions, Suggested Activities
Workbook: Pages 193–204
 Review Questions, Problems/Activities
Teacher's Resources:
 Chapter 17 Pretest
 Chapter 17 Teaching Strategy
 Chapter 17 Posttest

Teaching Strategy
- **Knowledge Assessment.** Administer the Chapter 17 Pretest. Correct the test and return. Highlight topics in which the individual student is deficient.
- Prepare Display #1.
- Review chapter objectives.
- Discuss fireplace design considerations.
- Present hearth, fire chamber, damper, and smoke shelf.
- Prepare Display #2.
- Assign Problem 17-1 and Problem 17-2 in the workbook.
- Discuss framing around the fireplace and chimney.
- Assign Suggested Activity #2 in the text.
- Prepare Display #3.
- Present fireplace specifications for other designs.
- Discuss prefabricated metal fireplaces and stoves.
- Review fireplace/chimney terms.
- Assign one or more of the remaining Suggested Activities in the text or Problem 17-3 in the workbook.
- **Chapter Review.** Assign Review Questions in the text. Discuss the correct answers. Assign Review Questions in the workbook. Have students check their own answers.
- **Evaluation.** Administer Chapter 17 Posttest. Correct the test and return. Return graded problems with comments.

Answers to Review Questions, Text
Page 387
1. Single face, two face opposite, two face adjacent, three face, and prefabricated metal.
2. hearth
3. The fireplace is likely to smoke into the room.
4. smoke shelf
5. smoke chamber
6. 1/10th
7. increase (or improve)
8. 2'
9. The chimney will be warmer and a warmer chimney functions better than a cold chimney.
10. 2"

11. shed water from the chimney and down the roof
12. angle steel
13. single-face fireplace
14. two-face adjacent fireplace
15. wall-mounted, prefabricated metal fireplace
16. local
17. Radiant and circulating.
18. Baffles, long smoke paths, and heat exchange devices.

Answers to Workbook Questions
Page 193

Part I: Completion

1. wood
2. noncombustible
3. deep
4. shallow
5. cleanout
6. back; sides
7. damper
8. damper
9. chimney
10. flue
11. Efficiency
12. 1/10th
13. better
14. free-standing
15. 2
16. noncombustible
17. decreased
18. saddle (or cricket)
19. Single-face fireplaces
20. three-way
21. circulating
22. 35%

Part II: Multiple Choice

1. C. 16"
2. A. 8"
3. B. Very efficient.
4. D. All of the above.
5. C. Basically a pyramid with the back side usually vertical.
6. A. Clay.
7. C. 4"
8. A. 8"
9. B. 16" × 16"
10. A. 2'
11. D. Angle steel.
12. B. Opens on the front and either left or right side.
13. D. A and B.
14. C. Heat exchange devices.

Part III: Short Answer/Listing

1. Single face, two-face opposite, two-face adjacent, three-face, and prefabricated metal.
2. Firebrick.
3. Fireclay is a fire-resistant, mortar-like refractory material used as a bonding agent between the firebrick.
4. It must be designed properly so that smoke and hot gases will go into the throat and up the chimney.
5. Cool air is drawn into the chamber, where it is heated and then returned through registers above the fireplace.
6. The smoke shelf causes cold air flowing down the chimney to be deflected upward into the rising warm air.
7. Smoke chambers are usually constructed of brick or other masonry.
8. Select a flue that has at least 1/10th the cross-sectional area of the fireplace opening.
9. When the height of the flue is less than 14' and when the flue is sheltered by trees or buildings.
10. Several flues may be within a single chimney.
11. Gas furnace, gas water heater, incinerator, and one for each fireplace.
12. Double headers and trimmers.
13. A saddle or cricket should be built on the high side of the chimney to shed water. Flashing can be placed around the chimney.
14. To improve the room-heating efficiency of an existing masonry fireplace.
15. Wood and coal.
16. Radiant stoves pass heat through the air with no assistance. Circulating stoves use radiant heat and airflow to distribute heat.
17. Circulating.
18. Answer may include any three: Simple box stoves, Franklin stoves, potbelly stoves, and some parlor stoves.

19. Cover the opening with a piece of sheet metal.
20. Increasing the height of the chimney increases the draft.

Part IV: Matching

1. F. Hearth.
2. D. Fireclay.
3. C. Ash dump.
4. A. Ash chamber.
5. B. Damper.
6. K. Smoke shelf.
7. J. Smoke chamber.
8. E. Flue.
9. H. Saddle.
10. G. Lintel.
11. I. Single-face.
12. O. Two-face opposite.
13. N. Two-face adjacent.
14. M. Three-face.
15. L. Stove.

Part V: Problems/Activities

1. Solution on page 298 of this manual.
2. Solution on page 299 of this manual.
3. Solution on page 300 of this manual.

Answers to Chapter 17 Pretest

Completion

1. 4"
2. Fireclay
3. chimney
4. round
5. sparks
6. smoke chamber

Multiple Choice

1. B. 20% to 30%
2. C. 16"
3. D. damper
4. B. flue
5. C. 6" or 8"
6. B. noncombustible
7. A. steel and cast iron

Short Answer

1. Radiant and circulating
2. Single-face, two-face opposite, two-face adjacent, three-face, and prefabricated metal.

3. The fireplace is likely to smoke into the room.
4. It will increase the draft.
5. Below the fireplace floor.
6. 2'
7. Little heat will be reflected into the room.
8. Fireplace, gas furnace, gas water heater, and incinerator.
9. Choose a flue that has a cross-sectional area of at least 1/10th the area of the fireplace opening.

Answers to Chapter 17 Posttest

Completion

1. sparks
2. Fireclay
2. smoke chamber
4. round
5. 4"
6. chimney

Multiple Choice

1. C. 16"
2. B. noncombustible
3. D. damper
4. C. 6" or 8"
5. A. steel and cast iron
6. B. flue
7. B. 20% to 30%

Short Answer

1. Single-face, two-face opposite, two-face adjacent, three-face, and prefabricated metal.
2. Little heat will be reflected into the room.
3. The fireplace is likely to smoke into the room.
4. Below the fireplace floor.
5. Choose a flue that has a cross-sectional area of at least 1/10th the area of the fireplace opening.
6. It will increase the draft.
7. 2'
8. Fireplace, gas furnace, gas water heater, and incinerator.
9. Radiant and circulating

Workbook Solution

1.

Directions:
Study the pictorial section of a fireplace and chimney below and identify each of the materials, parts, etc., indicated by the leaders. Use these specific notes:

> Ash pit
> Ash dump
> Cleanout door
> Damper
> Double header
> Face brick
> Firebrick
> Floor joist

> Smoke chamber
> Smoke shelf
> Steel lintel
> Stone hearth
> 4" Reinforced concrete inner hearth
> Minimum thickness of walls of fire chamber is 8"
> Flue lining

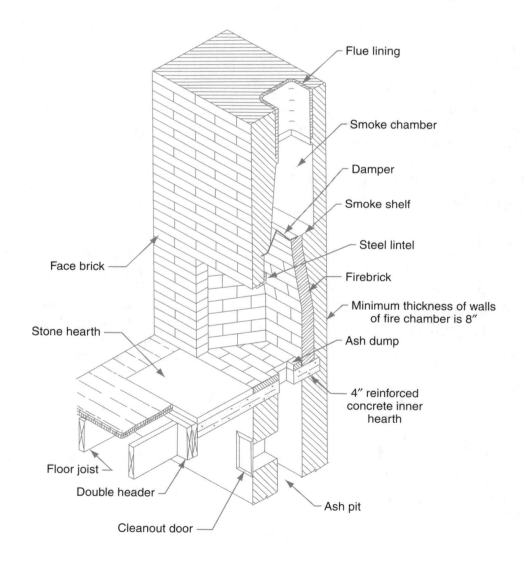

Flue lining

Smoke chamber

Damper

Smoke shelf

Steel lintel

Firebrick

Minimum thickness of walls of fire chamber is 8"

Ash dump

4" reinforced concrete inner hearth

Face brick

Stone hearth

Floor joist

Double header

Cleanout door

Ash pit

Directions:
Using the Design Data for Single Face Fireplaces chart in Figure 17-15 in the text, fill in the dimensions represented on the drawings for a 40" wide fireplace and modular flue liner. Do not scale the drawings to arrive at these dimensions.

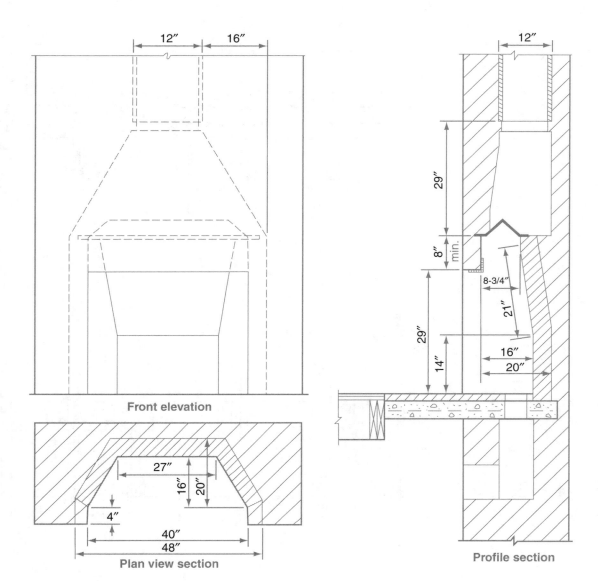

Front elevation

Plan view section

Profile section

3.

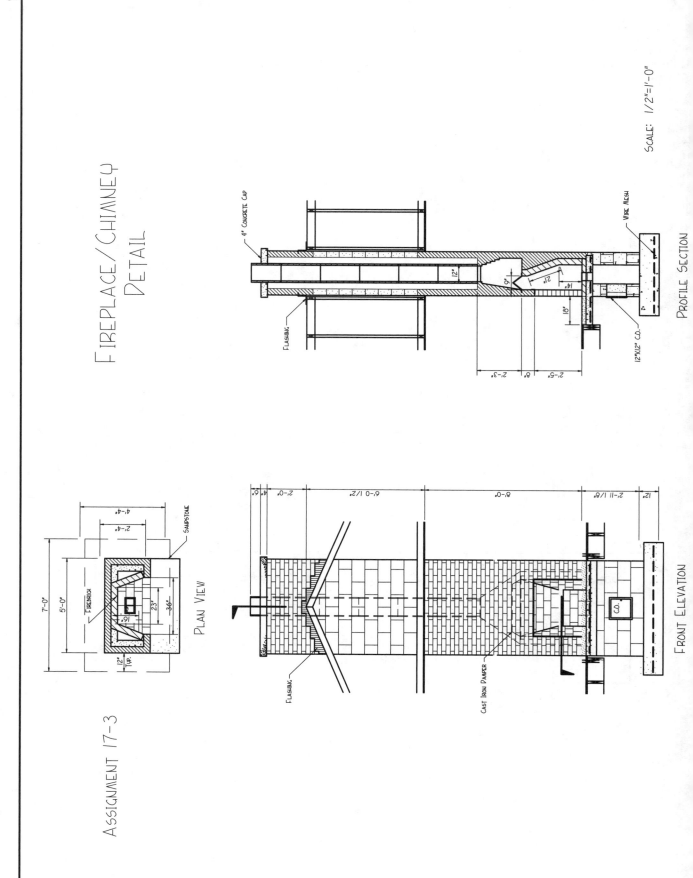

FIREPLACE/CHIMNEY DETAIL

ASSIGNMENT 17-3

Chapter 17 Pretest
Fireplaces, Chimneys, and Stoves

Name _____

Period _____**Date** _____**Score** _____

Completion
Complete each sentence with the proper response. Place your answer on the space provided.

1. Each flue with a liner requires at least _____ of masonry on all sides.

2. _____ is a fire-resistant mortar.

3. The _____ is a freestanding structure.

4. Flue liners are available in square, rectangular, and _____ shapes.

5. The function of the outer hearth is to protect the floor from _____.

6. The _____ is the area just above the smoke shelf.

1. _____

2. _____

3. _____

4. _____

5. _____

6. _____

Multiple Choice
Choose the answer that correctly completes the statement. Write the corresponding letter in the space provided.

_____ 1. Low-efficiency stoves range from _____ efficient.

    A. 10% to 20%
    B. 20% to 30%
    C. 30% to 40%
    D. 40% to 50%

_____ 2. The hearth should extend at least _____ in front of the fireplace.

    A. 8″
    B. 12″
    C. 16″
    D. 20″

_____ 3. Every fireplace should have a _____ to regulate the flow of air and to stop drafts of cold air when the fireplace is not in operation.

    A. throat
    B. lintel
    C. flue liner
    D. damper

_____ 4. Each fireplace must have its own _____.

    A. room
    B. flue
    C. Both A and B.
    D. None of the above.

_____ 5. The damper is placed _____ above the top of the fireplace opening.

    A. 2″ or 4″
    B. 4″ or 6″
    C. 6″ or 8″
    D. 8″ or 10″

_____ 6. A hearth should be constructed from a _____ material.

    A. sturdy
    B. noncombustible
    C. cementitious
    D. fireclay

_____ 7. Dampers are produced in both _____.

    A. steel and cast iron
    B. steel and aluminum
    C. cast iron and aluminum
    D. cast iron and slate

Short Answer

Answer the following questions.

1. What are the two main types of wood- and coal-burning stoves? _____

2. Identify five types of fireplaces that are used in homes. _____

3. What is the expected result if the fire chamber is too shallow? _____

4. How will increasing the height of a flue affect the draft of a fireplace? _____

5. Where is the ash dump usually located? _____

6. How high should the flue generally extend above the roof? _____

7. What is the expected result when a fire chamber is too deep? _____

8. List four devices that require a flue. _____

9. What is the rule of thumb to follow in selecting the proper flue size for a particular fireplace opening? _____

Chapter 17 Posttest
Fireplaces, Chimneys, and Stoves

Name _____

Period _____ Date _____ Score _____

Completion

Complete each sentence with the proper response. Place your answer on the space provided.

1. The function of the outer hearth is to protect the floor from _____.

1. _____

2. _____ is a fire-resistant mortar.

2. _____

3. The _____ is the area just above the smoke shelf.

3. _____

4. Flue liners are available in square, rectangular, and _____ shapes.

4. _____

5. Each flue with a liner requires at least _____ of masonry on all sides.

5. _____

6. The _____ is a freestanding structure.

6. _____

Multiple Choice

Choose the answer that correctly completes the statement. Write the corresponding letter in the space provided.

_____ 1. The hearth should extend at least _____ in front of the fireplace.

   A. 8"
   B. 12"
   C. 16"
   D. 20"

_____ 2. A hearth should be constructed from a _____ material.

   A. sturdy
   B. noncombustible
   C. cementitious
   D. fireclay

_____ 3. Every fireplace should have a _____ to regulate the flow of air and to stop drafts of cold air when the fireplace is not in operation.

   A. throat
   B. lintel
   C. flue liner
   D. damper

_____ 4. The damper is placed _____ above the top of the fireplace opening.

   A. 2" or 4"
   B. 4" or 6"
   C. 6" or 8"
   D. 8" or 10"

_____ 5. Dampers are produced in both _____.

    A. steel and cast iron
    B. steel and aluminum
    C. cast iron and aluminum
    D. cast iron and slate

_____ 6. Each fireplace must have its own _____.

    A. room
    B. flue
    C. Both A and B.
    D. None of the above.

_____ 7. Low-efficiency stoves range from _____ efficient.

    A. 10% to 20%
    B. 20% to 30%
    C. 30% to 40%
    D. 40% to 50%

Short Answer

Answer the following questions.

1. Identify five types of fireplaces that are used in homes. _____
_____
_____
_____

2. What is the expected result when a fire chamber is too deep?_____
_____

3. What is the expected result if the fire chamber is too shallow? _____
_____

4. Where is the ash dump usually located? _____

5. What is the rule of thumb to follow in selecting the proper flue size for a particular fireplace opening? _____

6. How will increasing the height of a flue affect the draft of a fireplace? _____
_____

7. How high should the flue generally extend above the roof? _____

8. List four devices that require a flue. _____
_____
_____

9. What are the two main types of wood- and coal-burning stoves? _____
_____

The Floor Plan
18

Objectives

After studying this chapter, the student will be able to:
- List the information required on a typical floor plan.
- Represent typical materials using standard architectural symbols.
- Design and draw a residential floor plan using accepted symbols and techniques.
- Dimension a floor plan in a clear and precise manner.
- Recognize the difference between a good and poor drawing of a floor plan.

Displays

1. **Sample floor plan.** Select a well-designed floor plan for display on the bulletin board. Be sure the plan illustrates proper techniques described in the text.
2. **Student work.** Display student work on the bulletin board. Select samples from the workbook assignments.

Instructional Materials

Text: Pages 389–408
   Review Questions, Suggested Activities
Workbook: Pages 205–218
   Review Questions, Problems/Activities
Teacher's Resources:
   Chapter 18 Pretest
   Chapter 18 Teaching Strategy
   Chapter 18 Posttest

Teaching Strategy

- **Knowledge Assessment.** Administer the Chapter 18 Pretest. Correct the test and return. Highlight topics in which the individual student is deficient.
- Prepare Display #1.
- Review chapter objectives.
- Present the definition and purpose of the floor plan.
- Identify the required information on a floor plan.

- Discuss location and size of walls.
- Present location and size of windows and doors, cabinets, appliances, and permanent fixtures.
- Cover stairs, fireplaces, walks, patios, and decks.
- Discuss room names and material symbols. Assign workbook Problem/Activity 18-1.
- Cover dimensioning floor plans, scale, and sheet identification.
- Assign workbook Problem/Activity 18-2. Prepare Display #2.
- Discuss the procedure for drawing the floor plan.
- Assign workbook Problem/Activity 18-3.
- Assign one or more of the Suggested Activities in the text.
- **Chapter Review.** Assign Review Questions in the text. Discuss the correct answers. Assign Review Questions in the workbook. Have students check their own answers. Make a transparency of the solution for Problem/Activity 18-1 and use for review.
- **Evaluation.** Administer Chapter 18 Posttest. Correct the test and return. Return graded problems with comments.

Answers to Review Questions, Text
Page 408

1. section
2. It identifies the location and dimensions of exterior and interior walls, windows, doors, major appliances, cabinets, fireplaces, and other fixed features of the house.
3. 1/4" = 1'-0"
4. 6"
5. centers
6. opening
7. With hidden (dashed) lines.
8. Direction of flight, number of risers, and width of the stairs.

9. a) Plaster.
   b) Aluminum or rigid insulation.
   c) Batt insulation.
   d) Dimensional lumber.
   e) Common brick.
   f) Cast concrete.
10. 0'-4"; 4"
11. space diagram
12. center
13. symbols library
14. Automatic wall generation, repetitive use of symbols, dimensioning features, and elimination of hand lettering.

Answers to Workbook Questions

Page 205

Part I: Short Answer/Listing

1. Answer may include any nine: Exterior and interior walls; size and location of windows and doors; built-in cabinets and appliances; permanent fixtures; stairs; fireplaces; walks, patios, and decks; room names; material symbols; location and size dimensions; and drawing scale.
2. Basic size, location, direction of flight, number of risers, and width of the stairs.
3. Basic width, length, location, fireplace opening shape, and additional chimney flues.
4. The name of the room is required, but not the sizes of the rooms. It is, however, helpful to provide the sizes. The size should be placed below the room name.
5. They should be placed at least 3/4" from the view.
6. At the bottom of each drawing.
7. The number of the sheet should be placed in the lower-right corner.
8. Determine the requirements of the structure and record them as preliminary sketches.
9. Lay out the exterior walls.
10. The height between finished floors must be determined and the tread and riser height calculated.
11. Dimensions, notes, and room names should be added after the kitchen and bathroom fixtures are drawn.
12. Sheet number, name of drawing, scale, date, the name of the person for whom the drawing is made, and who made the drawing.
13. If the expansion is planned in the initial drawing, the overall appearance of the completed structure is more pleasing. Also, the number of changes required are minimized when the expansion takes place.
14. The weatherboard or sheathing but not the siding.
15. 1/2" + 3-1/2" + 3/4" + 1/2" = 5-1/4"
16. symbols

Part II: Multiple Choice

1. A. First.
2. C. Section view.
3. B. 5"
4. B. sash width
5. A. Actual.
6. C. Hidden line.
7. D. All of the above.
8. C. 3/16"
9. B. Above the line.
10. A. 1/4" or 3/8"
11. C. Both A and B.
12. C. Center.
13. A. 4'
14. D. 1/4" = 1'-0".
15. B. Interior walls.
16. A. The doors, windows, stairs, and fireplaces have been drawn.
17. C. Before the kitchen cabinets, appliances, and bathroom fixtures have been drawn.
18. A. 24"; 12"
19. D. When the drawing is almost complete.
20. C. Vary in width.
21. C. Style of drawing.

Part III: Matching

1. B. Floor plan.
2. D.
3. F.
4. G.
5. E.
6. C. Hidden line.
7. H.

8. J.

9. M.

10. L.

11. K.

12. I.

13. A. Dimensions.

Part IV: Completion

1. plumbing
2. 8"
3. **OFFSET; DOUBLE LINE**
4. centerline
5. windows and exterior doors
6. swing
7. Hatch patterns (symbols)
8. parallel
9. 2"
10. outside
11. outside; stud
12. width
13. simplified; detailed
14. type
15. hidden
16. exterior
17. construction
18. accuracy
19. edge
20. center

Part V: Problems/Activities

1. Solution on page 309 of this manual.
2. Solution on page 310 of this manual.
3. Solution on page 311 of this manual.

Answers to Chapter 18 Pretest

Completion

1. outside
2. floor
3. right
4. hidden
5. edges

Multiple Choice

1. C. 5-3/8"
2. B. 3/4"
3. A. partial dimensions do not add up to the total distance
4. C. locate dimensions where you would logically look for them
5. A. detailed
6. C. 1'-6"
7. D. section

Short Answer

1. Check the entire drawing for accuracy and completeness.
2. Because building material sizes are keyed to this dimension; to reduce waste.
3. 3/16"
4. Exterior and interior walls; size and location of windows and doors; built-in cabinets and appliances; permanent fixtures; stairs; fireplaces; walks, patios, and decks; room names; material symbols; location and size dimensions; and drawing scale.
5. When information cannot be represented by a conventional dimension or symbol.
6. 1/4" = 1'-0"
7. Automatic wall generation, repetitive use of symbols, dimensioning features, and elimination of hand lettering.

Answers to Chapter 18 Posttest

Completion

1. floor
2. hidden
3. outside
4. edges
5. right

Multiple Choice

1. D. section
2. C. 5-3/8"
3. A. detailed
4. C. locate dimensions where you would logically look for them
5. B. 3/4"
6. C. 1'-6"
7. A. partial dimensions do not add up to the total distance

Short Answer

1. Automatic wall generation, repetitive use of symbols, dimensioning features, and elimination of hand lettering.

2. Exterior and interior walls; size and location of windows and doors; built-in cabinets and appliances; permanent fixtures; stairs; fireplaces; walks, patios, and decks; room names; material symbols; location and size dimensions; and drawing scale.

3. Because building material sizes are keyed to this dimension; to reduce waste.

4. When information cannot be represented by a conventional dimension or symbol.

5. 3/16″

6. 1/4″ = 1′-0″

7. Check the entire drawing for accuracy and completeness.

Workbook Solution

Directions:

Complete the plan view of the following symbols that are used on typical residential floor plans.

BRICK VENEER ON FRAME

SOLID BRICK WALL

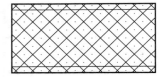

CONCRETE BLOCK WALL

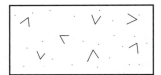

CASE CONCRETE WALL

ARCHWAY OR PLAIN OPENING

GLAZED TILE
SECTION

TERRAZZO
SECTION

SLATE
SECTION

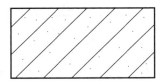

RUBBLE STONE
SECTION

SCALE: 1/4"=1'-0"

| FLOOR PLAN SYMBOLS | NAME: | 18-1 |

Workbook Solution

2.

18-

Directions:
Using the procedure discussed in the text, properly dimension the frame wall structure and the concrete wall structure examples. Note: The scale is 1/4" = 1'-0".

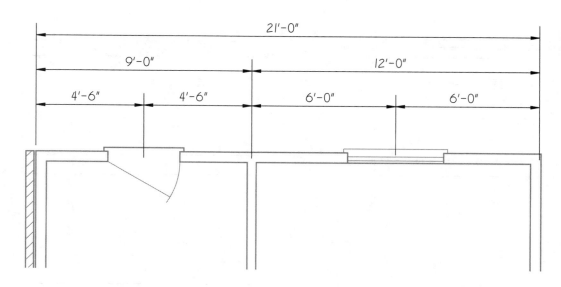

FRAME WALL CONSTRUCTION

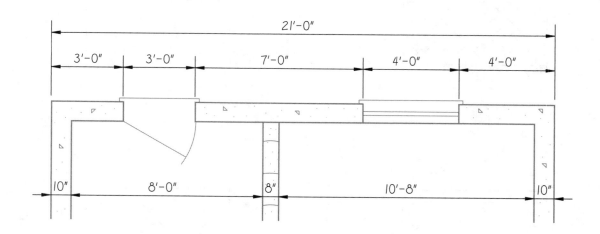

CONCRETE WALL CONSTRUCTION

DIMENSIONING FLOOR PLANS | NAME: | 18-

FLOOR PLAN

SCALE: 1/4"=1'-0"

NOTE: STANDARD DOOR OFFSET IS 6" UNLESS OTHERWISE SPECIFIED.

GARAGE FLOOR 4" BELOW HOUSE FLOOR

FLOOR DRAIN

GARAGE
11'-2" x 19'-4"

DINING AREA
9'-10" x 15'-8"

KITCHEN
11'-5" x 11'-8"

WORK TRIANGLE
17'-6"

D.W.

REF.

BAR

FAMILY ROOM
11'-10" x 16'-0"

LIVING ROOM
11'-4" x 17'-0"

PORCH
4" CONCRETE SLAB

BEDROOM # 3
10'-4" x 10'-10"

BATH
5'-0" x 13'-4"

TERRA COTTA TILE

FOYER
5'-7" x 11'-9"

LIN.

M. BEDROOM
13'-4" x 15'-5"

M. BATH
5'-6" x 11'-5"

BEDROOM # 2
13'-4" x 15'-2"

32'-0"

21'-0"

20'-0"

8'-0"

6'-0"

6'-0"

12'-0"

6'-0"

6'-0"

6'-0"

28'-0"

16'-0"

8'-0"

64'-0"

12'-0"

6'-0"

15'-0"

27'-0"

36'-0"

64'-0"

5'-6"

11'-6"

6'-0"

12'-0"

6'-0"

3'-0"

4'-0"

7'-3"

17'-0"

12'-0"

3'-0"

3'-0"

6'-0"

36'-0"

5'-6"

2'-9"

2'-9"

3'-0"

8'-0"

16'-0"

8'-0"

6'-0"

6'-0"

6'-0"

4'-0"

4'-0"

8'-0"

3'-0"

6'-0"

3'-0"

6'-0"

6'-0"

3'-0"

3'-0"

6'-0"

12'-0"

14'-0"

6'-0"

14'-0"

34'-0"

Chapter 18 Pretest
The Floor Plan

Name _____

Period _____**Date** _____**Score** _____

Completion

Complete each sentence with the proper response. Place your answer on the space provided.

1. Exterior frame walls are dimensioned to the _____ of the stud wall.

2. The _____ plan is the one plan to which all trade-workers refer.

3. Dimensions on a floor plan should read from the bottom and _____ side.

4. A plain opening or archway is shown using a(n) _____ linetype (symbol) on a floor plan.

5. Windows in a masonry wall are dimensioned to the _____ of the opening.

1. _____

2. _____

3. _____

4. _____

5. _____

Multiple Choice

Choose the answer that correctly completes the statement. Write the corresponding letter in the space provided.

_____ 1. An exterior frame wall composed of 5/8″ siding, 3/4″ insulation board, 2″ × 4″ studs, and 1/2″ dry wall is exactly _____ thick.

    A. 3-7/8″
    B. 6″
    C. 5-3/8″
    D. 5-7/8″

_____ 2. Dimensions should be a minimum of _____ from the floor plan view.

    A. 1/2″
    B. 3/4″
    C. 1″
    D. 2″

_____ 3. One of the most frequent errors in dimensioning is that _____.

    A. partial dimensions do not add up to the total distance
    B. the numbers cannot be read
    C. dimensions face the wrong direction
    D. dimensions are too close together

_____ 4. A good policy to follow when locating dimensions on a floor plan is to _____.

    A. group them all together in one corner
    B. leave out everything that may be obvious
    C. locate dimensions where you would logically look for them
    D. follow your hunches

_____ 5. Some symbols are simplified while others are _____.

    A. detailed
    B. abbreviated
    C. described
    D. None of the above.

_____ 6. Which of the following dimension forms is correct for floor plans?

    A. 0'-1/2"
    B. 6.125"
    C. 1'-6"
    D. 10.6'

_____ 7. The floor plan is actually a(n) _____ drawing.

    A. elevation
    B. pictorial
    C. top view
    D. section

Short Answer

Answer the following questions.

1. What is the very last thing to do when drawing a floor plan? _____
_____

2. Why should the overall lengths of major wall segments be multiples of 4'? _____
_____

3. What is the recommended height for lettering room names? _____
_____

4. List eleven basic features commonly shown on a floor plan. _____
_____
_____
_____
_____
_____

5. When are notes used instead of dimensions? _____

6. What is the usual scale of a residential floor plan? _____

7. List four features of CADD that reduce design and drafting time to a fraction of that required for manual drafting._____

_____

_____

_____

Chapter 18 Posttest
The Floor Plan

Name _____

Period _____ **Date** _____ **Score** _____

Completion

Complete each sentence with the proper response. Place your answer on the space provided.

1. The _____ plan is the one plan to which all trade-workers refer.

1. _____

2. A plain opening or archway is shown using a(n) _____ linetype (symbol) on a floor plan.

2. _____

3. Exterior frame walls are dimensioned to the _____ of the stud wall.

3. _____

4. Windows in a masonry wall are dimensioned to the _____ of the opening.

4. _____

5. Dimensions on a floor plan should read from the bottom and _____ side.

5. _____

Multiple Choice

Choose the answer that correctly completes the statement. Write the corresponding letter in the space provided.

_____ 1. The floor plan is actually a(n) _____ drawing.

    A. elevation
    B. pictorial
    C. top view
    D. section

_____ 2. An exterior frame wall composed of 5/8" siding, 3/4" insulation board, 2" × 4" studs, and 1/2" dry wall is exactly_____ thick.

    A. 3-7/8"
    B. 6"
    C. 5-3/8"
    D. 5-7/8"

_____ 3. Some symbols are simplified while others are _____.

    A. detailed
    B. abbreviated
    C. described
    D. None of the above.

_____ 4. A good policy to follow when locating dimensions on a floor plan is to _____.

    A. group them all together in one corner
    B. leave out everything that may be obvious
    C. locate dimensions where you would logically look for them
    D. follow your hunches

_____ 5. Dimensions should be a minimum of ____ from the floor plan view.

    A. 1/2″
    B. 3/4″
    C. 1″
    D. 2″

_____ 6. Which of the following dimension forms is correct for floor plans?

    A. 0′-1/2″
    B. 6.125″
    C. 1′-6″
    D. 10.6′

_____ 7. One of the most frequent errors in dimensioning is that _____.

    A. partial dimensions do not add up to the total distance
    B. the numbers cannot be read
    C. dimensions face the wrong direction
    D. dimensions are too close together

Short Answer

Answer the following questions.

1. List four features of CADD that reduce design and drafting time to a fraction of that required for manual drafting._____

_____

_____

_____

2. List eleven basic features commonly shown on a floor plan. _____

_____

_____

_____

_____

_____

3. Why should the overall lengths of major wall segments be multiples of 4′?_____

_____

4. When are notes used instead of dimensions? _____

5. What is the recommended height for lettering room names? _____

_____

6. What is the usual scale of a residential floor plan? _____

7. What is the very last thing to do when drawing a floor plan?_____

_____

Roof Designs

19

Objectives

After studying this chapter, the student will be able to:

- Name and sketch ten different types of basic roof designs.
- Describe the construction of a typical frame roof.
- Draw a roof that has a typical roof slope (pitch).
- Interpret information found on a rafter span chart.
- Explain the importance of proper attic ventilation and roof flashing.
- Compile the appropriate information to order roof trusses for a house.

Displays

1. **Roof Styles**. Create a bulletin board display of interesting roof designs using photos or pictures cut from magazines. Identify each roof design.
2. **Roofing Materials**. Display typical roof covering products such as asphalt shingles, cedar shakes, terra cotta tile, slate, and metal roofing.
3. **Cornice Models**. Show cornice models built by students for Activity #3 in the Suggested Activities in the text.
4. **Roof Trusses**. Build scale models of various roof trusses for display in the classroom.

Instructional Materials

Text: Pages 409–430
   Review Questions, Suggested Activities
Workbook: Pages 219–232
   Questions, Problems/Activities
Teacher's Resources:
   Chapter 19 Pretest
   Chapter 19 Teaching Strategy
   Chapter 19 Posttest

Teaching Strategy

- **Knowledge Assessment:** Administer the Chapter 19 Pretest. Correct the test and return. Highlight the topics in which the individual student is deficient.
- Prepare Display #1.
- Review the chapter objectives.
- Compare and contrast the different types of roofs.
- Discuss traditional frame roof construction.
- Assign Problem 19-1 and Problem 19-2 in the workbook.
- Cover rake and gable ends.
- Prepare Display #2.
- Assign Problem 19-3 in the workbook.
- Prepare Display #3.
- Discuss roof trusses, ventilation, and flashing.
- Assign Problem 19-4 in the workbook.
- Discuss gutters and downspouts, roof sheathing, and roofing.
- Prepare Display #4.
- Assign one or more of the Suggested Activities in the text.
- **Chapter Review:** Assign the Review Questions in the text. Discuss the correct answers. Assign the questions in the workbook. Have students check their own answers. Make a transparency of the solution to Problem 19-3 in the workbook and use for review.
- **Evaluation:** Administer the Chapter 19 Posttest. Correct the test and return. Return graded problems with comments.

Answers to Review Questions, Text
Page 429

1. Gable, hip, flat, shed, mansard, gambrel, butterfly, A-frame, folded plate, and curved panel. (Also acceptable: Winged gable, Dutch hip, parasol, warped, and free form.)

2. to support the roofing material
3. rafter
4. 48'
5. the inside of one exterior stud wall, the inside of the opposite exterior stud wall
6. run
7. Pitch = Rise/Clear Span
8. 12:12 or 1/2
9. The distance to be spanned, the spacing of the rafters, and the weight to be supported.
10. four
11. cornice
12. Open, box, and close.
13. To prevent moisture accumulation under the roof sheathing and to cool the attic/house.
14. 1/300th
15. Answer may include any two of the following: Aluminum, copper, and galvanized sheet steel.
16. 1/2"
17. Answer may include any two of the following: Asphalt shingles, wood shingles, tile, slate, roll roofing, copper, aluminum, galvanized steel, layers of felt and tar, and rubber membrane roofing.
18. 235
19. It permits wide, unsupported spans and uses a minimum amount of material.
20. W-type truss, king-post or K-post truss, and scissors truss.
21. The span, roof pitch, spacing of the trusses, and anticipated roof load.
22. It is used to fasten the members of a wood truss together.
23. Asphalt laminate shingles and metal roofs.

Answers to Workbook Questions
Page 219

Part I: Multiple Choice

1. D. All of the above.
2. A. flat
3. C. They extend from the ridge of the roof to the plate or beyond.
4. B. asphalt shingles
5. C. 6" and 12"
6. A. close
7. B. Generally, 2" × 4" lumber is used in lightweight wood roof trusses.

8. A. At least 6 square feet.
9. D. All of the above.
10. C. 3/4"
11. A. asphalt
12. C. 12'

Part II: Matching

1. F. Gable
2. H. Hip
3. E. Flat
4. O. Shed
5. I. Mansard
6. A. A-frame
7. J. Pitch
8. B. Clear span
9. L. Rise
10. M. Run
11. C. Cornice
12. K. Rake
13. G. Gusset
14. D. Flashing
15. N. Sheathing

Part III: Short Answer/Listing

1. It is made of layers of roofing felt and tar, or some other material such as rubber topped with gravel.
2. Ridge cut, seat cut, plumb cut, and tail cut.
3. The distance to be spanned, the spacing of the rafters, and the weight to be supported.
4. In low-pitched roofs, rafters may also serve as a base for the finished ceiling.
5. Exposed-beam construction, contemporary, or rustic designs.
6. Where the overhangs are very wide.
7. It is nailed to the underside of the rafters.
8. Wide overhangs protect the sidewall and reduce the frequency of painting.
9. A narrow box cornice is normally used for a colonial or Cape Cod.
10. The span, roof pitch, spacing of the trusses, and anticipated roof load.
11. Added ceiling insulation, added ventilation, and less moisture condensation.
12. Use louvered openings in the gable ends and along the underside of the overhang or use ridge ventilators.
13. Planks, individual boards, or another approved panel product.
14. Asphalt laminate shingles and metal roofing.

Part IV: Completion

1. flat
2. 3:12
3. gambrel
4. pitches
5. 4
6. gable
7. open
8. narrow
9. sloped
10. rake
11. king-post or K-post
12. moisture
13. 18"
14. ogee
15. face grain
16. felt
17. Flashing
18. cornice

Part V: Problems/Activities

1. Solution on page 322 of this manual.
2. Solution on page 323 of this manual.
3. Solution on page 324 of this manual.
4. Solution on page 325 of this manual.

Answers to Chapter 19 Pretest

Completion

1. less steep
2. wall plate
3. cornice
4. rise, run
5. 4

Multiple Choice

1. B. 24"
2. A. rake
3. A. shed
4. B. warped
5. D. flat
6. B. rafters
7. A. rise by the span
8. C. slate
9. C. run
10. D. barn
11. B. ventilation
12. B. gable

Short Answer

1. The narrow box, wide box with lookouts, and wide box without lookouts.
2. Open, box, and close.
3. Aluminum, copper, galvanized sheet steel, roll roofing, and small metal edging used to act as a drip edge.
4. Flashing should be used where the roof comes in contact with a wood or masonry wall, chimney, or roof valley, and at the edge of the roof.
5. Planks, individual boards, plywood, and other approved panel products.

Answers to Chapter 19 Posttest

Completion

1. 4
2. wall plate
3. rise, run
4. less steep
5. cornice

Multiple Choice

1. B. gable
2. A. shed
3. D. barn
4. B. warped
5. B. rafters
6. C. run
7. A. rise by the span
8. D. flat
9. C. slate
10. A. rake
11. B. ventilation
12. B. 24"

Short Answer

1. Open, box, and close.
2. The narrow box, wide box with lookouts, and wide box without lookouts.
3. Flashing should be used where the roof comes in contact with a wood or masonry wall, chimney, or roof valley, and at the edge of the roof.
4. Aluminum, copper, galvanized sheet steel, roll roofing, and small metal edging used to act as a drip edge.
5. Planks, individual boards, plywood, and other approved panel products.

Workbook Solution

1.

Directions:
Identify the elements indicated in the partial roof framing plan below.

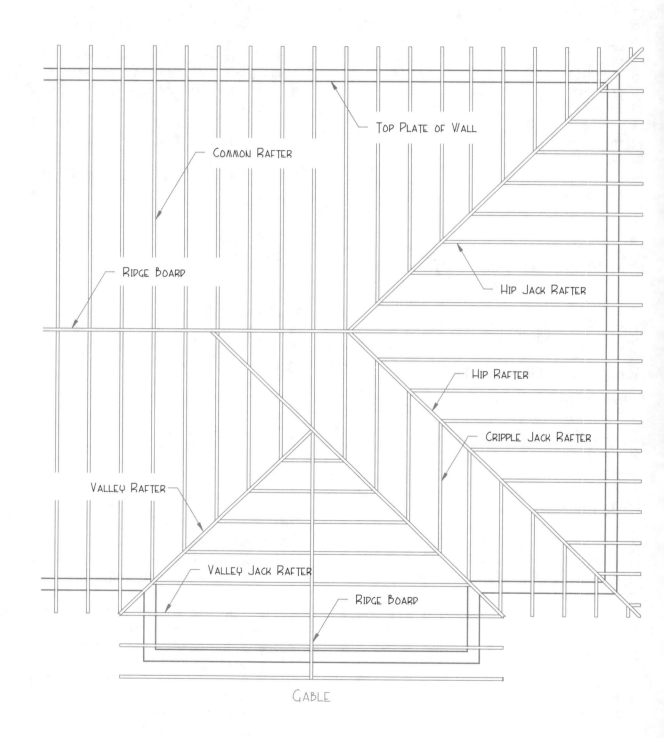

Top Plate of Wall

Common Rafter

Ridge Board

Hip Jack Rafter

Hip Rafter

Cripple Jack Rafter

Valley Rafter

Valley Jack Rafter

Ridge Board

Gable

SCALE: 1/4"=1'-0"

ROOF FRAMING PARTS   NAME: 19

Workbook Solution

Directions:

A. Construct the ceiling joist (2″ × 6″) and rafter (2″ × 4″) layout for a cottage that has a clear span of 19′–3 1/2″, a roof slope of 6:12, and an 18″ overhang. Dimension the rise and run and show the roof slope triangle.

B. Instead of ceiling joists and rafters, show the roof structure using W-type or King-post roof trusses. Dimension as above.

A

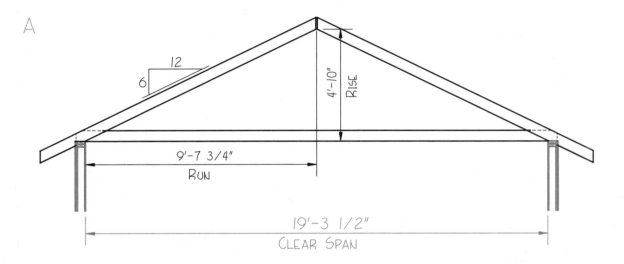

12

6

4′-10″ RISE

9′-7 3/4″
RUN

19′-3 1/2″
CLEAR SPAN

B

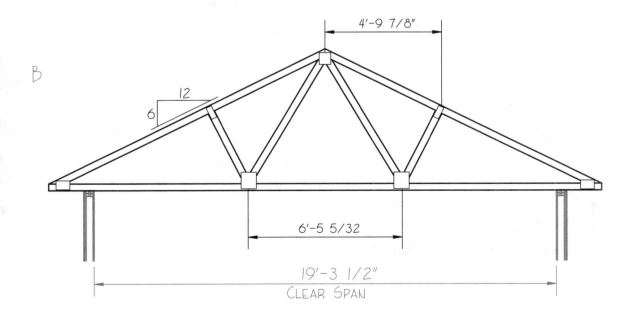

4′-9 7/8″

12

6

6′-5 5/32

19′-3 1/2″
CLEAR SPAN

ROOF SLOPE	NAME:	19-2

3.

Directions:
Draw a large scale (1″ = 1′-0″) section through a wide box cornice with lookouts. Incorporate the following dimensions and features in your drawing:

> 2″ × 4″ stud wall with 3/4″ RF insulation and horizontal siding on the outside and 1/2″ drywall inside.
> 24″ overhang (outside of insulation to end of rafters) with ventilation.
> 2″ × 6″ rafters and 2″ × 8″ ceiling joists.
> 1/2″ plywood roof sheathing, redwood fascia board, and asphalt shingles.

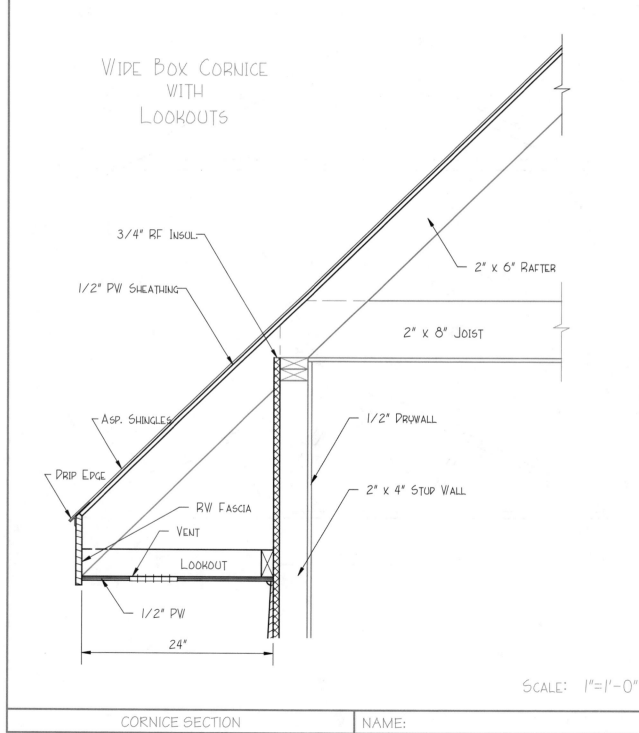

WIDE BOX CORNICE
WITH
LOOKOUTS

3/4″ RF INSUL.

1/2″ PW SHEATHING

2″ × 6″ RAFTER

2″ × 8″ JOIST

ASP. SHINGLES

1/2″ DRYWALL

DRIP EDGE

2″ × 4″ STUD WALL

RW FASCIA

VENT

LOOKOUT

1/2″ PW

24″

SCALE: 1″=1′-0″

| CORNICE SECTION | NAME: | 19 |

ASSIGNMENT 19-4

ENGINEERED WOOD ROOF TRUSSES

RIDGE LINE

VALLEY LINE

16" x 16" CHIMNEY

16" x 16" CHIMNEY

20" x 20" FRAMED OPENING

LOOKOUT RAFTERS

24"
TYP.

24"
TYP.

RIDGE LINE

NOTE: USE LATERAL AND DIAGONAL BRACING AS NEEDED
OR REQUIRED BY LOCAL CODE.
SHEATHING IS 1/2" CDX PLYWOOD OR EQUIVALENT.

SCALE: 1/4"=1'-0"

GUSSET PLATE

12
5

12
5

12
5

5'-0"

24'-0"

ROOF FRAMING PLAN

TRUSS DETAIL   SCALE: 1/2"=1'-0"

Chapter 19 Pretest
Roof Designs

Name _____

Period _____**Date** _____**Score** _____

Completion

Complete each sentence with the proper response. Place your answer on the space provided.

1. When comparing the steepness of roof pitches, an 8:12 slope is _____ than a 12:12 slope.

1. _____

2. The rise of a roof is the vertical distance measured from the top of the _____ to the underside of the rafters.

2. _____

3. A gable roof has a _____ formed on two sides of the building.

3. _____

4. The slope diagram represents the ratio between the _____ and _____ of the roof.

4. _____

_____

5. A lightweight roofing is one that weighs less than _____ pounds per square foot.

5. _____

Multiple Choice

Choose the answer that correctly completes the statement. Write the corresponding letter in the space provided.

_____ 1. Most wood roof trusses are designed to be placed _____ OC.

    A. 18″
    B. 24″
    C. 30″
    D. 36″

_____ 2. The _____ is the extension of a gable roof beyond the end wall of the house.

    A. rake
    B. soffit
    C. overhang
    D. fascia

_____ 3. A _____ roof is similar to a flat roof, but has more pitch.

    A. shed
    B. gable
    C. mansard
    D. butterfly

_____ 4. The _____ roof is an example of a modern roof that is experimental for residential housing structures.

    A. butterfly
    B. warped
    C. gambrel
    D. hip

_____ 5. A _____ roof is the most economical roof to construct.

    A. A-frame
    B. mansard
    C. curved panel
    D. flat

_____ 6. In typical gable roof construction, the _____ support the roof covering.

    A. top plates
    B. rafters
    C. ceiling joists
    D. soffits

_____ 7. The fractional pitch of a roof is calculated by dividing the _____.

    A. rise by the span
    B. span by the rise
    C. run by the span
    D. span by the run

_____ 8. A roof covering of _____ is an example of heavy roofing.

    A. roll roofing
    B. asphalt shingles
    C. slate
    D. All of the above.

_____ 9. The _____ of a roof is one-half of the span.

    A. pitch
    B. rise
    C. run
    D. slope

_____ 10. A gambrel roof is sometimes called a _____ roof.

    A. French
    B. winged gable
    C. folded plate
    D. barn

_____ 11. If sufficient _____ is not provided in the attic, moisture will probably form on the underside of the roof sheathing.

    A. headroom
    B. ventilation
    C. insulation
    D. heating ducts

_____ 12. The _____ roof is a very popular type of roof because it is easy to build, sheds water well, provides for ventilation, and is applicable to a variety of house shapes and designs.

  A. folded plate
  B. gable
  C. A-frame
  D. flat

Short Answer

Provide brief answers to the following questions.

1. Identify the three types of box cornices. _____

_____

_____

2. List the three types of cornices frequently used in residential buildings. _____

_____

_____

3. What common materials are frequently used as roof flashing? _____

_____

_____

_____

4. Where should flashing be used on a roof? _____

_____

_____

_____

5. What materials are generally used as roof sheathing? _____

_____

_____

_____

Chapter 19 Posttest
Roof Designs

Name _____

Period _____**Date** _____**Score** _____

Completion

Complete each sentence with the proper response. Place your answer on the space provided.

1. A lightweight roofing is one that weighs less than _____ pounds per square foot.

1. _____

2. The rise of a roof is the vertical distance measured from the top of the _____ to the underside of the rafters.

2. _____

3. The slope diagram represents the ratio between the _____ and _____ of the roof.

3. _____

_____

4. When comparing the steepness of roof pitches, an 8:12 slope is _____ than a 12:12 slope.

4. _____

5. A gable roof has a _____ formed on two sides of the building.

5. _____

Multiple Choice

Choose the answer that correctly completes the statement. Write the corresponding letter in the space provided.

_____ 1. The _____ roof is a very popular type of roof because it is easy to build, sheds water well, provides for ventilation, and is applicable to a variety of house shapes and designs.

A. folded plate
B. gable
C. A-frame
D. flat

_____ 2. A _____ roof is similar to a flat roof, but has more pitch.

A. shed
B. gable
C. mansard
D. butterfly

_____ 3. A gambrel roof is sometimes called a _____ roof.

A. French
B. winged gable
C. folded plate
D. barn

_____ 4. The _____ roof is an example of a modern roof that is experimental for residential housing structures.

    A. butterfly
    B. warped
    C. gambrel
    D. hip

_____ 5. In typical gable roof construction, the _____ support the roof covering.

    A. top plates
    B. rafters
    C. ceiling joists
    D. soffits

_____ 6. The _____ of a roof is one-half of the span.

    A. pitch
    B. rise
    C. run
    D. slope

_____ 7. The fractional pitch of a roof is calculated by dividing the _____.

    A. rise by the span
    B. span by the rise
    C. run by the span
    D. span by the run

_____ 8. A _____ roof is the most economical roof to construct.

    A. A-frame
    B. mansard
    C. curved panel
    D. flat

_____ 9. A roof covering of _____ is an example of heavy roofing.

    A. roll roofing
    B. asphalt shingles
    C. slate
    D. All of the above.

_____ 10. The _____ is the extension of a gable roof beyond the end wall of the house.

    A. rake
    B. soffit
    C. overhang
    D. fascia

_____ 11. If sufficient _____ is not provided in the attic, moisture will probably form on the underside of the roof sheathing.

    A. headroom
    B. ventilation
    C. insulation
    D. heating ducts

_____ 12. Most wood roof trusses are designed to be placed _____ OC.

    A. 18″
    B. 24″
    C. 30″
    D. 36″

Short Answer

Provide brief answers to the following questions.

1. List the three types of cornices frequently used in residential buildings. _____

    _____

    _____

2. Identify the three types of box cornices. _____

    _____

    _____

3. Where should flashing be used on a roof? _____

    _____

    _____

    _____

4. What common materials are frequently used as roof flashing? _____

    _____

    _____

    _____

5. What materials are generally used as roof sheathing? _____

    _____

    _____

    _____

Elevations

20

Objectives

After studying this chapter, the student will be able to:

- List features that should be included on an exterior elevation.
- Identify the dimensions commonly shown on elevations.
- Explain symbols that are often found on elevations.
- Draw a typical exterior elevation that demonstrates proper techniques.

Displays

1. **Front Elevations.** Select a well-designed front elevation of a residential structure and display it on the bulletin board. Include the floor plan if available.
2. **Student Work.** Display student work on the bulletin board. Use completed workbook assignments.

Instructional Materials

Text: Pages 431–447
 Review Questions, Suggested Activities
Workbook: Pages 233–244
 Review Questions, Problems/Activities
Teacher's Resources:
 Chapter 20 Pretest
 Chapter 20 Teaching Strategy
 Chapter 20 Posttest

Teaching Strategy

- **Knowledge assessment.** Administer Chapter 20 Pretest. Correct the test and return. Highlight topics in which the individual student is deficient.
- Prepare Display #1.
- Review chapter objectives.
- Discuss the definition and purpose of exterior elevations.
- Present required information, elevation identification, grade line, floors, and ceilings.
- Discuss walls, windows, and doors.
- Assign workbook Problem 20-1.
- Discuss roof features.
- Prepare Display #2.
- Assign workbook Problems/Activities 20-2 and 20-3.
- Present dimensions, notes, and symbols.
- Discuss the procedure for drawing an elevation. Assign workbook Problem/Activity 20-4.
- Assign one or more of the Suggested Activities in the text.
- **Chapter Review.** Assign Review Questions in the text. Discuss the correct answers. Assign Review Questions in the workbook. Have students check their own answers. Make transparencies of solutions to Problems/Activities 20-1 and 20-3 and use for review.
- **Evaluation.** Administer Chapter 20 Posttest. Correct the test and return. Return graded problems with comments.

Answers to Review Questions, Text

Page 447

1. To show the finished appearance of a given side of the building and furnish vertical height dimensions.
2. Four; Front, rear, left side, right side (or east, west, north, south).
3. grade line
4. hidden
5. 8'-0"
6. 7'-6"; 8'-0"
7. 6'-2"
8. 8"
9. Height dimensions can be projected from the typical wall section.
10. 6'-10"
11. On an elevation that shows the angle of the roof.
12. 2'-0"
13. By projecting from a typical wall section.
14. By projecting from a floor plan.
15. **SCALE**

Answers to Workbook Questions

Page 233

Part I: Completion

1. details
2. structure side
3. hidden
4. 4"
5. centerline
6. typical wall section
7. slope triangle
8. elevation
9. 1/4" = 1'-0".
10. floor
11. horizontal
12. scale

Part II: Short Answer/Listing

1. To show the finished appearance of each side of the house as well as exterior materials desired. Also, to illustrate the vertical height dimensions about basic features of the house.
2. Answer may include any four: Grade lines, finished floor and ceiling levels, location of exterior wall corners, windows and doors, roof features, vertical dimensions of important features, porches, decks and patios, and material symbols.
3. In the finished-floor-to-finished-ceiling distance, the first floor measurement is 8'-0", while the second floor measurement is 7'-6" or 8'-0". The construction dimension is measured from the top of the subfloor to the top of the wall plate; the first floor is usually 8'-1 1/2" while the second floor is usually 7'-7 1/2" or 8'-1 1/2". The latter method usually does not require any calculations and is generally preferred by carpenters.
4. This practice protects the framing members from moisture.
5. The lower face of the head jamb is considered the height of the opening. This dimension is usually 6'-10" from the top of the subfloor.
6. Highest.
7. B. Lay out the desired slope starting from the top-inside corner of the wall plate. A line from this point to the ridge will determine the underside. Note: A variation of this procedure will be necessary for certain roof trusses. D. Measure the amount of desired overhang. Do not forget to add the thickness of roof sheathing. E. Repeat the procedure for the other side of the roof. A. Locate the top of the upper wall plate and the centerline of the proposed ridge location. The ridge is usually in the center between the exterior walls. C. Measure the width of the rafter perpendicular to the bottom edge and draw the top edge parallel to the bottom edge of the rafter.
8. Answer may include any four: Thickness of the footing, distance from the footing to the grade, distances from finished floors to finished ceilings, overhang width, height of the top of windows and doors, and height of chimney above the roof. Other dimensions may be required for details such as deck railing, retaining walls, and planters.
9. The dimensions, notes, and symbols are the last details added to the elevation drawing and drawn before the title block.

Part III: Multiple Choice

1. B. Plot or site plan.
2. A. 8'-0".
3. C. Object
4. D. All of the above.
5. B. Roof pitch symbol.
6. B. section drawing
7. D. After the vertical and horizontal lines have been drawn and the features have been darkened.

Part IV: Problems/Activities

1. Solution on page 336 of this manual.
2. Solution on page 337 of this manual.
3. Solution on page 338 of this manual.
4. Solution on page 339 of this manual.

Answers to Chapter 20 Pretest

Completion

1. windows
2. Elevation
3. object
4. Window
5. 8'-0"

Multiple Choice
1. C. Either A or B.
2. D. grade line
3. A. 8″
4. A. front
5. A. 6′-10″
6. B. vertical height
7. B. 1/4″ = 1′-0″
8. B. hidden lines

Short Answer
1. By structure side or by compass points.
2. Because they may interfere with the other information if drawn earlier.
3. Answer may include any nine: Identification of the specific side of the house that the elevation represents, grade lines, finished floor and ceiling levels, location of exterior wall corners, windows and doors, roof features, vertical dimensions of important features, porches, decks and patios, and material symbols.
4. Projected from the floor plan.
5. **SCALE**

Answers to Chapter 20 Posttest
Completion
1. Elevation
2. 8′-0″
3. object
4. windows
5. Window

Multiple Choice
1. D. grade line
2. B. hidden lines
3. A. 8″
4. A. 6′-10″
5. C. Either A or B.
6. B. vertical height
7. A. front
8. B. 1/4″ = 1′-0″

Short Answer
1. Answer may include any nine: Identification of the specific side of the house that the elevation represents, grade lines, finished floor and ceiling levels, location of exterior wall corners, windows and doors, roof features, vertical dimensions of important features, porches, decks and patios, and material symbols.
2. By structure side or by compass points.
3. Projected from the floor plan.
4. Because they may interfere with the other information if drawn earlier.
5. **SCALE**

1.

Directions:
Draw an elevation view of each of the exterior wall materials indicated below. Symbols should be drawn at 1/4" = 1'-0" scale.

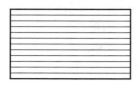

BRICK

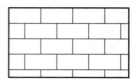

CONCRETE BLOCK

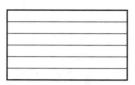

HORIZONTAL SIDING

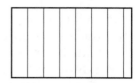

VERTICAL SIDING

STUCCO

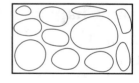

RUBBLE STONE

CAST CONCRETE

GLASS PANEL

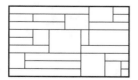

ASHLAR STONE

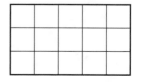

12" CERAMIC TILE

| EXTERIOR ELEVATION SYMBOLS | NAME: | 2(|

Workbook Solution

Directions:
Complete the partial front elevation of the two-story colonial below. See Figures 20-1 and 20-2 for ideas.

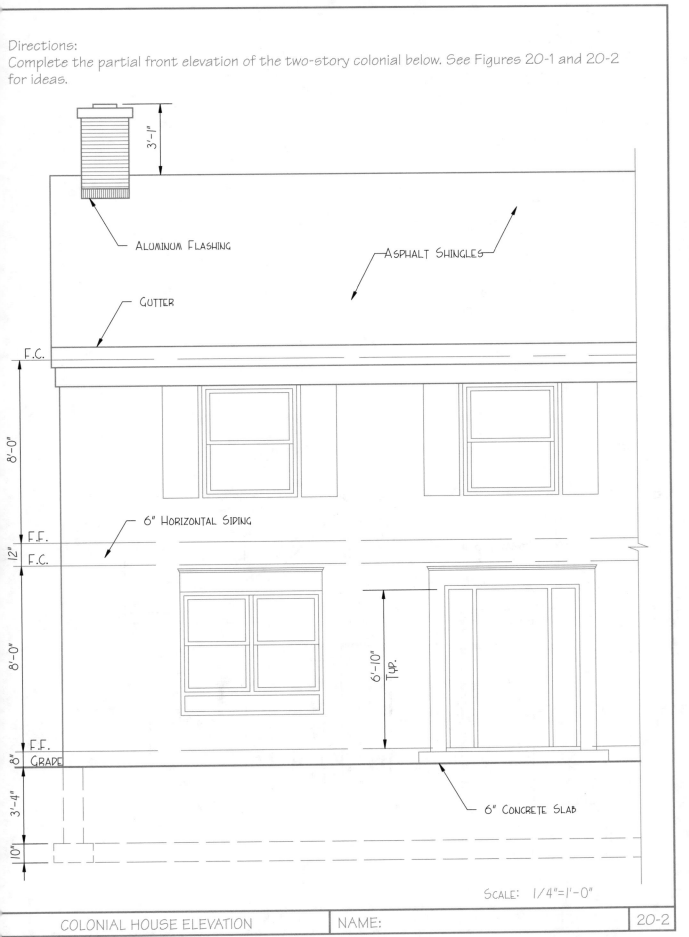

3'-1"

Aluminum Flashing

Asphalt Shingles

Gutter

F.C.

8'-0"

6" Horizontal Siding

F.F.

12"

F.C.

8'-0"

6'-10"
Typ.

F.F.

8"

Grade

3'-4"

6" Concrete Slab

10"

Scale: 1/4"=1'-0"

COLONIAL HOUSE ELEVATION   NAME: 20-2

3.

Directions:
Draw a complete front elevation for the garden house shown below using the following information: thickened-edge slab 24″ deep, floor-to-ceiling height of 8′-0″, 6′-10″ to top of windows and doors, 12″ overhang with bottom of soffit level with finished ceiling (truss construction), floor 4″ above the grade, 12:12 roof slope asphalt shingles, 6″ fascia, vertical siding (rough sawn 12″ boards with 1″ channel), four-panel doors. Follow the procedure described in Chapter 20 in the text.

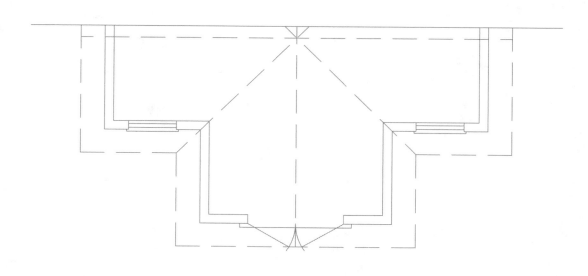

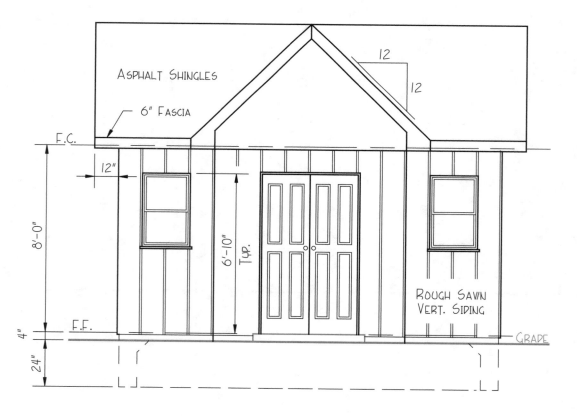

ASPHALT SHINGLES

12 / 12

6″ FASCIA

F.C.

12″

8′-0″

6′-10″ Typ.

F.F.

4″

24″

ROUGH SAWN VERT. SIDING

GRADE

SCALE: 1/4″=1′-0

GARDEN HOUSE ELEVATION   NAME: 20-

TYPICAL SOLUTION

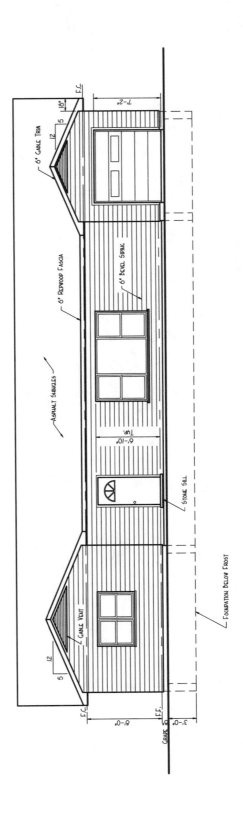

FRONT ELEVATION

SCALE: 1/4"=1'-0"

Chapter 20 Pretest
Elevations

Name _____

Period _____ **Date** _____ **Score** _____

Completion

Complete each sentence with the proper response. Place your answer on the space provided.

1. Tops of exterior doors are usually the same height as tops of _____.

   1. _____

2. _____ drawings provide height information about basic features of the house.

   2. _____

3. All visible wall corners are shown on the elevation using _____ lines.

   3. _____

4. _____ swing is shown on an elevation.

   4. _____

5. The minimum recommended height for garage ceilings is _____.

   5. _____

Multiple Choice

Choose the answer that correctly completes the statement. Write the corresponding letter in the space provided.

_____ 1. Roof angle is shown on the elevation using the _____.

   A. slope triangle
   B. fractional pitch
   C. Either A or B.
   D. None of the above

_____ 2. The reference point of most elevations is the _____.

   A. finish floor level
   B. eaves line
   C. top of the foundation wall
   D. grade line

_____ 3. Most codes require that the top of the foundation wall be at least _____ above the grade.

   A. 8″
   B. 10″
   C. 12″
   D. 14″

_____ 4. Material symbols are shown extensively on the _____ elevation(s).

   A. front
   B. four
   C. front and right side
   D. front and rear

_____ 5. The lower face of the head jamb of an exterior door is usually _____ from the top of the subfloor.

    A. 6'-10"
    B. 6'-8"
    C. 6'-6"
    D. 6'-4"

_____ 6. Dimensions on the elevation drawing are mainly _____ dimensions.

    A. location
    B. vertical height
    C. size
    D. Dimensions are not used on the elevation.

_____ 7. The usual scale of an exterior elevation is _____.

    A. 1/8" = 1'-0"
    B. 1/4" = 1'-0"
    C. 3/8" = 1'-0"
    D. 1/2" = 1'-0"

_____ 8. Features on an elevation that are below the grade line are shown as _____.

    A. centerlines
    B. hidden lines
    C. object lines
    D. phantom lines

Short Answer

Answer the following questions.

1. What are the two methods commonly used to identify a particular elevation? _____
_____

2. Why are material symbols usually drawn last on an elevation? _____
_____
_____

3. List nine features that are commonly included on elevation drawings. _____
_____
_____
_____
_____

4. How are the locations of windows, doors, and walls determined on an elevation?
_____

5. Which CADD command is typically used to change the size of a detail from 1" = 1'-0" to 1/4" = 1'-0"? _____

Chapter 20 Posttest
Elevations

Name _____

Period _____ **Date** _____ **Score** _____

Completion

Complete each sentence with the proper response. Place your answer on the space provided.

1. _____ drawings provide height information about basic features of the house.

1. _____

2. The minimum recommended height for garage ceilings is _____.

2. _____

3. All visible wall corners are shown on the elevation using _____ lines.

3. _____

4. Tops of exterior doors are usually the same height as tops of _____.

4. _____

5. _____ swing is shown on an elevation.

5. _____

Multiple Choice

Choose the answer that correctly completes the statement. Write the corresponding letter in the space provided.

_____ 1. The reference point of most elevations is the _____.

   A. finish floor level
   B. eaves line
   C. top of the foundation wall
   D. grade line

_____ 2. Features on an elevation that are below the grade line are shown as _____.

   A. centerlines
   B. hidden lines
   C. object lines
   D. phantom lines

_____ 3. Most codes require that the top of the foundation wall be at least _____ above the grade.

   A. 8″
   B. 10″
   C. 12″
   D. 14″

_____ 4. The lower face of the head jamb of an exterior door is usually _____ from the top of the subfloor.

   A. 6′-10″
   B. 6′-8″
   C. 6′-6″
   D. 6′-4″

_____ 5. Roof angle is shown on the elevation using the _____.

    A. slope triangle
    B. fractional pitch
    C. Either A or B.
    D. None of the above

_____ 6. Dimensions on the elevation drawing are mainly _____ dimensions.

    A. location
    B. vertical height
    C. size
    D. Dimensions are not used on the elevation.

_____ 7. Material symbols are shown extensively on the _____ elevation(s).

    A. front
    B. four
    C. front and right side
    D. front and rear

_____ 8. The usual scale of an exterior elevation is _____.

    A. $1/8'' = 1'\text{-}0''$
    B. $1/4'' = 1'\text{-}0''$
    C. $3/8'' = 1'\text{-}0''$
    D. $1/2'' = 1'\text{-}0''$

Short Answer

Answer the following questions.

1. List nine features that are commonly included on elevation drawings. _____

_____

_____

_____

_____

2. What are the two methods commonly used to identify a particular elevation? _____

_____

3. How are the locations of windows, doors, and walls determined on an elevation?

_____

4. Why are material symbols usually drawn last on an elevation? _____

_____

_____

5. Which CADD command is typically used to change the size of a detail from $1'' = 1'\text{-}0''$ to $1/4'' = 1'\text{-}0''$? _____

Residential Electrical
21

Objectives

After studying this chapter, the student will be able to:
- Define typical residential electrical terms.
- Plan for the electrical needs of a modern home.
- Identify and explain the three types of electrical circuits used in a residential structure.
- Calculate circuit requirements for a residence.
- Explain the advantages and disadvantages of low voltage exterior lighting.

Displays

1. **Electrical Hardware.** Show a collection of electrical hardware commonly used in residential electrical systems, such as switches, boxes, and outlets.
2. **Electrical Circuits.** Prepare a bulletin board illustrating the circuits in a house and the equipment, appliances, and lighting that they serve.

Instructional Materials

Text: Pages 449–463
    Review Questions, Suggested Activities
Workbook: Pages 245–254
    Review Questions, Problems/Activities
Teacher's Resources:
    Chapter 21 Pretest
    Chapter 21 Teaching Strategy
    Chapter 21 Posttest

Teaching Strategy

- **Knowledge Assessment.** Administer Chapter 21 Pretest. Correct the test and return. Highlight topics in which the individual student is deficient.
- Prepare Display #1.
- Review chapter objectives.
- Review electrical terms.
- Discuss the service entrance and distribution panel.

- Discuss branch circuits.
- Prepare Display #2.
- Assign workbook Problem 21-1.
- Discuss circuit requirements and outlets and switches.
- Assign workbook Problem 21-2.
- Discuss ground-fault circuit interrupter (GFCI) devices.
- Present low voltage exterior lighting.
- Assign one or more of the Suggested Activities in the text.
- **Chapter Review.** Assign Review Questions in the text. Discuss the correct answers. Assign Review Questions in the workbook. Have students check their own answers. Make transparencies of solutions to Problems/Activities 21-1 and 21-2 and use for review.
- **Evaluation.** Administer Chapter 21 Posttest. Correct the test and return. Return graded problems with comments.

Answers to Review Questions, Text

Page 462

1. voltage
2. circuit breakers; fuses
3. conductor
4. watts, which is a measure of work
5. three
6. 10; 12
7. copper
8. Number 12
9. Fire; also, increased resistance due to heat and thus wasted electricity.
10. 14
11. to disconnect all current to the house
12. 100
13. circuit breaker
14. Lighting circuits, special appliance circuits, and individual appliance circuits.
15. two
16. 20
17. three
18. 800

19. two
20. 12; 20
21. 2400 watts
22. Answer may include any five: Air conditioner, attic fan, clothes dryer, clothes washer, countertop oven, dishwasher, furnace, garbage disposal, range, table saw, water heater, and water pump.
23. circuit breaker
24. three
25. 6
26. three-way
27. shielded
28. Answer may include any three: Lights, wire, controllers, and transformers.
29. voltage drop
30. Considered safer for outdoor use, easier to install, and uses less energy.

Answers to Workbook Questions
Page 245

Part I: Multiple Choice
1. C. 3
2. D. 12
3. B. Circuit breakers
4. A. 120
5. C. 2400
6. D. All of the above.
7. B. 8'
8. C. Ground-fault circuit interrupters.
9. B. 2
10. A. 12

Part II: Short Answer/Listing
1. Two voltages are available; 120 and 240 volts.
2. Fire.
3. Main disconnect switch or breaker.
4. Answer may contain any two: To accommodate switches and outlets which are not designed for large wires; if one branch loses service, the remaining branches are available to provide service to other parts of the house; and so appliances that use smaller amounts of current have the proper fuse protection.
5. Answer may contain any three (others are possible): Range, water heater, washer, dryer, water pump, and table saw.
6. $40' \times 56' = 2240$ square feet ÷ 400 square feet per circuit = 5.6, or 6 lighting circuits
7. $40' \times 50' = 2000$ square feet
Lighting circuits:
2000 square feet ×
   3 watts per square foot   = 6000 watts
Special appliance circuits:
3 circuits @ 2400 watts each = 7200 watts
Individual appliance circuits:
   Electric range with oven = 12,000 watts
   Refrigerator   = 300 watts
   Washer   = 700 watts
   Electric dryer   = 5000 watts
   Dishwasher   = 1200 watts
   Garbage disposal   = 300 watts
   Furnace   = 800 watts
   Water heater   = 2000 watts
   Total   = 35,500 watts
35,500 watts ÷ 240 volts = 147.92, or 150 amp service
8. Lighting fixtures, convenience outlets, switches, and joints where wire is spliced should be housed in electrical boxes.
9. Answer may include any two: Entrances, garages, stairs, and rooms that have more than one entrance.

Part III: Completion
1. service
2. 200
3. appliance
4. 20
5. 120; 240
6. weatherproof
7. 48"; 30"; 40"
8. shower; bathtub
9. dimmer

Part IV: Matching
1. B. Circuit
2. M. Watt
3. A. Ampere
4. C. Circuit breaker or fuse
5. K. Voltage
6. G. Ohm
7. I. Service entrance
8. J. Service panel
9. D. Conductor
10. H. Service drop
11. F. Lighting outlet
12. E. Convenience outlet or receptacle
13. L. Voltage drop

Part V: Problems/Activities

1. Solution on page 349 of this manual.
2. Solution on page 350 of this manual.

Answers to Chapter 21 Pretest

Completion

1. 120; 240
2. Voltage
3. larger
4. 10'
5. 12

Multiple Choice

1. B. meter
2. C. 100
3. C. 3
4. C. 2400
5. C. in the distribution panel
6. A. 3
7. B. 12" or 18"
8. B. electrical box

Short Answer

1. Answer may be any one of the following: **Kitchen.** All countertop receptacles within a 6' straight-line distance from the sink must have GFCI protection. **Bathroom.** All receptacles installed in bathrooms must have GFCI protection. **Garage.** Every receptacle in a garage must have GFCI protection unless it is not readily accessible, such as a receptacle located on the ceiling for a garage door opener or one servicing a plug-in appliance occupying dedicated space, such as a freezer. **Outdoors.** All receptacles installed outdoors that are readily accessible and within 6'-6" of grade level must have GFCI protection. **Unfinished basements and crawlspaces at or below grade level.** All receptacles installed in these locations must have GFCI protection except for a dedicated branch circuit for a plug-in appliance, a laundry circuit, or a single receptacle supplying a permanently installed sump pump.
2. Lighting circuits, special appliance circuits, and individual appliance circuits.
3. Any permanently connected 120V appliance that is rated over 1400 watts or has an automatically-starting electric motor requires an individual appliance circuit.
4. 30" to 40"
5. weatherproof
6. To control a fixture from two locations.
7. 2
8. An understanding of related terms, electrical requirements for lighting and appliances, code restrictions, and safety considerations.

Matching

1. C. One amp under one volt of pressure.
2. F. The main distribution box that receives the electricity and distributes it to various parts of the house.
3. E. Conductors and fittings that bring electricity to the dwelling.
4. I. Service conductors from the power lines to the point of attachment to the structure.
5. G. An outlet designed to provide use of a lighting fixture.
6. A. A device connected to a circuit to permit electricity to be drawn off for appliances.
7. D. Material that allows the flow of electricity.
8. H. A safety device that opens an electric circuit if overloaded.
9. B. The path of electricity that flows from the source to one or more outlets and then back to the source.
10. J. Unit of current used to measure the amount of electricity flowing through a conductor per unit of time.

Answers to Chapter 21 Posttest

Completion

1. Voltage
2. 120; 240
3. 10'
4. larger
5. 12

Multiple Choice

1. C. 3
2. B. meter
3. C. in the distribution panel
4. C. 100
5. C. 2400

6. A. 3
7. B. electrical box
8. B. 12″ or 18″

Short Answer

1. An understanding of related terms, electrical requirements for lighting and appliances, code restrictions, and safety considerations.
2. Lighting circuits, special appliance circuits, and individual appliance circuits.
3. 2
4. Any permanently connected 120V appliance that is rated over 1400 watts or has an automatically-starting electric motor requires an individual appliance circuit.
5. weatherproof
6. 30″ to 40″
7. Answer may be any one of the following: **Kitchen.** All countertop receptacles within a 6′ straight-line distance from the sink must have GFCI protection. **Bathroom.** All receptacles installed in bathrooms must have GFCI protection. **Garage.** Every receptacle in a garage must have GFCI protection unless it is not readily accessible, such as a receptacle located on the ceiling for a garage door opener or one servicing a plug-in appliance occupying dedicated space, such as a freezer. **Outdoors.** All receptacles installed outdoors that are readily accessible and within 6′-6″ of grade level must have GFCI protection. **Unfinished basements and crawlspaces at or below grade level.** All receptacles installed in these locations must have GFCI protection except for a dedicated branch circuit for a plug-in appliance, a laundry circuit, or a single receptacle supplying a permanently installed sump pump.
8. To control a fixture from two locations.

Matching

1. J. Unit of current used to measure the amount of electricity flowing through a conductor per unit of time.
2. B. The path of electricity that flows from the source to one or more outlets and then back to the source.
3. D. Material that allows the flow of electricity.
4. H. A safety device that opens an electric circuit if overloaded.
5. G. An outlet designed to provide use of a lighting fixture.
6. A. A device connected to a circuit to permit electricity to be drawn off for appliances.
7. I. Service conductors from the power lines to the point of attachment to the structure.
8. E. Conductors and fittings that bring electricity to the dwelling.
9. F. The main distribution box that receives the electricity and distributes it to various parts of the house.
10. C. One amp under one volt of pressure.

Workbook Solution

Directions:
Label each of the electrical circuits below as to wire size, voltage, and amperage (overcurrent protection). See the completed example for format.

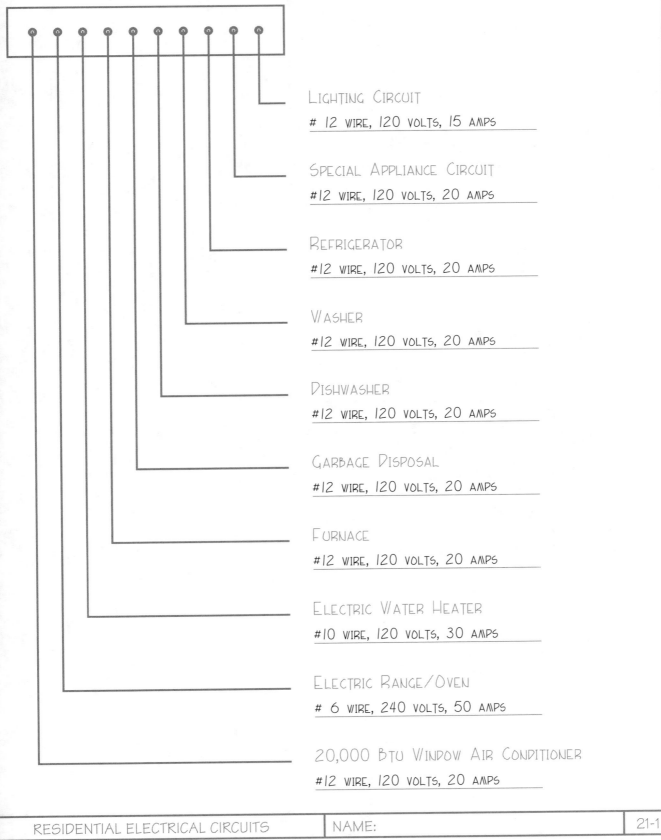

LIGHTING CIRCUIT
12 WIRE, 120 VOLTS, 15 AMPS

SPECIAL APPLIANCE CIRCUIT
#12 WIRE, 120 VOLTS, 20 AMPS

REFRIGERATOR
#12 WIRE, 120 VOLTS, 20 AMPS

WASHER
#12 WIRE, 120 VOLTS, 20 AMPS

DISHWASHER
#12 WIRE, 120 VOLTS, 20 AMPS

GARBAGE DISPOSAL
#12 WIRE, 120 VOLTS, 20 AMPS

FURNACE
#12 WIRE, 120 VOLTS, 20 AMPS

ELECTRIC WATER HEATER
#10 WIRE, 120 VOLTS, 30 AMPS

ELECTRIC RANGE/OVEN
6 WIRE, 240 VOLTS, 50 AMPS

20,000 BTU WINDOW AIR CONDITIONER
#12 WIRE, 120 VOLTS, 20 AMPS

| RESIDENTIAL ELECTRICAL CIRCUITS | NAME: | 21-1 |

2.

Directions:
Plan the location of switches and outlets for each of the situations below.

A. Ceiling outlet fixture with
single-pole switch

B. Ceiling outlet fixture switched
from two locations.

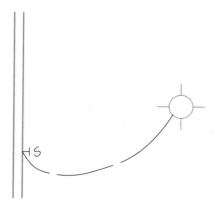

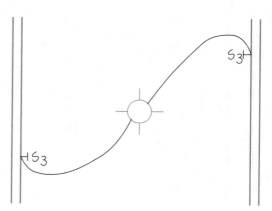

C. Room with switched ceiling outlet fixture and duplex outlets approximately 6 feet apart
along the walls.

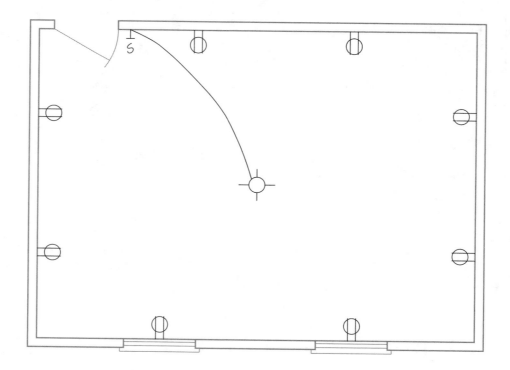

Chapter 21 Pretest
Residential Electrical

Name_____

Period _____Date _____Score _____

Completion

Complete each sentence with the proper response. Place your answer on the space provided.

1. A residence may have _____ or _____ volt service.

1. _____

2. _____ is the pressure that forces current through a wire.

2. _____

3. Number 2 wire is _____ in size than Number 4.

3. _____

4. The service drop must be at least _____ above the ground at all points.

4. _____

5. Number _____ wire is recommended for branch lighting circuits.

5. _____

Multiple Choice

Choose the answer that correctly completes the statement. Write the corresponding letter in the space provided.

_____ 1. The most common arrangement of electrical service to a house is with the service conductors first terminating at the _____.

A. service panel
B. meter
C. distribution box
D. ground post

_____ 2. The National Electrical Code recommends that a minimum of _____ amp service be provided for all residences.

A. 50
B. 75
C. 100
D. 150

_____ 3. A 240 volt service requires _____ wires.

A. 1
B. 2
C. 3
D. 4

_____ 4. How many watts of lighting capacity can be provided by a Number 12 copper wire with a 20 amp overcurrent protection in a 120 volt system?

A. 1200
B. 1800
C. 2400
D. 3000

_____ 5. The main disconnect switch is usually located _____.

    A. in the meter
    B. at the last utility pole
    C. in the distribution panel
    D. at the service drop

_____ 6. The NEC requires a minimum of _____ watts of lighting power for each square foot of floor space.

    A. 3
    B. 6
    C. 9
    D. 12

_____ 7. The height of most convenience outlets is _____ above the floor.

    A. 6″ or 12″
    B. 12″ or 18″
    C. 18″ or 24″
    D. 24″ or 36″

_____ 8. All convenience outlets, switches, and joints where wires are spliced must be housed in a(n) _____.

    A. fuse box
    B. electrical box
    C. distribution panel
    D. conduit

Short Answer

Answer the following questions.

1. A ground fault circuit interrupter can be installed in any receptacle or as a circuit breaker in the distribution panel. Give a specific example of where a GFCI should be installed. _____

_____

2. Name the three types of branch circuits used in a residence. _____

_____

_____

3. Why would an appliance require an individual appliance circuit? _____

_____

4. What is the typical height of switches on the wall for use by a person seated in a wheelchair?

_____

5. What type of outlets are used outside the house? _____

6. Why would three-way switches be used? _____

_____

7. What is the minimum number of special appliance circuits that should be provided in the kitchen? _____

8. Name four factors that must be understood in order to plan for the electrical needs of a home.

_____

_____

_____

Matching

Select the answer that correctly matches each term. Place your answer in the space provided.

A. A device connected to a circuit to permit electricity to be drawn off for appliances.
B. The path of electricity that flows from the source to one or more outlets and then back to the source.
C. One amp under one volt of pressure.
D. Material that allows the flow of electricity.
E. Conductors and fittings that bring electricity to the dwelling.
F. The main distribution box that receives the electricity and distributes it to various parts of the house.
G. An outlet designed to provide use of a lighting fixture.
H. A safety device that opens an electric circuit if overloaded.
I. Service conductors from the power lines to the point of attachment to the structure.
J. Unit of current used to measure the amount of electricity flowing through a conductor per unit of time.

_____ 1. Watt

_____ 2. Service panel

_____ 3. Service entrance

_____ 4. Service drop

_____ 5. Lighting outlet

_____ 6. Convenience outlet or receptacle

_____ 7. Conductor

_____ 8. Circuit breaker or fuse

_____ 9. Circuit

_____ 10. Ampere

Chapter 21 Posttest
Residential Electrical

Name _____

Period _____**Date** _____**Score** _____

Completion

Complete each sentence with the proper response. Place your answer on the space provided.

1. _____ is the pressure that forces current through a wire.

1. _____

2. A residence may have _____ or _____ volt service.

2. _____

3. The service drop must be at least _____ above the ground at all points.

3. _____

4. Number 2 wire is _____ in size than Number 4.

4. _____

5. Number _____ wire is recommended for branch lighting circuits.

5. _____

Multiple Choice

Choose the answer that correctly completes the statement. Write the corresponding letter in the space provided.

_____ 1. A 240 volt service requires _____ wires.

    A. 1
    B. 2
    C. 3
    D. 4

_____ 2. The most common arrangement of electrical service to a house is with the service conductors first terminating at the _____.

    A. service panel
    B. meter
    C. distribution box
    D. ground post

_____ 3. The main disconnect switch is usually located _____.

    A. in the meter
    B. at the last utility pole
    C. in the distribution panel
    D. at the service drop

_____ 4. The National Electrical Code recommends that a minimum of _____ amp service be provided for all residences.

    A. 50
    B. 75
    C. 100
    D. 150

_____ 5. How many watts of lighting capacity can be provided by a Number 12 copper wire with a 20 amp overcurrent protection in a 120 volt system?

    A. 1200
    B. 1800
    C. 2400
    D. 3000

_____ 6. The NEC requires a minimum of _____ watts of lighting power for each square foot of floor space.

    A. 3
    B. 6
    C. 9
    D. 12

_____ 7. All convenience outlets, switches, and joints where wires are spliced must be housed in a(n) _____.

    A. fuse box
    B. electrical box
    C. distribution panel
    D. conduit

_____ 8. The height of most convenience outlets is _____ above the floor.

    A. 6″ or 12″
    B. 12″ or 18″
    C. 18″ or 24″
    D. 24″ or 36″

Short Answer

Answer the following questions.

1. Name four factors that must be understood in order to plan for the electrical needs of a home.

_____

_____

_____

2. Name the three types of branch circuits used in a residence._____

_____

_____

3. What is the minimum number of special appliance circuits that should be provided in the kitchen? _____

4. Why would an appliance require an individual appliance circuit?_____

_____

5. What type of outlets are used outside the house? _____

6. What is the typical height of switches on the wall for use by a person seated in a wheelchair?

_____

7. A ground fault circuit interrupter can be installed in any receptacle or as a circuit breaker in the distribution panel. Give a specific example of where a GFCI should be installed. _____
_____

8. Why would three-way switches be used? _____
_____

Matching

Select the answer that correctly matches each term. Place your answer in the space provided.

A. A device connected to a circuit to permit electricity to be drawn off for appliances.
B. The path of electricity that flows from the source to one or more outlets and then back to the source.
C. One amp under one volt of pressure.
D. Material that allows the flow of electricity.
E. Conductors and fittings that bring electricity to the dwelling.

F. The main distribution box that receives the electricity and distributes it to various parts of the house.
G. An outlet designed to provide use of a lighting fixture.
H. A safety device that opens an electric circuit if overloaded.
I. Service conductors from the power lines to the point of attachment to the structure.
J. Unit of current used to measure the amount of electricity flowing through a conductor per unit of time.

_____ 1. Ampere

_____ 2. Circuit

_____ 3. Conductor

_____ 4. Circuit breaker or fuse

_____ 5. Lighting outlet

_____ 6. Convenience outlet or receptacle

_____ 7. Service drop

_____ 8. Service entrance

_____ 9. Service panel

_____ 10. Watt

Information, Communication, and Security Wiring

Objectives

After studying this chapter, the student will be able to:
- Identify the features related to information, communication, and security that should be considered when designing a new home.
- List the types of lines or cables used in residential telephone systems.
- Define common terms associated with information, communication, and security wiring.
- List the components of a security system designed to protect residential property.
- Discuss the components of a home automation system.
- Describe the elements of a low-voltage switching system.

Displays

1. **Security Wiring Components**. Collect as many typical wiring components of a security system as you can. Display them with identification for student examination.
2. **Home Automation**. Display a working home automation system and allow the students to experiment with its operation.

Instructional Materials

Text: Pages 465–481
  Review Questions, Suggested Activities
Workbook: Pages 255–262
  Questions, Problems/Activities
Teacher's Resources:
  Chapter 22 Pretest
  Chapter 22 Teaching Strategy
  Chapter 22 Posttest

Teaching Strategy

- **Knowledge Assessment:** Administer the Chapter 22 Pretest. Correct the test and return. Highlight the topics in which the individual student is deficient.
- Prepare Display #1.
- Review the chapter objectives.
- Discuss modern technology features for home applications and cover their functions.
- Discuss information and communication wiring.
- Discuss data and video conductors.
- Assign Problem 22-1 in the workbook.
- Assign Problem 22-2 in the workbook.
- Cover home automation.
- Prepare Display #2.
- Discuss low-voltage switching.
- Assign one of the Suggested Activities in the text.
- **Chapter Review:** Assign the Review Questions in the text. Discuss the correct answers. Assign the questions in the workbook. Have students check their own answers. Make a transparency of the solution to Problem 22-1 in the workbook and use for review.
- **Evaluation:** Administer the Chapter 22 Posttest. Correct the test and return. Return graded problems with comments.

Answers to Review Questions, Text

Page 480

1. cable pair
2. C. ribbon stranded wire
3. D. black, green, red, yellow
4. three
5. 6, 20
6. unshielded twisted-pair (UTP) cable (Also acceptable: Category 5 or Cat 5 cable)
7. T568B
8. A. 285 feet
9. Radio Grade 6 (RG-6)
10. doors
11. perimeter
12. Smoke

13. A. network
14. Answer may include any three of the following: Hard-wired systems, power line technology, structured wiring, and combination systems.
15. RJ-45
16. 24

Answers to Workbook Questions

Page 255

Part I: Matching

1. E. Relays
2. A. Cable pair
3. D. RG-6 cable
4. F. Signaling circuits
5. C. Hard-wired system
6. G. UTP cable
7. B. Digital data
8. H. Wiring closet

Part II: Completion

1. alarm
2. motion
3. perimeter
4. power line
5. structured
6. 20
7. telephone
8. 2, 6
9. RG-6
10. panic button
11. network

Part III: Multiple Choice

1. C. spiral ribbon
2. B. 285 feet
3. D. None of the above.
4. D. RJ-45
5. D. 24
6. C. three

Part IV: Problems/Activities

1. Solution on page 360 of this manual.
2. Evaluate the plan according to principles discussed in the text.

Answers to Chapter 22 Pretest

Completion

1. wiring
2. cable pair
3. three
4. 16
5. Category 5 or Cat 5
6. Digital
7. signal
8. network

Multiple Choice

1. B. T568B
2. A. Radio Grade 6
3. D. Category 5
4. C. 24
5. A. yellow

Matching

1. E. Has eight conductors of Number 24 wire bundled inside a PVC jacket.
2. D. High-quality video cable.
3. A. Devices that supply the electrical power to buzzers, doorbells, and warning devices.
4. B. A type of automation system more likely to be found in commercial or industrial applications than in residential applications.
5. F. The first line of defense of a security system designed to protect the occupants as well as the property.
6. C. Electrically operated switches.

Short Answer

1. Monitoring functions, switching (activating) functions, programming functions, communication/recording functions, and alarm functions.
2. Class 1 Circuits
3. Answer may include any three of the following: Cable TV, digital cable, digital satellite, cable modems, and in-home security cameras (video applications).
4. Because the values of digital data are specific, data can be transmitted, received, and recreated with no loss of content. By contrast, analog data is always received with noise added into the content.
5. motion detectors
6. Hardware modules to switch electrical equipment on or off, a computer interface to send commands to the modules, and a software program to control the interfaced hardware.
7. Evaluate responses individually.

Answers to Chapter 22 Posttest

Completion

1. cable pair
2. three
3. 16
4. Category 5 or Cat 5
5. network
6. wiring
7. Digital
8. signal

Multiple Choice

1. D. Category 5
2. B. T568B
3. A. yellow
4. A. Radio Grade 6
5. C. 24

Matching

1. D. Devices that supply the electrical power to buzzers, doorbells, and warning devices.
2. B. A type of automation system more likely to be found in commercial or industrial applications than in residential applications.
3. F. The first line of defense of a security system designed to protect the occupants as well as the property.
4. E. Electrically operated switches.
5. A. Has eight conductors of Number 24 wire bundled inside a PVC jacket.
6. C. High-quality video cable.

Short Answer

1. Class 1 Circuits
2. Answer may include any three of the following: Cable TV, digital cable, digital satellite, cable modems, and in-home security cameras (video applications).
3. motion detectors
4. Monitoring functions, switching (activating) functions, programming functions, communication/recording functions, and alarm functions.
5. Because the values of digital data are specific, data can be transmitted, received, and recreated with no loss of content. By contrast, analog data is always received with noise added into the content.
6. Evaluate responses individually.
7. Hardware modules to switch electrical equipment on or off, a computer interface to send commands to the modules, and a software program to control the interfaced hardware.

Workbook Solution

1.

Directions:
Draw each of the symbols specified below as shown in the completed example.
Scale is 1/4" = 1'-0".

A	MD	⊙
AUDIO OUTLET	MOTION DETECTOR	FLOOR OUTLET

V	DA	◁D
VIDEO OUTLET	DOOR ALARM	DATA OUTLET

F	⟨S⟩	◁I
FIRE ALARM	SMOKE DETECTOR	INTERCOM

F◁	⟨H⟩	Ⓙ
FIRE HORN	THERMAL SENSOR	JUNCTION BOX

⊓	⊞	
DISCONNECT SWITCH	SECURITY KEY PAD	GFCI OUTLET

⊘	V/F	S
TRANSFORMER	SPRINKLER	SPEAKER OUTLET

SECURITY SYMBOLS	NAME:	22

Chapter 22 Pretest
Information, Communication, and Security Wiring

Name _____

Period _____**Date** _____**Score** _____

Completion

Complete each sentence with the proper response. Place your answer on the space provided.

1. All cables from a high-tech security system are routed to a single location called a(n) _____ cabinet.

2. Telephone lines are two wires called a(n) _____.

3. The National Electrical Code recognizes _____ classes of signaling circuits.

4. The conductors used for buzzers, bells, and chimes range in size from Number _____ to Number 20.

5. Unshielded twisted-pair (UTP) cable is the same as _____ cable.

6. _____ data refers to information that is converted to only a few specific values, commonly described as "1s and 0s."

7. Twisted-pair wire is a product in which each pair of wires is twisted together to preserve _____ quality.

8. In a home automation system, a(n) _____ enables products to "talk" and "listen" to one another.

1. _____

2. _____

3. _____

4. _____

5. _____

6. _____

7. _____

8. _____

Multiple Choice

Choose the answer that correctly completes the statement. Write the corresponding letter in the space provided.

_____ 1. The most common cable/wiring standard for new construction is:

    A. T568A
    B. T568B
    C. T-568A
    D. T-568B

_____ 2. _____ is a type of coaxial cable.

    A. Radio Grade 6
    B. Bell wire
    C. Category 3
    D. Category 5

_____ 3. A standard RJ-45 jack is used with _____ cable.

    A. Radio Grade 6
    B. Bell wire
    C. Category 3
    D. Category 5

_____ 4. In low-voltage switching, switch conductors carry _____ volts.

    A. 6
    B. 12
    C. 24
    D. 120

_____ 5. The colors used for four-wire telephone cable are black, green, red, and _____.

    A. yellow
    B. white
    C. blue
    D. orange

Matching

Match the correct term with its description listed below. Place the corresponding letter on the space provided.

A. Devices that supply the electrical power to buzzers, doorbells, and warning devices.
B. A type of automation system more likely to be found in commercial or industrial applications than in residential applications.
C. Electrically operated switches.
D. High-quality video cable.
E. Has eight conductors of Number 24 wire bundled inside a PVC jacket.
F. The first line of defense of a security system designed to protect the occupants as well as the property.

_____ 1. UTP cable

_____ 2. RG-6 quad shield

_____ 3. Signaling circuits

_____ 4. Hard-wired system

_____ 5. Perimeter system

_____ 6. Relays

Short Answer

Provide brief answers to the following questions.

1. List five general areas used to classify modern technology features and functions that might be considered when designing a new home. _____

_____

_____

_____

2. Which class of signaling circuits describes circuits where power is not to exceed 30V and 1000VA? _____

3. List three uses for RG-6 cable. _____

_____

_____

4. How does the transmission of content vary between digital data and analog data? _____

_____

_____

_____

5. What types of devices provide the final line of defense for home security systems? _____

_____

6. Identify the three components typically included in a basic power line technology system.

_____

_____

7. List three questions that may be considered when planning a home automation/security system. _____

_____

_____

_____

_____

Chapter 22 Posttest
Information, Communication, and Security Wiring

Name _____

Period _____ Date _____ Score _____

Completion

Complete each sentence with the proper response. Place your answer on the space provided.

1. Telephone lines are two wires called a(n) _____.

1. _____

2. The National Electrical Code recognizes _____ classes of signaling circuits.

2. _____

3. The conductors used for buzzers, bells, and chimes range in size from Number _____ to Number 20.

3. _____

4. Unshielded twisted-pair (UTP) cable is the same as _____ cable.

4. _____

5. In a home automation system, a(n) _____ enables products to "talk" and "listen" to one another.

5. _____

6. All cables from a high-tech security system are routed to a single location called a(n) _____ cabinet.

6. _____

7. _____ data refers to information that is converted to only a few specific values, commonly described as "1s and 0s."

7. _____

8. Twisted-pair wire is a product in which each pair of wires is twisted together to preserve _____ quality.

8. _____

Multiple Choice

Choose the answer that correctly completes the statement. Write the corresponding letter in the space provided.

_____ 1. A standard RJ-45 jack is used with _____ cable.

    A. Radio Grade 6
    B. Bell wire
    C. Category 3
    D. Category 5

_____ 2. The most common cable/wiring standard for new construction is:

    A. T568A
    B. T568B
    C. T-568A
    D. T-568B

_____ 3. The colors used for four-wire telephone cable are black, green, red, and _____.

    A. yellow
    B. white
    C. blue
    D. orange

_____ 4. _____ is a type of coaxial cable.

    A. Radio Grade 6
    B. Bell wire
    C. Category 3
    D. Category 5

_____ 5. In low-voltage switching, switch conductors carry _____ volts.

    A. 6
    B. 12
    C. 24
    D. 120

Matching

Match the correct term with its description listed below. Place the corresponding letter on the space provided.

A. Has eight conductors of Number 24 wire bundled inside a PVC jacket.
B. A type of automation system more likely to be found in commercial or industrial applications than in residential applications.
C. High-quality video cable.
D. Devices that supply the electrical power to buzzers, doorbells, and warning devices.
E. Electrically operated switches.
F. The first line of defense of a security system designed to protect the occupants as well as the property.

_____ 1. Signaling circuits

_____ 2. Hard-wired system

_____ 3. Perimeter system

_____ 4. Relays

_____ 5. UTP cable

_____ 6. RG-6 quad shield

Short Answer

Provide brief answers to the following questions.

1. Which class of signaling circuits describes circuits where power is not to exceed 30V and 1000VA? _____

2. List three uses for RG-6 cable. _____

_____

_____

3. What types of devices provide the final line of defense for home security systems? _____
_____

4. List five general areas used to classify modern technology features and functions that might be considered when designing a new home. _____
_____
_____
_____

5. How does the transmission of content vary between digital data and analog data? _____
_____
_____
_____

6. List three questions that may be considered when planning a home automation/security system. _____
_____
_____
_____
_____

7. Identify the three components typically included in a basic power line technology system.
_____
_____

The Electrical Plan
23

Objectives

After studying this chapter, the student will be able to:

- Describe an electrical plan and identify its features.
- Identify typical electrical symbols found on a residential electrical plan.
- Draw an electrical plan for a residential structure using manual drafting techniques.
- Draw an electrical plan for a residential structure using CADD.

Displays

1. **Electrical Plan.** Select an outstanding example of a residential electrical plan. Display it on the bulletin board for the class to study.
2. **Code Requirements.** Display the National Electrical Code book and other local requirements that affect the design of a residential electrical system.

Instructional Materials

Text: Pages 483–490
   Review Questions, Suggested Activities
Workbook: Pages 263–272
   Review Questions, Problems/Activities
Teacher's Resources:
   Chapter 23 Pretest
   Chapter 23 Teaching Strategy
   Chapter 23 Posttest

Teaching Strategy

- **Knowledge Assessment.** Administer the Chapter 23 Pretest. Correct the test and return. Highlight topics in which the individual student is deficient.
- Prepare Display #1.
- Review chapter objectives.
- Discuss the definition and purpose of the electrical plan.
- Present required information on an electrical plan.

- Discuss the service entrance.
- Assign workbook Problem 23-1.
- Cover switches, convenience outlets, and lighting.
- Prepare Display #2.
- Discuss branch circuits.
- Assign workbook Problem 23-2.
- Discuss the procedure for drawing an electrical plan.
- Assign workbook Problem 23-3.
- Assign one or more of the Suggested Activities in the text.
- **Chapter Review.** Assign Review Questions in the text. Discuss the correct answers. Assign Review Questions in the workbook. Have students check their own answers. Make transparencies of solutions to Problems/Activities 23-1 and 23-2 and use for review.
- **Evaluation.** Administer Chapter 23 Posttest. Correct the test and return. Return graded problems with comments.

Answers to Review Questions, Text *Page 490*

1. The service entrance capacity, meter and distribution panel location, placement and type of switches, location and type of lighting fixtures, special electrical equipment, number and types of circuits, electrical fixture schedule, symbols and a legend, and notes that help to describe the system.
2. (either of the following) Where the wires attach to the house or where the largest amounts of electricity will be used.
3. outside
4. a) Flush-mounted distribution panel.
   b) Three-way switch.
   c) Push button.
   d) Telephone.
   e) Duplex convenience outlet.
5. On-off toggle, quiet, mercury, push button, dimmer, and delayed action.
6. severe shock

7. identify the fixtures to be used
8. incandescent; fluorescent
9. To achieve proper line width when plotting.

Answers to Workbook Questions

Page 263

Part I: Short Answer/Listing

1. To show the location and type of electrical equipment to be used.
2. Answer may include any five: The service entrance capacity, meter and distribution panel location, placement and type of switches, location and type of lighting fixtures, special electrical equipment, number and types of circuits, electrical fixture schedule, symbols and a legend, and notes.
3. On-off toggle switch.
4. A regular outlet remains "hot" all the time while a switched outlet may be switched from "hot" to no power.
5. A ceiling fixture should be planned in the dining room centered over the table. Fluorescent lights may be used for kitchens, bathrooms, and workshops. Recessed lighting fixtures are convenient for foyers, hallways, and special emphasis areas.
6. Beside the symbol representing the distribution panel.
7. A. Weatherproof outlet.
   B. Appliance receptacle.
   C. Split-wired outlet.
   D. 240 volt outlet.
   E. Telephone junction box.
   F. Electric service meter.
   G. Electrical distribution box.
   H. Duplex receptacle outlet.
   I. Telephone.
   J. Single-pole switch.
   K. Three-way switch.
   L. Fluorescent fixture.

Part II: Completion

1. plan
2. National Electrical Code (NEC)
3. Traffic
4. two
5. fluorescent

6. lighting

Part III: Multiple Choice

1. B. Floor plan.
2. A. It is less expensive and more efficient.
3. C. Hidden line or centerline drawn with an irregular curve.
4. D. Exterior fixtures.
5. A. Lighting fixture schedule.

Part IV: Problems/Activities

1. Solution on page 370 of this manual.
2. Solution on page 371 of this manual.
3. Solution on page 372 of this manual.

Answers to Chapter 23 Pretest

Completion

1. shorter
2. two
3. floor
4. weatherproof
5. close

Multiple Choice

1. B. exterior
2. C. duplex
3. A. on-off toggle

Short Answer

1. Type, manufacturer, catalog number, number required, mounting height, watts, and remarks.
2. Answer may include any five: Meter, distribution panel box, electric outlets, switches, special electrical features, the number and types of circuits in the home, and lighting schedule.
3. Incandescent and fluorescent.
4. Hidden line or centerline.

Matching

1. A. Ceiling outlet fixture.
2. F. Recessed outlet fixture.
3. D. Fluorescent fixture.
4. I. Telephone.
5. J. Thermostat.
6. C. Duplex receptacle outlet.
7. H. Split-wired duplex receptacle outlet.
8. K. 240 volt outlet.
9. L. Weatherproof duplex outlet.
10. G. Single-pole switch.
11. E. Push button.

12. B. Chimes.

Answers to Chapter 23 Posttest

Completion
1. floor
2. close
3. shorter
4. weatherproof
5. two

Multiple Choice
1. A. on-off toggle
2. C. duplex
3. B. exterior

Short Answer
1. Answer may include any five: Meter, distribution panel box, electric outlets, switches, special electrical features, the number and types of circuits in the home, and lighting schedule.
2. Hidden line or centerline.

3. Incandescent and fluorescent.
4. Type, manufacturer, catalog number, number required, mounting height, watts, and remarks.

Matching
1. I. Ceiling outlet fixture.
2. D. Recessed outlet fixture.
3. L. Fluorescent fixture.
4. A. Telephone.
5. F. Thermostat.
6. J. Duplex receptacle outlet.
7. E. Split-wired duplex receptacle outlet.
8. B. 240 volt outlet.
9. K. Weatherproof duplex outlet.
10. H. Single-pole switch.
11. C. Push button.
12. G. Chimes.

Workbook Solution

1.

CEILING OUTLET
FIXTURE

RECESSED OUTLET
FIXTURE

FAN HANGER
OUTLET

JUNCTION
BOX

DUPLEX RECEPTACLE
OUTLET

QUADRUPLEX
RECEPTACLE OUTLET

SPLIT-WIRED
DUPLEX RECEPTACLE OUTLET

SPECIAL PURPOSE
SINGLE RECEPTACLE OUTLET

 W/P

WEATHERPROOF
DUPLEX OUTLET

240 VOLT
OUTLET

 S

SINGLE-POLE
SWITCH

 S₃

THREE-WAY
SWITCH

PUSH BUTTON

CH.

CHIMES

S_D

DIMMER SWITCH

THERMOSTAT

TELEPHONE

FLUORESCENT FIXTURE

| ELECTRICAL SYMBOLS | NAME: | 23- |

Workbook Solution

Directions:
Using the garage floor plan below, prepare an electrical plan that includes the following features:

> Three-way switch for two ceiling outlet fixtures.
> Switch for two outside lights on either side of the garage door.
> Four duplex outlets on garage side walls (two each side).
> Two duplex outlets above the workbench.
> Garage door opener outlet and switch.

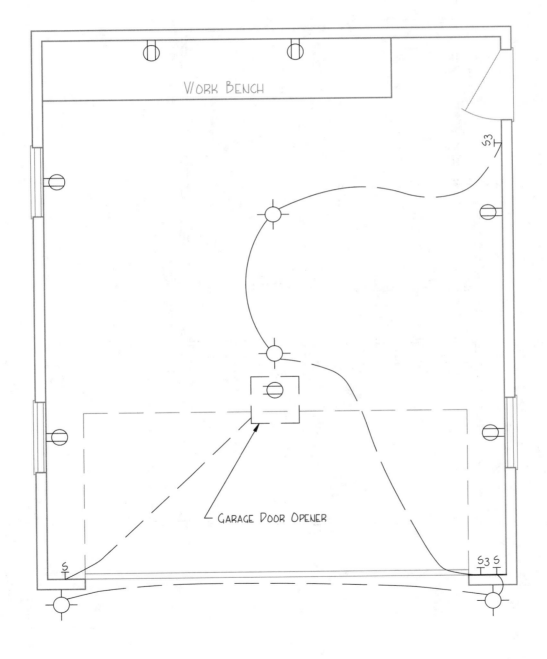

WORK BENCH

S_3

GARAGE DOOR OPENER

S

S_3 S

GARAGE ELECTRICAL PLAN	NAME:	23-2

3.

TYPICAL SOLUTION

ELECTRICAL PLAN

SCALE: 1/4"=1'-0"

TELEPHONE JUNCTION BOX

ELECTRIC SERVICE METER
240 VOLTS, 150 AMPS.

ELECTRICAL DISTRIBUTION PANEL

GARAGE
DOOR
OPENER

GARAGE
11'-2" x 19'-4"

KITCHEN
11'-5" x 11'-8"

P.W.

REF.

BAR

WP

PATIO

FAMILY ROOM
11'-10" x 16'-0"

PUBLIC AREA
9'-10" x 15'-8"

WP

HEAT
PUMP

BEDROOM # 3
10'-4" x 10'-10"

CL.

LIVING ROOM
11'-4" x 17'-0"

PORCH

4" CONCRETE SLAB

TO DRIVEWAY LIGHTS

BATH
5'-0" x 13'-4"

CL.

CL.

LIN.

CL.

FOYER
5'-7" x 11'-0"

CL.

CLOSET

WP

M. BEDROOM
13'-4" x 15'-5"

M. BATH
5'-6" x 11'-8"

BEDROOM # 2
13'-4" x 15'-2"

CIRCUIT DATA

LIGHTING CIRCUITS:
4 PROVIDING 1800 WATTS EACH = 7200 WATTS
SPECIAL APPLIANCE CIRCUITS:
2 PROVIDING 2400 WATTS EACH = 4800 WATTS
INDIVIDUAL APPLIANCE CIRCUITS:
1 FOR REFRIGERATOR = 2400 WATTS
1 FOR GARBAGE DISPOSER = 2400 WATTS
1 FOR DISHWASHER = 2400 WATTS
1 FOR WASHER AND GAS DRYER = 2400 WATTS
1 FOR HEAT PUMP = 7200 WATTS
1 FOR ELECTRIC RANGE = 12000 WATTS
1 FOR ELECTRIC HOT WATER HEATER = 5000 WATTS
1 FOR FUTURE USE = 2400 WATTS
DISTRIBUTION PANEL:
150 AMP, 16 CIRCUIT CAPACITY

Chapter 23 Pretest
The Electrical Plan

Name _____

Period _____ **Date** _____ **Score** _____

Completion
Complete each sentence with the proper response. Place your answer on the space provided.

1. Voltage drops are reduced with _____ runs.

2. Most 120 volt convenience outlets have _____ receptacles.

3. The electrical plan is usually traced from the _____ plan.

4. Electric meters are _____ and designed for exterior installation.

5. The main breaker should be located _____ to the meter.

1. _____

2. _____

3. _____

4. _____

5. _____

Multiple Choice
Choose the answer that correctly completes the statement. Write the corresponding letter in the space provided.

_____ 1. Lighting fixtures that are located outside the house must be _____ fixtures.

    A. higher quality
    B. exterior
    C. typical
    D. made from brass

_____ 2. Most outlets in the home are 120 volt _____ type.

    A. simplex
    B. quiet
    C. duplex
    D. mercury

_____ 3. The least expensive type of switch used to switch lights is the _____ switch.

    A. on-off toggle
    B. quiet
    C. mercury
    D. dimmer

Short Answer
Answer the following questions.

1. List seven pieces of information that are generally shown on a lighting fixture schedule._____

_____

_____

_____

_____

2. List five features commonly shown on the electrical plan. _____

_____

_____

3. What are the two types of lights generally used in homes? _____

_____

4. Which two linetypes (symbols) are used to show the connection of switches to fixtures? ____

_____

Matching

Select the answer that correctly matches each term. Place your answer in the space provided.

A. Ceiling outlet fixture.
B. Chimes.
C. Duplex receptacle outlet.
D. Fluorescent fixture.
E. Push button.
F. Recessed outlet fixture.

G. Single-pole switch.
H. Split-wired duplex receptacle outlet.
I. Telephone.
J. Thermostat.
K. 240 volt outlet.
L. Weatherproof duplex outlet.

_____ 1.

_____ 2.

_____ 3.

_____ 4.

_____ 5.

_____ 6.

_____ 7.

_____ 8.

_____ 9.

_____ 10.

_____ 11.

_____ 12.

Chapter 23 Posttest
The Electrical Plan

Name _____

Period _____ **Date** _____ **Score** _____

Completion

Complete each sentence with the proper response. Place your answer on the space provided.

1. The electrical plan is usually traced from the _____ plan.

2. The main breaker should be located _____ to the meter.

3. Voltage drops are reduced with _____ runs.

4. Electric meters are _____ and designed for exterior installation.

5. Most 120 volt convenience outlets have _____ receptacles.

1. _____

2. _____

3. _____

4. _____

5. _____

Multiple Choice

Choose the answer that correctly completes the statement. Write the corresponding letter in the space provided.

_____ 1. The least expensive type of switch used to switch lights is the _____ switch.

    A. on-off toggle
    B. quiet
    C. mercury
    D. dimmer

_____ 2. Most outlets in the home are 120 volt _____ type.

    A. simplex
    B. quiet
    C. duplex
    D. mercury

_____ 3. Lighting fixtures that are located outside the house must be _____ fixtures.

    A. higher quality
    B. exterior
    C. typical
    D. made from brass

Short Answer

Answer the following questions.

1. List five features commonly shown on the electrical plan. _____

_____

_____

2. Which two linetypes (symbols) are used to show the connection of switches to fixtures? ____
   _____

3. What are the two types of lights generally used in homes? _____
   _____

4. List seven pieces of information that are generally shown on a lighting fixture schedule.____
   _____
   _____
   _____
   _____

Matching

Select the answer that correctly matches each term. Place your answer in the space provided.

A. Telephone.
B. 240 volt outlet.
C. Push button.
D. Recessed outlet fixture.
E. Split-wired duplex receptacle outlet.
F. Thermostat.

G. Chimes.
H. Single-pole switch.
I. Ceiling outlet fixture.
J. Duplex receptacle outlet.
K. Weatherproof duplex outlet.
L. Fluorescent fixture.

____ 1.

____ 2.

____ 3.

____ 4.

____ 5.

____ 6.

____ 7.

____ 8.

____ 9.

____ 10.

____ 11.

____ 12.

Residential Plumbing
24

Objectives

After studying this chapter, the student will be able to:

- Discuss the purpose of a residential plumbing system.
- Identify the elements contained in a residential water supply system.
- Identify the elements of a residential water and waste removal system.
- Explain the operation of various in-house water treatment systems.
- Explain the layout of a private sewage disposal system.

Displays

1. **Plumbing Supplies.** Collect examples of galvanized steel, copper, and plastic pipe and fittings that are used in residential plumbing systems. Display these for examination by the class.
2. **Code Requirements.** Prepare a bulletin board display using excerpts from the plumbing code enforced in your area. Highlight areas of particular importance.

Instructional Materials

Text: Pages 491–504
  Review Question, Suggested Activities
Workbook: Pages 273–282
  Review Questions, Problems/Activities
Teacher's Resources:
  Chapter 24 Pretest
  Chapter 24 Teaching Strategy
  Chapter 24 Posttest

Teaching Strategy

- **Knowledge Assessment.** Administer Chapter 24 Pretest. Correct the test and return. Highlight topics in which the individual student is deficient.
- Prepare Display #1.
- Review chapter objectives.
- Discuss the water supply system.
- Assign workbook Problem 24-1.

- Discuss the water and waste removal systems.
- Assign workbook Problem 24-2.
- Discuss fixtures.
- Present the private sewage disposal system.
- Assign workbook Problem 24-3.
- Discuss the septic tank and disposal field.
- Present calculation of disposal field size.
- Assign one or more of the Suggested Activities in the text.
- **Chapter Review.** Assign Review Questions in the text. Discuss the correct answers. Assign Review Questions in the workbook. Have students check their own answers. Make transparencies of the solutions to Problems/Activities 24-1 and 24-2 and use for review.
- **Evaluation.** Administer Chapter 24 Posttest. Correct the test and return. Return graded problems with comments.

Answers to Review Questions, Text

Page 503

1. The water supply, water and waste removal, and fixtures that facilitate the use of water.
2. building main
3. hose bib
4. cold water branch line
5. Answer may include any two: Threaded galvanized steel pipe, plastic, and copper tubing.
6. 3/4"
7. cushion the water flow and reduce pipe noise during use
8. Each main line, branch line, and fixture.
9. gravity
10. 4"
11. soil stack
12. secondary
13. house
14. trap
15. cleanout

16. stack wall
17. sump pump
18. plumbing fixture
19. The septic tank and the disposal field.
20. Adequate area and proper soil.
21. 75
22. 750 (or 1-1/2 times the sewage flow from the house over a 24-hour period)
23. garbage disposal
24. receive sewage in liquid form from the septic tank and allow it to seep into the soil
25. Dry and porous soil containing sand or gravel.
26. 1″ in 50′
27. percolation

Answers to Workbook Questions

Page 273

Part I: Matching

1. B. Building main
2. D. Hot water branch
3. G. Main stacks
4. H. Secondary stacks
5. A. Branch main
6. E. House sewer
7. C. Cleanout
8. K. Vent stack
9. I. Stack wall
10. J. Sump
11. F. Percolation test

Part II: Completion

1. Water treatment
2. blocked
3. shutoff
4. 6″
5. turns
6. main; secondary
7. disposal
8. bedrooms
9. 2′

Part III: Short Answer/Listing

1. Water supply, water and waste removal, and fixtures.
2. Pipes should be installed along interior walls. When pipes are installed along exterior walls, they should be insulated to prevent freezing.
3. Special heavy-duty copper tubing with soldered or flare-type joints.
4. An on-demand water heater is a small electric heating unit placed under a sink or lavatory where only small amounts of hot water are needed. The heater produces hot water instantly. Only a cold water line needs to be piped to the unit.
5. As many as possible and practical.
6. It is removed through the soil/vent stack, which protrudes about 12″ above the roof.
7. It removes about 75% of the solids from the sewage by bacterial action before discharging the sewage into the disposal field. It also provides storage space for the settled solids while they undergo digestive action.
8. To receive sewage in liquid form from the septic tank and allow it to seep into the soil.
9. 3 bedrooms x 500 square foot per bedroom = 1500 square feet for disposal field

Part IV: Multiple Choice

1. A. Are smaller than main lines.
2. B. 3/4″
3. D. Cushion the water flow and reduce pipe noise during use.
4. C. gravity
5. B. 4″
6. B. fixtures
7. A. 1 acre
8. C. 750
9. C. Water supply well.

Part V: Problems/Activities

1. Solution on page 380 of this manual.
2. Solution on page 381 of this manual.
3. Solution on page 382 of this manual.

Answers to Chapter 24 Pretest

Completion

1. Frost-free
2. city water main; private water source
3. top
4. smaller
5. reverse osmosis

Multiple Choice

1. C. 6″
2. B. building main

3. A. air compression
4. B. under the vanity
5. C. cleanout
6. D. smooth
7. D. house sewer
8. A. not under pressure
9. B. percolation tests
10. B. soil stack
11. A. prevent gases from escaping through the fixture drain into the house
12. A. stack wall
13. D. hot water heater

Short Answer

1. The fixtures.
2. 75%
3. Threaded galvanized steel pipe, plastic pipe, and copper pipe (tubing).
4. Answer may include any four: Cast iron, copper, brass alloy, fiber, and plastic pipe.
5. Water supply system, water and waste removal system, and fixtures.
6. Septic tank and disposal field.
7. Each main line, branch line, and fixture.

Answers to Chapter 24 Posttest

Completion

1. city water main; private water source
2. smaller
3. Frost-free
4. top
5. reverse osmosis

Multiple Choice

1. B. building main
2. D. hot water heater
3. A. air compression
4. C. 6"
5. B. under the vanity
6. D. smooth
7. A. not under pressure
8. B. soil stack
9. D. house sewer
10. A. prevent gases from escaping through the fixture drain into the house
11. C. cleanout
12. A. stack wall
13. B. percolation tests

Short Answer

1. Water supply system, water and waste removal system, and fixtures.
2. Threaded galvanized steel pipe, plastic pipe, and copper pipe (tubing).
3. Each main line, branch line, and fixture.
4. Answer may include any four: Cast iron, copper, brass alloy, fiber, and plastic pipe.
5. The fixtures.
6. Septic tank and disposal field.
7. 75%

Workbook Solution

1.

Directions:
Using the simplified house section below, draw the schematic of a residential water supply system. Connect each fixture to the cold water and hot water mains (where appropriate). Complete the system to the building main. Label each pipe as to size and name. Include shutoff valves for each branch line and fixture. Provide a hose bib and air chamber at each faucet. See Figure 24-1 in the text for a typical layout.

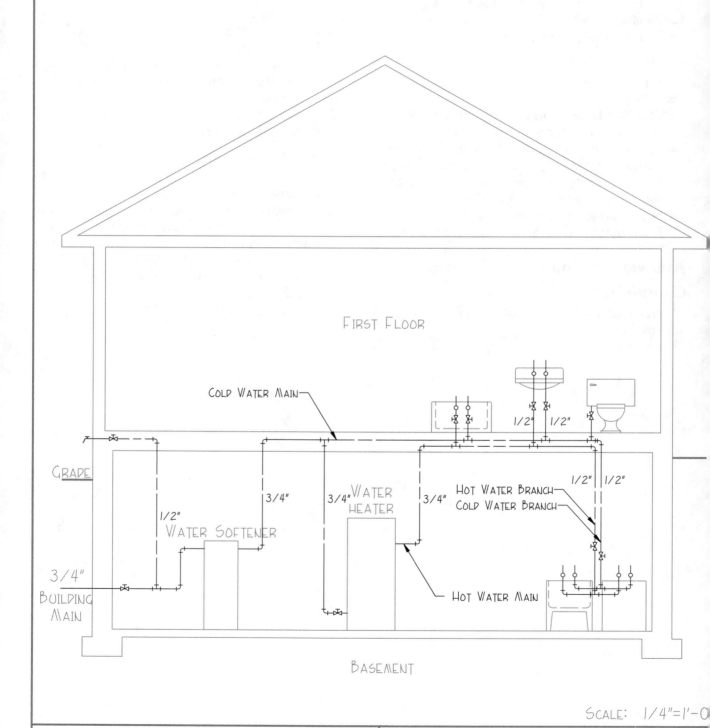

FIRST FLOOR

COLD WATER MAIN

1/2"   1/2"

GRADE

1/2"   1/2"

3/4"

3/4" WATER HEATER

3/4"

HOT WATER BRANCH

COLD WATER BRANCH

1/2"

WATER SOFTENER

3/4"

BUILDING MAIN

HOT WATER MAIN

BASEMENT

SCALE: 1/4"=1'-0

| WATER SUPPLY SYSTEM | NAME: | 24 |

Workbook Solution

Directions:
Using the simplified house section below, draw the schematic of a residential water and waste removal system. Connect each fixture to the house drain and connect the house drain to the house sewer. Provide a 4″ vent stack through the roof and label each part of the system showing size of pipe used. Study Figure 24-8 in your text for a layout. Remember, this is a gravity system.

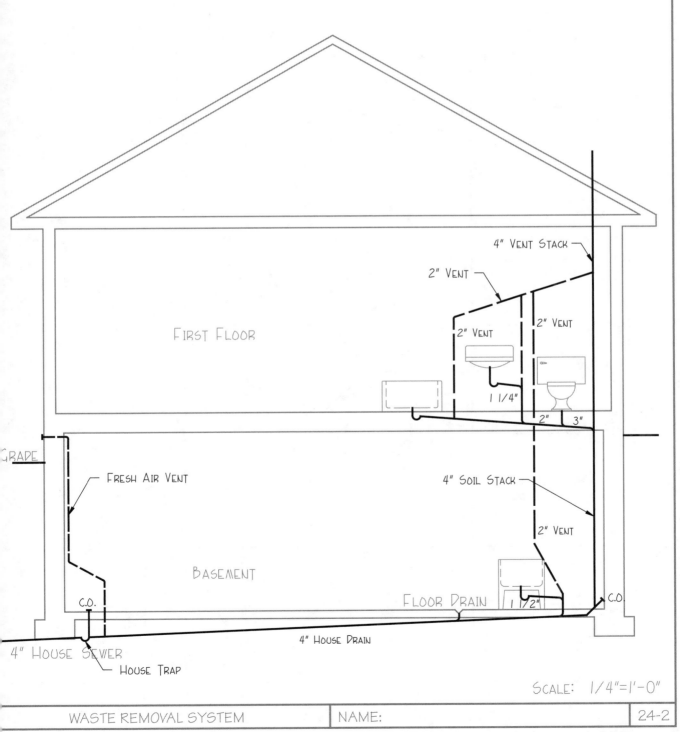

SCALE: 1/4″=1′-0″

WASTE REMOVAL SYSTEM	NAME:	24-2

Workbook Solution

3.

Directions:
Suppose you purchased Lot #2 in the subdivision below and wish to install a private well for household use. The surrounding lots have wells and septic systems already and your lot has the septic tank and disposal field in place. The local code specifies a minimum distance of 150' from the disposal field and 75' from the septic tank to the well. Indicate the area on your lot where the well can be placed.

SCALE: 1"=50'-0"

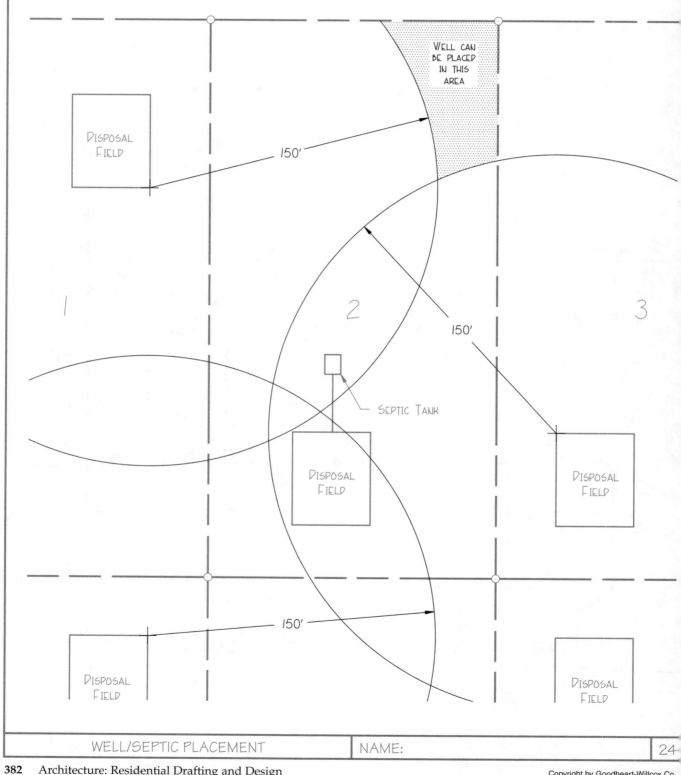

WELL/SEPTIC PLACEMENT   NAME: 24-

Chapter 24 Pretest
Residential Plumbing

Name _____

Period _____**Date** _____**Score** _____

Completion

Complete each sentence with the proper response. Place your answer on the space provided.

1. _____ hose bibs are available for use in cold climates.

2. A residential water supply system begins at the _____ or a(n) _____.

3. Large pipes should pass through the _____ of a joist and the joist should be blocked.

4. Branch lines are _____ in size than main lines.

5. In a(n) _____ water treatment system, the line pressure forces water through a thin semipermeable membrane.

1. _____

2. _____

   _____

3. _____

4. _____

5. _____

Multiple Choice

Choose the answer that correctly completes the statement. Write the corresponding letter in the space provided.

_____ 1. Generally, cold and hot water branch lines are placed about _____ apart.

   A. 2"
   B. 4"
   C. 6"
   D. 8"

_____ 2. In the water supply system, the pipe that enters the house is known as the _____.

   A. branch main
   B. building main
   C. water supply line
   D. branch line

_____ 3. Many codes require that a(n) _____ chamber be located at each faucet.

   A. air compression
   B. water storage
   C. water purification
   D. noise

_____ 4. Small, on-demand hot water heaters are located _____.

   A. in the basement
   B. under the vanity
   C. in a closet
   D. near the water storage tank

_____ 5. Each stack requires a _____ located at the base of the stack.

    A. 45° elbow
    B. closet bend
    C. cleanout
    D. trap

_____ 6. Drain lines are generally _____ inside with minimum projections and sharp turns.

    A. glazed
    B. rubber lined
    C. zinc coated
    D. smooth

_____ 7. Once the house drain passes outside of the house, it is called the _____.

    A. septic line
    B. secondary stack
    C. main stack
    D. house sewer

_____ 8. Unlike the water supply system, the drainage system is _____.

    A. not under pressure
    B. not so important
    C. the last thing to be planned
    D. installed by apprentices.

_____ 9. The suitability of the soil for a disposal field must be determined by _____.

    A. well drilling records
    B. percolation tests
    C. compaction tests
    D. history of the area

_____ 10. A vertical drain pipe that collects waste from one or more fixtures is called a _____.

    A. house sewer
    B. soil stack
    C. vent pipe
    D. cleanout

_____ 11. Traps are installed below each fixture except water closets, which have internal traps, to _____.

    A. prevent gases from escaping through the fixture drain into the house
    B. aid in draining the water
    C. reduce sound
    D. slow the flow of water

_____ 12. When a wall is constructed of 2″ × 6″ studs to house a 4″ cast iron pipe, this wall is called a _____.

    A. stack wall
    B. soil wall
    C. vent wall
    D. sewer wall

_____ 13. The hot water main emerges from the _____.

    A. water storage tank
    B. hot water branch line
    C. hose bib
    D. hot water heater

Short Answer

Answer the following questions.

1. What are the most obvious parts of the plumbing system? _____

_____

2. About what percentage of the solids are removed in the septic tank by bacterial action?

_____

3. Identify three types of pipe that are commonly used in the water supply system.

_____

_____

4. Identify the types of pipe that are commonly used for the waste removal system in a residential structure. _____

_____

_____

5. List the three principal parts of a residential plumbing installation. _____

_____

_____

_____

6. What are the two parts of a private sewage disposal system? _____

_____

7. Where should shutoff valves be used in a water supply system? _____

_____

_____

Chapter 24 Posttest
Residential Plumbing

Name _____

Period _____ **Date** _____ **Score** _____

Completion

Complete each sentence with the proper response. Place your answer on the space provided.

1. A residential water supply system begins at the _____ or a(n) _____.

1. _____

   _____

2. Branch lines are _____ in size than main lines.

2. _____

3. _____ hose bibs are available for use in cold climates.

3. _____

4. Large pipes should pass through the _____ of a joist and the joist should be blocked.

4. _____

5. In a(n) _____ water treatment system, the line pressure forces water through a thin semipermeable membrane.

5. _____

Multiple Choice

Choose the answer that correctly completes the statement. Write the corresponding letter in the space provided.

_____ 1. In the water supply system, the pipe that enters the house is known as the _____.

   A. branch main
   B. building main
   C. water supply line
   D. branch line

_____ 2. The hot water main emerges from the _____.

   A. water storage tank
   B. hot water branch line
   C. hose bib
   D. hot water heater

_____ 3. Many codes require that a(n) _____ chamber be located at each faucet.

   A. air compression
   B. water storage
   C. water purification
   D. noise

_____ 4. Generally, cold and hot water branch lines are placed about _____ apart.

   A. 2″
   B. 4″
   C. 6″
   D. 8″

_____ 5. Small, on-demand hot water heaters are located _____.

    A. in the basement
    B. under the vanity
    C. in a closet
    D. near the water storage tank

_____ 6. Drain lines are generally _____ inside with minimum projections and sharp turns.

    A. glazed
    B. rubber lined
    C. zinc coated
    D. smooth

_____ 7. Unlike the water supply system, the drainage system is _____.

    A. not under pressure
    B. not so important
    C. the last thing to be planned
    D. installed by apprentices.

_____ 8. A vertical drain pipe that collects waste from one or more fixtures is called a _____.

    A. house sewer
    B. soil stack
    C. vent pipe
    D. cleanout

_____ 9. Once the house drain passes outside of the house, it is called the _____.

    A. septic line
    B. secondary stack
    C. main stack
    D. house sewer

_____ 10. Traps are installed below each fixture except water closets, which have internal traps, to _____.

    A. prevent gases from escaping through the fixture drain into the house
    B. aid in draining the water
    C. reduce sound
    D. slow the flow of water

_____ 11. Each stack requires a _____ located at the base of the stack.

    A. 45° elbow
    B. closet bend
    C. cleanout
    D. trap

_____ 12. When a wall is constructed of 2″ × 6″ studs to house a 4″ cast iron pipe, this wall is called a _____.

    A. stack wall
    B. soil wall
    C. vent wall
    D. sewer wall

_____ 13. The suitability of the soil for a disposal field must be determined by _____.
- A. well drilling records
- B. percolation tests
- C. compaction tests
- D. history of the area

Short Answer

Answer the following questions.

1. List the three principal parts of a residential plumbing installation. _____

_____

_____

_____

2. Identify three types of pipe that are commonly used in the water supply system.

_____

_____

3. Where should shutoff valves be used in a water supply system? _____

_____

_____

4. Identify the types of pipe that are commonly used for the waste removal system in a residential structure. _____

_____

_____

5. What are the most obvious parts of the plumbing system? _____

_____

6. What are the two parts of a private sewage disposal system? _____

_____

7. About what percentage of the solids are removed in the septic tank by bacterial action?

_____

The Plumbing Plan
25

Objectives

After studying this chapter, the student will be able to:
- Explain the purpose of a residential plumbing plan.
- Identify the components of a residential plumbing plan.
- Draw plumbing symbols and fixtures on a plumbing plan using proper techniques.
- Develop a residential plumbing plan.
- Compile a plumbing fixture schedule.

Displays

1. **Plumbing Plan**. Select a residential plumbing plan that illustrates good layout and design. Display the plan on the bulletin board.
2. **Student Work**. Display some of the best student work submitted on the bulletin board using assignments from the workbook.

Instructional Materials

Text: Pages 505–514
   Review Questions, Suggested Activities
Workbook: Pages 283–292
   Questions, Problems/Activities
Teacher's Resources:
   Chapter 25 Pretest
   Chapter 25 Teaching Strategy
   Chapter 25 Posttest

Teaching Strategy

- **Knowledge Assessment:** Administer the Chapter 25 Pretest. Correct the test and return. Highlight the topics in which the individual student is deficient.
- Prepare Display #1.
- Review the chapter objectives.
- Review the definition, purpose, and required information for the plumbing plan.
- Discuss waste lines and vent stacks.
- Discuss water supply lines.
- Discuss drain and fixture locations and pipe sizes and types.
- Present information included in the plumbing fixture schedule.
- Discuss the use of symbols, legends, and notes.
- Assign Problem 25-1 in the workbook.
- Present the procedure for drawing a plumbing plan.
- Assign Problems 25-2 and 25-3 in the workbook.
- Prepare Display #2.
- Assign one or more of the Suggested Activities in the text.
- **Chapter Review:** Assign the Review Questions in the text. Discuss the correct answers. Assign the questions in the workbook. Have students check their own answers. Make transparencies of solutions to Problems 25-1 and 25-2 in the workbook and use for review.
- **Evaluation:** Administer the Chapter 25 Posttest. Correct the test and return. Return graded problems with comments.

Answers to Review Questions, Text

Page 514

1. It shows the location, size, and type of all plumbing equipment to be used.
2. Proper location and sufficient size.
3. the waste line network
4. water closet
5. 3"
6. gravity
7. 3/4"
8. storm sewer
9. The average amount of water used, peak loads, water pressure on the line, and length of the pipe run.
10. inside diameter (ID)
11. Type L
12. plumbing fixture schedule
13. Drain, waste, and vent.
14. The inclusion of a piping symbols library.
15. Gas lines and in-house vacuum systems.

Answers to Workbook Questions
Page 283

Part I: Completion
1. plan
2. electrical
3. 1/4
4. wider
5. shutoff
6. L
7. manufacturer
8. building main
9. storm sewer
10. drain, waste, and vent

Part II: Short Answer/Listing
1. Waste lines and vent stacks, water supply lines, drain and plumbing fixture locations, the size and type of pipe to be used, proper plumbing symbols, a plumbing fixture schedule, and notes required to describe the system.
2. They should be connected to the building main before it reaches the softener.
3. Two or more plans.
4. Plumbing for fixtures should be located in order to provide access for servicing.
5. It refers to the approximate inside diameter of the pipe.
6. Identifying symbols, names of plumbing fixtures, number required, pipe connection sizes, and remarks.
7. The information is recorded in general notes on the plumbing plan in a prominent place such as above the title block.
8. hidden
9. A.
10. A legend is used to explain nonstandard or uncommon symbols on a plumbing plan.

Part III: Multiple Choice
1. B. floor plan
2. C. waste line network
3. B. 3/8"
4. A. plot
5. B. floor drain in a plan view

Part IV: Problems/Activities
1. Solution on page 392.
2. Solution on page 393.

3. Evaluate solution based on principles discussed in the text.

Answers to Chapter 25 Pretest
Completion
1. larger
2. size
3. floor
4. water closet
5. electrical

Multiple Choice
1. B. 3"
2. C. 1/4" per foot
3. B. L
4. C. gravity
5. A. building main
6. D. All of the above.

Short Answer
1. Split-level and two-story.
2. The local code or the National Plumbing Code.
3. Drain, waste, and vent.
4. Waste lines and vent stacks, water supply lines, drain and plumbing fixture locations, the size and type of pipe to be used, proper plumbing symbols, a plumbing fixture schedule, and notes required to describe the system.
5. The storm sewer or a dry well.
6. Identifying symbols, names of plumbing fixtures, number required, pipe connection sizes, and remarks.

Answers to Chapter 25 Posttest
Completion
1. floor
2. electrical
3. size
4. water closet
5. larger

Multiple Choice
1. B. 3"
2. C. gravity
3. C. 1/4" per foot
4. A. building main
5. B. L
6. D. All of the above.

Short Answer

1. Waste lines and vent stacks, water supply lines, drain and plumbing fixture locations, the size and type of pipe to be used, proper plumbing symbols, a plumbing fixture schedule, and notes required to describe the system.
2. Split-level and two-story.
3. The storm sewer or a dry well.
4. The local code or the National Plumbing Code.
5. Identifying symbols, names of plumbing fixtures, number required, pipe connection sizes, and remarks.
6. Drain, waste, and vent.

Workbook Solution

1.

Directions:
Directions:
Draw the plan view symbol for each of the plumbing symbols listed below. The scale for these symbols is 1/4″ = 1′-0″.

SOIL STACK	GATE VALVE	COUPLING OR SLEEVE
ELBOW TURNED UP	ELBOW TURNED DOWN	TEE TURNED UP
METER	HOSE BIB	TEE TURNED DOWN
CLEANOUT	FLOOR DRAIN	TEE HORIZONTAL

C.W.

COLD WATER LINE

G

GAS LINE

H.W.

HOT WATER LINE

S

SPRINKLER LINE

SOIL OR WASTE LINE

VENT PIPE

| PLUMBING SYMBOLS | NAME: | 2 |

Workbook Solution

Directions:
Show the typical piping arrangement for the two situations below. Use proper symbols and show tees, elbows, etc.

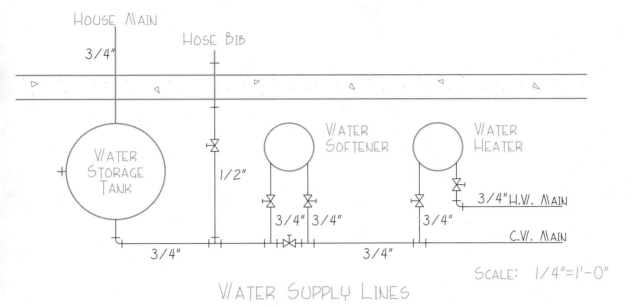

WATER SUPPLY LINES

SCALE: 1/4"=1'-0"

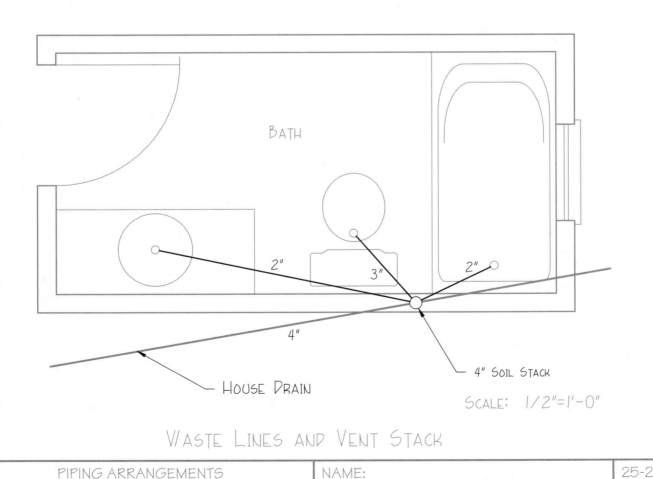

WASTE LINES AND VENT STACK

SCALE: 1/2"=1'-0"

PIPING ARRANGEMENTS	NAME:	25-2

Chapter 25 Pretest
The Plumbing Plan

Name_____

Period _____Date _____Score _____

Completion

Complete each sentence with the proper response. Place your answer on the space provided.

1. Waste lines are _____ in size than water supply lines.

2. Proper location and sufficient _____ are the major considerations in planning the waste lines.

3. The plumbing plan is generally traced from the _____ plan.

4. A main stack must be designated for each _____.

5. The plumbing system should be coordinated with the _____ and climate control systems.

1. _____

2. _____

3. _____

4. _____

5. _____

Multiple Choice

Choose the answer that correctly completes the statement. Write the corresponding letter in the space provided.

_____ 1. The minimum waste line size for a water closet is _____.

    A. 2″
    B. 3″
    C. 4″
    D. 5″

_____ 2. Waste lines are usually sloped about _____ to facilitate even flow.

    A. 1/16″ per foot
    B. 1/8″ per foot
    C. 1/4″ per foot
    D. 1/2″ per foot

_____ 3. Type _____ copper pipe is a medium weight pipe usually used for inside hot and cold water lines.

    A. K
    B. L
    C. M
    D. DWV

_____ 4. Waste lines depend on _____ to move the waste.

    A. vacuum
    B. pressure
    C. gravity
    D. All of the above.

_____ 5. Hose bibs and other fixtures that do not require softened or filtered water should be connected to the _____ before it reaches the softener.

    A. building main
    B. cold water main
    C. hot water branch line
    D. cold water branch line

_____ 6. The proper pipe size for a given installation will depend on _____.

    A. the water pressure on the line
    B. the average amount of water used
    C. the length of the pipe run
    D. All of the above.

Short Answer

Provide brief answers to the following questions.

1. What types of house designs may require two plumbing plans? _____

_____

_____

2. Where can the clearance dimensions and minimum space requirements for fixtures be found?

_____

_____

3. What does a DWV designation on copper pipe mean? _____

_____

4. List the required information on a plumbing plan. _____

_____

_____

_____

_____

5. What are floor drains usually connected to? _____

_____

6. What information is generally shown on a plumbing fixture schedule? _____

_____

_____

_____

Chapter 25 Posttest
The Plumbing Plan

Name _____

Period _____**Date** _____**Score** _____

Completion

Complete each sentence with the proper response. Place your answer on the space provided.

1. The plumbing plan is generally traced from the _____ plan.

1. _____

2. The plumbing system should be coordinated with the _____ and climate control systems.

2. _____

3. Proper location and sufficient _____ are the major considerations in planning the waste lines.

3. _____

4. A main stack must be designated for each _____.

4. _____

5. Waste lines are _____ in size than water supply lines.

5. _____

Multiple Choice

Choose the answer that correctly completes the statement. Write the corresponding letter in the space provided.

_____ 1. The minimum waste line size for a water closet is _____.

   A. 2″
   B. 3″
   C. 4″
   D. 5″

_____ 2. Waste lines depend on _____ to move the waste.

   A. vacuum
   B. pressure
   C. gravity
   D. All of the above.

_____ 3. Waste lines are usually sloped about _____ to facilitate even flow.

   A. 1/16″ per foot
   B. 1/8″ per foot
   C. 1/4″ per foot
   D. 1/2″ per foot

_____ 4. Hose bibs and other fixtures that do not require softened or filtered water should be connected to the _____ before it reaches the softener.

   A. building main
   B. cold water main
   C. hot water branch line
   D. cold water branch line

_____ 5. Type _____ copper pipe is a medium weight pipe usually used for inside hot and cold water lines.

    A. K
    B. L
    C. M
    D. DWV

_____ 6. The proper pipe size for a given installation will depend on _____.

    A. the water pressure on the line
    B. the average amount of water used
    C. the length of the pipe run
    D. All of the above.

Short Answer

Provide brief answers to the following questions.

1. List the required information on a plumbing plan. _____

    _____

    _____

    _____

    _____

2. What types of house designs may require two plumbing plans? _____

    _____

    _____

3. What are floor drains usually connected to? _____

    _____

4. Where can the clearance dimensions and minimum space requirements for fixtures be found?

    _____

    _____

5. What information is generally shown on a plumbing fixture schedule? _____

    _____

    _____

    _____

6. What does a DWV designation on copper pipe mean? _____

    _____

Residential Climate Control
26

Objectives

After studying this chapter, the student will be able to:
- Discuss the components of a complete climate control system.
- List the advantages and disadvantages of various types of residential heating systems.
- Perform heat loss calculations for a typical residential structure.
- Select building materials that will provide the best insulation properties.

Displays

1. **Typical Residential Climate Control Systems.** Create a bulletin board display from manufacturer's literature showing typical residential climate control systems. Identify each system.
2. **Advantages and Disadvantages of Climate Control Systems.** Using charts developed by students in response to Suggested Activity #5 in the text, show the advantages and disadvantages of each of the typical residential climate control systems.

Instructional Materials

Text: Pages 515–537
   Review Questions, Suggested Activities
Workbook: Pages 293–300
   Review Questions, Problems/Activities
Teacher's Resources:
   Chapter 26 Pretest
   Chapter 26 Teaching Strategy
   Chapter 26 Posttest

Teaching Strategy

- **Knowledge Assessment.** Administer the Chapter 26 Pretest. Correct the test and return. Highlight topics in which the individual student is deficient.
- Prepare Display #1.
- Review chapter objectives.

- Discuss temperature control.
- Assign workbook Problem 26-1.
- Discuss humidity control and air circulation and cleaning.
- Discuss forced-air systems.
- Present hydronic systems.
- Discuss electric radiant systems.
- Discuss heat pumps.
- Present heat loss calculations.
- Assign workbook Problem 26-2.
- Assign one or more of the Suggested Activities in the text.
- **Chapter Review.** Assign Review Questions in the text. Discuss the correct answers. Assign Review Questions in the workbook. Have students check their own answers. Make transparencies of the solutions to Problems/Activities 26-1 and 26-2 and use for review.
- **Evaluation.** Administer Chapter 26 Posttest. Correct the test and return. Return graded problems with comments.

Answers to Review Questions, Text
Page 537

1. Temperature control, humidity control, air circulation, and air cleaning.
2. Answer may include any five: Adequate insulation, proper ventilation, solar orientation of the house, weatherstripping windows and doors, overhangs, landscaping, and special glass.
3. relative humidity
4. 50
5. Throat and skin irritations are likely and furniture may crack and separate at the glue joints.
6. Wood doors, windows, and drawers can swell and not operate smoothly and water is likely to condense on windows, which may cause damage to the woodwork.
7. dehumidifier
8. Forced-air, hydronic, electric radiant, and heat pumps.

9. It heats air in a furnace and forces it through pipes or ducts to all parts of the house.
10. Upflow, counterflow, and horizontal.
11. An automatic sensing device that sends a signal to the furnace or air conditioner at a temperature set by the homeowner.
12. Boiler, water pipes, and radiators or radiant panels.
13. Answer may include any three: Each room may be controlled individually, absence of noise transmitted from room to room, no registers to occupy wall space, no drafts, it is clean, it is quiet, and it is efficient.
14. electric radiant system
15. refrigeration
16. Compressor-condenser.

Answers to Workbook Questions
Page 293
Part I: Short Answer/Listing
1. In the ceiling, in the exterior walls, and under the floor.
2. Crawl space and attic.
3. Dehumidifier.
4. Forced-air, hydronic, electric radiant, and heat pumps.
5. Relatively inexpensive to purchase and install, quickly provides adequate amounts of heat, humidification is simple, and the ductwork may be used for central air conditioning.
6. Zoned heating; each zone or area has a separate furnace and thermostat.
7. Forced-air and hydronic.
8. Heat pump; They are not efficient in areas where the temperature drops below 30°F.

Part II: Multiple Choice
1. C. Rigid foam
2. B. landscaping
3. A. Humidifiers
4. B. forced-air system.
5. A. thermostat
6. C. one-pipe
7. A. The temperature of each room can be controlled individually.
8. C. Both A and B.
9. D. heat pump
10. B. microprocessor

Part III: Completion
1. insulation
2. solar
3. more
4. Air cleaning
5. horizontal
6. radiant
7. Resistance
8. heat pump

Part IV: Matching
1. G. Relative humidity
2. A. Btu
3. H. Resistivity
4. I. U factor
5. C. Heat loss
6. D. Infiltration
7. B. Design temperature difference
8. E. Inside design temperature
9. F. Outside design temperature

Part V: Problems/Activities
1. Solution on page 402 of this manual.
2. Solution on page 403 of this manual.

Answers to Chapter 26 Pretest
Completion
1. Light
2. Landscaping
3. Ventilation
4. Weatherstripping
5. heating; cooling

Multiple Choice
1. B. south
2. C. 50%
3. B. dehumidifier
4. D. forced-air
5. A. each room can be controlled individually
6. C. refrigeration
7. A. exposed surfaces of the house
8. C. resistivity
9. C. $1.00 \div 16.63 = .060$
10. D. All of the above.
11. A. more
12. B. moisture content is too high in the house
13. A. dust and foreign particles
14. B. thermostat
15. C. resistance wiring
16. B. mild
17. B. microprocessor

Short Answer

1. To prevent the transfer of heat or cold from one location to another.
2. Throat and skin irritations are likely.
3. Standard upflow, counterflow, and horizontal.
4. The availability of fuels, temperature variations, cost of installation and maintenance, type of house, and personal preference of the owner.
5. Temperature control, humidity control, air circulation, and air cleaning.
6. The ratio (percentage) of water vapor in the atmosphere to the amount required to saturate it at a given temperature.
7. Forced-air, hydronic, electric radiant, and heat pumps.
8. Boiler, water pipes, and radiators or radiant panels.

Answers to Chapter 26 Posttest

Completion

1. heating; cooling
2. Ventilation
3. Light
4. Weatherstripping
5. Landscaping

Multiple Choice

1. D. All of the above.
2. B. south
3. A. more
4. C. 50%
5. B. moisture content is too high in the house

6. B. dehumidifier
7. A. dust and foreign particles
8. D. forced-air
9. B. thermostat
10. A. each room can be controlled individually
11. C. resistance wiring
12. C. refrigeration
13. B. mild
14. A. exposed surfaces of the house
15. C. resistivity
16. C. $1.00 \div 16.63 = .060$
17. B. microprocessor

Short Answer

1. Temperature control, humidity control, air circulation, and air cleaning.
2. To prevent the transfer of heat or cold from one location to another.
3. The ratio (percentage) of water vapor in the atmosphere to the amount required to saturate it at a given temperature.
4. Throat and skin irritations are likely.
5. Forced-air, hydronic, electric radiant, and heat pumps.
6. Standard upflow, counterflow, and horizontal.
7. Boiler, water pipes, and radiators or radiant panels.
8. The availability of fuels, temperature variations, cost of installation and maintenance, type of house, and personal preference of the owner.

Workbook Solution

1.

Directions:
Add insulation to the crawl space/first floor section below to maximize resistance to heat loss. The following areas are suggested for consideration: RF insulation on the outside of the stud wall, batt insulation between the studs and between the floor joists, sill sealer, and RF insulation either inside or outside of the foundation wall.

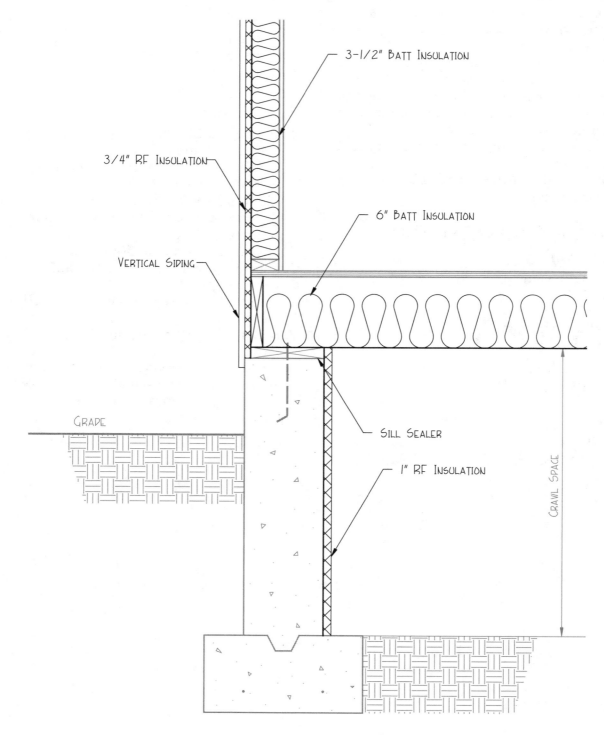

3-1/2" BATT INSULATION

3/4" RF INSULATION

6" BATT INSULATION

VERTICAL SIDING

SILL SEALER

1" RF INSULATION

GRADE

CRAWL SPACE

SCALE: 1"=1'-0

HEAT LOSS REDUCTION   NAME:

Workbook Solution

Directions:
Calculate the heat loss for the exterior wall below and fill in the values as indicated. The wall has no windows or doors.

Wall Area Calculation:
Total wall area = 8'-0" × 12'-0" = 96 square feet
Window and door area = 0 square feet
Net wall area = 96 square feet

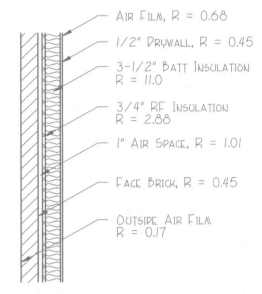

AIR FILM, R = 0.68

1/2" DRYWALL, R = 0.45

3-1/2" BATT INSULATION
R = 11.0

3/4" RF INSULATION
R = 2.88

1" AIR SPACE, R = 1.01

FACE BRICK, R = 0.45

OUTSIDE AIR FILM
R = 0.17

Resistivity of Wall Materials:

4" Face brick	=	0.45
1" Air space	=	1.01
3/4" RF insulation	=	2.88
3-1/2" Batt insulation	=	11.00
1/2" Drywall	=	0.45
Outside air film	=	0.17
Inside air film	=	0.68
Total resistivity	=	16.64

U Factor for Net Wall Area:
1.00 divided by total resistivity = 0.060
Therefore, U factor for net wall = 0.060

Design Temperature Difference:

Inside design temperature	=	70°
Outside design temperature	=	5°
Design temperature difference	=	65°

Btu/H for Net Wall:
Net wall area × U factor × temperature difference
96 square feet × 0.060 × 65° = 374.4 Btu/H

Therefore, the heat loss for the 8'-0" × 12'-0" wall is 374.4 Btu/H.

Chapter 26 Pretest
Residential Climate Control

Name _____

Period _____ **Date** _____ **Score** _____

Completion

Complete each sentence with the proper response. Place your answer on the space provided.

1. _____-colored roofing materials absorb less heat from the sun.

2. _____ not only serves to improve the appearance of a home, but may be used to block cold winds and provide shade.

3. _____ reduces the temperature and moisture content in the house.

4. _____ seals small cracks around doors and windows to reduce heat loss.

5. Temperature control includes both _____ and _____.

1. _____

2. _____

3. _____

4. _____

5. _____

_____

Multiple Choice

Choose the answer that correctly completes the statement. Write the corresponding letter in the space provided.

_____ 1. In cold climates, an attempt should be made to place all large areas of glass on the _____ side of the house away from the cold winter winds and in a position to take advantage of the winter sun.

A. north
B. south
C. east
D. west

_____ 2. A comfortable humidity level is around _____ when the temperature is about 75°F.

A. 25%
B. 35%
C. 50%
D. 60%

_____ 3. A(n) _____ may be used to remove water vapor from the air in a house.

A. humidifier
B. dehumidifier
C. air filtering system
D. hydrometer

_____ 4. The _____ heating system is popular because it is relatively inexpensive to purchase and install, provides heat in adequate amounts quickly, the ducts may be used in a central air conditioning system, and humidification is simple.

    A. hydronic
    B. solar warm water
    C. electric radiant
    D. forced-air

_____ 5. One of the major advantages of a hydronic heating system is that _____.

    A. each room can be controlled individually
    B. humidification is easy
    C. it is the least expensive to operate
    D. the system is inexpensive to install

_____ 6. Heat pumps are essentially _____ units that pump or transfer natural heat from air or water to heat or cool the house.

    A. hot air engine
    B. condensing
    C. refrigeration
    D. None of the above.

_____ 7. Before the proper size of heating or cooling unit can be determined, heat loss calculations are required for _____.

    A. exposed surfaces of the house
    B. all interior space of the house
    C. the heating unit
    D. None of the above.

_____ 8. Ability of a material to resist the transfer of heat or cold is called its _____.

    A. U factor
    B. infiltration
    C. resistivity
    D. design temperature difference

_____ 9. The U factor for one square foot of material that has a resistivity of 16.63 is _____.

    A. $1.00 \times 16.63 = 16.63$
    B. $16.63 \div 100 = .1663$
    C. $1.00 \div 16.63 = .060$
    D. $16.63 \times 100 = 1663$

_____ 10. The efficiency of the heating or cooling system is affected by the _____ of the house.

    A. solar orientation
    B. ventilation
    C. insulation
    D. All of the above.

_____ 11. Air will hold _____ water vapor when the temperature is high than (as) when the temperature is low.

    A. more
    B. less
    C. about the same amount of
    D. Temperature makes no difference.

_____ 12. When water condenses on the inside of windows, it generally indicates that the _____.

    A. temperature is too low in the house
    B. moisture content is too high in the house
    C. furnace needs repair because carbon dioxide is being produced
    D. heating system is working well

_____ 13. Air cleaning devices remove _____ from the air in the house.

    A. dust and foreign particles
    B. viruses
    C. moisture
    D. All of the above.

_____ 14. Furnace operation is controlled by a _____.

    A. manometer
    B. thermostat
    C. multiflow valve
    D. timer

_____ 15. Electric radiant systems use _____ to produce heat.

    A. radio waves
    B. atomic energy
    C. resistance wiring
    D. evaporation units

_____ 16. Heat pumps are highly efficient in _____ climates.

    A. very cold
    B. mild
    C. all
    D. Climate is not a factor.

_____ 17. Programmable thermostats have a _____ and can automatically control a home's heating and cooling systems.

    A. mercury switch
    B. microprocessor
    C. telephone port
    D. satellite connection

Name _____

Short Answer

Answer the following questions.

1. What is the function of insulation? _____
   _____

2. When the humidity is too low in a house, what is the physical effect on a person? _____
   _____

3. Identify the three basic types of forced-air furnaces available for residential installations. ___
   _____

4. List five factors that should be considered in choosing the "right" heating system for a particular home. _____
   _____
   _____

5. Identify the four elements of a complete climate control system. _____
   _____
   _____
   _____

6. What is relative humidity? _____
   _____

7. Name the four basic types of heating systems most commonly used in residential structures.
   _____
   _____
   _____

8. What are the three main parts of a hydronic system? _____
   _____
   _____

Chapter 26 Posttest
Residential Climate Control

Name _____

Period _____Date _____Score _____

Completion

Complete each sentence with the proper response. Place your answer on the space provided.

1. Temperature control includes both _____ and _____.

    1. _____

       _____

2. _____ reduces the temperature and moisture content in the house.

    2. _____

3. _____-colored roofing materials absorb less heat from the sun.

    3. _____

4. _____ seals small cracks around doors and windows to reduce heat loss.

    4. _____

5. _____ not only serves to improve the appearance of a home, but may be used to block cold winds and provide shade.

    5. _____

Multiple Choice

Choose the answer that correctly completes the statement. Write the corresponding letter in the space provided.

_____ 1. The efficiency of the heating or cooling system is affected by the _____ of the house.

    A. solar orientation
    B. ventilation
    C. insulation
    D. All of the above.

_____ 2. In cold climates, an attempt should be made to place all large areas of glass on the _____ side of the house away from the cold winter winds and in a position to take advantage of the winter sun.

    A. north
    B. south
    C. east
    D. west

_____ 3. Air will hold _____ water vapor when the temperature is high than (as) when the temperature is low.

    A. more
    B. less
    C. about the same amount of
    D. Temperature makes no difference.

_____ 4. A comfortable humidity level is around _____ when the temperature is about 75°F.

    A. 25%
    B. 35%
    C. 50%
    D. 60%

_____ 5. When water condenses on the inside of windows, it generally indicates that the _____.

    A. temperature is too low in the house
    B. moisture content is too high in the house
    C. furnace needs repair because carbon dioxide is being produced
    D. heating system is working well

_____ 6. A(n) _____ may be used to remove water vapor from the air in a house.

    A. humidifier
    B. dehumidifier
    C. air filtering system
    D. hydrometer

_____ 7. Air cleaning devices remove _____ from the air in the house.

    A. dust and foreign particles
    B. viruses
    C. moisture
    D. All of the above.

_____ 8. The _____ heating system is popular because it is relatively inexpensive to purchase and install, provides heat in adequate amounts quickly, the ducts may be used in a central air conditioning system, and humidification is simple.

    A. hydronic
    B. solar warm water
    C. electric radiant
    D. forced-air

_____ 9. Furnace operation is controlled by a _____.

    A. manometer
    B. thermostat
    C. multiflow valve
    D. timer

_____ 10. One of the major advantages of a hydronic heating system is that _____.

    A. each room can be controlled individually
    B. humidification is easy
    C. it is the least expensive to operate
    D. the system is inexpensive to install

_____ 11. Electric radiant systems use _____ to produce heat.

    A. radio waves
    B. atomic energy
    C. resistance wiring
    D. evaporation units

_____ 12. Heat pumps are essentially _____ units that pump or transfer natural heat from air or water to heat or cool the house.

    A. hot air engine
    B. condensing
    C. refrigeration
    D. None of the above.

_____ 13. Heat pumps are highly efficient in _____ climates.

    A. very cold
    B. mild
    C. all
    D. Climate is not a factor.

_____ 14. Before the proper size of heating or cooling unit can be determined, heat loss calculations are required for _____.

    A. exposed surfaces of the house
    B. all interior space of the house
    C. the heating unit
    D. None of the above.

_____ 15. Ability of a material to resist the transfer of heat or cold is called its _____.

    A. U factor
    B. infiltration
    C. resistivity
    D. design temperature difference

_____ 16. The U factor for one square foot of material that has a resistivity of 16.63 is _____.

    A. $1.00 \times 16.63 = 16.63$
    B. $16.63 \div 100 = .1663$
    C. $1.00 \div 16.63 = .060$
    D. $16.63 \times 100 = 1663$

_____ 17. Programmable thermostats have a _____ and can automatically control a home's heating and cooling systems.

    A. mercury switch
    B. microprocessor
    C. telephone port
    D. satellite connection

Short Answer

Answer the following questions.

1. Identify the four elements of a complete climate control system. _____

_____

_____

_____

2. What is the function of insulation? _____

_____

3. What is relative humidity? _____

_____

4. When the humidity is too low in a house, what is the physical effect on a person? _____

_____

5. Name the four basic types of heating systems most commonly used in residential structures.

_____

_____

_____

6. Identify the three basic types of forced-air furnaces available for residential installations. ___

_____

7. What are the three main parts of a hydronic system? _____

_____

_____

8. List five factors that should be considered in choosing the "right" heating system for a particular home. _____

_____

_____

Climate Control Plan

Objectives

After studying this chapter, the student will be able to:

- List features included on a residential climate control plan.
- Plan the ductwork for a typical forced-air system.
- Select an appropriate heating or cooling unit for a given structure.
- Draw a climate control plan using proper symbols and conventions.

Displays

1. **Climate Control Plan**. Display a complete climate control plan on the bulletin board. Select a plan that illustrates the drawing procedures described in the text.
2. **Student Work**. Display samples of student work from workbook assignments on the bulletin board.

Instructional Materials

Text: Pages 539–547
  Review Questions, Suggested Activities
Workbook: Pages 301–308
  Questions, Problems/Activities
Teacher's Resources:
  Chapter 27 Pretest
  Chapter 27 Teaching Strategy
  Chapter 27 Posttest

Teaching Strategy

- **Knowledge Assessment:** Administer the Chapter 27 Pretest. Correct the test and return. Highlight the topics in which the individual student is deficient.
- Prepare Display #1.
- Review the chapter objectives.
- Discuss the definition and purpose of a climate control plan and address the information required.
- Discuss the distribution system.
- Assign Problems 27-1 and 27-2 in the workbook.

- Discuss thermostats and climate control equipment.
- Prepare Display #2.
- Discuss schedules, calculations, and notes.
- Present the procedure for drawing a climate control plan.
- Assign one or more of the Suggested Activities in the text.
- **Chapter Review:** Assign the Review Questions in the text. Discuss the correct answers. Assign the questions in the workbook. Have students check their own answers. Make a transparency of the solution to Problem 27-1 in the workbook and use for review.
- **Evaluation:** Administer the Chapter 27 Posttest. Correct the test and return. Return graded problems with comments.

Answers to Review Questions, Text

Page 547

1. It shows the location, size, and type of heating, cooling, ventilating, humidification, and air cleaning equipment and the required piping or ducts.
2. Size and location of the distribution system, location of thermostats and registers or baseboard convectors, climate control equipment location and type, an equipment schedule, heat loss calculations, and any general or specific notes needed to fully describe the system.
3. Ducts, pipes
4. $1/4'' = 1'$
5. The conditioned air (heated or cooled) is concentrated where it is needed most—along the outside walls.
6. If the room is over 180 square feet.
7. Extended plenum and radial.
8. 6″, 8″
9. $10'' \times 8''$
10. wall stack
11. three
12. Equipment schedule, register schedule.

Answers to Workbook Questions

Page 301

Part I: Multiple Choice

1. C. floor plan
2. B. The location of thermostats and registers or baseboard convectors.
3. A. It concentrates heating or cooling along outside walls.
4. B. 8″
5. B. The size of the baseboard unit or convector cabinet.

Part II: Completion

1. plan
2. pipes
3. 15
4. extended plenum
5. 8″ × 26″
6. schedule
7. hidden
8. 1/4″ = 1′-0″

Part III: Short Answer/Listing

1. The location, size, and type of heating, cooling, ventilating, humidification, and air cleaning equipment and the required piping or ducts.
2. Ducts are drawn as close to scale as possible while pipes are shown as single lines and are not drawn to scale.
3. Two or more.
4. The extended plenum system.
5. 2″
6. One.
7. The total area of all round register ducts.
8. The thermostat should be located on an inside partition in a place where the temperature will be representative of the room(s) as a whole.
10. The type of heating and cooling system(s) must be determined and heat loss calculated for each room.

Part IV: Problems/Activities

1. Solution on page 415 of this manual.
2. Solution on page 416 of this manual.

Answers to Chapter 27 Pretest

Completion

1. perimeter
2. baseboard unit or convector cabinet
3. extended plenum
4. forced-air
5. electrical
6. partition
7. thermostat

Multiple Choice

1. C. 15′
2. A. wall stack
3. B. 1/4″ = 1′-0″
4. B. extended plenum
5. A. 8″ × 14″

Answers to Chapter 27 Posttest

Completion

1. electrical
2. perimeter
3. extended plenum
4. partition
5. baseboard unit or convector cabinet
6. forced-air
7. thermostat

Multiple Choice

1. B. 1/4″ = 1′-0″
2. A. 8″ × 14″
3. C. 15′
4. B. extended plenum
5. A. wall stack

Workbook Solution

↓ W.A.

WARM AIR SUPPLY

↑ C.A.

COLD AIR RETURN

SECOND FLOOR SUPPLY

SECOND FLOOR RETURN

12″ x 18″ ⟶

12″ x 18″ DUCT/FLOW

DUCT CHANGE IN SIZE

T

THERMOSTAT

H

HUMIDISTAT

R

RADIATOR

CONVECTOR

CONVECTOR

REGISTER

REGISTER

CEILING DUCT OUTLET

SCALE: 1/4″=1′-0″

CLIMATE CONTROL SYMBOLS   NAME: 27-1

2.

SCALE: 1/4"=1'-0"

Assignment # 27-2

Chapter 27 Pretest
Climate Control Plan

Name _____

Period _____**Date** _____**Score** _____

Completion

Complete each sentence with the proper response. Place your answer on the space provided.

1. A _____ system of outlets provides uniform heating or cooling.

2. For hydronic heating, the size of the _____ required will depend on the heat loss calculated for a given area.

3. A 6″ or 8″ round duct may be used to supply a register in the _____ system.

4. Inlets are required for _____ systems.

5. The climate control plan should be closely coordinated with the structural, plumbing, and _____ aspects of the home.

6. A thermostat should be located on an inside _____ in a place where the temperature will be representative of the room as a whole.

7. Each automatic climate control system requires at least one _____.

1. _____

2. _____

3. _____

4. _____

5. _____

6. _____

7. _____

Multiple Choice

Choose the answer that correctly completes the statement. Write the corresponding letter in the space provided.

_____ 1. If a room has more than _____ of exterior wall, then two or more outlets should be used.

    A. 5′
    B. 10′
    C. 15′
    D. 20′

_____ 2. A vertical duct designed to fit between the studs is called a _____.

    A. wall stack
    B. feeder stack
    C. feeder duct
    D. thin duct

_____ 3. The scale used to draw a residential climate control plan is generally _____ scale.

    A. 1/8″ = 1′-0″
    B. 1/4″ = 1′-0″
    C. 3/8″ = 1′-0″
    D. 1/2″ = 1′-0″

_____ 4. Two basic types of ductwork systems are the radial system and the _____ system.

    A. round pipe
    B. extended plenum
    C. perimeter
    D. underground

_____ 5. If a rectangular plenum is to serve six 6″ round ducts, the plenum duct should be _____.

    A. 8″ × 14″
    B. 8″ × 16″
    C. 8″ × 18″
    D. 8″ × 20″

Chapter 27 Posttest
Climate Control Plan

Name _____

Period _____**Date** _____**Score** _____

Completion
Complete each sentence with the proper response. Place your answer on the space provided.

1. The climate control plan should be closely coordinated with the structural, plumbing, and _____ aspects of the home.

2. A _____ system of outlets provides uniform heating or cooling.

3. A 6″ or 8″ round duct may be used to supply a register in the _____ system.

4. A thermostat should be located on an inside _____ in a place where the temperature will be representative of the room as a whole.

5. For hydronic heating, the size of the _____ required will depend on the heat loss calculated for a given area.

6. Inlets are required for _____ systems.

7. Each automatic climate control system requires at least one _____.

1. _____

2. _____

3. _____

4. _____

5. _____

6. _____

7. _____

Multiple Choice
Choose the answer that correctly completes the statement. Write the corresponding letter in the space provided.

_____ 1. The scale used to draw a residential climate control plan is generally _____.

    A. 1/8″ = 1′-0″
    B. 1/4″ = 1′-0″
    C. 3/8″ = 1′-0″
    D. 1/2″ = 1′-0″

_____ 2. If a rectangular plenum is to serve six 6″ round ducts, the plenum duct should be _____.

    A. 8″ × 14″
    B. 8″ × 16″
    C. 8″ × 18″
    D. 8″ × 20″

_____ 3. If a room has more than _____ of exterior wall, then two or more outlets should be used.

    A. 5′
    B. 10′
    C. 15′
    D. 20′

_____ 4. Two basic types of ductwork systems are the radial system and the _____ system.

    A. round pipe
    B. extended plenum
    C. perimeter
    D. underground

_____ 5. A vertical duct designed to fit between the studs is called a _____.

    A. wall stack
    B. feeder stack
    C. feeder duct
    D. thin duct

Solar Space Heating

28

Objectives

After studying this chapter, the student will be able to:
- Describe the two basic types of solar space heating.
- Explain how a passive solar space-heating system works.
- Compare direct, indirect, and isolated passive solar-gain systems.
- Identify the two most frequently used active solar systems.
- List the advantages and disadvantages of solar space heating.

Displays

1. **Solar Energy Systems.** Prepare a bulletin board display from materials secured from manufacturers of active solar energy systems. Warm air as well as warm water systems should be represented.
2. **Collector Plates.** Display a collection of solar collector elements from a variety of flat plate collectors. Contact manufacturers for samples.

Instructional Materials

Text: Pages 549–562
  Review Questions, Suggested Activities
Workbook: Pages 309–316
  Review Questions, Problems/Activities
Teacher's Resources:
  Chapter 28 Pretest
  Chapter 28 Teaching Strategy
  Chapter 28 Posttest

Teaching Strategy

- **Knowledge Assessment.** Administer Chapter 28 Pretest. Correct the test and return. Highlight topics in which the individual student is deficient.
- Prepare Display #1.
- Review chapter objectives.
- Introduce passive solar systems.
- Discuss direct gain systems.
- Present indirect gain systems.
- Discuss isolated gain systems.
- Assign workbook Problem 28-1.
- Introduce active solar systems.
- Prepare Display #2.
- Discuss warm air solar systems.
- Assign workbook Problem 28-2.
- Discuss warm water solar systems.
- Discuss advantages and disadvantages of solar heating.
- Assign one or more of the Suggested Activities in the text.
- **Chapter Review.** Assign Review Questions in the text. Discuss the correct answers. Assign Review Questions in the workbook. Have students check their own answers. Make transparencies of the solutions for Problems/Activities 28-1 and 28-2 and use for review.
- **Evaluation.** Administer Chapter 28 Posttest. Correct the test and return. Return graded problems with comments.

Answers to Review Questions, Text

Page 562

1. Passive solar systems and active solar systems.
2. Convection, conduction, and radiation.
3. Direct gain, indirect gain, and isolated gain or sun space systems.
4. Large areas of south-facing glazing (glass or other material) permit large amounts of sunlight to enter the interior space of the dwelling to directly heat the air inside.
5. It stores heat and helps modulate temperature within a structure.
6. Answer may include any three: Water, concrete, stone, and adobe.
7. A cubic foot of water.
8. Indirect gain systems heat the interior space by storing heat in a thermal mass, then releasing the heat into the interior space; direct gain systems heat the air in the living space directly.

9. Large drums that are painted black can be filled with water and stacked in an area that receives direct sunlight.
10. Trombe
11. The result of a fluid expanding and rising.
12. indirect
13. They are expensive and their effectiveness is reduced over time.
14. It collects and stores solar energy in an area outside of the living space.
15. Answer may include any two: Less interior space is dedicated to heat collection devices, large areas of interior space are not exposed to the sun, and heat collected is easier to control.
16. isolated
17. Active solar space heating involves collecting heat from solar radiation and then using pumps, fans, or other devices to distribute the heat to desired locations; a passive system does not have any mechanical components.
18. Warm air systems and warm water systems.
19. From 15% to 65%.
20. absorber
21. flat
22. Aluminum.
23. Flat black.
24. Stone.
25. south
26. blower
27. Proper sun orientation for large glass areas, roof overhang lengths, adequate insulation, adequate thermal mass, and concern for airflow inside a structure.
28. Corrosion and freezing.
29. double
30. liquid-to-air

Answers to Workbook Questions

Page 309

Part I: Completion

1. passive
2. direct
3. outside
4. isolated
5. active
6. absorber plate
7. thermal mass

8. warm water
9. efficiency

Part II: Short Answer/Listing

1. Passive and active.
2. To help modulate temperature extremes within the structure.
3. The appearance and noise created by expansion and contraction caused by heating and cooling may be offensive and problems may arise with evaporation, corrosion, and leaking.
4. Double glazing of glass, plastic, or fiberglass; minimized air infiltration; and thick concrete floors that are isolated from the foundation and soil beneath.
5. An airtight box, have a highly transparent glazing, and have sufficient insulation to retain its heat during cold weather.
6. Between 50° and 60°.
7. A set of controls activates a blower that moves the heated air into the living spaces.
8. The corrosive action of water and higher pressure than associated with an air-type system warrant greater concern in the design and construction of the water collectors. Also, freezing should be prevented by using a mixture of antifreeze and water, installing a drain-down procedure, or using nonwater fluids.

Part III: Multiple Choice

1. C. Is a type of passive solar system.
2. B. Use a large thermal mass located between the sun and living space to collect and store heat.
3. A. Reverse thermosiphoning.
4. D. All of the above.
5. B. Warm air solar system.
6. B. Aluminum.
7. A. Sufficiently large to store enough heat for three days of cloudy weather.
8. C. Large insulated tank usually located in the basement or crawl space.
9. B. Liquid-to-air heat exchangers such as baseboard convectors.

Part IV: Matching

1. F. Solar radiation
2. B. Convection
3. A. Conduction
4. E. Radiation

5. I. Trombe wall
6. H. Thermosiphoning
7. J. Water storage wall
8. D. Glauber's salt
9. G. Sun space
10. C. Flat plate collector

Part V: Problems/Activities

1. Solution on page 425 of this manual.
2. Solution on page 426 of this manual.

Answers to Chapter 28 Pretest

Completion

1. Direct
2. fuel
3. small
4. gain
5. Active

Multiple Choice

1. A. thermosiphoning
2. C. isolated gain
3. B. Convection
4. A. greenhouse or sun space
5. A. conduction
6. B. active solar
7. C. radiation
8. C. absorber plate
9. D. water
10. D. copper
11. B. indirect gain
12. B. phase change

Short Answer

1. Direct gain systems, indirect gain systems, and isolated gain systems.
2. Passive and active solar systems.
3. Trombe wall and water storage wall.
4. Convection, conduction, and radiation.
5. It is inexpensive and can store large amounts of heat.
6. Thick, interior, masonry walls, floors, and furnishings.
7. Solar energy is collected and stored in an area outside of the living space. Thermosiphoning moves warm air into the dwelling while cool air returns to the collector to be warmed again.
8. Tilt and orientation of the solar collector.
9. A bank of collectors, a warm water storage tank, a pump to circulate the water, some form of heat exchange device in the living

space, and controls for operating the system.
10. Corrosive action of water, higher pressure, and threat of freezing.
11. Warm air systems and warm water systems.
12. A large box or crawl space area filled with stone.

Answers to Chapter 28 Posttest

Completion

1. fuel
2. Active
3. gain
4. Direct
5. small

Multiple Choice

1. B. Convection
2. A. conduction
3. C. radiation
4. D. water
5. B. indirect gain
6. A. thermosiphoning
7. B. phase change
8. C. isolated gain
9. A. greenhouse or sun space
10. B. active solar
11. C. absorber plate
12. D. copper

Short Answer

1. Passive and active solar systems.
2. Convection, conduction, and radiation.
3. Direct gain systems, indirect gain systems, and isolated gain systems.
4. Thick, interior, masonry walls, floors, and furnishings.
5. Trombe wall and water storage wall.
6. It is inexpensive and can store large amounts of heat.
7. Solar energy is collected and stored in an area outside of the living space. Thermosiphoning moves warm air into the dwelling while cool air returns to the collector to be warmed again.
8. Warm air systems and warm water systems.
9. Tilt and orientation of the solar collector.
10. A large box or crawl space area filled with stone.

11. A bank of collectors, a warm water storage tank, a pump to circulate the water, some form of heat exchange device in the living space, and controls for operating the system.
12. Corrosive action of water, higher pressure, and threat of freezing.

Workbook Solution

Directions:
Complete each of the simplified structures below to illustrate the type of passive solar system indicated.

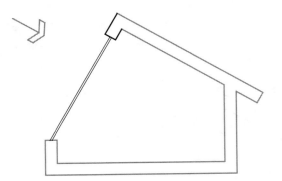

DIRECT GAIN SLOPED WALL

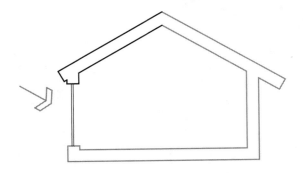

DIRECT GAIN VERTICAL WALL

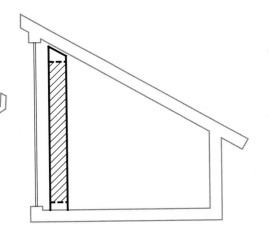

INDIRECT GAIN TROMBE WALL

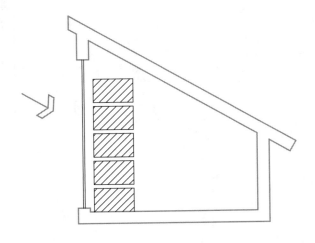

INDIRECT GAIN DRUM WALL

PASSIVE SOLAR HEATING

NAME:

Workbook Solution

2.

Directions:
Add solar collectors on the roof, thermal storage with blower in the basement, and connecting ducts to the simplified partial structure below. Show the collectors as 6" thick and 8' long, the ducts as 6" in diameter, and the storage as 4' × 8'. See Figure 28-13 for design layout.

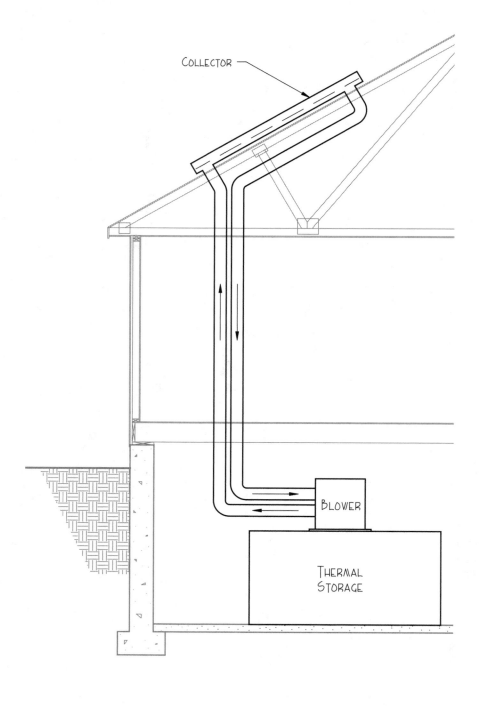

COLLECTOR

BLOWER

THERMAL
STORAGE

ACTIVE SOLAR SYSTEM	NAME:	28

Chapter 28 Pretest
Solar Space Heating

Name _____

Period _____ **Date** _____ **Score** _____

Completion

Complete each sentence with the proper response. Place your answer on the space provided.

1. _____ gain systems are the most popular type of passive solar space heating systems.

2. Increased heating costs and dwindling _____ supplies are reasons to consider solar space heating.

3. Frame walls have little mass and, therefore, store _____ amounts of heat.

4. The word _____ refers to the way heat is extracted from solar radiation.

5. _____ solar systems use pumps or fans to distribute heat.

1. _____

2. _____

3. _____

4. _____

5. _____

Multiple Choice

Choose the answer that correctly completes the statement. Write the corresponding letter in the space provided.

_____ 1. The result of a fluid expanding and rising is called _____.

    A. thermosiphoning
    B. reverse thermosiphoning
    C. conduction
    D. transformation

_____ 2. Solar systems that collect and store solar energy in an area outside of the living space are known as _____ systems.

    A. direct gain
    B. indirect gain
    C. isolated gain
    D. remote gain

_____ 3. _____ is the transfer of heat by a moving fluid.

    A. Conduction
    B. Convection
    C. Radiation
    D. Saturation

_____ 4. A _____ is an example of an isolated gain system.

    A. greenhouse or sun space
    B. Trombe wall
    C. drum wall
    D. None of the above.

_____ 5. The flow of heat through an object by transferring heat from one molecule to another is _____.

    A. conduction
    B. convection
    C. radiation
    D. osmosis

_____ 6. A(n) _____ heating system utilizes pumps, fans, or other devices to distribute the heat to desired locations.

    A. passive solar
    B. active solar
    C. isolated gain
    D. None of the above.

_____ 7. The flow of heat from a warm source through space in waves of infrared or visible light energy is _____.

    A. conduction
    B. convection
    C. radiation
    D. None of the above.

_____ 8. Every solar collector has some type of _____ that is designed to absorb heat from solar radiation.

    A. storage
    B. glazing
    C. absorber plate
    D. heater element

_____ 9. Which one of the following materials is capable of storing the most heat per cubic foot of volume?

    A. adobe
    B. concrete
    C. stone
    D. water

_____ 10. The most efficient material commonly used for warm air absorber plates is _____.

    A. aluminum
    B. steel
    C. ceramic
    D. copper

_____ 11. In a(n) _____ system, a large thermal mass is placed between the sun and the living space.

    A. direct gain
    B. indirect gain
    C. isolated gain
    D. None of the above.

_____ 12. A _____ material such as Glauber's salt has some possible advantages as a thermal storage material.

    A. state shift
    B. phase change
    C. solid liquid
    D. wet dry

Short Answer

Answer the following questions.

1. Name the three most common types of passive solar systems. _____
_____

2. What are the two basic methods or systems that have evolved to capture solar energy for space heating?_____

3. Identify two types of walls that are used in indirect gain systems._____
_____

4. By which three means is heat distributed in a passive solar heating system?_____
_____

5. Give two reasons why water is frequently used as a thermal mass._____
_____

6. What structural elements or additional items are generally used to form the large thermal mass required for direct gain systems? _____
_____
_____

7. Briefly explain how an isolated gain passive solar system works. _____
_____
_____
_____
_____

8. In addition to the design and construction of the absorber plate, what two other factors are important to ensure maximum heat collection? _____
_____

9. What are the five basic parts of a warm water solar system?_____

_____

_____

_____

10. What concerns are present in warm water systems that are not present in warm air systems?

_____

_____

11. What are the two basic types of active solar space heating systems? _____

_____

12. What type of thermal storage is generally used with a warm air active solar space heating
   system?_____

_____

Chapter 28 Posttest
Solar Space Heating

Name _____

Period _____**Date** _____**Score** _____

Completion

Complete each sentence with the proper response. Place your answer on the space provided.

1. Increased heating costs and dwindling _____ supplies are reasons to consider solar space heating.

2. _____ solar systems use pumps or fans to distribute heat.

3. The word _____ refers to the way heat is extracted from solar radiation.

4. _____ gain systems are the most popular type of passive solar space heating systems.

5. Frame walls have little mass and, therefore, store _____ amounts of heat.

1. _____

2. _____

3. _____

4. _____

5. _____

Multiple Choice

Choose the answer that correctly completes the statement. Write the corresponding letter in the space provided.

_____ 1. _____is the transfer of heat by a moving fluid.

A. Conduction
B. Convection
C. Radiation
D. Saturation

_____ 2. The flow of heat through an object by transferring heat from one molecule to another is _____.

A. conduction
B. convection
C. radiation
D. osmosis

_____ 3. The flow of heat from a warm source through space in waves of infrared or visible light energy is _____.

A. conduction
B. convection
C. radiation
D. None of the above.

_____ 4. Which one of the following materials is capable of storing the most heat per cubic foot of volume?

    A. adobe
    B. concrete
    C. stone
    D. water

_____ 5. In a(n) _____ system, a large thermal mass is placed between the sun and the living space.

    A. direct gain
    B. indirect gain
    C. isolated gain
    D. None of the above.

_____ 6. The result of a fluid expanding and rising is called _____.

    A. thermosiphoning
    B. reverse thermosiphoning
    C. conduction
    D. transformation

_____ 7. A _____ material such as Glauber's salt has some possible advantages as a thermal storage material.

    A. state shift
    B. phase change
    C. solid liquid
    D. wet dry

_____ 8. Solar systems that collect and store solar energy in an area outside of the living space are known as _____ systems.

    A. direct gain
    B. indirect gain
    C. isolated gain
    D. remote gain

_____ 9. A _____ is an example of an isolated gain system.

    A. greenhouse or sun space
    B. Trombe wall
    C. drum wall
    D. None of the above.

_____ 10. A(n) _____ heating system utilizes pumps, fans, or other devices to distribute the heat to desired locations.

    A. passive solar
    B. active solar
    C. isolated gain
    D. None of the above.

_____ 11. Every solar collector has some type of _____ that is designed to absorb heat from solar radiation.

   A. storage
   B. glazing
   C. absorber plate
   D. heater element

_____ 12. The most efficient material commonly used for warm air absorber plates is _____.

   A. aluminum
   B. steel
   C. ceramic
   D. copper

Short Answer

Answer the following questions.

1. What are the two basic methods or systems that have evolved to capture solar energy for space heating? _____

2. By which three means is heat distributed in a passive solar heating system? _____

_____

3. Name the three most common types of passive solar systems. _____

_____

4. What structural elements or additional items are generally used to form the large thermal mass required for direct gain systems? _____

_____

_____

5. Identify two types of walls that are used in indirect gain systems. _____

_____

6. Give two reasons why water is frequently used as a thermal mass. _____

_____

7. Briefly explain how an isolated gain passive solar system works. _____

_____

_____

_____

8. What are the two basic types of active solar space heating systems? _____

_____

9. In addition to the design and construction of the absorber plate, what two other factors are important to ensure maximum heat collection? _____

_____

10. What type of thermal storage is generally used with a warm air active solar space heating system?_____

_____

11. What are the five basic parts of a warm water solar system?_____

_____

_____

_____

12. What concerns are present in warm water systems that are not present in warm air systems?

_____

_____

Nontraditional Structures

29

Objectives

After studying this chapter, the student will be able to:

- Explain the purpose of a large thermal mass in earth-sheltered dwellings.
- List important site considerations for earth-sheltered buildings.
- Explain why soil type is a major concern in the design of an earth-sheltered structure.
- Summarize design variations of earth-sheltered dwellings.
- Explain why a dome structure generally has less heat loss than a conventional structure of comparable size.
- Diagram how a typical dome provides free interior space.
- Describe how a typical dome is constructed.
- List several advantages and disadvantages of dome homes.

Displays

1. **Soil Types.** Create a display of typical soil types found in your local area. Identify those which are most suitable for earth-sheltered dwellings. Use samples collected by students in Suggested Activity #2 in the text.
2. **Earth-sheltered Dwellings.** Create a bulletin board display composed of photos/pictures of earth-sheltered dwellings. Identify each type of dwelling.
3. **Dome Homes.** Create a bulletin board display of photos of dome homes which are available from manufacturers. Show floor plans and finished products.
4. **Dome Models.** Display dome home models built by past students as a part of Suggested Activity #5 in the text.

Instructional Materials

Text: Pages 565–578
Review Questions, Suggested Activities

Workbook: Pages 317–330
Review Questions, Problems/Activities
Teacher's Resources:
Chapter 29 Pretest
Chapter 29 Teaching Strategy
Chapter 29 Posttest

Teaching Strategy

- **Knowledge Assessment.** Administer the Chapter 29 Pretest. Correct the test and return. Highlight topics in which the individual student is deficient.
- Prepare Display #1.
- Review chapter objectives.
- Introduce site considerations.
- Discuss orientation on the site and topography as a design consideration.
- Discuss soil and groundwater considerations.
- Present energy conservation and structural systems.
- Discuss the cost of earth-sheltered dwellings.
- Introduce design variations of earth-sheltered dwellings.
- Assign workbook Problem/Activity 29-1.
- Discuss the slope design, atrium design, and penetrational design.
- Assign workbook Problem/Activity 29-2.
- Prepare Display #2.
- Cover the advantages and disadvantages of earth-sheltered housing.
- Prepare Display #3.
- Introduce dome structures.
- Discuss dome variations.
- Assign Suggested Activity #2 in the text.
- Discuss typical dome construction.
- Cover advantages and disadvantages of domes.
- Assign workbook Problems/Activities 29-3 and 29-4.
- Prepare Display #4.
- Assign one or more of the remaining Suggested Activities in the text.

- **Chapter Review.** Assign Review Questions in the text. Discuss the correct answers. Assign Review Questions in the workbook. Have students check their own answers.
- **Evaluation.** Administer the Chapter 29 Posttest. Correct the test and return. Return graded problems with comments.

Answers to Review Questions, Text

Page 577

1. Orientation to sun and wind, topography, soil type, groundwater level, and the load-bearing elements of the structure must be designed to withstand the pressure of earth and heavy roof loads.
2. south
3. Vegetation, shutters, and overhangs.
4. The structure must be shielded from winter winds and, at the same time, provide for ventilation in the summer.
5. northwest
6. Contour of the land, trees, streams, and other natural features.
7. The potential energy savings derived from the structure.
8. Soft or loose deposits, expansive clay, or soft clay (if a deep excavation).
9. 62.4 pounds per square foot for each foot of depth.
10. surface area
11. Earth placed against the walls and on the roof reduces heat loss in winter by effectively reducing the exposed surface area.
12. Conventional flat roof systems and somewhat unconventional systems that use vault and dome shapes.
13. Slope, atrium, and penetrational designs.
14. Penetrational.
15. atrium
16. R. Buckminster Fuller
17. triangular
18. Efficient system that is strong and versatile; open, obstruction-free floor space; factory production; requires less energy for heating and air conditioning; economical to build; interior is exciting and fun to decorate due to the varied shapes and surfaces.
19. Reduced exposed exterior surface.
20. 26'; 60'
21. triangle
22. pentagons; hexagons
23. A crane is needed to lift the assembled structure into place or to lift the final panel into place if the structure is assembled in place. Depending on the construction method used, it will be used to either place the shell of the dome on the foundation or to put the top hexagon in place.
24. Answer may include any two: Basement, crawl space, or slab foundation.
25. Support the structure and provide headspace on the second level.

Answers to Workbook Questions

Page 317

Part I: Short Answer/Listing

1. Orientation to the sun and wind, topography, type of soil, and groundwater level.
2. Southeast.
3. Earth-sheltered houses are usually heavier and placed deeper into the earth than conventional houses. Excessive groundwater is a problem for this type of dwelling.
4. It swells when wet and produces very high pressure that can damage the structure.
5. The shape or geometry of the plan and the earth mass around the structure.
6. Conventional roof systems use cast-in-place concrete slabs, concrete planks, and wood or steel post and beam systems. Unconventional systems can support heavier loads and include concrete or steel culvert shapes and domes.
7. The slope design is usually a very energy efficient solution due to the continuous earth mass, windows on the south side, and reduced wind on the structure.
8. About 30% less.
9. To decrease the number of components, eliminate the high level of accuracy needed to join a large number of small triangles, and because windows and doors are not easily incorporated into a plan that uses small triangles.

10. Four hexagons and three trapezoids.
11. Crane.
12. They support the entire structure while providing additional headroom on the second floor.
13. The structure is generally stronger and requires less energy to heat than conventional rectangular shapes covering the same floor space.

Part II: Multiple Choice

1. C. Solar energy may be used to heat the interior space.
2. A. sloping
3. B. Bearing capacity and tendency to expand when wet.
4. D. Compacted sand or gravel.
5. A. Has a small surface area exposed.
6. D. All of the above.
7. A. Better suited for warm climates.
8. B. Their high resistance to fire damage.
9. A. Triangle.
10. B. The structure of the dome is self supporting.
11. C. Hexagons, pentagons, and trapezoids.
12. B. angles
13. D. All of the above.
14. A. wing

Part III: Completion

1. south
2. deciduous
3. fine
4. good
5. large
6. slope
7. penetrational
8. R. Buckminster Fuller
9. asphalt
10. precut

Part IV: Problems/Activities

1. Solution on page 439 of this manual.
2. Solution on page 440 of this manual.
3. Evaluate the solution based on the application of good design, accuracy, and quality of work.
4. Evaluate the solution based on the application of good design, accuracy, and quality of work.

Answers to Chapter 29 Pretest

Completion

1. northwest
2. contour
3. Vegetation
4. 30%
5. supports
6. Earth

Multiple Choice

1. A. similar to conventional construction
2. B. riser
3. B. southeast
4. B. 60′
5. B. 62.4
6. B. atrium
7. C. 30%
8. D. All of the above.
9. C. bolted
10. A. soil-bearing capacity
11. B. sand or gravel
12. A. slope

Short Answer

1. Its bearing capacity and tendency to expand when wet.
2. Orientation to sun and wind; topography; type of soil; groundwater level; and load-bearing elements of the structure.
3. Conventional flat roof systems (cast-in-place concrete slabs, concrete planks, post and beam systems) and unconventional roof systems (vault and dome shapes).
4. The penetrational design.
5. Slope design, atrium design, and penetrational design.
6. Long expected life span of the building, low maintenance costs, less cost for heating and cooling, and high resistance to fire.
7. Asphalt shingles and cedar shakes.
8. Domes provide structural superiority, unobstructed floor space, low cost, factory production, and reduced energy needs.
9. Answer may include any four: Very efficient system that is strong and versatile; provides an open, obstruction-free floor space; factory production speeds assembly/construction; requires less

energy for heating or cooling for the same area; economical to build; and interior is exciting and fun to decorate.
10. Basement, crawl space, or slab foundation.

Answers to Chapter 29 Posttest

Completion

1. Earth
2. northwest
3. contour
4. Vegetation
5. 30%
6. supports

Multiple Choice

1. A. soil-bearing capacity
2. B. southeast
3. B. sand or gravel
4. B. 62.4
5. A. slope
6. B. atrium
7. C. 30%
8. B. 60'
9. D. All of the above.
10. A. similar to conventional construction
11. C. bolted
12. B. riser

Short Answer

1. Orientation to sun and wind; topography; type of soil; groundwater level; and load-bearing elements of the structure.
2. Its bearing capacity and tendency to expand when wet.
3. Conventional flat roof systems (cast-in-place concrete slabs, concrete planks, post and beam systems) and unconventional roof systems (vault and dome shapes).
4. Slope design, atrium design, and penetrational design.
5. The penetrational design.
6. Long expected life span of the building, low maintenance costs, less cost for heating and cooling, and high resistance to fire.
7. Domes provide structural superiority, unobstructed floor space, low cost, factory production, and reduced energy needs.
8. Asphalt shingles and cedar shakes.
9. Basement, crawl space, or slab foundation.
10. Answer may include any four: Very efficient system that is strong and versatile; provides an open, obstruction-free floor space; factory production speeds assembly/construction; requires less energy for heating or cooling for the same area; economical to build; and interior is exciting and fun to decorate.

Directions:

Draw a simplified section view of a single-level residential structure of the slope design for the site indicated below by the dotted line. (See Figure 29-8 in the text.) The plan should incorporate the following: 8′ ceiling, 24′ depth (front to back), 2′ of soil on top of a 1′ thick ceiling, glass wall on south side, and 4′ bubble-type skylight near the rear of the home. Scale is 1/8″ = 1′-0″.

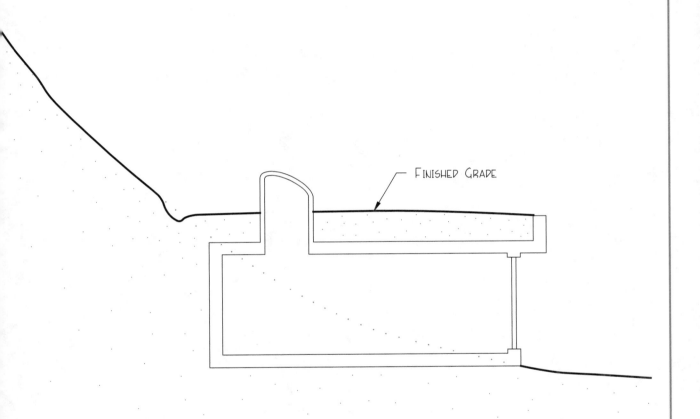

FINISHED GRADE

SCALE: 1/8″=1′-0″

EARTH-SHELTERED HOME | NAME: | 29-1

Workbook Solution

2.

Winter wind from NW, summer breezes from SE, and sun from S.

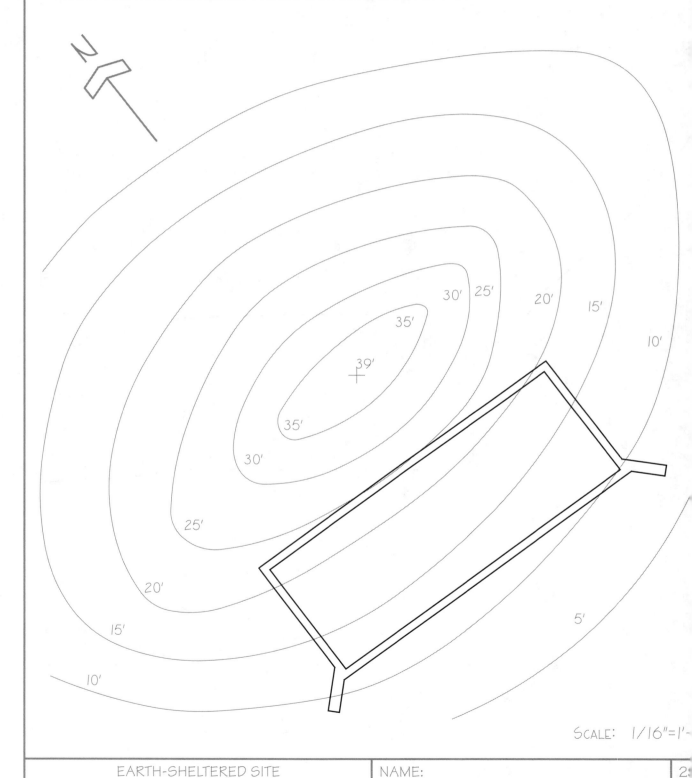

30' 25' 20' 15' 10'

35'

39'

35'

30'

35'

25'

20'

15'

10'

5'

SCALE: 1/16"=1'-

EARTH-SHELTERED SITE	NAME:	2

Chapter 29 Pretest
Nontraditional Structures

Name _____

Period _____**Date** _____**Score** _____

Completion

Complete each sentence with the proper response. Place your answer on the space provided.

1. Winter winds in the northern hemisphere are primarily from the _____.

1. _____

2. Patterns of water runoff are dependent on site _____.

2. _____

3. _____ on the site is desirable for beautification as well as for erosion and noise reduction.

3. _____

4. Heat loss in a dome is reduced about _____ over a rectangular structure with the same amount of area.

4. _____

5. A dome does not require interior or exterior _____.

5. _____

6. _____ is capable of providing a large thermal mass and may act as an insulator.

6. _____

Multiple Choice

Choose the answer that correctly completes the statement. Write the corresponding letter in the space provided.

_____ 1. The construction of individual panels used in residential dome structures is _____.

    A. similar to conventional construction
    B. similar to aircraft construction
    C. only performed in a factory
    D. None of the above.

_____ 2. Some dome models have _____ walls to support the entire structure while providing additional headroom on the second floor.

    A. wing
    B. riser
    C. dwarf
    D. flying

_____ 3. Summer breezes in the northern hemisphere are generally from the _____.

    A. northeast
    B. southeast
    C. northwest
    D. southwest

_____ 4. Manufactured dome homes are generally available in diameter ranging from 26′ to
_____.

    A. 50′
    B. 60′
    C. 70′
    D. 80′

_____ 5. When soil is saturated with water, it presents a pressure of _____ pounds per square
foot for each foot of depth.

    A. 50.2
    B. 62.4
    C. 74.6
    D. 100

_____ 6. The _____ design of earth-sheltered home places living areas around a central court-
yard with all windows opening into the courtyard.

    A. slope
    B. atrium
    C. penetrational
    D. unidirectional

_____ 7. The dome reduces the quantity of building materials needed per square foot of usable
area by about _____ over conventional construction.

    A. 10%
    B. 20%
    C. 30%
    D. 40%

_____ 8. Most manufactured dome homes are not true geodesic domes, rather variations that
are composed of _____.

    A. isosceles triangles
    B. trapezoids
    C. pentagons and hexagons
    D. All of the above.

_____ 9. Individual panels in a dome structure are usually _____ together.

    A. nailed
    B. glued
    C. bolted
    D. clamped

_____ 10. Of the following, which one is *not* an important design consideration related to the
energy efficiency of an earth-sheltered dwelling?

    A. soil-bearing capacity
    B. prevailing wind
    C. orientation to the sun
    D. landscaping

_____ 11. Generally, _____ is recommended for backfill against the wall of an earth-sheltered dwelling.

    A. clay
    B. sand or gravel
    C. peat
    D. inorganic silt

_____ 12. The earth-sheltered structure known as the _____ design maximizes earth cover around the dwelling by placing all windows and doors on one side of the structure.

    A. slope
    B. atrium
    C. penetrational
    D. unidirectional

Short Answer

Answer the following questions.

1. What are the two important soil characteristics that should be evaluated before deciding on a site for an earth-sheltered dwelling? _____

2. Name five design aspects that are important for earth-sheltered structures. _____

3. Which two basic systems are to support the roof load used in earth-sheltered structures? ___

4. Which earth-sheltered design provides window openings and access at various points around the structure? _____

5. What are the three basic design variations of earth-sheltered dwellings? _____

6. List four advantages of earth-sheltered housing. _____

7. Which two popular materials are generally used to weatherproof the exterior of a dome home? _____

8. List five attributes of residential dome structures. _____

9. List four advantages of the dome structure. _____

_____

_____

_____

10. Which type(s) of foundation(s) may be used for a dome structure? _____

_____

Chapter 29 Posttest
Nontraditional Structures

Name_____

Period _____Date _____Score _____

Completion
Complete each sentence with the proper response. Place your answer on the space provided.

1. _____ is capable of providing a large thermal mass and may act as an insulator.

1. _____

2. Winter winds in the northern hemisphere are primarily from the _____.

2. _____

3. Patterns of water runoff are dependent on site _____.

3. _____

4. _____ on the site is desirable for beautification as well as for erosion and noise reduction.

4. _____

5. Heat loss in a dome is reduced about _____ over a rectangular structure with the same amount of area.

5. _____

6. A dome does not require interior or exterior _____.

6. _____

Multiple Choice
Choose the answer that correctly completes the statement. Write the corresponding letter in the space provided.

_____ 1. Of the following, which one is *not* an important design consideration related to the energy efficiency of an earth-sheltered dwelling?

A. soil-bearing capacity
B. prevailing wind
C. orientation to the sun
D. landscaping

_____ 2. Summer breezes in the northern hemisphere are generally from the _____.

A. northeast
B. southeast
C. northwest
D. southwest

_____ 3. Generally, _____ is recommended for backfill against the wall of an earth-sheltered dwelling.

A. clay
B. sand or gravel
C. peat
D. inorganic silt

_____ 4. When soil is saturated with water, it presents a pressure of _____ pounds per square foot for each foot of depth.

    A. 50.2
    B. 62.4
    C. 74.6
    D. 100

_____ 5. The earth-sheltered structure known as the _____ design maximizes earth cover around the dwelling by placing all windows and doors on one side of the structure.

    A. slope
    B. atrium
    C. penetrational
    D. unidirectional

_____ 6. The _____ design of earth-sheltered home places living areas around a central court-yard with all windows opening into the courtyard.

    A. slope
    B. atrium
    C. penetrational
    D. unidirectional

_____ 7. The dome reduces the quantity of building materials needed per square foot of usable area by about _____ over conventional construction.

    A. 10%
    B. 20%
    C. 30%
    D. 40%

_____ 8. Manufactured dome homes are generally available in diameter ranging from 26′ to _____.

    A. 50′
    B. 60′
    C. 70′
    D. 80′

_____ 9. Most manufactured dome homes are not true geodesic domes, rather variations that are composed of _____.

    A. isosceles triangles
    B. trapezoids
    C. pentagons and hexagons
    D. All of the above.

_____ 10. The construction of individual panels used in residential dome structures is _____.

    A. similar to conventional construction
    B. similar to aircraft construction
    C. only performed in a factory
    D. None of the above.

_____ 11. Individual panels in a dome structure are usually _____ together.

    A. nailed
    B. glued
    C. bolted
    D. clamped

_____ 12. Some dome models have _____ walls to support the entire structure while providing additional headroom on the second floor.

    A. wing
    B. riser
    C. dwarf
    D. flying

Short Answer

Answer the following questions.

1. Name five design aspects that are important for earth-sheltered structures. _____
_____
_____

2. What are the two important soil characteristics that should be evaluated before deciding on a site for an earth-sheltered dwelling?_____
_____

3. Which two basic systems are to support the roof load used in earth-sheltered structures? ___
_____
_____

4. What are the three basic design variations of earth-sheltered dwellings? _____
_____
_____

5. Which earth-sheltered design provides window openings and access at various points around the structure? _____

6. List four advantages of earth-sheltered housing. _____
_____
_____

7. List five attributes of residential dome structures. _____
_____
_____
_____

8. Which two popular materials are generally used to weatherproof the exterior of a dome home?_____

9. Which type(s) of foundation(s) may be used for a dome structure? _____

_____

10. List four advantages of the dome structure. _____

_____

_____

_____

New Products and Methods of Construction

Objectives

After studying this chapter, the student will be able to:

- Describe the proper application of exterior insulation finish systems.
- Explain the advantages and disadvantages of foam core structural sandwich panels in residential construction.
- Select an appropriate alternative to traditional formed concrete wall systems.
- Describe alternative concrete block construction products.
- Describe the key elements in a frost-protected shallow foundation.
- Identify deck materials that are weather-resistant.
- Discuss the advantages and disadvantages of the Hebel Wall System.

Displays

1. **Exterior Insulation Finish Systems**. Display a cutaway model section of a typical application of EIFS. Identify the various materials used in the application.
2. **Structural Foam Sandwich Panels**. Collect samples of structural foam sandwich panels and display for student examination.
3. **Concrete Wall Systems**. Display examples of innovative concrete wall systems that are designed to increase thermal performance.

Instructional Materials

Text: Pages 579–596
   Review Questions, Suggested Activities
Workbook: Pages 331–336
   Questions, Problems/Activities
Teacher's Resources:
   Chapter 30 Pretest
   Chapter 30 Teaching Strategy
   Chapter 30 Posttest

Teaching Strategy

- **Knowledge Assessment:** Administer the Chapter 30 Pretest. Correct the test and return. Highlight the topics in which the individual student is deficient.
- Prepare Display #1.
- Review the chapter objectives.
- Discuss exterior insulation finish systems.
- Prepare Display #2.
- Discuss structural foam sandwich panels.
- Prepare Display #3.
- Discuss concrete wall systems.
- Present alternatives to traditional concrete wall systems.
- Discuss alternative concrete block construction products.
- Assign one or more of the Suggested Activities in the text.
- Assign Problem 30-1 in the workbook.
- **Chapter Review:** Assign the Review Questions in the text. Discuss the correct answers. Assign the questions in the workbook. Have students check their own answers.
- **Evaluation:** Administer the Chapter 30 Posttest. Correct the test and return. Return graded assignments with comments.

Answers to Review Questions, Text

Page 596

1. Synthetic stucco.
2. Answer may include any three of the following: Construction time is reduced, design freedom is increased, thermal performance of the wall is improved, air infiltration is reduced, and the finished result is very attractive and popular.
3. Two strong, stiff skins are adhered to a foam core that is 3-1/2" to 11-1/4" thick.
4. e) All of the above are concerns.
5. 3-1/2", 5-1/2", or 7-1/4"

6. To improve the thermal performance of concrete walls.
7. R-20
8. 4′ long by 8′ wide by 5-1/2″ thick
9. To place a fill material in the block cores as the wall is built.
10. Along the stem wall and horizontally away from the bottom of the foundation wall.
11. Tropical hardwoods and synthetic decking.
12. Hebel blocks are 8″ × 8″ × 24″ and weigh between 30 and 34 pounds each.

Answers to Workbook Questions

Page 331

Part I: Short Answer/Listing

1. Along the stem wall and horizontally away from the bottom of the foundation wall.
2. Tropical hardwoods and synthetic decking.
3. Synthetic stucco.
4. Polymer-based (PB) and polymer-modified (PM).
5. Hebel blocks are 8″ × 8″ × 24″ and weigh from 30 to 34 pounds each.
6. 3-1/2″, 5-1/2″, or 7-1/4″.
7. Answer may include any two of the following: Meranti, cambara, bater, and pelawon.
8. High-density polyethylene.
9. Answer may include any two of the following: The cost is higher, there is a confusing array of products, and some products require special installation procedures.
10. Answer may include any two of the following: Florida, Georgia, South Carolina, Alabama, Mississippi, Louisiana, Texas, and California.
11. Structural foam sandwich panels are structural members made of two strong, stiff skins adhered to a foam core that is 3-1/2″ to 11-1/4″ thick.
12. To improve thermal performance.
13. Concrete cast between two rigid polystyrene foam panels and interlocking blocks of plastic foam insulation that are stackable and whose hollow cores are filled with concrete.

14. Answer may include any three of the following: Construction time is reduced because the blocks are insulated and ready for use, thermal performance is greatly improved because no concrete webs extend through the block to act as a thermal bridge, blocks are made to standard dimensions, and the blocks can be made in any architectural finish.

Part II: Multiple Choice

1. D. Integra™
2. A. The flexibility reduces the need for numerous control joints.
3. A. Durability over time.
4. C. SmartBlock™
5. C. 4′ × 8′

Part III: Completion

1. oriented strand board
2. concrete masonry unit
3. 24
4. southern yellow pine

Part IV: Problems/Activities

1. Evaluate solution based on the application of good design, accuracy, and quality of work.

Answers to Chapter 30 Pretest

Completion

1. Slab
2. termite
3. wood-plastic
4. southern yellow pine
5. Ipe

Multiple Choice

1. B. Installation details are flexible.
2. A. The flexibility reduces the need for numerous control joints.
3. A. They are the same size as regular concrete blocks.
4. C. ultra-lightweight
5. D. All of the above.
6. B. 20
7. C. SmartBlock™
8. C. 4′ × 8′

Short Answer

1. The UL fire rating is eight hours compared to about one hour for frame wall construction.

2. It moves the frost line away from the house.
3. It eliminates the need for horizontal insulation around the foundation wall.
4. Proprietary connectors hold the foam insulation panel in place while the concrete is cast.
5. The manufacturer must post tension the wall system and must install the polyurethane insulation.
6. A crane.
7. Well-managed forests or plantations.
8. Answer may include any three of the following: Dark red meranti, light red meranti, white meranti, and yellow meranti.
9. Weather and insects.
10. Structural foam sandwich panels are structural members made of two strong, stiff skins adhered to a foam core that is 3-1/2″ to 11-1/4″ thick.
11. Speed of erection, superior energy performance, strength, and less moisture migration.
12. 3-1/2″, 5-1/2″, or 7-1/4″
13. Concrete cast between two rigid polystyrene foam panels and interlocking blocks of plastic foam insulation that are stackable and whose hollow cores are filled with concrete.
14. Answer may include any three of the following: Construction time is reduced because the blocks are insulated and ready for use, thermal performance is greatly improved because no concrete webs extend through the block to act as a thermal bridge, blocks are made to standard dimensions, and the blocks can be made in any architectural finish.

Answers to Chapter 30 Posttest

Completion

1. wood-plastic
2. termite
3. Ipe
4. southern yellow pine
5. Slab

Multiple Choice

1. D. All of the above.
2. B. Installation details are flexible.
3. A. The flexibility reduces the need for numerous control joints.
4. C. 4′ × 8′
5. C. ultra-lightweight
6. C. SmartBlock™
7. B. 20
8. A. They are the same size as regular concrete blocks.

Short Answer

1. Answer may include any three of the following: Construction time is reduced because the blocks are insulated and ready for use, thermal performance is greatly improved because no concrete webs extend through the block to act as a thermal bridge, blocks are made to standard dimensions, and the blocks can be made in any architectural finish.
2. Well-managed forests or plantations.
3. Speed of erection, superior energy performance, strength, and less moisture migration.
4. The UL fire rating is eight hours compared to about one hour for frame wall construction.
5. Answer may include any three of the following: Dark red meranti, light red meranti, white meranti, and yellow meranti.
6. It moves the frost line away from the house.
7. Concrete cast between two rigid polystyrene foam panels and interlocking blocks of plastic foam insulation that are stackable and whose hollow cores are filled with concrete.
8. Proprietary connectors hold the foam insulation panel in place while the concrete is cast.
9. Structural foam sandwich panels are structural members made of two strong, stiff skins adhered to a foam core that is 3-1/2″ to 11-1/4″ thick.
10. The manufacturer must post tension the wall system and must install the polyurethane insulation.
11. 3-1/2″, 5-1/2″, or 7-1/4″
12. It eliminates the need for horizontal insulation around the foundation wall.
13. Weather and insects.
14. A crane.

Chapter 30 Pretest
New Products and Methods of Construction

Name _____

Period _____ Date _____ Score _____

Completion
Complete each sentence with the proper response. Place your answer on the space provided.

1. _____ foundations are the norm in the South.

2. Borate-treated EPS is designed to repel _____ infestation.

3. Synthetic decking materials are made from recycled plastic or _____ composites.

4. Pressure-treated softwoods such as _____ are the most used decking material today.

5. Pau Lope® is the trade name for _____.

1. _____

2. _____

3. _____

4. _____

5. _____

Multiple Choice
Choose the answer that correctly completes the statement. Write the corresponding letter in the space provided.

_____ 1. Which of the following is *not* an advantage of exterior insulation finish systems (EIFS)?

    A. Thermal performance of the wall is improved.
    B. Installation details are flexible.
    C. Air infiltration is reduced.
    D. All of the above.

_____ 2. Which of the following is a characteristic of EIFS PB systems?

    A. The flexibility reduces the need for numerous control joints.
    B. They can tolerate prolonged wetting.
    C. They are usually thicker than 1/4″.
    D. They are called hard-coat systems.

_____ 3. Which of the following characteristics is not representative of Hebel blocks?

    A. They are the same size as regular concrete blocks.
    B. They are inorganic.
    C. They are made in an autoclave.
    D. They are 70% to 80% air.

_____ 4. Hebel blocks are classified as _____ concrete.

    A. cinder block
    B. specialty
    C. ultra-lightweight
    D. regular

_____ 5. Which of the following is an area of concern about structural foam sandwich panels?

    A. Their durability over time.
    B. Insect infestation.
    C. Small ridge lines may be visible on a roof where the panels join.
    D. All of the above.

_____ 6. Insulating concrete walls claim an R-value of _____.

    A. 10
    B. 20
    C. 30
    D. 40

_____ 7. Which product listed below may be described as interlocking blocks of plastic foam insulation that are stackable and whose hollow cores are filled with concrete?

    A. Lite-Form™
    B. Thermomass™
    C. SmartBlock™
    D. Plasti-Fab Enermizer Building Systems™

_____ 8. What is the standard size of a welded-wire sandwich panel?

    A. $2' \times 4'$
    B. $4' \times 4'$
    C. $4' \times 8'$
    D. $4' \times 16'$

Short Answer

Provide brief answers to the following questions.

1. How does the fire rating of a Hebel wall compare to that of a traditional frame wall? _____
_____
_____

2. What is the primary function of the horizontal insulation around a frost-protected shallow foundation? _____
_____

3. If the climate has fewer than 2500 heating degree days, what effect does this have on the construction of a frost-protected shallow foundation? _____
_____
_____

4. What is the key ingredient in the Thermomass™ insulated concrete wall system?
_____
_____

5. What two functions must the manufacturer perform in the Integra™ wall system? _____
_____
_____

Name _____

6. What large piece of equipment may be needed to install structural foam sandwich panels?

_____

7. Well-managed tropical hardwoods used in weather-resistant decking come from what two sources? _____

_____

8. What are three types of meranti (Philippine mahogany)? _____

_____

_____

9. What are the two main reasons that deck materials deteriorate? _____

_____

10. Describe the construction of a structural foam sandwich panel. _____

_____

_____

11. Identify four advantages of structural foam sandwich panels. _____

_____

_____

12. What are the typical wall thicknesses of sandwich wall panels?_____

_____

13. Describe the two main categories of insulated concrete wall forms._____

_____

_____

_____

14. List three advantages of the Therma-Lock™ block system. _____

_____

_____

_____

Chapter 30 Posttest
New Products and Methods of Construction

Name _____

Period _____ Date _____ Score _____

Completion

Complete each sentence with the proper response. Place your answer on the space provided.

1. Synthetic decking materials are made from recycled plastic or _____ composites.

1. _____

2. Borate-treated EPS is designed to repel _____ infestation.

2. _____

3. Pau Lope® is the trade name for _____.

3. _____

4. Pressure-treated softwoods such as _____ are the most used decking material today.

4. _____

5. _____ foundations are the norm in the South.

5. _____

Multiple Choice

Choose the answer that correctly completes the statement. Write the corresponding letter in the space provided.

_____ 1. Which of the following is an area of concern about structural foam sandwich panels?

    A. Their durability over time.
    B. Insect infestation.
    C. Small ridge lines may be visible on a roof where the panels join.
    D. All of the above.

_____ 2. Which of the following is *not* an advantage of exterior insulation finish systems (EIFS)?

    A. Thermal performance of the wall is improved.
    B. Installation details are flexible.
    C. Air infiltration is reduced.
    D. All of the above.

_____ 3. Which of the following is a characteristic of EIFS PB systems?

    A. The flexibility reduces the need for numerous control joints.
    B. They can tolerate prolonged wetting.
    C. They are usually thicker than 1/4″.
    D. They are called hard-coat systems.

_____ 4. What is the standard size of a welded-wire sandwich panel?

    A. 2′ × 4′
    B. 4′ × 4′
    C. 4′ × 8′
    D. 4′ × 16′

_____ 5. Hebel blocks are classified as _____ concrete.

    A. cinder block
    B. specialty
    C. ultra-lightweight
    D. regular

_____ 6. Which product listed may be described as interlocking blocks of plastic foam insulation that are stackable and whose hollow cores are filled with concrete?

    A. Lite-Form™
    B. Thermomass™
    C. SmartBlock™
    D. Plasti-Fab Enermizer Building Systems™

_____ 7. Insulating concrete walls claim an R-value of _____.

    A. 10
    B. 20
    C. 30
    D. 40

_____ 8. Which of the following characteristics is not representative of Hebel blocks?

    A. They are the same size as regular concrete blocks.
    B. They are inorganic.
    C. They are made in an autoclave.
    D. They are 70% to 80% air.

Short Answer

Provide brief answers to the following questions.

1. List three advantages of the Therma-Lock™ block system. _____

_____

_____

2. Well-managed tropical hardwoods used in weather-resistant decking come from what two sources? _____

_____

3. Identify four advantages of structural foam sandwich panels. _____

_____

4. How does the fire rating of a Hebel wall compare to that of a traditional frame wall?_____

_____

5. What are three types of meranti (Philippine mahogany)? _____

_____

Name _____

6. What is the primary function of the horizontal insulation around a frost-protected shallow foundation? _____

_____

7. Describe the two main categories of insulated concrete wall forms. _____

_____

_____

8. What is the key ingredient in the Thermomass™ insulated concrete wall system?

_____

_____

9. Describe the construction of a structural foam sandwich panel. _____

_____

_____

10. What two functions must the manufacturer perform in the Integra™ wall system? _____

_____

_____

11. What are the typical wall thicknesses of sandwich wall panels? _____

_____

12. If the climate has fewer than 2500 heating degree days, what effect does this have on the construction of a frost-protected shallow foundation? _____

_____

_____

13. What are the two main reasons that deck materials deteriorate? _____

_____

14. What large piece of equipment may be needed to install structural foam sandwich panels?

_____

Modular Applications
31

Objectives

After studying this chapter, the student will be able to:
- List the advantages of modular applications in the construction industry.
- Apply modular concepts to the design of a simple residence.
- Describe panelized construction.
- Explain industrialized housing.

Displays

1. **Modular Applications.** Prepare a bulletin board that shows a variety of modular applications such as modular components, preassembled panels, room modules, etc.
2. **Student Designs.** Display the modular garage designs created by past students for Suggested Activity #4 in the text.
3. **Manufacturer Literature.** Show literature from manufacturers of standard roof and wall panels. See Suggested Activity #3 in text for sources.

Instructional Materials

Text: Pages 597–605
   Review Questions, Suggested Activities
Workbook: Pages 337–340
   Review Questions, Problems/Activities
Teacher's Resources:
   Chapter 31 Pretest
   Chapter 31 Teaching Strategy
   Chapter 31 Posttest

Teaching Strategy

- **Knowledge Assessment.** Administer Chapter 31 Pretest. Correct the test and return. Highlight topics in which the individual student is deficient.
- Prepare Display #1.
- Review chapter objectives.
- Introduce modular construction.
- Cover standardization and modular components.
- Assign Suggested Activity #4 in the text.
- Discuss industrialized housing.
- Prepare Display #2 and/or #3.
- Assign workbook Problem/Activity 31-1.
- Assign one or more of the remaining Suggested Activities in the text.
- **Chapter Review.** Assign Review Questions in the text. Discuss the correct answers. Assign Review Questions in the workbook. Have students check their own answers. Make a transparency of the solution to Problem/Activity 31-1 and use for review.
- **Evaluation.** Administer the Chapter 31 Posttest. Correct the test and return. Return graded problems with comments.

Answers to Review Questions, Text

Page 604

1. Precut lumber, factory-built wall assemblies, modular components, and industrialized housing.
2. modular-size
3. modular components
4. Answer may include any four: Design freedom and aesthetic appeal, high strength-to-weight ratios, uniform quality, more efficient use of materials, lower cost, and reduced time required for installation.
5. a) 4" cube
   b) 4'-0" cube or 12 standard modules on each side
   c) 16" cube or 24" cube
6. 4"
7. 16"
8. arrowhead; dot
9. at the top of the subfloor
10. houses built in a factory
11. This dimension provides adequate width for a fair size room and 14' is the

maximum width that most states will allow on the highway.

12. Jigs and fixtures are used to cut and fit parts together, thus accuracy is improved. Better-quality lumber is usually used because a warped board will not fit the jig properly.

Answers to Workbook Questions

Page 337

Part I: Completion

1. stick-built
2. modular
3. 16"
4. dot
5. components
6. industrialized housing

Part II: Short Answer/Listing

1. Less time and cost in house construction.
2. Major module, which is a 4'-0" cube or 12 standard modules, and minor module, which is a 16" or 24" cube.
3. modular grid
4. Building parts that have been preassembled either in a plant or on-site.
5. Answer may include any three: Design freedom and aesthetic appeal, high strength-to-weight ratios, uniform quality, more efficient use of materials, lower cost, and reduced time required for installation.
6. Jigs and fixtures are used to cut and fit parts, thus accuracy is improved. Better-quality lumber is usually used because a warped board will not fit the jig properly.

Part III: Multiple Choice

1. C. Industrialized housing.
2. B. minor
3. A. On grid lines.
4. B. Modular components.
5. C. Jigs and fixtures are used to cut and fit parts together.
6. A. The modules are usually complete with plumbing, wiring, finished floors, and doors.

Part IV: Problems/Activities

1. Solution on page 462 of this manual.

Answers to Chapter 31 Pretest

Completion

1. 12
2. Industrialized housing
3. panel
4. 4"
5. standard

Multiple Choice

1. B. 4"
2. D. 48"
3. B. arrowhead
4. D. All of the above.
5. C. 14'
6. B. jigs and fixtures
7. B. standardization
8. C. 16" and 24"
9. A. on a grid line
10. D. centered on
11. A. industrialized housing

Short Answer

1. Plumbing, wiring, finished floors, and doors and windows.
2. Answer may include any two: Kitchen, bath, and living room.
3. Answer may include any five: Design freedom and aesthetic appeal, high strength-to-weight ratios, uniform quality, more efficient use of materials, lower cost, and reduced time required for installation.

Answers to Chapter 31 Posttest

Completion

1. Industrialized housing
2. 4"
3. panel
4. standard
5. 12

Multiple Choice

1. B. standardization
2. B. 4"
3. C. 16" and 24"
4. D. 48"
5. A. on a grid line
6. B. arrowhead
7. D. centered on
8. D. All of the above.

9. A. industrialized housing
10. C. 14'
11. B. jigs and fixtures

Short Answer

1. Answer may include any five: Design freedom and aesthetic appeal, high strength-to-weight ratios, uniform quality, more efficient use of materials, lower cost, and reduced time required for installation.
2. Plumbing, wiring, finished floors, and doors and windows.
3. Answer may include any two: Kitchen, bath, and living room.

Workbook Solution

1.

Directions:

Using the modular grid below, draw the plan view wall framing plan for a 10'-0" × 12'-0" frame storage building with siding. Be sure to apply the modular concepts presented in the text. Provide an access door at least 36" wide and two windows in your design. The scale is 1/2" = 1'-0".

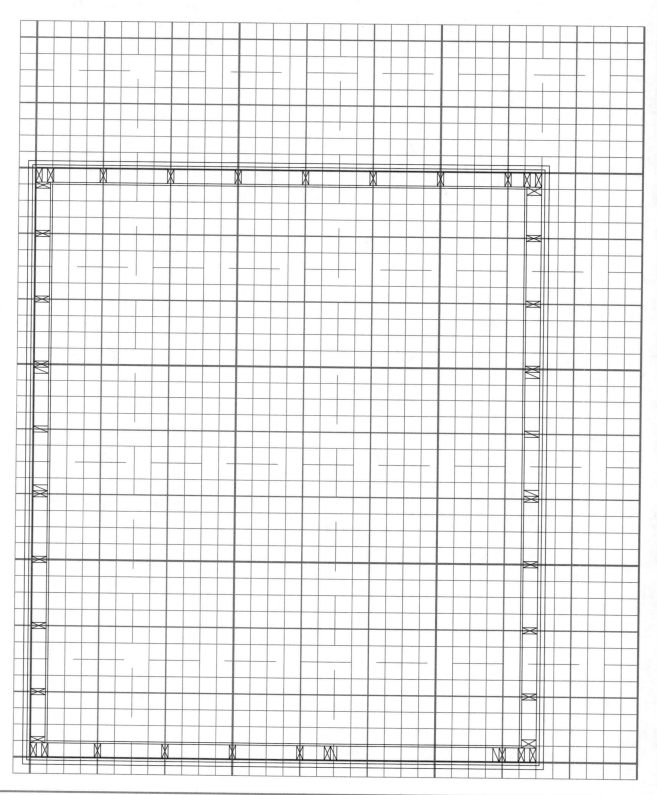

MODULAR CONSTRUCTION   NAME: 31-

Chapter 31 Pretest
Modular Applications

Name _____

Period _____**Date** _____**Score** _____

Completion

Complete each sentence with the proper response. Place your answer on the space provided.

1. The major module is 4'-0" or _____ standard modules.

2. _____ refers to houses constructed in a factory.

3. Modular _____ components are usually produced in widths ranging from 16" to 196" in multiples of 16".

4. In the modular concept, lengths must be multiples of _____.

5. A modular plan includes length, width, and height using the _____ module.

1. _____

2. _____

3. _____

4. _____

5. _____

Multiple Choice

Choose the answer that correctly completes the statement. Write the corresponding letter in the space provided.

_____ 1. All modules are multiples of _____ and each is a cube.

    A. 2"
    B. 4"
    C. 8"
    D. 12"

_____ 2. In the modular system, exterior walls are generally multiples of _____, if feasible.

    A. 12"
    B. 24"
    C. 36"
    D. 48"

_____ 3. Dimensions terminating on a grid line are shown with a(n) _____ terminator.

    A. dot
    B. arrowhead
    C. slash
    D. Any symbol desired can be used as the terminator.

_____ 4. Which of the following is an example of a typical modular component?

    A. Floor panels.
    B. Roof panels.
    C. Wall sections.
    D. All of the above.

_____ 5. The ideal width of a factory-built housing module is _____ because it is large enough for a room and is the maximum width most states will allow on the highway.

    A. 10′
    B. 12′
    C. 14′
    D. 16′

_____ 6. The accuracy and quality of factory-built homes is better than traditional construction because of the use of better quality lumber and _____ are used to cut and fit parts.

    A. gang saws
    B. jigs and fixtures
    C. lasers
    D. None of the above.

_____ 7. Successful application of the modular concept to on-site construction or factory-built homes requires _____.

    A. more costly homes
    B. standardization
    C. fewer design possibilities
    D. increased construction time

_____ 8. Minor modules are _____.

    A. 8″ and 12″
    B. 12″ and 16″
    C. 16″ and 24″
    D. 24″ and 36″

_____ 9. When using a modular grid to develop modular drawings, details should begin and terminate _____.

    A. on a grid line
    B. wherever is convenient
    C. where the room layout dictates
    D. None of the above.

_____ 10. Partitions are usually _____ grid lines on a modular grid.

    A. not related to
    B. between
    C. beside one or more
    D. centered on

_____ 11. The term _____ refers to houses built in a factory.

    A. industrialized housing
    B. stick-built
    C. modular components
    D. precut lumber

Name _____

Short Answer

Answer the following questions.

1. Most factory-built modules are more than an empty shell. List four features that are included in a typical module. _____

   _____

   _____

2. Give two examples of a module within a module. _____

   _____

3. List five advantages of prefabricated panels. _____

   _____

   _____

   _____

Chapter 31 Posttest
Modular Applications

Name _____

Period _____ Date _____ Score _____

Completion

Complete each sentence with the proper response. Place your answer on the space provided.

1. _____ refers to houses constructed in a factory.

2. In the modular concept, lengths must be multiples of _____.

3. Modular _____ components are usually produced in widths ranging from 16″ to 196″ in multiples of 16″.

4. A modular plan includes length, width, and height using the _____ module.

5. The major module is 4′-0″ or _____ standard modules.

1. _____

2. _____

3. _____

4. _____

5. _____

Multiple Choice

Choose the answer that correctly completes the statement. Write the corresponding letter in the space provided.

_____ 1. Successful application of the modular concept to on-site construction or factory-built homes requires _____.

    A. more costly homes
    B. standardization
    C. fewer design possibilities
    D. increased construction time

_____ 2. All modules are multiples of _____ and each is a cube.

    A. 2″
    B. 4″
    C. 8″
    D. 12″

_____ 3. Minor modules are _____.

    A. 8″ and 12″
    B. 12″ and 16″
    C. 16″ and 24″
    D. 24″ and 36″

_____ 4. In the modular system, exterior walls are generally multiples of _____, if feasible.

    A. 12″
    B. 24″
    C. 36″
    D. 48″

_____ 5. When using a modular grid to develop modular drawings, details should begin and terminate _____.

    A. on a grid line
    B. wherever is convenient
    C. where the room layout dictates
    D. None of the above.

_____ 6. Dimensions terminating on a grid line are shown with a(n) _____ terminator.

    A. dot
    B. arrowhead
    C. slash
    D. Any symbol desired can be used as the terminator.

_____ 7. Partitions are usually _____ grid lines on a modular grid.

    A. not related to
    B. between
    C. beside one or more
    D. centered on

_____ 8. Which of the following is an example of a typical modular component?

    A. Floor panels.
    B. Roof panels.
    C. Wall sections.
    D. All of the above.

_____ 9. The term _____ refers to houses built in a factory.

    A. industrialized housing
    B. stick-built
    C. modular components
    D. precut lumber

_____ 10. The ideal width of a factory-built housing module is _____ because it is large enough for a room and is the maximum width most states will allow on the highway.

    A. 10'
    B. 12'
    C. 14'
    D. 16'

_____ 11. The accuracy and quality of factory-built homes is better than traditional construction because of the use of better quality lumber and _____ are used to cut and fit parts.

    A. gang saws
    B. jigs and fixtures
    C. lasers
    D. None of the above.

Name _____

Short Answer

Answer the following questions.

1. List five advantages of prefabricated panels. _____

   _____

   _____

   _____

2. Most factory-built modules are more than an empty shell. List four features that are included in a typical module. _____

   _____

   _____

3. Give two examples of a module within a module._____

   _____

Perspective Drawings

32

Objectives

After studying this chapter, the student will be able to:

- Explain the purpose of a perspective drawing.
- Explain the difference between one-, two-, and three-point perspectives.
- Prepare a one- or two-point perspective drawing using the office method.
- Explain how changing the viewing position, angle, and height alters the perspective.
- Describe how to create a perspective using CADD.

Displays

1. **Perspective drawings.** Create a display using one- and two-point perspective drawings from previous classes or your own work. Label each drawing as to type of perspective and rendering technique used.
2. **Perspectives of homes.** Use perspective drawings of homes cut from magazines to create a bulletin board display. Use samples submitted by past students as a part of Suggested Activity #3 in the text.

Instructional Materials

Text: Pages 607–635
　Review Questions, Suggested Activities
Workbook: Pages 341–360
　Review Questions, Problems/Activities
Teacher's Resources:
　Chapter 32 Pretest
　Chapter 32 Teaching Strategy
　Chapter 32 Posttest

Teaching Strategy

- **Knowledge Assessment.** Administer Chapter 32 Pretest. Correct the test and return. Highlight topics in which the individual student is deficient.
- Prepare Display #1.
- Review chapter objectives.
- Introduce pictorial drawings.
- Introduce perspectives.
- Discuss two-point perspective.
- Draw several objects on the chalkboard using the step-by-step procedure discussed in the text. Assign workbook Problems/Activities 32-1, 32-2, 32-3, and 32-4.
- Discuss one-point perspectives.
- Prepare Display #2.
- Draw several objects on the chalkboard using the step-by-step procedure discussed in the text. Assign workbook Problems/Activities 32-5, 32-6, 32-7, and 32-8.
- Discuss perspective grids.
- Discuss and demonstrate drawing complex features in perspective.
- Assign one or more of the Suggested Activities in the text.
- **Chapter Review.** Assign Review Questions in the text. Discuss the correct answers. Assign Review Questions in the workbook. Have students check their own answers. Make transparencies of the solutions to Problems/Activities 32-1 and 32-5 and use for review.
- **Evaluation.** Administer Chapter 32 Posttest. Correct the test and return. Return graded problems with comments.

Answers to Review Questions, Text

Page 634

1. Isometric, oblique, and perspective.
2. One-point (parallel), two-point (angular), and three-point (oblique).
3. two-point perspective
4. elevation
5. height of the observer's eye
6. touches the picture plane
7. larger
8. station point

9. The distance from the station point to the picture plane is the distance between the observer and the picture plane.
10. elevation
11. horizon line
12. two
13. The size of the perspective is larger.
14. 30° on one side and 60° on the other
15. cone of vision
16. distorted
17. Ground level, 5' or 6', and 30'.
18. The distance is decreased.
19. interior
20. Sight lines must be projected from the station point in the elevation to the object to determine the height in the perspective.
21. Limited freedom in choosing the position of the station point and placement of the picture plane.
22. Superimposing a grid over the object in the plan and elevation views and projecting points to the perspective view, then connecting the points.

Answers to Workbook Questions
Page 341
Part I: Matching
1. C. Perspective
2. H. Three-point perspective
3. A. Ground line
4. B. Horizon line
5. E. Picture plane
6. G. Station point
7. I. True length line
8. J. Vanishing points
9. F. Rendering
10. D. Perspective grid

Part II: Short Answer/Listing
1. **One-point perspectives:** Usually interior drawings, for example, furniture layouts. **Two-point perspectives:** Usually exterior views of residential structures. **Three-point perspectives:** Usually exterior views of tall commercial structures.
2. Elevation drawing, plan drawing, and perspective drawing.
3. Two.
4. 30° on one side and 60° on the other side.

5. The proper height will depend on the particular object and which features are to be emphasized.
6. They are parallel.
7. Draw two construction lines from the station point to the picture plane line parallel to the sides of the object in the plan view. Drop vertical lines from the point where the construction lines cross the picture plane line to the horizon line. These points are the left and right vanishing points.
8. First draw the object as though it had sharp lines and then soften the corners freehand or with a French or irregular curve.

Part III: Multiple Choice
1. C. parallel
2. B. The perspective of the object will be above the ground line.
3. A. They generate a photo-like drawing that is very accurate in detail.
4. C. 30° and 45°.
5. C. Both A and B.
6. B. ground line

Part IV: Completion
1. station point
2. larger
3. station point
4. 20' to 30'
5. plan view
6. true length (TL)
7. one
8. points
9. 3D
10. rendering

Part V: Problems/Activities
1. A. Plan view.
   B. Picture plane.
   C. Cone of vision.
   D. Station point.
   E. Horizon line.
   F. Right vanishing point.
   G. Elevation view.
   H. Ground line.
   I. Perspective.
   J. Left vanishing point.
2. Solution on page 472 of this manual.

3. Solution on page 473 of this manual.
4. Evaluate solution based on accuracy and quality of view.
5. Solution on page 474 of this manual.
6. Solution on page 475 of this manual.
7. Solution on page 476 of this manual.
8. Evaluate the solution based on how well it communicates the idea and accuracy of the construction.

Answers to Chapter 32 Pretest

Completion

1. angular
2. ground plane
3. isometric; perspective
4. picture plane
5. Vanishing

Multiple Choice

1. D. station point
2. B. height of the observer's eye above the ground
3. D. true size
4. B. 30°–45°
5. D. All of the above.
6. A. picture plane
7. B. two
8. A. ground line
9. C. station point
10. D. true-length line
11. B. horizon line and ground line

Short Answer

1. Tall, commercial buildings.
2. At the station point.
3. Exterior views.
4. Superimpose a grid or series of points over the object (surface). Then, connect the points with a French or irregular curve.
5. One-point or parallel perspective, two-point or angular perspective, and three-point or oblique perspective.
6. Elevation drawing, plan drawing, and perspective drawing.
7. Two.

8. The drawing will be distorted and unrealistic.
9. Generally, only a few seconds are required.

Answers to Chapter 32 Posttest

Completion

1. ground plane
2. isometric; perspective
3. Vanishing
4. angular
5. picture plane

Multiple Choice

1. B. two
2. D. station point
3. A. ground line
4. B. height of the observer's eye above the ground
5. C. station point
6. D. true size
7. D. true-length line
8. B. 30°–45°
9. B. horizon line and ground line
10. D. All of the above.
11. A. picture plane

Short Answer

1. One-point or parallel perspective, two-point or angular perspective, and three-point or oblique perspective.
2. Tall, commercial buildings.
3. Elevation drawing, plan drawing, and perspective drawing.
4. At the station point.
5. Two.
6. Exterior views.
7. The drawing will be distorted and unrealistic.
8. Superimpose a grid or series of points over the object (surface). Then, connect the points with a French or irregular curve.
9. Generally, only a few seconds are required.

Workbook Solution

2.

Directions:
Draw a two-point perspective of the object using the setup provided. Show all construction lines, but use wider visible object lines. Omit hidden lines from the pictorial.

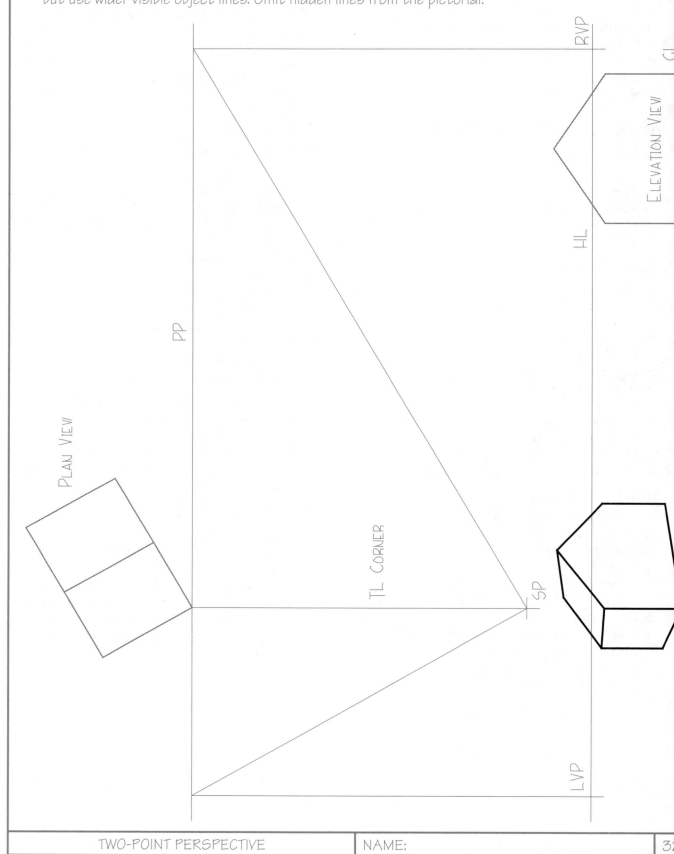

RVP

GL

ELEVATION VIEW

HL

PP

PLAN VIEW

TL CORNER

SP

LVP

| TWO-POINT PERSPECTIVE | NAME: | 3 |

Workbook Solution

Directions:
Draw a two-point perspective of the object as indicated. Show all construction lines, but use wider visible object lines. Omit hidden lines in the pictorial.

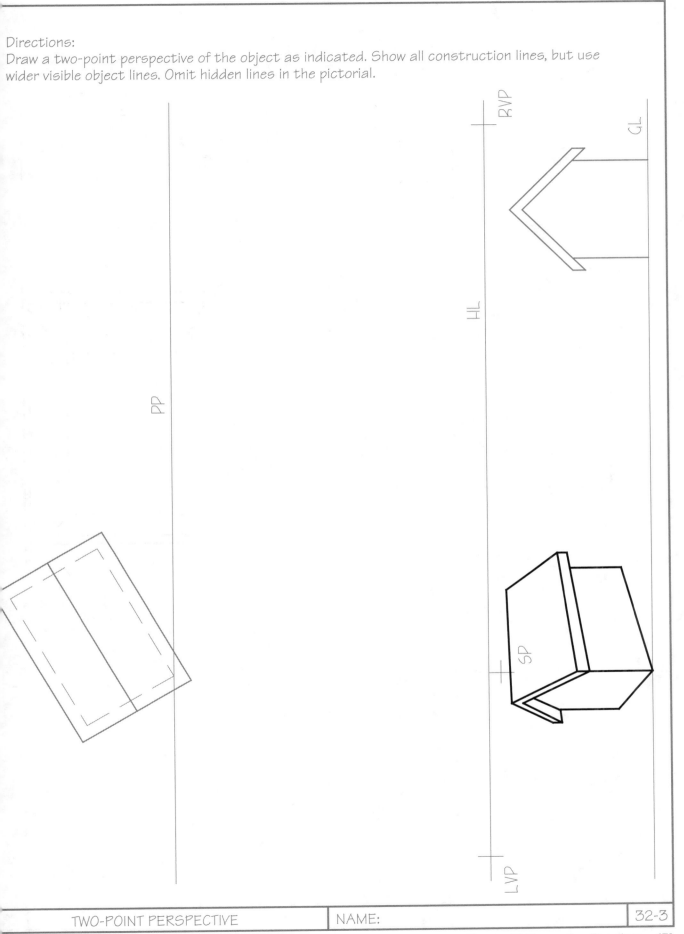

TWO-POINT PERSPECTIVE

NAME:

32-3

5.

Directions:
Complete the one-point perspective drawing below using the procedure described in the text.
Show your construction using light construction lines. Darken the visible object lines.

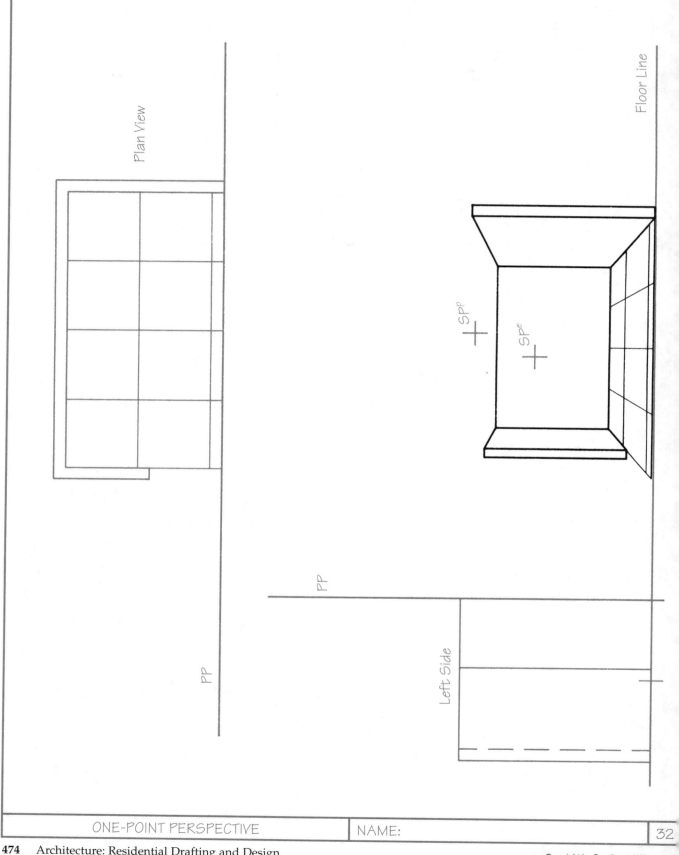

Plan View

PP

Floor Line

SP^p

SP^e

PP

Left Side

ONE-POINT PERSPECTIVE

NAME:

32

Workbook Solution

Directions:

Draw a one-point perspective of the room, table, and rug indicated below. Show construction lines as very light lines. Darken visible object lines and omit hidden lines.

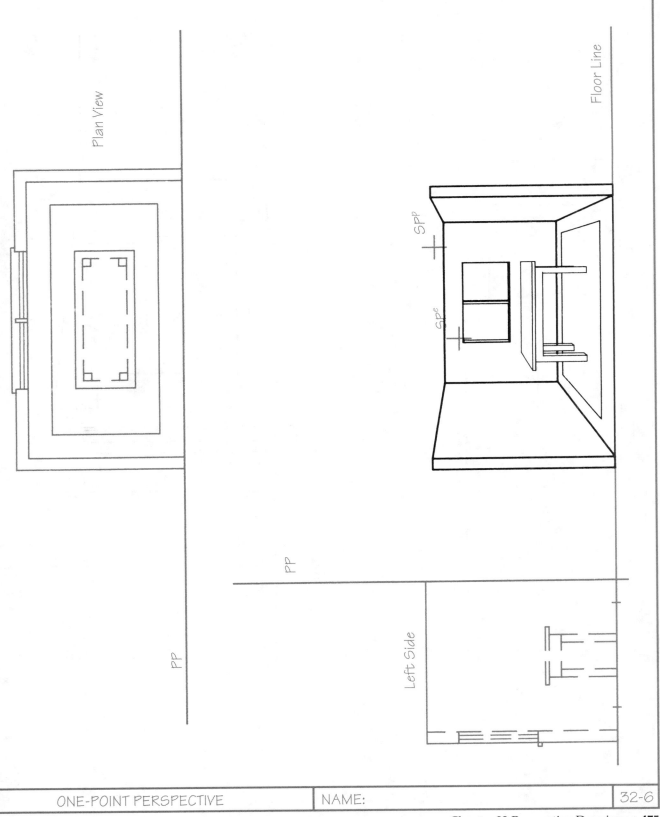

Plan View

PP

Floor Line

SPP

SP

PP

Left Side

Workbook Solution

7.

Draw a one-point perspective of the room and contents (simplified furniture pieces) below. Show construction lines as very light lines. Darken visible object lines and omit hidden lines.

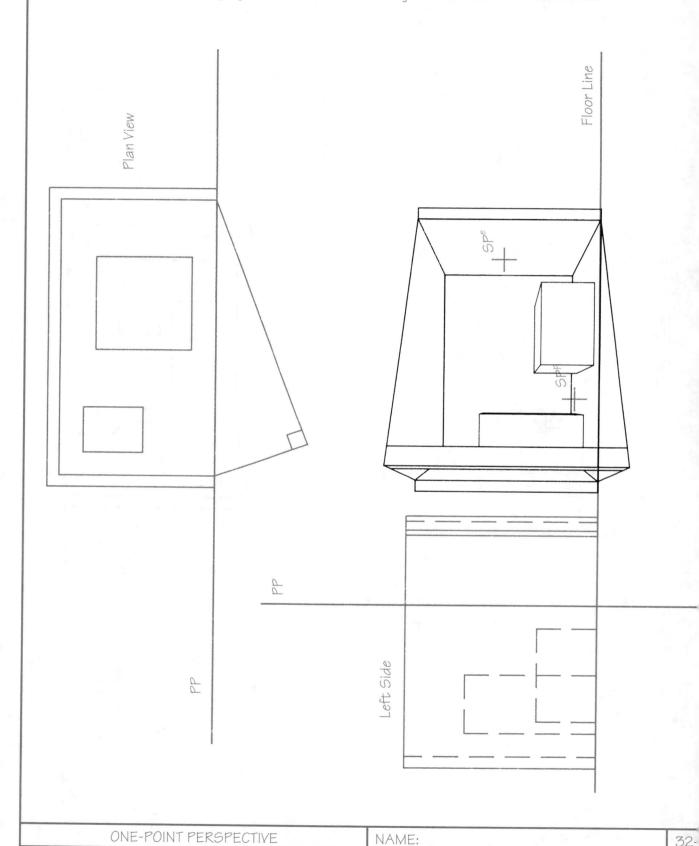

Plan View

PP

Floor Line

SP

SP

PP

Left Side

ONE-POINT PERSPECTIVE   NAME: 32-

Chapter 32 Pretest
Perspective Drawings

Name _____

Period _____**Date** _____**Score** _____

Completion
Complete each sentence with the proper response. Place your answer on the space provided.

1. A two-point perspective is also called a(n) _____ perspective.

2. The picture plane is perpendicular to the _____.

3. Three types of pictorial drawings commonly used for communication purposes are _____, oblique, and _____.

4. The _____ is a transparent plane on which the perspective is drawn.

5. _____ points are always located on the horizon line in one- and two-point perspectives.

1. _____

2. _____

3. _____

   _____

4. _____

5. _____

Multiple Choice
Choose the answer that correctly completes the statement. Write the corresponding letter in the space provided.

_____ 1. In drawing perspectives, the _____ is the location of the observer's eye.

   A. vanishing point
   B. horizon line
   C. picture plane
   D. station point

_____ 2. The distance between the ground line and horizon line represents the _____.

   A. height of the object
   B. height of the observer's eye above the ground
   C. distance the observer is away from the object
   D. None of the above.

_____ 3. Any portion of the object that touches the picture plane will be _____ in the perspective drawing.

   A. hidden from view
   B. larger than scale
   C. smaller than scale
   D. true size

_____ 4. In most instances, the station point is positioned so that it forms a cone of vision of _____ with respect to the object.

    A. 15°–30°
    B. 30°–45°
    C. 45°–60°
    D. over 60°

_____ 5. One-point perspectives are well suited for _____.

    A. room and furniture layouts
    B. kitchen cabinet pictorial details
    C. interior space studies
    D. All of the above.

_____ 6. In drawing a one-point perspective, both views of the station point must be the same distance from the _____.

    A. picture plane
    B. horizon line
    C. ground line
    D. edge of the paper

_____ 7. A two-point perspective has _____ vanishing points.

    A. one
    B. two
    C. three
    D. zero

_____ 8. The _____ represents the horizontal ground plane.

    A. ground line
    B. elevation line
    C. height line
    D. picture plane

_____ 9. The picture plane is normally located between the object and _____.

    A. horizon line
    B. ground line
    C. station point
    D. right side view

_____ 10. It is always necessary to find at least one _____ in a two-point perspective drawing so that height measurements may be made.

    A. side of the object
    B. full-size view
    C. angular view
    D. true-length line

_____ 11. The height of the observer's eye is represented by the distance between the _____.

    A. horizon line and picture plane
    B. horizon line and ground line
    C. ground line and picture plane
    D. station point and picture plane

Name _____

Short Answer

Answer the following questions.

1. Which type of structures are three-point perspectives used for? _____
   _____

2. Where do the visual rays or sight lines begin? _____
   _____

3. What type of view is the two-point perspective especially suited for? _____
   _____

4. What general approach may be used to draw circular or irregular objects in perspective?
   _____

5. List the three basic types of perspectives. _____
   _____
   _____

6. What are the three parts of a perspective layout? _____
   _____
   _____

7. How many views of the station point are usually shown in a one-point perspective? _____
   _____

8. What will the result be if the station point is too close to the object? _____
   _____

9. How long does it usually take to create a perspective from a 3D model with a CADD program
   once the model is complete? _____
   _____

Chapter 32 Posttest
Perspective Drawings

Name _____

Period _____ **Date** _____ **Score** _____

Completion

Complete each sentence with the proper response. Place your answer on the space provided.

1. The picture plane is perpendicular to the _____.   1. _____

2. Three types of pictorial drawings commonly used for communication purposes are _____, oblique, and _____.   2. _____

   _____

3. _____ points are always located on the horizon line in one- and two-point perspectives.   3. _____

4. A two-point perspective is also called a(n) _____ perspective.   4. _____

5. The _____ is a transparent plane on which the perspective is drawn.   5. _____

Multiple Choice

Choose the answer that correctly completes the statement. Write the corresponding letter in the space provided.

_____ 1. A two-point perspective has _____ vanishing points.

   A. one
   B. two
   C. three
   D. zero

_____ 2. In drawing perspectives, the _____ is the location of the observer's eye.

   A. vanishing point
   B. horizon line
   C. picture plane
   D. station point

_____ 3. The _____ represents the horizontal ground plane.

   A. ground line
   B. elevation line
   C. height line
   D. picture plane

_____ 4. The distance between the ground line and horizon line represents the _____.

   A. height of the object
   B. height of the observer's eye above the ground
   C. distance the observer is away from the object
   D. None of the above.

_____ 5. The picture plane is normally located between the object and _____.

    A. horizon line
    B. ground line
    C. station point
    D. right side view

_____ 6. Any portion of the object that touches the picture plane will be _____ in the perspective drawing.

    A. hidden from view
    B. larger than scale
    C. smaller than scale
    D. true size

_____ 7. It is always necessary to find at least one _____ in a two-point perspective drawing so that height measurements may be made.

    A. side of the object
    B. full-size view
    C. angular view
    D. true-length line

_____ 8. In most instances, the station point is positioned so that it forms a cone of vision of _____ with respect to the object.

    A. 15°–30°
    B. 30°–45°
    C. 45°–60°
    D. over 60°

_____ 9. The height of the observer's eye is represented by the distance between the _____.

    A. horizon line and picture plane
    B. horizon line and ground line
    C. ground line and picture plane
    D. station point and picture plane

_____ 10. One-point perspectives are well suited for _____.

    A. room and furniture layouts
    B. kitchen cabinet pictorial details
    C. interior space studies
    D. All of the above.

_____ 11. In drawing a one-point perspective, both views of the station point must be the same distance from the _____.

    A. picture plane
    B. horizon line
    C. ground line
    D. edge of the paper

Name _____

Short Answer

Answer the following questions.

1. List the three basic types of perspectives. _____
_____
_____

2. Which type of structures are three-point perspectives used for?_____
_____

3. What are the three parts of a perspective layout? _____
_____
_____

4. Where do the visual rays or sight lines begin? _____
_____

5. How many views of the station point are usually shown in a one-point perspective? _____
_____

6. What type of view is the two-point perspective especially suited for?_____
_____

7. What will the result be if the station point is too close to the object? _____
_____

8. What general approach may be used to draw circular or irregular objects in perspective? ___
_____

9. How long does it usually take to create a perspective from a 3D model with a CADD program once the model is complete? _____
_____

Presentation Drawings
33

Objectives

After studying this chapter, the student will be able to:
- Explain the purpose of a presentation drawing.
- List methods commonly used to increase the degree of realism in a presentation plan.
- Render presentation drawings using a variety of methods.
- Explain entourage.
- Describe lighting for a CADD 3D model to be rendered.
- Explain walkthrough animation.

Displays

1. **Architectural Renderings**. Collect renderings of architectural structures and display them in the classroom to provide examples of style and inspiration. Use samples submitted by students as a part of Suggested Activity #2 in text.
2. **Student Renderings**. Use student work to create a bulletin board display of renderings, as detailed in Suggested Activity #6 in the text.

Instructional Materials

Text: Pages 637–660
Review Questions, Suggested Activities
Workbook: Pages 361–370
Questions, Problems/Activities
Teacher's Resources:
Chapter 33 Pretest
Chapter 33 Teaching Strategy
Chapter 33 Posttest

Teaching Strategy

- **Knowledge Assessment.** Administer the Chapter 33 Pretest. Correct the test and return. Highlight the topics in which the individual student is deficient.
- Prepare Display #1. Review the chapter objectives.
- Introduce presentation drawings.
- Introduce rendering.
- Discuss pencil rendering and ink rendering.
- Assign Problems 33-1 and 33-2 in the workbook.
- Discuss watercolor rendering.
- Assign Suggested Activity #6 in the text.
- Discuss tempera, colored pencil, magic marker, and scratchboard rendering.
- Prepare Display #2.
- Discuss appliqué and airbrush rendering.
- Discuss entourage and types of presentation plans—exterior perspectives, rendered elevations, plot plans, floor plans, and sections.
- Assign Problems 33-3 and 33-4 in the workbook.
- Assign one or more of the remaining Suggested Activities in the text.
- **Chapter Review.** Assign the Review Questions in the text. Discuss the correct answers. Assign the questions in the workbook. Have students check their own answers.
- **Evaluation.** Administer the Chapter 33 Posttest. Correct the test and return. Return graded problems with comments.

Answers to Review Questions, Text
Page 659

1. Rendering
2. Answer may include any six of the following: Airbrush, appliqué, CADD, colored pencil, felt-tipped pen, ink, pencil, scratchboard, tempera, watercolor, or a combination of these methods.
3. Pencil rendering
4. ink
5. appliqué
6. An airbrush is simply an air nozzle that sprays paint or colored ink.
7. To add to the realism of a drawing and show an architectural structure in its proper setting.

8. Key light, fill light, and backlight.
9. Answer may include any five of the following: Exterior perspective, rendered elevation, presentation plot plan, presentation floor plan, rendered section, and walkthrough animation.
10. orthographic
11. Furniture arrangement, space utilization, and conveniences.
12. A walkthrough animation shows an animated view of how a building would appear to a person actually walking through it.
13. A flyby animation is essentially the same type of animation as a walkthrough, except it shows what the exterior of a building would look like to a person in a plane flying by or in a car driving by.
14. Answer may include any two of the following: Size of the animation, length of the animation, special effects, material complexity, and number of shadow-casting lights in the scene.
15. a) A frame on which an important action takes place.
    b) A frame in between keyframes.
    c) Where animated movement data are stored by the computer for a keyframe.

Answers to Workbook Questions
Page 361
Part I: Short Answer/Listing
1. Presentation drawings are more realistic in appearance than construction drawings.
2. Answer may include any four of the following: Exterior and interior perspectives, rendered elevations, presentation plot plans, floor plans, and sections.
3. Appliqué rendering is accomplished by attaching a pressure-sensitive transparent film on top of the drawing sheet.
4. The observer's position with respect to each surface.

Part II: Multiple Choice
1. B. Pencil
2. B. Ink
3. D. Airbrush
4. C. Scratchboard
5. D. to remove shadows

Part III: Completion
1. Tempera
2. scratchboard
3. entourage
4. plot
5. key
6. light source
7. walkthrough animation
8. keyframe

Part IV: Problems/Activities
1. Evaluate solution based on realism and accuracy. Display student work that best demonstrates the art of pencil rendering.
2. Evaluate solution based on realism and accuracy. Display student work that best illustrates the art of ink rendering.
3. Evaluate solution based on realism and accuracy.
4. Evaluate solution based on realism and accuracy.

Answers to Chapter 33 Pretest
Completion
1. Entourage
2. water-soluble
3. scratchboard
4. walkthrough
5. pencil
6. wash

Multiple Choice
1. A. felt-tipped pen
2. B. Airbrush
3. B. ink
4. C. scratchboard
5. D. It is used to remove shadows.

Short Answer
1. appliqué
2. Furniture arrangement, space utilization, and conveniences.
3. A keyframe is a frame on which an important action takes place. An animation key stores data corresponding to movement and is created or "set" on each keyframe.
4. Lines are scratched through a special black coating on illustration board to reveal a white background. The result is a drawing of white lines on a black background.
5. To show the finished structure and to present various parts of the building in a

form that is more meaningful than construction drawings.
6. They are faster to draw and satisfactory if presented well.
7. The angle of the sun must be determined first.

Answers to Chapter 33 Posttest

Completion

1. wash
2. walkthrough
3. scratchboard
4. pencil
5. water-soluble
6. Entourage

Multiple Choice

1. B. ink
2. D. It is used to remove shadows.
3. A. felt-tipped pen
4. C. scratchboard
5. B. Airbrush

Short Answer

1. They are faster to draw and satisfactory if presented well.
2. Lines are scratched through a special black coating on illustration board to reveal a white background. The result is a drawing of white lines on a black background.
3. appliqué
4. To show the finished structure and to present various parts of the building in a form that is more meaningful than construction drawings.
5. Furniture arrangement, space utilization, and conveniences.
6. A keyframe is a frame on which an important action takes place. An animation key stores data corresponding to movement and is created or "set" on each keyframe.
7. The angle of the sun must be determined first.

Chapter 33 Pretest
Presentation Drawings

Name _____

Period _____**Date** _____**Score** _____

Completion

Complete each sentence with the proper response. Place your answer on the space provided.

1. _____ refers to surroundings such as trees, shrubs, cars, people, and terrain.

2. Tempera paint is a type of _____ paint.

3. A(n) _____ is a special white illustration board with a black coating used in rendering.

4. A(n) _____ animation shows an animated view of how a building would appear to a person actually walking through it.

5. Probably the easiest type of rendering is _____ rendering.

6. In watercolor rendering, a light _____ is achieved by using very little paint with lots of water.

1. _____

2. _____

3. _____

4. _____

5. _____

6. _____

Multiple Choice

Choose the answer that correctly completes the statement. Write the corresponding letter in the space provided.

_____ 1. Presentation plot plans are frequently rendered using the _____ technique.

    A. felt-tipped pen
    B. tempera
    C. scratchboard
    D. pencil

_____ 2. _____ renderings require a great deal of practice to produce high-quality work.

    A. Pencil
    B. Airbrush
    C. Felt-tipped pen
    D. Appliqué

_____ 3. Renderings to be used for reproduction are best done with _____.

    A. pencil
    B. ink
    C. felt-tipped pens
    D. watercolors

_____ 4. A(n) _____ rendering produces white lines on a black background.

    A. ink
    B. felt-tipped pen
    C. scratchboard
    D. appliqué

_____ 5. In triangle lighting, which of the following is true of the fill light?

    A. It provides most of the illumination.
    B. It is placed in front of the scene.
    C. It is placed toward the rear of the scene.
    D. It is used to remove shadows.

Short Answer

Provide brief answers to the following questions.

1. What type of rendering is accomplished by attaching a pressure-sensitive transparent film over a drawing? _____

2. List three typical features presentation floor plans may be used to emphasize. _____

3. What is the difference between a keyframe and an animation key? _____

4. How are scratchboard renderings produced? _____

5. What are the primary uses of a presentation drawing? _____

6. Why are elevations frequently used instead of exterior perspectives for presentation purposes? _____

7. What is the first thing you need to decide when planning to shade the surfaces of an object?
_____

Chapter 33 Posttest
Presentation Drawings

Name _____

Period _____**Date** _____**Score** _____

Completion
Complete each sentence with the proper response. Place your answer on the space provided.

1. In watercolor rendering, a light _____ is achieved by using very little paint with lots of water.

1. _____

2. A(n) _____ animation shows an animated view of how a building would appear to a person actually walking through it.

2. _____

3. A(n) _____ is a special white illustration board with a black coating used in rendering.

3. _____

4. Probably the easiest type of rendering is _____ rendering.

4. _____

5. Tempera paint is a type of _____ paint.

5. _____

6. _____ refers to surroundings such as trees, shrubs, cars, people, and terrain.

6. _____

Multiple Choice
Choose the answer that correctly completes the statement. Write the corresponding letter in the space provided.

_____ 1. Renderings to be used for reproduction are best done with _____.

    A. pencil
    B. ink
    C. felt-tipped pens
    D. watercolors

_____ 2. In triangle lighting, which of the following is true of the fill light?

    A. It provides most of the illumination.
    B. It is placed in front of the scene.
    C. It is placed toward the rear of the scene.
    D. It is used to remove shadows.

_____ 3. Presentation plot plans are frequently rendered using the _____ technique.

    A. felt-tipped pen
    B. tempera
    C. scratchboard
    D. pencil

_____ 4. A(n) _____ rendering produces white lines on a black background.

    A. ink
    B. felt-tipped pen
    C. scratchboard
    D. appliqué

_____ 5. _____ renderings require a great deal of practice to produce high-quality work.

    A. Pencil
    B. Airbrush
    C. Felt-tipped pen
    D. Appliqué

Short Answer

Provide brief answers to the following questions.

1. Why are elevations frequently used instead of exterior perspectives for presentation purposes?_____

_____

_____

2. How are scratchboard renderings produced? _____

_____

_____

_____

3. What type of rendering is accomplished by attaching a pressure-sensitive transparent film over a drawing? _____

4. What are the primary uses of a presentation drawing?_____

_____

_____

_____

5. List three typical features presentation floor plans may be used to emphasize. _____

_____

_____

_____

6. What is the difference between a keyframe and an animation key? _____

_____

_____

_____

7. What is the first thing you need to decide when planning to shade the surfaces of an object?

_____

Architectural Models
34

Objectives

After studying this chapter, the student will be able to:
- Explain the various types of architectural models used to represent residential structures.
- List the features commonly included in a presentation model.
- Summarize the steps for constructing a balsa wood model.

Displays

1. **Architectural Models.** Display several architectural models in the classroom for examination.
2. **Model Materials.** Collect typical architectural model materials and display them on the bulletin board. Label each material.
3. **Model Fixtures.** Display model fixtures carved by past students as required in Suggested Activity #4 in the text.

Instructional Materials

Text: Pages 661–673
  Review Questions, Suggested Activities
Workbook: Pages 371–376
  Review Questions, Problems/Activities
Teacher's Resources:
  Chapter 34 Pretest
  Chapter 34 Teaching Strategy
  Chapter 34 Posttest

Teaching Strategy

- **Knowledge Assessment.** Administer Chapter 34 Pretest. Correct the test and return. Highlight topics in which the individual student is deficient.
- Prepare Display #1.
- Review chapter objectives.
- Discuss structural models and presentation models.
- Present materials used in model construction.
- Prepare Display #2.
- Cover the procedure for constructing a balsa model.
- Assign workbook Problems/Activities 34-1, 34-2, and 34-3.
- Prepare Display #3.
- Assign one or more of the Suggested Activities in the text.
- **Chapter Review.** Assign Review Questions in the text. Discuss the correct answers. Assign Review Questions in the workbook. Have students check their own answers.
- **Evaluation.** Administer Chapter 34 Posttest. Correct the test and return. Return graded problems with comments.

Answers to Review Questions, Text
Page 671

1. Small scale solid model, structural model, and presentation model.
2. 1/4″ = 1′-0″
3. Foam board (Styrofoam®), cardboard or illustration board, and balsa wood.
4. Obtain a set of plans for the home that are drawn as a scale of 1/4″ = 1′-0″.
5. flat
6. 30″ × 30″ or 30″ × 36″
7. 3/4″
8. 3/16″ or 1/4″
9. 1/8″
10. Dark
11. By carving it to form furniture and major fixtures.

Answers to Workbook Questions
Page 371

Part I: Multiple Choice

1. A. small scale solid
2. C. 1/2″ = 1′-0″ or 1″ = 1′-0″
3. B. It can be finished to resemble various exterior building materials.
4. A. floor plan
5. B. 1/8″

6. D. White; soft pastel

Part II: Completion

1. 1/8″ = 1′-0″.
2. presentation
3. balsa
4. 30″ × 36″
5. mitered
6. Plexiglas®
7. model
8. sheathing
9. sponge; twigs

Part III: Short Answer/Listing

1. Small scale solid models, structural models, and presentation models.
2. A structural model.
3. 1/4″ = 1′-0″
4. Plaster of Paris, Styrofoam®, and cardboard.
5. Floor plan and elevations.
6. 3/16″ or 1/4″
7. By using copper or aluminum foil.
8. Painted with a water-base paint and then wiped.
9. Sandpaper.

Part IV: Problems/Activities

1. Evaluate the model according to the construction techniques suggested in the text.
2. Evaluate the model according to techniques discussed in the text and the actual construction procedures the student followed.
3. Provide students with specific instructions on building techniques, methods, and materials. Evaluate the model according to construction techniques suggested in the text.

Answers to Chapter 34 Pretest

Completion

1. small scale solid
2. presentation
3. appearance
4. structural
5. Plants

Multiple Choice

1. D. presentation
2. B. balsa wood
3. C. mitered
4. A. soap or wood
5. C. structural
6. D. All of the above.
7. A. floor plan and elevations

Short Answer

1. 1/4″ = 1′-0″
2. By using strips of sandpaper glued to the roof.
3. Small scale solid model.
4. Two coats of bright green paint with grass flock sprinkled on before the second coat dries.

Answers to Chapter 34 Posttest

Completion

1. appearance
2. small scale solid
3. structural
4. presentation
5. Plants

Multiple Choice

1. C. structural
2. D. presentation
3. D. All of the above.
4. B. balsa wood
5. A. floor plan and elevations
6. C. mitered
7. A. soap or wood

Short Answer

1. Small scale solid model.
2. 1/4″ = 1′-0″
3. Two coats of bright green paint with grass flock sprinkled on before the second coat dries.
4. By using strips of sandpaper glued to the roof.

Chapter 34 Pretest
Architectural Models

Name _____

Period _____**Date** _____**Score** _____

Completion

Complete each sentence with the proper response. Place your answer on the space provided.

1. Very little detail is shown on _____ models.

2. Most residential models are _____ models.

3. Models are useful in checking the finished _____ of an architectural design.

4. Part of the siding and roofing is left off a(n) _____ model.

5. _____ may be purchased or fabricated from sponge and/or twigs.

1. _____

2. _____

3. _____

4. _____

5. _____

Multiple Choice

Choose the answer that correctly completes the statement. Write the corresponding letter in the space provided.

_____ 1. The purpose of a _____ model is to show the appearance of the finished building as realistically as possible.

    A. small scale solid
    B. structural
    C. large scale solid
    D. presentation

_____ 2. A good material for presentation architectural models is _____ because it is easy to cut, can be sanded, and does not easily warp.

    A. cardboard
    B. balsa wood
    C. illustration board
    D. plaster of Paris

_____ 3. On a presentation model, wall corners that are _____ jointed present a neater appearance.

    A. butt
    B. dovetail
    C. mitered
    D. pin

_____ 4. Furniture and major fixtures can be carved from _____.

    A. soap or wood
    B. plaster of Paris
    C. stone
    D. glass

_____ 5. A _____ model is usually built at 1/2″ = 1′-0″ or 1″ = 1′-0″ scale to show the basic construction.

    A. small scale solid
    B. large scale solid
    C. structural
    D. presentation

_____ 6. Which one of the following materials are commonly used for architectural model construction?

    A. Foam board.
    B. Balsa wood.
    C. Cardboard or illustration board.
    D. All of the above.

_____ 7. The two plans or drawings that are generally sufficient to build an architectural model are the _____.

    A. floor plan and elevations
    B. floor plan and foundation plan
    C. floor plan and plot plan
    D. plot plan and elevations

Short Answer

Answer the following questions.

1. At which scale are presentation models usually built? _____

2. How can an asphalt shingle roof be represented? _____

_____

3. Which type of architectural model is used to show how a building will relate to surrounding buildings? _____

4. How can grass be represented on an architectural model?_____

_____

Chapter 34 Posttest
Architectural Models

Name _____

Period _____**Date** _____**Score** _____

Completion

Complete each sentence with the proper response. Place your answer on the space provided.

1. Models are useful in checking the finished _____ of an architectural design.

   1. _____

2. Very little detail is shown on _____ models.

   2. _____

3. Part of the siding and roofing is left off a(n) _____ model.

   3. _____

4. Most residential models are _____ models.

   4. _____

5. _____ may be purchased or fabricated from sponge and/or twigs.

   5. _____

Multiple Choice

Choose the answer that correctly completes the statement. Write the corresponding letter in the space provided.

_____ 1. A _____ model is usually built at 1/2″ = 1′-0″ or 1″ = 1′-0″ scale to show the basic construction.

   A. small scale solid
   B. large scale solid
   C. structural
   D. presentation

_____ 2. The purpose of a _____ model is to show the appearance of the finished building as realistically as possible.

   A. small scale solid
   B. structural
   C. large scale solid
   D. presentation

_____ 3. Which one of the following materials are commonly used for architectural model construction?

   A. Foam board.
   B. Balsa wood.
   C. Cardboard or illustration board.
   D. All of the above.

_____ 4. A good material for presentation architectural models is _____ because it is easy to cut, can be sanded, and does not easily warp.

    A. cardboard
    B. balsa wood
    C. illustration board
    D. plaster of Paris

_____ 5. The two plans or drawings that are generally sufficient to build an architectural model are the _____.

    A. floor plan and elevations
    B. floor plan and foundation plan
    C. floor plan and plot plan
    D. plot plan and elevations

_____ 6. On a presentation model, wall corners that are _____ jointed present a neater appearance.

    A. butt
    B. dovetail
    C. mitered
    D. pin

_____ 7. Furniture and major fixtures can be carved from _____.

    A. soap or wood
    B. plaster of Paris
    C. stone
    D. glass

Short Answer

Answer the following questions.

1. Which type of architectural model is used to show how a building will relate to surrounding buildings? _____

2. At which scale are presentation models usually built? _____

3. How can grass be represented on an architectural model?_____

_____

4. How can an asphalt shingle roof be represented? _____

_____

Material and Tradework Specifications

35

Objectives

After studying this chapter, the student will be able to:
- Explain the purpose of material and tradework specifications.
- List the sources of specification guides.
- Identify the format followed by typical contract specification sheets.
- Use a *Description of Materials* form.

Displays

1. **Contract Specifications.** Secure a set of contract specifications from a local builder or loan officer. Display it on the bulletin board for student examination.
2. **Description of Materials.** Display a set of *Description of Materials* for a structure to be built in your area. Check with a builder or local lumber company for a sample or visit the Department of Veterans Affairs web site.

Instructional Materials

Text: Pages 675–684
   Review Questions, Suggested Activities
Workbook: Pages 377–380
   Review Questions, Problems/Activities
Teacher's Resources:
   Chapter 35 Pretest
   Chapter 35 Teaching Strategy
   Chapter 35 Posttest

Teaching Strategy

- **Knowledge Assessment.** Administer Chapter 35 Pretest. Correct the test and return. Highlight topics in which the individual student is deficient.
- Prepare Display #1.
- Review chapter objectives.
- Introduce material and tradework specifications.
- Present specification formats.
- Review examples of specifications.
- Prepare Display #2.
- Present the *Description of Materials* form.
- Assign workbook Problem/Activity 35-1.
- Assign one or more of the Suggested Activities in the text.
- **Chapter Review.** Assign Review Questions in the text. Discuss the correct answers. Assign Review Questions in the workbook. Have students check their own answers.
- **Evaluation**. Administer Chapter 35 Posttest. Correct the test and return. Return graded problems with comments.

Answers to Review Questions, Text

Page 684

1. A description of the materials to be used, list of required building operations, notes relative to cash allowances for such items as lighting fixtures and hardware that are to be selected by the owner, an indication that all of the specifications refer to the detailed plans of the working drawings, a statement or agreement on the quality of tradeworker's skill, and liability covered by the contractor during construction.
2. To allow the clients to express their own personal tastes and preferences.
3. sale
4. contract
5. Lighting fixtures, hardware, and other items that are to be selected by the owner.
6. To provide a definition of quality.
7. Construction details found on the working drawings do not need to be repeated in the specifications.

Answers to Workbook Questions

Page 377

Part I: Answer/Listing

1. Material specifications.
2. Specification sheets.

3. Have detailed tradework specifications prepared; both client and contractor must agree to theses specifications.
4. From an architect, the American Institute of Architects, or the Department of Veterans Affairs.
5. The contractor.

Part II: Completion

1. specifications
2. architect; client
3. building
4. owner
5. brand

Part III: Problems/Activities

1. Evaluate the form according to its completeness and thoroughness.

Answers to Chapter 35 Pretest

Completion

1. binding
2. Specifications
3. architect
4. *Description of Materials*
5. Quality; tradework

Multiple Choice

1. D. All of the above.
2. A. sale
3. C. details and products
4. B. American Institute of Architects
5. B. Millwork

Answers to Chapter 35 Posttest

Completion

1. architect
2. binding
3. *Description of Materials*
4. Quality; tradework
5. Specifications

Multiple Choice

1. C. details and products
2. B. American Institute of Architects
3. D. All of the above.
4. B. Millwork
5. A. sale

Chapter 35 Pretest
Material and Tradework Specifications

Name _____

Period _____**Date** _____**Score** _____

Completion

Complete each sentence with the proper response. Place your answer on the space provided.

1. Specifications and working drawings are legally _____ on both the contractor and the owner.

1. _____

2. _____ outline the liability covered by the contractor during construction.

2. _____

3. The _____ is generally responsible for the preparation of material and tradework specifications.

3. _____

4. The VA form _____ has become one of the leading guides for writing specifications.

4. _____

5. _____ and _____ are more difficult to define than material specifications.

5. _____

_____

Multiple Choice

Choose the answer that correctly completes the statement. Write the corresponding letter in the space provided.

_____ 1. Specification forms generally include _____.

   A. a description of the materials to be used
   B. list of required building operations
   C. notes relative to cash allowances for such items as lighting fixtures
   D. All of the above.

_____ 2. The architect generally writes the complete specifications for a house when the house is being constructed for _____.

   A. sale
   B. a specific client
   C. Both A and B.
   D. None of the above.

_____ 3. The specifications provide written information on _____ that supplement(s) the drawings and become part of the complete set of building plans.

   A. building procedures
   B. subcontractors to be used
   C. details and products
   D. None of the above.

_____ 4. Standard specification forms are available from the Department of Veterans Affairs and the _____.

     A. Lumberman's Association
     B. American Institute of Architects
     C. American Plywood Association
     D. Builders of America

_____ 5. Which of the following are usually major headings under building operations in the specification?

     A. Countertops
     B. Millwork
     C. Drywall
     D. Glazing

Chapter 35 Posttest
Material and Tradework Specifications

Name _____

Period _____**Date** _____**Score** _____

Completion

Complete each sentence with the proper response. Place your answer on the space provided.

1. The _____ is generally responsible for the preparation of material and tradework specifications.

1. _____

2. Specifications and working drawings are legally _____ on both the contractor and the owner.

2. _____

3. The VA form _____ has become one of the leading guides for writing specifications.

3. _____

4. _____ and _____ are more difficult to define than material specifications.

4. _____

_____

5. _____ outline the liability covered by the contractor during construction.

5. _____

Multiple Choice

Choose the answer that correctly completes the statement. Write the corresponding letter in the space provided.

_____ 1. The specifications provide written information on _____ that supplement(s) the drawings and become part of the complete set of building plans.

   A. building procedures
   B. subcontractors to be used
   C. details and products
   D. None of the above.

_____ 2. Standard specification forms are available from the Department of Veterans Affairs and the _____.

   A. Lumberman's Association
   B. American Institute of Architects
   C. American Plywood Association
   D. Builders of America

_____ 3. Specification forms generally include _____.

   A. a description of the materials to be used
   B. list of required building operations
   C. notes relative to cash allowances for such items as lighting fixtures
   D. All of the above.

_____ 4. Which of the following are usually major headings under building operations in the specification?

    A. Countertops
    B. Millwork
    C. Drywall
    D. Glazing

_____ 5. The architect generally writes the complete specifications for a house when the house is being constructed for _____.

    A. sale
    B. a specific client
    C. Both A and B.
    D. None of the above.

Estimating Building Cost

36

Objectives

After studying this chapter, the student will be able to:

- Explain the process of estimating the building cost.
- Generate a typical materials list for a simple structure.
- Estimate the cost of a residential structure using the square foot or cubic foot method.

Displays

1. **Plan and Estimated Cost**. Select a simple house plan and calculate an estimated building cost. Put the plan and cost estimate on the bulletin board for examination by students.
2. **Pay Rates for Skilled Trades**. Create a display using current rates charged by skilled tradespersons. See Suggested Activity #3 in the text.

Instructional Materials

Text: Pages 685–693
   Review Questions, Suggested Activities
Workbook: Pages 381–390
   Questions, Problems/Activities
Teacher's Resources:
   Chapter 36 Pretest
   Chapter 36 Teaching Strategy
   Chapter 36 Posttest

Teaching Strategy

- **Knowledge Assessment.** Administer the Chapter 36 Pretest. Correct the test and return. Highlight the topics in which the individual student is deficient.
- Prepare Display #1.
- Review the chapter objectives.
- Discuss preliminary estimates.
- Discuss estimates that are more accurate.
- Prepare Display #2.
- Assign Problem 36-1 in the workbook.
- Assign one or more of the Suggested Activities in the text.
- **Chapter Review.** Assign the Review Questions in the text. Discuss the correct answers. Assign the questions in the workbook. Have students check their own answers.
- **Evaluation.** Administer the Chapter 36 Posttest. Correct the test and return. Return graded problems with comments.

Answers to Review Questions, Text

Page 693

1. The square foot method and the cubic foot method.
2. $66.67
3. By using the material takeoff method.
4. Building permit, plumbing permit, electrical permit, and health permit.
5. publications, general contractors, and subcontractors
6. the supplier where the materials will be purchased

Answers to Workbook Questions

Page 381

Part I: Completion

1. estimating
2. builders
3. total area
4. specifications
5. height

Part II: Short Answer/Listing

1. A ranch-style home is more expensive to build than a two-story home that provides the same area of living space.
2. Yes.
3. Answer may include any two of the following: Fees for permits, fees for hookups, and the cost of insurance to protect materials and workers.
4. Determine the quantity, quality, and cost of materials required, and the cost of labor

for installation. Also, include an allowance for material waste, supervision, and overhead.

5. The order of the headings usually follows the construction sequence.

6. Building permit, plumbing permit, electrical permit, and health permit.

Part III: Multiple Choice

1. C. one-half
2. B. $164,000
3. D. 3,800 cubic feet
4. D. 60% to 80%

Part IV: Problems/Activities

1. Evaluate materials list according to completeness and accuracy.

Answers to Chapter 36 Pretest

Completion

1. total area
2. volume
3. construction
4. takeoff
5. electrical
6. 1440
7. constant

Multiple Choice

1. B. $10,000
2. B. $82,000
3. C. one-half
4. A. 11,520
5. D. 60% to 80%

Short Answer

1. Answer may include any two of the following: Fees for permits, fees for hookups, and the cost of insurance to protect materials and workers.
2. Compute the number of square feet in the house.
3. Material price fluctuations and labor overruns.

Answers to Chapter 36 Posttest

Completion

1. construction
2. takeoff
3. total area
4. volume
5. 1440
6. electrical
7. constant

Multiple Choice

1. D. 60% to 80%
2. B. $82,000
3. A. 11,520
4. C. one-half
5. B. $10,000

Short Answer

1. Compute the number of square feet in the house.
2. Answer may include any two of the following: Fees for permits, fees for hookups, and the cost of insurance to protect materials and workers.
3. Material price fluctuations and labor overruns.

Chapter 36 Pretest
Estimating Building Cost

Name _____

Period _____**Date** _____**Score** _____

Completion

Complete each sentence with the proper response. Place your answer on the space provided.

1. The square foot method produces an estimate of the building cost based on the _____ in the house.

1. _____

2. The cubic foot method produces an estimate of the building cost based on the _____ of the house.

2. _____

3. The order of the headings on a materials list usually coincides with the _____ sequence.

3. _____

4. Making a cost estimate by determining the quantity, quality, and cost of materials to be used and the cost of labor required for installation is called material _____.

4. _____

5. Most areas require a building permit, plumbing permit, _____ permit, and health permit for construction.

5. _____

6. A house that is 24′ × 60′ and has a detached garage of 20′ × 20′ has _____ square feet of living space.

6. _____

7. When calculating the cost of a home, most builders use a different _____ for each house style and adjust it for special features.

7. _____

Multiple Choice

Choose the answer that correctly completes the statement. Write the corresponding letter in the space provided.

_____ 1. Using the square foot method, how much would a garage cost to build if the rate were $25 per square foot and the garage were 20′ × 20′ in size?

    A. $5,000
    B. $10,000
    C. $15,000
    D. $20,000

_____ 2. Using the square foot method, a 24′ × 60′ house with a 20′ × 20′ detached garage would cost how much to build if the cost per square foot were $50 for the living space?

    A. $72,000
    B. $82,000
    C. $92,000
    D. $102,000

_____ 3. The cost of a garage is calculated at _____ the cost per square foot of the living area using the square foot method.

    A. one-eighth
    B. one-fourth
    C. one-half
    D. three-fourths

_____ 4. The volume of the living space of a 24' × 60' ranch home with standard height ceilings is _____ cubic feet.

    A. 11,520
    B. 12,960
    C. 14,400
    D. 15,840

_____ 5. It is reasonable to expect the labor cost to build a new home to be from _____ of the total cost.

    A. 30% to 50%
    B. 40% to 60%
    C. 50% to 70%
    D. 60% to 80%

Short Answer

Provide brief answers to the following questions.

1. In addition to materials and labor, what are two other items that should be included in the cost of building a house? _____

_____

2. What is the first step used to produce an estimate of the building cost when applying the square foot method? _____

_____

3. List two reasons why the final building cost may vary from the estimate. _____

_____

_____

Chapter 36 Posttest
Estimating Building Cost

Name _____

Period _____ **Date** _____ **Score** _____

Completion
Complete each sentence with the proper response. Place your answer on the space provided.

1. The order of the headings on a materials list usually coincides with the _____ sequence.

1. _____

2. Making a cost estimate by determining the quantity, quality, and cost of materials to be used and the cost of labor required for installation is called material _____.

2. _____

3. The square foot method produces an estimate of the building cost based on the _____ in the house.

3. _____

4. The cubic foot method produces an estimate of the building cost based on the _____ of the house.

4. _____

5. A house that is 24′ × 60′ and has a detached garage of 20′ × 20′ has _____ square feet of living space.

5. _____

6. Most areas require a building permit, plumbing permit, _____ permit, and health permit for construction.

6. _____

7. When calculating the cost of a home, most builders use a different _____ for each house style and adjust it for special features.

7. _____

Multiple Choice
Choose the answer that correctly completes the statement. Write the corresponding letter in the space provided.

_____ 1. It is reasonable to expect the labor cost to build a new home to be from _____ of the total cost.

   A. 30% to 50%
   B. 40% to 60%
   C. 50% to 70%
   D. 60% to 80%

_____ 2. Using the square foot method, a 24′ × 60′ house with a 20′ × 20′ detached garage would cost how much to build if the cost per square foot were $50 for the living space?

   A. $72,000
   B. $82,000
   C. $92,000
   D. $102,000

_____ 3. The volume of the living space of a 24′ × 60′ ranch home with standard height ceilings is _____ cubic feet.

    A. 11,520
    B. 12,960
    C. 14,400
    D. 15,840

_____ 4. The cost of a garage is calculated at _____ the cost per square foot of the living area using the square foot method.

    A. one-eighth
    B. one-fourth
    C. one-half
    D. three-fourths

_____ 5. Using the square foot method, how much would a garage cost to build if the rate were $25 per square foot and the garage were 20′ × 20′ in size?

    A. $5,000
    B. $10,000
    C. $15,000
    D. $20,000

Short Answer

Provide brief answers to the following questions.

1. What is the first step used to produce an estimate of the building cost when applying the square foot method? _____

_____

2. In addition to materials and labor, what are two other items that should be included in the cost of building a house? _____

_____

3. List two reasons why the final building cost may vary from the estimate. _____

_____

_____

Architectural Remodeling, Renovation, and Preservation

Objectives

After studying this chapter, the student will be able to:

- List the reasons that people remodel and the factors they should consider before beginning a remodeling project.
- Compare the five main types of remodeling according to cost, complexity, and time required.
- Evaluate the needs of a family and select an appropriate type of remodeling.
- Explain renovation.
- Identify three types of historical preservation.
- Explain the role of the family, interior designer, architect, and contractor in a remodeling, renovation, or preservation project.

Displays

1. **Remodeling Costs.** Collect cost data for common remodel materials, labor costs, and permit fees for your area of the country. Prepare a display that will help students to understand the real costs involved in remodeling a home.
2. **Remodeling Plans.** Display several remodeling plans that could be used as models for architectural drafters. If possible, show both manual and CADD drawings.

Instructional Materials

Text: Pages 695–713
    Review Questions, Suggested Activities
Workbook: Pages 391–396
    Review Questions, Problems/Activities
Teacher's Resources:
    Chapter 37 Pretest
    Chapter 37 Teaching Strategy
    Chapter 37 Posttest

Teaching Strategy

- **Knowledge Assessment.** Administer Chapter 37 Pretest. Correct the test and return. Highlight topics in which the individual student is deficient.
- Prepare Display #1.
- Review chapter objectives.
- Discuss choosing to remodel.
- Present types of remodeling.
- Assign workbook Problem/Activity 37-1.
- Prepare Display #2.
- Assign one of the Suggested Activities in the text.
- Discuss historic preservation.
- Discuss remodeling plans.
- **Chapter Review.** Assign Review Questions in the text. Discuss the correct answers. Assign Review Questions in the workbook. Have students check their own answers. Make transparencies of good solutions to Problem/Activity 37-1 and use for review.
- **Evaluation.** Administer Chapter 37 Posttest. Correct the test and return. Return graded problems with comments.

Answers to Review Questions, Text

Page 713

1. New family members may need their own bedrooms; entertaining may become more common, requiring more adequate kitchen and living spaces; increases in income may result in more disposable income and spur the desire for updated styles and appliances; as the work schedules of family members become busier, a more efficient home may be needed; and older homes may need newer equipment or better insulation to keep up with higher fuel prices.
2. They may have close ties with neighbors, schools, and community organizations;

the home may also hold sentimental value; time and money invested on landscaping may make moving not worthwhile; and the high cost of building.

3. Cost, time, and effort required to remodel.
4. Changing lived-in areas, making unused space livable, adding on, buying to remodel, and preserving an historic home.
5. 7'
6. Providing temporary load-bearing support and checking for plumbing and wiring within the wall.
7. If the more expensive house has sound wiring, plumbing, and structural members but the cheaper one does not, the cheaper house may actually cost more to renovate or remodel in the long run.
8. Determining the weak and strong points of the present home; evaluating the existing plumbing, heating/cooling, wiring, and insulation; developing a rough sketch; and developing a finished plan.
9. Adaptive reuse
10. Restoration, preservation through remodeling, adaptive reuse.

Answers to Workbook Questions
Page 391

Part I: Matching
1. F. Adaptive reuse.
2. H. Historic preservation.
3. E. Dormer.
4. B. Attic.
5. A. Remodeling.
6. C. Restoration.
7. G. Dehumidifying system.
8. D. Moisture barrier.

Part II: Completion
1. unused
2. Kitchen
3. bathroom
4. appliances
5. basement
6. damp
7. outside
8. 7'
9. attic
10. exterior

Part III: Short Answer/Listing
1. New family members may need their own bedrooms; entertaining may become more common; requiring more adequate kitchen and living spaces; increases in income may result in more disposable income and spur the desire for updated styles and appliances; as the work schedules of family members become busier, a more efficient home may be needed; and older homes may need newer equipment or better insulation to keep up with higher fuel prices.
2. Cost, time, and effort required.
3. Changing lived-in areas, making unused space livable, adding on, buying to remodel, and preserving an historic home.
4. Update or add appliances, improve the use of space, improve traffic patterns, increase the availability of storage, and improve the efficiency of the work triangle.
5. Answer may include any four: Updating fixtures, enlarging the room by moving a wall, adding storage space, adding natural lighting and ventilation through skylights, and new floor and wall treatments for easier maintenance.
6. Garages, porches, attics, and unfinished basements.
7. The roof must be removed and then replaced, the foundation and first floor walls must be strong enough to support the weight, and stairways connecting the first and second floors must be built.
8. (answers may vary) Changing an old factory building or warehouse into housing units.
9. Appraising the original house, determining the desired and needed changes, and drawing plans.
10. Interior designer, architect, and building contractor.

Part IV: Problems/Activities
1. Evaluate the plan according to principles suggested in the text.

Answers to Chapter 37 Pretest

Completion

1. architect
2. contractor
3. rehab
4. interior designer
5. architect

Multiple Choice

1. D. changed lived-in areas
2. A. bathroom
3. B. renovated
4. D. All of the above.
5. A. interior designer
6. B. HVAC
7. B. kitchen
8. C. rewiring

Answers to Chapter 37 Posttest

Completion

1. rehab
2. architect
3. architect
4. interior designer
5. contractor

Multiple Choice

1. D. All of the above.
2. C. rewiring
3. D. changed lived-in areas
4. B. HVAC
5. A. bathroom
6. B. kitchen
7. B. renovated
8. A. interior designer

Chapter 37 Pretest
Architectural Remodeling, Renovation, and Preservation

Name _____

Period _____ **Date** _____ **Score** _____

Completion

Complete each sentence with the proper response. Place your answer on the space provided.

1. The _____ makes final drawings of the proposed plan.

2. The _____ schedules subcontractors as needed.

3. Renovation is often called _____.

4. The _____ helps select fabric samples.

5. The _____ supervises the remodeling work.

1. _____

2. _____

3. _____

4. _____

5. _____

Multiple Choice

Choose the answer that correctly completes the statement. Write the corresponding letter in the space provided.

_____ 1. The least complex type of remodeling generally involves _____.

    A. restoration
    B. adding on
    C. adaptive reuse
    D. changing lived-in areas

_____ 2. When converting an attic into a bedroom, a(n) _____ should also be added.

    A. bathroom
    B. fire escape
    C. outside entrance
    D. dormer

_____ 3. If a structure is returned to its original condition using current styles, new materials, and state of the art appliances, it is _____.

    A. adapted for reuse
    B. restored
    C. renovated
    D. remodeled

_____ 4. When considering remodeling to add space and deciding where to add it, the _____ should be considered.

    A. type of space needed
    B. location of rooms in the existing home
    C. availability of space in the existing home
    D. All of the above.

_____ 5. A professional that can help translate housing needs and desires into plans and provide advice on appropriate colors, materials, and furnishings that fit within a budget is a(n) _____.

    A. interior designer
    B. architect
    C. building contractor
    D. carpenter

_____ 6. To ensure proper heating and cooling of a remodeled area, it may be wise to consult a(n) _____ professional for this aspect of the project.

    A. sheet metal
    B. HVAC
    C. electrical
    D. gas/fuel

_____ 7. The _____ is the most remodeled room in the house and usually the most expensive to remodel.

    A. bathroom
    B. kitchen
    C. bedroom
    D. family room

_____ 8. When remodeling a kitchen, _____ is necessary if several new appliances are added or major appliances are moved.

    A. new flooring
    B. new wall coverings
    C. rewiring
    D. None of the above.

Chapter 37 Posttest
Architectural Remodeling, Renovation, and Preservation

Name _____

Period _____ **Date** _____ **Score** _____

Completion

Complete each sentence with the proper response. Place your answer on the space provided.

1. Renovation is often called _____.

2. The _____ supervises the remodeling work.

3. The _____ makes final drawings of the proposed plan.

4. The _____ helps select fabric samples.

5. The _____ schedules subcontractors as needed.

1. _____

2. _____

3. _____

4. _____

5. _____

Multiple Choice

Choose the answer that correctly completes the statement. Write the corresponding letter in the space provided.

_____ 1. When considering remodeling to add space and deciding where to add it, the _____ should be considered.

    A. type of space needed
    B. location of rooms in the existing home
    C. availability of space in the existing home
    D. All of the above.

_____ 2. When remodeling a kitchen, _____ is necessary if several new appliances are added or major appliances are moved.

    A. new flooring
    B. new wall coverings
    C. rewiring
    D. None of the above.

_____ 3. The least complex type of remodeling generally involves _____.

    A. restoration
    B. adding on
    C. adaptive reuse
    D. changing lived-in areas

_____ 4. To ensure proper heating and cooling of a remodeled area, it may be wise to consult a(n) _____ professional for this aspect of the project.

    A. sheet metal
    B. HVAC
    C. electrical
    D. gas/fuel

_____ 5. When converting an attic into a bedroom, a(n) _____ should also be added.

    A. bathroom
    B. fire escape
    C. outside entrance
    D. dormer

_____ 6. The _____ is the most remodeled room in the house and usually the most expensive to remodel.

    A. bathroom
    B. kitchen
    C. bedroom
    D. family room

_____ 7. If a structure is returned to its original condition using current styles, new materials, and state of the art appliances, it is _____.

    A. adapted for reuse
    B. restored
    C. renovated
    D. remodeled

_____ 8. A professional that can help translate housing needs and desires into plans and provide advice on appropriate colors, materials, and furnishings that fit within a budget is a(n) _____.

    A. interior designer
    B. architect
    C. building contractor
    D. carpenter

Designing for Health and Safety

Objectives

After studying this chapter, the student will be able to:
- Identify fire hazards around the home and explain preventative measures.
- Explain the hazards associated with carbon monoxide and discuss preventative measures.
- Explain the hazards associated with radon in residential housing and describe preventative measures.
- Discuss problems in residential structures associated with excess moisture.
- Describe the dangers associated with weather- and nature-related events such as earthquakes, floods, tornadoes, and hurricanes.
- List steps that can be taken to mitigate the damage and destruction of weather- and nature-related events.

Displays

1. **Fire Prevention.** Prepare a bulletin board display that shows the key elements of a home fire prevention program.
2. **CO and Radon Detection.** Display equipment and plans for protecting a home from dangerous levels of CO and radon.
3. **Weather-Related Hazards.** Prepare a large map of the US that shows areas most prone to damage from flooding, tornadoes, hurricanes, and earthquakes.

Instructional Materials

Text: Pages 715–738
  Review Questions, Suggested Activities
Workbook: Pages 397–402
  Questions, Problems/Activities
Teacher's Resources:
  Chapter 38 Pretest
  Chapter 38 Teaching Strategy
  Chapter 38 Posttest

Teaching Strategy

- **Knowledge Assessment.** Administer the Chapter 38 Pretest. Correct the test and return. Highlight the topics in which the individual student is deficient.
- Prepare Display #1.
- Review the chapter objectives.
- Discuss design measures for health and safety.
- Assign one of the Suggested Activities in the text.
- Discuss smoke and fire detection, fire prevention, and fire code.
- Prepare Display #2.
- Discuss carbon monoxide and radon.
- Discuss moisture and mold problems.
- Prepare Display #3.
- Discuss weather- and nature-related safety.
- Assign Problem 38-1 in the workbook.
- Discuss general home safety.
- Assign one or more of the remaining Suggested Activities in the text.
- **Chapter Review.** Assign the Review Questions in the text. Discuss the correct answers. Assign the questions in the workbook. Have students check their own answers. Make a transparency of the solution to Problem/Activity 38-1 and use for review.
- **Evaluation.** Administer the Chapter 38 Posttest. Correct the test and return. Return graded problems with comments.

Answers to Review Questions, Text

Page 737

1. D. All of the above are correct.
2. Answer may include any two of the following: In the living or family room, at the top of the stairwell between the first and second floors, and outside each bedroom.

3. two
4. B. Class B.
5. Carbon monoxide
6. Radon
7. Sealing joints, cracks, and other openings; installing an active, fan-driven radon-removal vent-pipe system; reducing the "stack" or "chimney" effect in basements.
8. Answer may include any four of the following: Damp spots on ceilings and the room side of exterior walls, water and frost on the inside surfaces of windows, moisture on basement sidewalls and floors, water-filled blisters on outside paint surfaces, and marbles of ice on attic floors resulting from condensation of water on points of nails through roof sheathing.
9. D. Drippy outside hose bib.
10. Molds
11. moisture (or water vapor)
12. mold
13. A. Stachybotrys atra.
14. flooding
15. New Madrid
16. B. April, May, and June.
17. C. 74 mph.
18. B. August and September.
19. B. Falls.

Answers to Workbook Questions
Page 397

Part I: Completion
1. home
2. fire
3. creosote
4. photoelectric
5. combustion
6. Flash
7. safe
8. surge
9. November
10. Falls

Part II: Short Answer/Listing
1. Answer may include any two of the following: Falling asleep while smoking, improperly using flammable materials to start a fire, operating unsafe electrical or heating equipment, and placing materials that will burn too close to a potential source of ignition.
2. Answer may include any three of the following: On each floor of the house, including the basement and finished attic; in the living room or family room; at the top of the stairwell between the first and second floors; and outside each bedroom.
3. Answer may include any four of the following: Headaches, drowsiness, fatigue, nausea, and vomiting.
4. Because water vapor is not visible and not easily detected until it condenses.
5. Answer may include any four of the following: Upper respiratory infections, breathing difficulties, coughing, sore throat, nasal and sinus congestion, and skin and eye irritation.
6. The foundation; horizontal members, such as floors; columns, posts, and other vertical members that transfer the weight of the structure to the foundation; and all points of connection.
7. Two.

Part III: Multiple Choice
1. D. grease
2. C. 15
3. D. Stachybotrys atra.
4. D. The southern half of Texas.
5. A. Floods.
6. D. Tornado Alley
7. C. 85%
8. B. April, May, and June.
9. B. 110
10. A. 74

Part IV: Problems/Activities
1. Solution on page 520 of this manual.

Answers to Chapter 38 Pretest
Completion
1. B
2. oxygen
3. uranium
4. mitigation
5. mold
6. falls
7. digestion

Multiple Choice

1. D. electrical devices
2. D. Drippy hose bib.
3. C. 36″
4. B. 74
5. C. New Madrid
6. D. 90
7. B. April through June.
8. D. flooding
9. C. 80%
10. C. Texas, Oklahoma, and Kansas.

Answers to Chapter 38 Posttest

Completion

1. uranium
2. mitigation
3. falls
4. digestion
5. oxygen
6. B
7. mold

Multiple Choice

1. C. 80%
2. C. 36″
3. D. 90
4. B. April through June.
5. D. Drippy hose bib.
6. C. Texas, Oklahoma, and Kansas.
7. C. New Madrid
8. D. flooding
9. B. 74
10. D. electrical devices

Workbook Solution

1.

Directions:
Match each of the health or safety concerns on the left with the common source, cause, or remedy on the right. Connect the matching descriptions with lines.

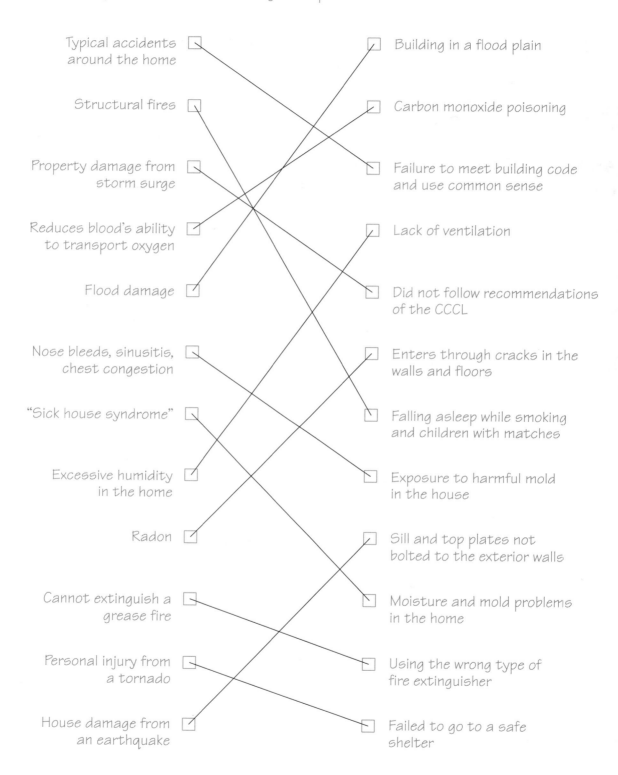

Typical accidents around the home

Structural fires

Property damage from storm surge

Reduces blood's ability to transport oxygen

Flood damage

Nose bleeds, sinusitis, chest congestion

"Sick house syndrome"

Excessive humidity in the home

Radon

Cannot extinguish a grease fire

Personal injury from a tornado

House damage from an earthquake

Building in a flood plain

Carbon monoxide poisoning

Failure to meet building code and use common sense

Lack of ventilation

Did not follow recommendations of the CCCL

Enters through cracks in the walls and floors

Falling asleep while smoking and children with matches

Exposure to harmful mold in the house

Sill and top plates not bolted to the exterior walls

Moisture and mold problems in the home

Using the wrong type of fire extinguisher

Failed to go to a safe shelter

Chapter 38 Pretest
Designing for Health and Safety

Name _____

Period _____**Date** _____**Score** _____

Completion

Complete each sentence with the proper response. Place your answer on the space provided.

1. A Class _____ fire extinguisher is used for a grease fire.

2. CO poisoning reduces the blood's ability to transport _____.

3. Radon comes from the natural decay of _____ found in soil, rock, and water.

4. Reducing radon is called radon _____.

5. Stachybotrys atra is a greenish-black _____.

6. About one-third of the accidental deaths that occur in US homes each year are from _____.

7. Molds break down plant materials by _____.

1. _____

2. _____

3. _____

4. _____

5. _____

6. _____

7. _____

Multiple Choice

Choose the answer that correctly completes the statement. Write the corresponding letter in the space provided.

_____ 1. Class C extinguishers are for use with fires involving _____.

   A. paper
   B. fabric
   C. burning liquids
   D. electrical devices

_____ 2. Which of the following is *not* generally a source of water vapor in the house?

   A. Roof leak.
   B. Wet plaster.
   C. Wet basement.
   D. Drippy hose bib.

_____ 3. Fire safety code requirements mandate that all stairs must be at least _____ wide.

   A. 28″
   B. 32″
   C. 36″
   D. 40″

_____ 4. A tropical storm is classified as a hurricane when sustained winds reach _____ miles per hour.

    A. 64
    B. 74
    C. 84
    D. 94

_____ 5. The area along the Mississippi River called the _____ region is an earthquake zone.

    A. Louisiana Delta
    B. Mississippi Valley
    C. New Madrid
    D. Missouri Basin

_____ 6. Long-term radon testing devices require more than _____ days.

    A. 30
    B. 50
    C. 70
    D. 90

_____ 7. Tornadoes are most frequent in the US during which months?

    A. January through March.
    B. April through June.
    C. July through September.
    D. October through December.

_____ 8. Which natural hazard is responsible for more property damage and deaths than any destructive force of nature in the US?

    A. fires
    B. tornadoes
    C. hurricanes
    D. flooding

_____ 9. What percentage of all fire deaths in the US occur in the home?

    A. 60%
    B. 70%
    C. 80%
    D. 90%

_____ 10. Which of the following states have more tornadoes than other states?

    A. Florida, Georgia, and Alabama.
    B. Missouri, Ohio, and Illinois.
    C. Texas, Oklahoma, and Kansas.
    D. Nebraska, North Dakota, and Minnesota.

Chapter 38 Posttest
Designing for Health and Safety

Name _____

Period _____ **Date** _____ **Score** _____

Completion

Complete each sentence with the proper response. Place your answer on the space provided.

1. Radon comes from the natural decay of _____ found in soil, rock, and water.

   1. _____

2. Reducing radon is called radon _____.

   2. _____

3. About one-third of the accidental deaths that occur in US homes each year are from _____.

   3. _____

4. Molds break down plant materials by _____.

   4. _____

5. CO poisoning reduces the blood's ability to transport _____.

   5. _____

6. A Class _____ fire extinguisher is used for a grease fire.

   6. _____

7. Stachybotrys atra is a greenish-black _____.

   7. _____

Multiple Choice

Choose the answer that correctly completes the statement. Write the corresponding letter in the space provided.

_____ 1. What percentage of all fire deaths in the US occur in the home?

   A. 60%
   B. 70%
   C. 80%
   D. 90%

_____ 2. Fire safety code requirements mandate that all stairs must be at least _____ wide.

   A. 28"
   B. 32"
   C. 36"
   D. 40"

_____ 3. Long-term radon testing devices require more than _____ days.

   A. 30
   B. 50
   C. 70
   D. 90

_____ 4. Tornadoes are most frequent in the US during which months?

    A. January through March.
    B. April through June.
    C. July through September.
    D. October through December.

_____ 5. Which of the following is *not* generally a source of water vapor in the house?

    A. Roof leak.
    B. Wet plaster.
    C. Wet basement.
    D. Drippy hose bib.

_____ 6. Which of the following states have more tornadoes than other states?

    A. Florida, Georgia, and Alabama.
    B. Missouri, Ohio, and Illinois.
    C. Texas, Oklahoma, and Kansas.
    D. Nebraska, North Dakota, and Minnesota.

_____ 7. The area along the Mississippi River called the _____ region is an earthquake zone.

    A. Louisiana Delta
    B. Mississippi Valley
    C. New Madrid
    D. Missouri Basin

_____ 8. Which natural hazard is responsible for more property damage and deaths than any destructive force of nature in the US?

    A. fires
    B. tornadoes
    C. hurricanes
    D. flooding

_____ 9. A tropical storm is classified as a hurricane when sustained winds reach _____ miles per hour.

    A. 64
    B. 74
    C. 84
    D. 94

_____ 10. Class C extinguishers are for use with fires involving _____.

    A. paper
    B. fabric
    C. burning liquids
    D. electrical devices

Career Opportunities

39

Objectives

After studying this chapter, the student will be able to:
- List various career options in architecture and residential construction.
- Compare the duties and educational requirements of various occupations in architecture and construction.
- Describe the type of objectives found in a model ethics code.
- Explain why job site safety is important.
- List leadership traits.
- Explain the advantages and disadvantages of entrepreneurship.

Displays

1. **Careers in Architecture and Construction.** Create a bulletin board display of typical career opportunities in architecture and construction. Use photos or descriptions of various careers.

Instructional Materials

Text: Pages 739–748
    Review Questions, Suggested Activities
Workbook: Pages 403–410
    Review Questions, Problems/Activities
Teacher's Resources:
    Chapter 39 Pretest
    Chapter 39 Teaching Strategy
    Chapter 39 Posttest

Teaching Strategy

- **Knowledge Assessment.** Administer the Chapter 39 Pretest. Correct the test and return. Highlight topics in which the individual student is deficient.
- Prepare Display #1.
- Review chapter objectives.
- Introduce career opportunities.
- Discuss the architect.
- Discuss architectural drafters and illustrators.
- Present information about the specifications writer and estimator.

- Discuss the surveyor and construction technologist.
- Discuss teaching architectural drawing.
- Assign workbook Problem/Activity 39-1.
- Assign one or more of the Suggested Activities in the text.
- **Chapter Review.** Assign Review Questions in the text. Discuss the correct answers. Assign Review Questions in the workbook. Have students check their own answers.
- **Evaluation.** Administer the Chapter 39 Posttest. Correct the test and return. Return graded problems with comments.

Answers to Review Questions, Text
Page 747

1. form; materials
2. To ensure that the person is qualified to design structures that meet the standards for safety, health, and property.
3. Answer may include any three: High schools, trade or vocational schools, community colleges, and universities.
4. estimator
5. land surveyor
6. Draw the details of working drawings and make tracings from original drawings that the architect or designer has prepared.
7. building contractor
8. specifications writer
9. To be successful over the long term.
10. Lack of adequate financing, poor management of the enterprise, and lack of knowledge required.

Answers to Workbook Questions
Page 403

Part I: Short Answer/Listing

1. Bachelor's degree from an accredited college or university.
2. Architectural illustrator.
3. A specifications writer may advance to this position from experience in the construction industry and related study.

4. Economics, structural materials, math, and computer experience.
5. Lack of adequate financing, poor management of the enterprise, and lack of knowledge required.
6. Testing the knowledge of workers to be sure they understand the proper use of their tools and machines; discussing safety procedures every few weeks; demonstrating safe work practices; developing a set of company safety rules; and enforcing safe work practices.
7. Work ethic.

Part II: Completion
1. architect
2. construction
3. estimator
4. surveyor
5. bachelor's
6. construction technologist

Part III: Multiple Choice
1. B. Design structures that meet the standards for health, safety, and property.
2. A. Be familiar with a CADD system.
3. C. Hardware, construction, and building materials.
4. D. All of the above.

Part IV: Matching
1. A. Architect
2. B. Architectural drafter
3. F. Specifications writer
4. D. Estimator
5. G. Surveyor
6. C. Construction technologist
7. E. Residential designer

Part V: Problems/Activities
1. **Architect**
   Duties: Work closely with the client in making preliminary drawings, sketches, etc.; prepare working drawings; assist the client in selecting a contractor; and periodically check on construction.
   Educational requirements: Generally, a bachelor's degree is required, but a two-year degree and several years of practical experience is sometimes acceptable; a license is required.

Architectural Drafter
Duties: Draw details of working drawings and make tracings from original drawings.
Educational requirements: Usually, several courses in architectural drafting and the use of CADD in high school or community college is sufficient to begin as an architectural drafter; often begin as junior drafters.

Architectural Illustrator
Duties: Prepare sketches, drawings, renderings, and illustrations for clients and publications such as commercial catalogs and advertisements.
Educational requirements: Similar to those of the architectural drafter or commercial artist.

Specifications Writer
Duties: Prepare all the necessary written information needed to describe materials, methods, and fixtures to be used in the structure.
Educational requirements: A college degree is usually required with an emphasis on drawings, materials, and building construction.

Estimator
Duties: Calculate the costs of materials and labor for a building; prepare all the paperwork necessary to inform the architect and/or builder of what the costs of the structure will be.
Educational requirements: A college degree with emphasis on mathematics and the use of computers is generally required; a background in economics and structural materials is also valuable.

Surveyor
Duties: Establish areas and boundaries of real estate property; involved with the planning and subdivision of land and the preparation of property descriptions.
Educational requirements: Normally, a bachelor's degree in surveying or civil engineering is required, but some community colleges and universities offer two year programs for surveying technicians.

Construction Technologist

Duties: Construction technologists are qualified for both technical and supervisory roles in the construction industry; specializations include estimation and bidding, quality control, site supervision, specifications writing, expediting, purchasing, and managing construction.

Educational requirements: A bachelor's degree in construction technology is required.

Teacher of Architectural Drafting

Duties: Teaching in high schools, trade or vocational schools, community colleges, and universities.

Educational requirements: A master's degree is required, or at least desired, to teach at most any level, but a doctorate is preferred for teaching at the university level; practical experience in the field is also a necessity.

Answers to Chapter 39 Pretest

Completion

1. estimator
2. license
3. Architectural illustration
4. architect
5. commercial

Multiple Choice

1. D. specifications writer
2. A. Construction technologist.
3. B. high school graduation with some courses in architectural drafting
4. C. a bachelor's degree
5. A. Land surveyor.
6. C. a bachelor's degree
7. D. All of the above.
8. B. architectural drafter
9. D. Makes an example of the worker who fails to meet the standards.
10. B. Having an excuse for poor work or unfinished work.

Short Answer

1. To provide direction and help in making decisions concerning the product or service.
2. So the business can be successful over the long term.

3. Testing the knowledge of workers to be sure they understand the proper use of their tools and machines; discussing safety procedures every few weeks; demonstrating safe work practices; developing a set of company safety rules; and enforcing state work practices.
4. The complex process of planning and designing a residential structure, codes, ordinances, design options, and product choices.

Answers to Chapter 39 Posttest

Completion

1. architect
2. license
3. commercial
4. Architectural illustration
5. estimator

Multiple Choice

1. C. a bachelor's degree
2. B. architectural drafter
3. B. high school graduation with some courses in architectural drafting
4. D. specifications writer
5. C. a bachelor's degree
6. A. Land surveyor.
7. D. All of the above.
8. A. Construction technologist.
9. B. Having an excuse for poor work or unfinished work.
10. D. Makes an example of the worker who fails to meet the standards.

Short Answer

1. The complex process of planning and designing a residential structure, codes, ordinances, design options, and product choices.
2. Testing the knowledge of workers to be sure they understand the proper use of their tools and machines; discussing safety procedures every few weeks; demonstrating safe work practices; developing a set of company safety rules; and enforcing state work practices.
3. To provide direction and help in making decisions concerning the product or service.
4. So the business can be successful over the long term.

Chapter 39 Pretest
Career Opportunities

Name _____

Period _____ **Date** _____ **Score** _____

Completion

Complete each sentence with the proper response. Place your answer on the space provided.

1. The professional who calculates the costs of materials and labor for a building is called a(n) _____.

1. _____

2. Architects must pass an examination to obtain a(n) _____ to practice.

2. _____

3. _____ is a specialized field that requires some art talent.

3. _____

4. The job of a(n) _____ requires a great deal of creativity and sensitivity to form and materials.

4. _____

5. Most architects design _____ buildings as part of their work.

5. _____

Multiple Choice

Choose the answer that correctly completes the statement. Write the corresponding letter in the space provided.

_____ 1. The job of the _____ is to prepare all the necessary written information needed to describe materials, methods, and fixtures to be used in the structure.

    A. architectural illustrator
    B. estimator
    C. construction technologist
    D. specifications writer

_____ 2. Which professional is qualified for both supervisory and technical roles in the construction industry?

    A. Construction technologist.
    B. Architectural drafter.
    C. Architectural illustrator.
    D. None of the above.

_____ 3. Educational requirements for an architectural drafter usually include _____.

    A. high school graduation
    B. high school graduation with some courses in architectural drafting
    C. two years of community college work
    D. bachelor's degree

_____ 4. The academic credentials required for an architect are generally _____.

    A. a few years of work experience
    B. an associate's degree
    C. a bachelor's degree
    D. a master's degree

_____ 5. Which professional establishes areas and boundaries of real estate property?

    A. Land surveyor.
    B. Construction technologist.
    C. Architectural drafter.
    D. None of the above.

_____ 6. The highest level of education required for an estimator is generally _____.

    A. only high school graduation
    B. an associate's degree in building construction
    C. a bachelor's degree
    D. None of the above.

_____ 7. Opportunities to teach architectural drafting exist in _____.

    A. high schools and trade or vocational schools
    B. community colleges
    C. universities
    D. All of the above.

_____ 8. A(n) _____ generally draws the details of working drawings and makes tracings from original drawings that the architect or designer has prepared.

    A. junior architect
    B. architectural drafter
    C. architectural illustrator
    D. construction technologist

_____ 9. Which of the following is *not* a quality of a successful leader?

    A. Has a vision.
    B. Is a role model.
    C. Checks the small things.
    D. Makes an example of the worker who fails to meet the standards.

_____ 10. Which of the following is an example of a poor work ethic?

    A. Admitting a mistake and learning from it.
    B. Having an excuse for poor work or unfinished work.
    C. Respecting a fellow worker's wishes.
    D. Agreeing to work overtime to complete a task.

Name _____

Short Answer

Answer the following questions.

1. Why should a business have well-defined goals? _____

_____

_____

2. What is the practical reason for establishing and adhering to a model ethics code? _____

_____

3. List five techniques that can be employed to sharpen concern for safety on the job. _____

_____

_____

_____

_____

_____

4. List five areas in which a residential designer should be knowledgeable. _____

_____

_____

_____

Chapter 39 Posttest
Career Opportunities

Name _____

Period _____**Date** _____**Score** _____

Completion

Complete each sentence with the proper response. Place your answer on the space provided.

1. The job of a(n) _____ requires a great deal of creativity and sensitivity to form and materials.

2. Architects must pass an examination to obtain a(n) _____ to practice.

3. Most architects design _____ buildings as part of their work.

4. _____ is a specialized field that requires some art talent.

5. The professional who calculates the costs of materials and labor for a building is called a(n) _____.

1. _____

2. _____

3. _____

4. _____

5. _____

Multiple Choice

Choose the answer that correctly completes the statement. Write the corresponding letter in the space provided.

_____ 1. The academic credentials required for an architect are generally _____.

    A. a few years of work experience
    B. an associate's degree
    C. a bachelor's degree
    D. a master's degree

_____ 2. A(n) _____ generally draws the details of working drawings and makes tracings from original drawings that the architect or designer has prepared.

    A. junior architect
    B. architectural drafter
    C. architectural illustrator
    D. construction technologist

_____ 3. Educational requirements for an architectural drafter usually include _____.

    A. high school graduation
    B. high school graduation with some courses in architectural drafting
    C. two years of community college work
    D. bachelor's degree

_____ 4. The job of the _____ is to prepare all the necessary written information needed to describe materials, methods, and fixtures to be used in the structure.

  A. architectural illustrator
  B. estimator
  C. construction technologist
  D. specifications writer

_____ 5. The highest level of education required for an estimator is generally _____.

  A. only high school graduation
  B. an associate's degree in building construction
  C. a bachelor's degree
  D. None of the above.

_____ 6. Which professional establishes areas and boundaries of real estate property?

  A. Land surveyor.
  B. Construction technologist.
  C. Architectural drafter.
  D. None of the above.

_____ 7. Opportunities to teach architectural drafting exist in _____.

  A. high schools and trade or vocational schools
  B. community colleges
  C. universities
  D. All of the above.

_____ 8. Which professional is qualified for both supervisory and technical roles in the construction industry?

  A. Construction technologist.
  B. Architectural drafter.
  C. Architectural illustrator.
  D. None of the above.

_____ 9. Which of the following is an example of a poor work ethic?

  A. Admitting a mistake and learning from it.
  B. Having an excuse for poor work or unfinished work.
  C. Respecting a fellow worker's wishes.
  D. Agreeing to work overtime to complete a task.

_____ 10. Which of the following is *not* a quality of a successful leader?

  A. Has a vision.
  B. Is a role model.
  C. Checks the small things.
  D. Makes an example of the worker who fails to meet the standards.

Name _____

Short Answer

Answer the following questions.

1. List five areas in which a residential designer should be knowledgeable. _____

   _____

   _____

   _____

2. List five techniques that can be employed to sharpen concern for safety on the job. _____

   _____

   _____

   _____

   _____

   _____

3. Why should a business have well-defined goals? _____

   _____

   _____

4. What is the practical reason for establishing and adhering to a model ethics code? _____

   _____